CW01572989

Country and Political Risk

Country and Political Risk
Practical Insights for Global Finance

Edited by Sam Wilkin

Published by Risk Books, a Division of Incisive Financial Publishing Ltd

Haymarket House
28–29 Haymarket
London SW1Y 4RX
Tel: +44 (0)20 7484 9700
Fax: +44 (0)20 7484 9800
E-mail: books@riskwaters.com
Sites: www.riskbooks.com
      www.riskwaters.com

Every effort has been made to secure the permission of individual copyright holders for inclusion.

© Incisive Media Investments Limited 2004

ISBN 1 904339 31 X

British Library Cataloguing in Publication Data
A catalogue record for this book is available from the British Library

Managing Editor: Laurie Donaldson
Development Editor: Tamsine Green
Copy Editor: Andrew John

Typeset by Mizpah Publishing Services Private Limited, Chennai, India

Printed and bound in Spain by Espacegraphic, Pamplona, Navarra

Contents

List of Contributors

Carl F. Adams is executive director of the Financial Standards Foundation Consultancy where his assignments have included: senior advisor for risk management to the IMF, the US National Intelligence Council, Oxford Analytica Ltd, Malcolm Binks Associates, The Korean Economic Institute, private sector financial institutions and rating agencies. He is past chairman of the Risk Management Association (RMA) New York chapter; a member of the Financial Task Force Committee of the Corporate Council on Africa; a participant in the Business Council of the UN; and a senior director of the Capital Markets Credit Analysts Society. He was global manager for country risk and director of portfolio risk management at Merrill Lynch for 11 years. Before that assignment, he was president and founder of Strategic Research International Inc. Prior to this, he was a vice president for ratings policy and economics analysis with Moody's Investors Service. His academic degrees are from the University of Oklahoma and New York University.

Michael Bates is director of consultancy and research with Oxford Analytica, an international consulting firm based in Oxford that advises clients on the implications of global political and economic developments. Previously he served as a Member of Parliament in the UK from 1992–97 and held a number of ministerial posts between 1994–97 including Paymaster General. Michael earned his MBA degree from the Saïd Business School, University of Oxford. He is a non-executive director of eStandards Forum Inc and Congregational and General plc. His published work includes *The Road to International Financial Stability*, edited by Benu Schnieder *et al*, Palgrave Macmillan, 2003.

Alessio Ciarlone works in the International Relations Office of the Bank of Italy. He is in charge of country risk assessment and he is a member of the "observatory" on emerging markets established within the office. Moreover, he follows the work of the World Bank on poverty and poverty-related issues. After joining the Bank of Italy, Alessio spent one year in the UK where he obtained a masters degree in economics from the University of York. Currently, he is a first-year student in the PhD programme on money, banking and finance organised by the University of Rome, Tor Vergata. His preferred research topics are international macro, international finance and poverty.

Stijn Claessens is Senior Adviser in the Financial Sector Vice-Presidency at the World Bank and Professor of International Finance Policy at the University of Amsterdam. Stijn has taught at New York University business school and has over fourteen years of experience at the World Bank. Over his career, Stijn has provided advice and participated in missions to emerging markets in Latin America, East Asia and the transition economies. His research on international finance issues has been published in the *Journal of Financial Economics, Journal of Finance* and *Quarterly Journal of Economics*. He is on the editorial board of the *World Bank Economic Review* and an associate editor of the *Journal of Financial Services Research*. He is also a fellow of the CEPR. Stijn has an MA from Erasmus University and a PhD from The Wharton School, University of Pennsylvania, both in business economics.

Guy Dunn is the Director of Research at the World Markets Research Centre (WMRC) in London. He devised WMRC's country risk rating system, and also designed a 12-factor country risk rating assessment on 202 countries for a World Bank project. Prior to joining WMRC, Guy worked at the risk consultancy Control Risks Group. He has written numerous articles on country risk and has had research published in the book *Russian Organized Crime*. Guy has worked in conjunction with many government bodies, including with the Dutch, Italian, Japanese and UK Foreign Ministries. He has spoken on country risk at conferences worldwide and has been frequently interviewed in the media. He also has spoken on country risk at the US State Department, the Royal Institute for International Affairs (Chatham House), The Royal United Services Institute (RUSI) and the US Library of Congress.

Therese Feng is a director at Fitch Ratings, Inc, where she covers Asian and Latin American sovereigns. Prior to joining the company, she worked at Duff & Phelps Credit Rating Co. on the sovereign creditworthiness of Asian countries. Therese was most recently a research fellow at the Kennedy School of Government at Harvard University. She has also undertaken economic research at the Yale Center for Law and Environmental Policy and Harvard Institute for International Development. Therese has conducted extensive research on the Chinese power sector. Her doctoral dissertation, *Controlling Air Pollution in China*, was published by Edward Elgar Press in 1999. Therese holds bachelor, master, and doctoral degrees from Yale University.

Jotaro Hamada is a lead risk management officer with the Multilateral Investment Guarantee Agency (MIGA), the World Bank Group's political risk insurer in Washington, DC. He has led the effort to build MIGA's enterprise-wide risk management infrastructure. Before joining MIGA,

Jotaro was an engagement manager with McKinsey & Company in both the Tokyo and Chicago offices, where he served clients in a wide range of industries on issues such as corporate strategy, cross-border M&A/strategic alliance and international business development. He received his MBA and a Master of International Affairs from Columbia University, and has a Bachelor of Liberal Arts from the University of Tokyo.

Campbell R. Harvey is the J. Paul Sticht Professor of International Business at the Fuqua School of Business, Duke University. He obtained his PhD from the University of Chicago. He is also a research associate of the National Bureau of Economic Research in Cambridge, Massachusetts. Campbell has received four Graham and Dodd Scrolls for excellence in financial writing from the Association of Investment Management and Research and two Roger F. Murray Prizes from the Institute for Research in Quantitative Finance (Q-Group). He has served, or still serves, as a consultant or principal to some of the world's leading asset management and consulting firms. He has published over 100 scholarly articles and books. From 2001 to 2004, Harvey served on the board of directors of the American Finance Association and the Western Finance Association. In addition to this, he is Editor of the *Review of Financial Studies* and the *Emerging Markets Review* and holds associate editorships in the *Financial Analysts Journal* as well as 14 academically oriented finance journals, including the *Journal of Financial Economics*.

Henning Haugerudbraaten is a former risk management officer with the Multilateral Investment Guarantee Agency (MIGA) of the World Bank Group in Washington, DC. Henning has worked on all aspects of MIGA's risk and financial management, including political risk insurance pricing, economic capital modelling, financial forecasting, liquidity assessment, and investment portfolio management. At MIGA, he was also responsible for political risk analysis of several East European countries. Henning, a CFA charter holder, holds a master's degree in international relations from Johns Hopkins University's School of Advanced International Studies (SAIS). He is currently an advisor in the investment management department of Norges Bank in Oslo, Norway.

Peter Heijmans is an economist at ABN AMRO Bank NV, serving for group risk management in the unit Emerging Markets Analysis and Multilateral Organisations. He joined the ABN AMRO Bank in June 2004. Prior to joining ABN AMRO, Peter served as a tax policy advisor at the Ministry of Finance in the Netherlands. He also spent two years at the Taxation and Customs Union Directorate-General (DG TAXUD) of the European Commission in Brussels, serving for the unit Economic Analysis of Taxation. During this time, Peter worked in the field of labour taxation and corporate income taxation, and was involved in the preparation of the joint DG TAXUD/EUROSTAT publication on the structures of the taxation systems in the European Union. Peter holds a degree in economics from the University of Tilburg in the Netherlands.

Andrew Hickman is a managing director and head of research and development for ERisk. He takes lead responsibility for design of risk measurement models in ERisk's software products and consulting assignments. His research focuses particularly on modelling low-frequency, high-severity events such as credit defaults and political risk insurance. Prior to ERisk, Andrew worked for Credit Suisse Financial Products, modelling counterparty credit exposure on structured derivatives spanning commodities, interest rates, equities and FX, in both emerging and developed markets. Before that, he was a consultant in Oliver, Wyman & Company's risk management practice. Andrew received a BSc in economics with concentrations in finance and political science from the University of Pennsylvania's Wharton School of Business.

Preston Keat is Research Director at Eurasia Group. He holds a PhD in political science from UCLA, an MSc from the London School of Economics, and a BA from the College of William and Mary. He has been deeply involved in the development of and reporting relating to the Deutsche Bank Eurasia Group Stability Index, a cutting edge tool for global market risk analysis. He has also published a range of articles on political and economic reform in Emerging Europe.

Ilya Khaykin is a former associate with ERisk. His work has focused on the development of risk models and the management of the implementation of these models in public and private sector insurers and banks. Ilya has worked in depth with the modelling of political, credit, interest rate, operational and mortality risks. Prior to ERisk he worked as a consultant at First Manhattan Consulting Group. Ilya holds a bachelor's degree in applied physics from Columbia University. He is currently pursuing graduate studies jointly at the Institut d'Etudes Politiques de Paris (Sciences Po) and at the London School of Economics in international conflict and security studies.

J. Marc Michel Léonard is chief economist and head of Aon Trade Credit's political risk consulting practice, where he oversees ATC's political and economic analysis. Prior to joining Aon, Michel was with Medley Global Advisors, a New York based political risk analysis firm founded by George Soros' chief policy strategist, where he provided advice on political and economic risks to senior managers at some of the world's top MNCs and investment banks. Michel started his career as an academic at the

University of Virginia, he has published widely in both academic and business publications and is a frequent commentator for national and international news media on issues including political risk assessment, how to minimise a firm's exposure to political risk, and how political risk informs currency strategy, financial markets, and Federal Reserve policy. A graduate of McGill University, he holds an MTS from Harvard University and an MA and PhD in political economy from the University of Virginia.

Alexander J. Motyl is Senior Analyst with Eurasia Group, and a Professor of political science, Deputy Director of the Center for Global Change and Governance, and Co-Director of the Central and East European Studies programme at Rutgers University, Newark. He has published widely on state stability, regime breakdown, revolutionary change, and nationalism.

Frank Packer joined the financial markets group at the Bank for International Settlements in 2003 as a senior economist, after more than three years as a director in the economic and market analysis group of Nikko Citigroup in Tokyo. Before that, he was seven years at the Federal Reserve Bank of New York (NY Fed) for seven years, most recently in the capital markets group. While at the NY Fed, he participated in two working groups reporting to the Research Task Force of the Basel Committee on Bank Supervision; one was on the supervisory lessons of the East Asian financial crisis, the other on the value of credit ratings. His long-term research interests include bankruptcy, credit ratings, initial public offerings, and the Japanese economy. He has a PhD and MS in finance and economics from Columbia University; his other degrees are from the University of Chicago (MBA) and Harvard (BA).

Luigi Ruggerone is currently Country Risk Manager at the risk management department of Banca Intesa, which he joined in 2003, after serving as Head of Emerging Markets Economics at the research department. He lives in Milan with his wife Alessandra and his son Luca. He received his degree at Università Cattolica del Sacro Cuore of Milan and completed an MSc and an MPhil in economics at the University of Warwick. In addition to the research regularly published with Banca Intesa, Luigi Ruggerone is author and co-author of various international monetary economics papers published in distinguished journals. He also teaches international economics at Università Cattolica del Sacro Cuore of Milan and monetary economics at Università di Bologna.

Khalid Sheikh joined ABN AMRO in 1987 as an economist, having worked as an economic and policy advisor at the Dutch Ministry of Foreign Affairs, and undertaken a Doctorandus at Erasmus University, Rotterdam. During his career with the bank he has occupied several research, strategic advisory and product development positions. Currently he is working at Group Risk Management and heads the emerging market analysis & multilateral organisation department of ABN AMRO. Khalid has also worked as Temporary Expat for the IMF on risk management issues and corporate governance. He also tutors at the post-graduate course of the Vrije Universiteit van Amsterdam and special workshops of IMF and the World Bank. Khalid has chaired the Bestuur Openbaar Onderwijs IJsselstein for four years. He holds a masters degree in developmènt economics from the Erasmus University in Rotterdam and a post-doctorate masters degree in financial economics from the Tilburg Institute of Academic Studies.

Martin Stone is a director in the counter terrorism & political risk division of Aon Special Risks. Previously, he worked as Head of Country & Political Risk consulting at Deloitte & Touche and prior to that, spent ten years at the international political and security risk consultancy Control Risks Group, latterly as Head of Research, and before that as Senior Middle East and North Africa analyst. Martin has spoken widely on political, country and terrorism risk in the UK, US, the Middle East, Japan and South Africa. He contributed an article on security risk analysis for the Financial Times' *Mastering Risk* series in 2000, and Columbia University Press published his book on the politics and sociology of Algeria in 1997. He has an MBA and an MA in Arabic from the University of Edinburgh.

Christian Stracke is the Head of Emerging Markets Research at CreditSights, an independent financial research firm with headquarters in New York. At CreditSights Christian is responsible for emerging markets sovereign strategy and economic research, with an emphasis on Latin America. Prior to joining CreditSights, Christian was Head of Latin America Strategy at Commerzbank Securities in New York. Christian has a special interest in the structural determinants of economic growth and sovereign credit quality, and has published articles in the *World Policy Journal* and the *Journal of International Affairs*. Christian is a graduate of the University of Chicago, and completed course work in a PhD programme in political science at New York University.

Chamaree Suthiphongchai earned her MBA in financial engineering from MIT Sloan School of Management. She joined the bank of Thailand in 1996 and is currently a senior analyst for the Financial Institutions Policy Group, where she specialises in derivatives, exotic derivatives, and other structured products. In 2003, during her employment at the Bank of Thailand, she joined the Bank for International Settlement as a visiting fellow.

Giorgio Trebeschi is a researcher at the International Relations Office at the Bank of Italy in Rome. His main duties include analysing and monitoring developments for research as well as for supervision and surveillance purposes. He was previously employed in the Financial Stability Wing at the Bank of England, where he carried out research related to market microstructure issues and published the following papers: *Equity Markets under stress: tests for arbitrage anomalies in the stock-futures basis*; proceedings from *The second joint central bank research conference on risk measurement and systemic risk* (co-authored with Joe Ganley, Bank of Japan); *Price formation and transparency on the London Stock Exchange* (co-authored with Victoria Saporta and Anne Vila, Bank of England). He holds a masters degree in finance from the University of London.

Sam Wilkin is Editor-in-Chief of Countryrisk.com, an online magazine dedicated to country and political risk analysis. He previously served as country risk advisor and head of US political risk consulting for Aon Trade Credit, a division of the Fortune 500 insurance brokerage Aon Corporation. Prior to joining Aon, he worked as Director of Country Analysis for Marvin Zonis & Associates, a political risk consultancy. Sam studied economics at Eckerd College and Waseda University in Tokyo. He received his MA in international relations from the University of Chicago. He is co-author of *The Kimchi Matters* (Agate, 2003), has authored numerous articles on political risk and is the 2004 alumni fellow for Eckerd College. Sam lives in Chicago.

Introduction

Sam Wilkin

Countryrisk.com

What is perhaps most fascinating about country risk is the variety of people the field attracts. Economists and political scientists are well represented, but also experts in finance, organisational behaviour, public policy and business management. Not to mention area studies specialists with in-depth knowledge of a country or region, as well as military and intelligence professionals for whom "country risk" represents the threat of war or state failure. To this, add lawyers, civil servants, former diplomats, bankers, brokers and even the occasional politician turned student of politics.

This diversity of backgrounds entails a diversity of approaches. With perspectives ranging from portfolio theory to critical theory, any volume on country risk inevitably stands the chance of becoming jumbled. I hope to avoid this pitfall by virtue of coherent organisation. The first section of this book, on country risk assessment, reviews various country risk assessment methodologies. In the second section, several practitioners demonstrate the art of country risk assessment in practice. The third section reviews the managerial challenges posed by country risk: risk mitigation and transfer, pricing risks on a portfolio basis and organising a firm's country risk function.

DEFINING COUNTRY RISK

Country risk is, broadly speaking, the risk of business loss due to country-specific factors, usually related to political and economic instability. But nearly every contributor to this volume has his or her own definition. This is as it should be. Ultimately, *the definition of country risk depends on the business activity being contemplated.* Different businesses have different country risk exposures.

Some types of country and political risk – especially for foreign direct investors – stem from "micro" risks. That is, risks specific to a single firm or investment. For instance, a host government's unilateral abrogation of a power-purchase agreement that puts an investor's power plant out of business, or discriminatory regulation that makes it impossible for a foreign factory to turn a profit.

This volume focuses, in the main, not on micro but on "macro" risks – macropolitical and macroeconomic events such as wars, revolutions and, most importantly, economic crises. These macro risks are of central concern in global banking and insurance. Most of the contributors to this volume represent the global finance community, a community whose interests have been underserved by previous books on country and political risk.

But also, these macro risks – and their assessment and management – are of universal interest. Managing macro threats, such as currency crises, is important to all investors and lenders in a way that managing micro threats, such as discriminatory taxation, is not. Hence this volume, by addressing macro risks, focuses on core country and political risk concerns common to all global businesses.

In the banking industry, which has the greatest representation in this book, country risk is generally defined as the risk of loss in cross-border lending stemming from factors that are, at least partially, under government control. This includes classic "sovereign risk" – the risk that a government will fail to honour its sovereign obligations, whether due to unwillingness or inability to pay – as well as "transfer risk" – generally, the risk of restrictions on the international transfer of funds. And finally, what is often called "collective debtor" risk, which refers to the threat – increasingly important in recent years – that countrywide events will cause simultaneous default by a large number of private debtors. Contributors to this volume also mention country investment and operational risks for banks. These are of growing importance because global banks increasingly conduct much of their business in – as well as lend to – geographically distant countries.

The concerns of fund managers – those who trade, research and hold foreign securities and equities – are also well represented in this book. In fund management, country risk represents "the general level of political, financial, and economic uncertainty in a country which impacts the value of the country's bonds and equities", in the words of Campbell Harvey's finance glossary. This is certainly a different type of risk from, say, default by foreign private creditors. The common ground with banking is that the concerns are at a macro level. Macropolitical and macroeconomic events move these markets, not small-scale regulatory decisions.

This volume also includes contributions from the political risk insurance industry – which no book on political risk would be complete without. In general, political risk brokers and underwriters concern themselves with micro risks, such as "expropriation" (government seizure of an investor's assets). But in this volume the insurance contributors also discuss macro issues. For instance, country-level determinants of expropriation, the organisation of the country risk function, and exchange transfer risk.

THE STRUCTURE OF THE BOOK
Assessing country risk
What causes emerging-markets crises – Mexico in 1994, Thailand in 1997, Russia in 1998, Brazil in 1999 – and can these meltdowns be predicted? The book begins with two surveys of the academic literature on the subject. In the first chapter, **Stijn Claessens** distils a complex and abstract literature on theories of currency and banking crises into a well-organised review. He also comments on the practical implications of these theories for crisis prevention and recovery.

In the second chapter, **Alessio Ciarlone** and **Giorgio Trebeschi** flip the coin and review the empirical models – the early-warning systems – that attempt to forecast coming crises. They focus on the smaller debt crisis literature, and the problem of developing an empirical definition of debt crises for early-warning research.

In the third chapter, **Khalid Sheikh** and **Peter Heijmans** discuss emerging global economic and regulatory trends from the perspective of global banking. They focus on how these trends affect country risk assessment. They consider the changing nature of emerging-markets crises, the causes of rising public debt levels, and whether, in light of these global trends, the New Basel Capital Accord might have some unintended consequences.

Then it is time for the consultants to have their say. The country risk analysis industry is home to a number of established and well-reputed firms, including the Economist Intelligence Unit, Control Risks, Business Monitor International and Political Risk Services. (Indeed, the country risk ratings produced by the *International Country Risk Guide*, a subsidiary of Political Risk Services, feature prominently in two chapters – 5 and 14 – in this volume.)

For this book, I decided to invite some of the newer country analysis firms – founded in the past ten years, and perhaps less familiar to readers – to put their best foot forward. One of these is Eurasia Group, which has made waves on Wall Street with its novel approach to emerging-markets analysis. In the fourth chapter, **Preston Keat** and **Alexander J. Motyl** run through the group's methodology for assessing state stability, and the performance of their approach during the Russian and Brazilian currency crises.

In the fifth chapter, **Campbell R. Harvey** takes country risk ratings from the International Country Risk Guide and puts them through their paces on decades of historical data on international equity returns. He updates his well-known "Political Risk, Economic Risk and Financial Risk" paper – now almost a decade old – with several new twists. This time he analyses individual country risk components, such as "ethnic tensions" and "democratic accountability", instead of overall ratings, and compares these against both market returns and a measure of the cost of capital, with some unexpected results.

Another new approach to assessing country risk is offered by eStandards Forum, an industry group that monitors countries' compliance with global regulatory best practices. The eStandards ratings of regulatory compliance are now being used as an unorthodox measure of country risk – most famously by the enormous California-based pension fund, CalPERS. In the sixth chapter, **Carl F. Adams** discusses the philosophy behind the use of standards compliance as a measure of country risk, explains the eStandards system and speculates on future trends.

The last chapter in the country risk assessment section of this book marks a departure from the typical format of a volume on country risk. While the contributors to this book are diverse – representing academia, banking, insurance, consulting, investment research and rating agencies – the scope of professionals with an interest in, and insight into, country analysis is even broader. The seventh chapter records interviews conducted with four of the world's leading country analysts representing Wall Street, academia, the intelligence community and a human rights pressure group. The topic is country analysis, broadly conceived.

Country risk cases

Assessing country risk is two parts science to one part art. The science includes economics and politics, but also finance, public policy, sociology, history and many other areas. Art also has a role, because the political and economic drivers of country risk are too complex and rooted in human psychology to admit accurate forecasting. Predicting the unpredictable is, ultimately, an art.

For the section of the book on country risk cases we invited several practitioners to demonstrate the art of country risk assessment. While the cases address markets of profound interest – Turkey, China, Brazil and Russia – each contributor was asked to highlight, in the first instance, their methodology and approach. The analysis will therefore remain relevant, even as the assessments themselves are inevitably overtaken by world events.

Luigi Ruggerone contributes the first case study, Chapter 8, a risk assessment, conducted in spring 2004 at Banca Intesa, for a potential foreign acquisition. The focus of the case study is the use of country risk scenarios in "stress testing" – assessing the financial impact of extreme events. The chapter makes the case for stress testing, lays out a stress-testing methodology and applies the methodology to the case of a potential acquisition in Turkey.

Chapter 9 is an analysis of China from a rating agency perspective by **Therese Feng**. Sovereign ratings – produced by Fitch Ratings, Moody's and Standard & Poor's – are arguably the most authoritative country risk assessments in existence. Sovereign rating upgrades and downgrades frequently move markets, and may even have regulatory implications for banks' cross-border exposures. This chapter is a detailed review of the internal and external political factors that Fitch Ratings consider when they assign their sovereign rating for China.

Like country risk analysis, emerging markets research is dominated by a few major firms: Goldman Sachs, JP Morgan, Merrill Lynch, UBS, CSFB, Deutsche Bank, Lehman Brothers. For this volume, I invited a contribution from CreditSights – a research firm whose independence is of increasing value in these days of Wall Street scandals. In Chapter 10, **Christian Stracke** offers an example of the art of emerging-market analysis, with an assessment of Brazil. His economic model of Brazil's total factor productivity has alarming implications for the country's long-term risk profile.

Another new voice is World Markets Research Centre, which has made a name for itself through its daily coverage of world events and rating system focused on on-the-ground risks. In Chapter 11, **Guy Dunn** applies a newly updated version of this rating system to Russia, demonstrating a rigorous approach to the often nebulous topic of operational risks.

Managing a country risk portfolio

The final section of the book shifts focus from consideration of risky countries to consideration of the global firms that operate there, and how these companies manage the attendant risks. In Chapter 12, **Michael Bates** presents a comprehensive review of best practices in country risk management, focusing on the techniques in use at global financial institutions. He covers all the bases: the changing risk environment, risk assessment approaches, case studies of setting and benchmarking internal country risk ratings, and various schemes for organising the country risk function.

Building on this last theme, in Chapter 13 **J. Marc Michel Léonard** takes a novel approach to the topic of country risk, considering the various lessons that models of human decision-making behaviour offer for country risk managers. Based on a survey of Global 500 firms, he draws up a profile of typical errors made in country risk management. He then explains the sources of these errors – rooted in organisational problems – and recommends steps that can prevent such organisational failures from recurring.

Political risk is an unusual line of insurance, and not simply because it protects against threats such as wars, riots, expropriations and nationalisations. Generally speaking, political risk underwriters are forced to set premiums based on educated guesswork, since there are insufficient data to allow for an actuarial approach.

In Chapter 14, **Jotaro Hamada, Henning Haugerudbraaten, Andrew Hickman and Ilya Khaykin** advance the state of the art in this area, by laying out a scheme for pricing political risks that is based on statistical modelling and an economic capital approach.

The last two chapters review tools for country and political risk transfer. In Chapter 15, **Martin Stone** unpacks the often misunderstood and conflated threats of currency inconvertibility and exchange transfer – pointing out, for instance, that most insurance claims in this area stem from incidents of passive blockage, not deliberate government action. The chapter offers insight into the definition and assessment of these risks, as well as advice on technical risk transfer issues.

Finally, in Chapter 16, **Frank Packer** and **Chamaree Suthiphongchai** review the development of a relatively new tool in the country risk manager's kit – sovereign credit default swaps (CDS). They provide a detailed review of the growth of this credit derivative, with breakdowns by region, rating, restructuring clause and maturity. They also compare CDS risk premiums with sovereign ratings, with interesting results.

ACKNOWLEDGEMENTS

Fortunately, in an edited volume, much of the credit goes precisely where due – to the authors, who produced excellent contributions, several of them advancing the state of the art in their fields, while holding positions of significant responsibility.

Several others must also be thanked. Luigi Ruggerone contributed a substantial amount of work in conceptualising this volume and inviting several important contributions. Without his efforts, this project simply would not have been possible (and he also delivered an excellent chapter). Stijn Claessens, Therese Feng, David Hale, Dan Lefkovitz, Michel Leonard, Martin Stone, Christian Stracke and Marvin Zonis all made useful suggestions on content and contributors. And finally, ample credit goes to Tamsine Green, the development editor at Risk Books who pushed this project forward from inception to completion.

REFERENCE

Harvey, C., and G. Morgenson, 2002, *The New York Times Dictionary of Money and Investing: The Essential Guide to the Language of the New Market* (New York: Times Books).

Section 1

Assessing Country Risk

Currency and Banking Crises: A Review of the Theories*

Stijn Claessens

World Bank

INTRODUCTION

The currency and banking crises in Latin America, Europe and Asia during the past three decades have generated substantial literature on their causes. The literature on these currency crises begins with models developed to explain those experienced by some Latin American countries in the late 1970s. These models view currency crises as being caused by weak economic fundamentals. Following the collapse of the European Monetary System in 1992, the so-called second-generation models of currency crises emerged. These models show that currency crises can occur due to certain government policy actions, self-fulfilling expectations of market participants and possibilities of multiple equilibriums, even in the absence of fundamental weaknesses. The theoretical currency crisis literature has expanded further since the 1997 Asian financial crisis. The so-called third-generation models view a currency crisis as a run on an economy or a financial panic.

In the case of banking crises, much of the theory focuses on special characteristics of banks – such as maturity and currency

*This chapter was originally prepared for the Asian Development Bank and presented at the Early Warning System Seminar, Beijing, 13 December, 2002, and at the Early Warning System Workshop, Beijing, 16 June, 2004. The author would like to thank the participants for very useful comments on the presentations and paper, and in particular Juzhong Zhuang for his comments on the paper. The paper was prepared while the author was at the University of Amsterdam. The opinions expressed do not represent those of the World Bank or the Asian Development Bank.

transformation, and asymmetric information – that make banks and the banking industry vulnerable to runs and collapses following adverse shocks of either domestic or external origin. A single bank run can by contagion lead to a systemic banking crisis. Institutional features of economies, such as excessive deposit insurance, poor supervision and weak corporate governance, are emphasised in the literature, as these are closely related to the incentives of bank managers to take on risks in lending operations and bank profitability.

This chapter reviews theories of currency and banking crises in some detail. The next section describes the three generations of currency crisis models. The section following looks at causes of banking crises. The last section concludes by outlining current thinking on how currency and (systemic) banking crises can be prevented and their impact limited.

THEORY OF CURRENCY CRISES

A review of the theory regarding currency crises is best done utilising the three generations of models. The first-generation models began with the seminal pieces by Krugman (1979) and Flood and Garber (1984), which were built on work by Salant and Henderson (1978). The key focus of these papers was that macro-policies, defined broadly, can (i) be inconsistent when combined with fixed or pegged exchange rates, (ii) lead to an unsustainable situation and (iii) be followed by a currency adjustment. These macro inconsistencies may include excessive domestic credit growth, fiscal weaknesses and poor economic performance, to mention only a few. The major contribution of these papers was not so much the fact that inconsistencies can lead to currency adjustments, as that is well understood. Rather, it was that there could be a sharp and sudden loss in foreign-exchange reserves when forward-looking market participants realised that the existing exchange rate was no longer viable indefinately.

The first generation of currency crisis models can be interpreted more broadly. It is not only that the policy inconsistencies can be macroeconomic: they can also be of a microeconomic or other nature. The inconsistencies with a fixed or pegged foreign-exchange rate can thus also be attributable to the presence of some structural weaknesses. For example, a decline in competitiveness as a result of poor labour upgrading can mean that a foreign-exchange target is no longer viable; a weakening of export prices due to new competition can make macro-policies – including the foreign-exchange target – more inconsistent. As such, the first-generation literature on currency crises can be seen to view currency crises as events caused by poor policies or structural weaknesses.

The second generation of currency crisis models began with Obstfeld (1986 and 1996; see also Krugman, 1997). Obstfeld stressed that there may be tradeoffs between the various policy objectives pursued by a country. For example, inflation and employment may face some tradeoffs, as in the traditional Phillips curve. The government may be indifferent between, say, an outcome of low inflation and high unemployment or an outcome of high inflation and low unemployment. The low-inflation equilibrium may be associated with a fixed exchange rate and the high-inflation outcome with a floating foreign-exchange regime or another fixed, but depreciated, exchange rate. If the government (or the country, more generally) is indifferent, either equilibrium may be sustained, thus opening up the possibility of multiple equilibriums, and associated sudden currency adjustments.

Prospective fiscal deficits caused by a collapse of a banking system and the need for a fiscal bailout may also trigger a currency crisis – the expectation of the government having to bail out a banking system may cause lenders to pull out funds, thus triggering the collapse of the currency and the crisis (see Burnside, Eichenbaum, Rebelo, 2001). This means that one can have self-fulfilling currency crises; that is, because of some events or actions (for example, by a speculator), the equilibrium may shift from a fixed regime to a floating regime or from one fixed exchange rate to another fixed but more depreciated rate.

There are other related models. Blanchard and Watson (1982) model the collapse of a stochastic speculative bubble that was itself a rational equilibrium. The bubble, however, was nevertheless *ex post* irrational and also had a positive probability of collapsing all along. Typically, this has been applied more to stock markets. In some cases, however, the exchange rate has displayed some of the same patterns, such as in Russia in the summer of 1998, when the exchange rate and the fiscal situation were being supported by large capital inflows that all along seemed to have a large probability of collapsing.

The theoretical currency crisis literature has expanded further since the 1997 East Asian financial crisis. The third-generation models view a currency crisis as a run on a country or a financial panic. In some sense, the country is subject to the equivalent of a bank run with the fixed (or pegged) exchange rate functioning as the equivalent of a fixed-deposit contract. As such, the literature builds on the seminal model of Diamond and Dybvig (1983) of bank runs. The first and most complete version of this analogy to the banking crisis literature is Chang and Velasco (2001).

More broadly, the third-generation model draws attention to the structure of claims on a country as it affects the risk of a financial crisis. Creditors, particularly those with short-term claims, can suddenly withdraw, leaving the country with an acute shortage of foreign exchange and liquidity. The withdrawal may be rational for each creditor given the lack of coordination among creditors – each individual's incentive is to withdraw first, fearing that others will withdraw even earlier. The effect for the country, however, is a loss of aggregate liquidity that triggers a currency or financial collapse.

Even more broadly, the third-generation models have drawn attention to the importance of balance-sheet effects for the sustainability of a currency target. Papers on this topic include Krugman (1999), Caballero and Krishnamurthy (2001), and Aghion, Bachetta and Banerjee (2000). In Krugman (1999), the argument is that balance-sheet mismatches can force banks or corporations to quickly generate demand for foreign exchange. With a large part of the financial sector or corporate sector seeking foreign exchange, however, pressure is put on the foreign-exchange rate. As the rate depreciates, more financial institutions or corporations may seek foreign exchange to cover open positions, stimulating even further aggregate outflows and thereby triggering a currency crisis. Caballero and Krishnamurthy (2001) point out that these events may be more likely in emerging markets because firms and banks there cannot easily collateralise their foreign-exchange assets or cashflow. As such, they have less ability to smooth shocks, and a relatively small event can trigger large capital outflows and a currency crisis.

There are many variations of the basic third-generation currency crisis models, all of which centre on balance-sheet effects and capital market imperfections. One such theory is the disorderly workout (Sachs, 1994a and 1994b and Miller and Zhang, 2000). This theory can be seen as the equivalent of a grab for assets in the absence of a domestic bankruptcy system, as in the case of a liquidity problem of a firm. Because an effective means of reorganising claims in case of an international liquidity problem does not exist, a disorderly workout can easily result when a country is hit by a small shock that ought to be only a liquidity shock. The liquidity shock may turn into an insolvency situation, however, because the corporations and financial institutions in the country, with no access to good restructuring mechanisms, will destroy value, creating a debt overhang.

An international bankruptcy regime for sovereign claims could prevent a liquidity shock for a government from becoming a solvency issue, and there has been much research and policy discussion under way recently in this area (such as the Sovereign Debt Restructuring Mechanism; see Krueger, 2002). Even when an international bankruptcy regime for sovereign claims could be introduced, the issue of restructuring remains for international claims on domestic corporations and financial institutions. For these, local insolvency regimes are often insufficient and, almost always, poorly equipped to deal with the large number of claims in a systemic crisis and the ensuing complexities of international restructuring.

Another type of currency crisis that has received attention under the third-generation models is the "moral-hazard-induced crisis". Excessive, overly risky investment by banks, other financial institutions or corporations may be induced by government behaviour or policy. Specifically, risky banks may be able to borrow cheaply as they have implicit or explicit guarantees from the government on their liabilities, that is, implicit or explicit deposit insurance. If they are or if they become undercapitalised and are weakly regulated, then the incentive for them to increase risk becomes great. Akerlof and Romer (1993) model what they call looting behaviour in the context of the US Savings and Loan crisis in the early 1980s. This model has been extended, although not always formally, to the situation of a currency crisis. The addition is that both foreign and domestic creditors go along with the risky behaviour of financial institutions or corporations, as they know that the government or international financial institutions will bail them out.

Krugman (1998) applies this model to the Asian crisis. Dooley (2000) generalises the model with any form of government guarantee. Johnson *et al* (2000) applies this to cases of weak corporate governance. They show that a framework of weak institutional corporate governance can mean that controlling shareholders become more interested in looting the firm when hit by a small shock. In turn, this can trigger a currency crisis. They provide empirical support for this across a number of countries as the degree of currency depreciation is related to the quality of the institutional framework.

A last form of recent currency crisis models, although not necessarily belonging to the third-generation models, has been related to the phenomenon of contagion in real and financial markets. It is obvious that global shocks, such as rises in interest rates or oil price changes, may affect a whole group of countries simultaneously and thus create turbulence on a large scale that may suggest spillovers but are really crises due to common shocks. There may also be other ways by which a crisis in one country spills over into other parts of the world. For example, these can be trade links invoking competitive devaluations. They can also be financial links related to things such as foreign direct investment where, for example, events in Thailand can trigger a crisis in Indonesia as Thai investors withdraw from Indonesia. The common lender channel is one specific form of this kind of contagion. In the East Asian financial crisis, Japan was found to transmit shocks in this way, while the US played a role in the Latin American crises. A crisis in one country may also teach investors something about fundamentals in other, similar countries. This is not necessarily contagion, but rather learning about the true model of risk. Following the Asian financial crisis, many observers have used the concept of a "wake-up call". In one sense, this concept and some of the other contagion models are more a part of first- or second-generation currency and banking crisis models.

Nonetheless, financial markets are frequently cited as the sole or main culprit of financial crises. As such, there may be an independent role for financial markets in causing financial crises. There are still two dimensions or situations to consider. One is when there is some rational behaviour in financial markets that, nevertheless, has perverse effects. Much of this would derive from coordination issues in financial markets – individuals may act rationally on their own, but collectively they may cause a bad outcome, such as a bank run. The degree of this behaviour can be affected by many institutional features, such as the prevalence of benchmarking on index portfolios among investment managers or the degree of agency issues among investment fund managers. Information asymmetries may aggravate the issue when investors follow insiders deemed to have better information. The other dimension is the truly irrational behaviour at the individual level. This irrational behaviour can include herding or prevalence of multiple equilibriums at the level of asset classes (for example, emerging markets at a given time are in or out of "fashion").

The distinction between the individually rational but collectively irrational and the individually irrational is theoretically unclear and often empirically impossible to prove. Debates still rage about whether the Asian financial crisis was caused by either form. Therefore, some have argued that it is more relevant to investigate whether there are policy interventions that can affect either type of behaviour. This still requires, however, a test to determine whether either effect is considered to have purely negative effects. After all, some forms of "contagion" represent a normal allocation of resources and good form of market discipline. Furthermore, each policy intervention raises its own tradeoffs, such as moral hazard in the case of an international lender as a last resort to counteract the individually rational but collectively irrational run on a country.

THEORY OF BANKING CRISES

There are two types of banking distress: individual and system-wide. The theory regarding causes of the first type takes a more micro view and has been applied extensively to the empirical models used mainly in developed countries to predict financial distress. Reviewing this theory is relevant here because individual banking distress can lead to systemic distress, depending upon various factors. Although the theory dealing with determinants of system-wide banking distress is somewhat similar to that regarding individual bank distress, there are some important differences and additions, several of which already have been reviewed under the theory of currency crises. A review of both types follows.

Much of the literature on bank runs has modelled the phenomenon as an asymmetric information problem between depositors and banks. Some consider these banking panics as random manifestations of mass hysteria or mob psychology, as discussed by Kindleberger (1978). This "pure panic" or "sunspot" theory of a bank run is formalised in Diamond and Dybvig (1983). They posit that illiquidity of assets provides the rationale for a bank's vulnerability to runs. Multiple equilibriums can exist where one of the equilibrium points is a bank run scenario arising from the panic of agents. They also show that a bank run can be self-fulfilling when depositors believe that other depositors are withdrawing their funds even without any initial deterioration of the bank's balance sheet.

In terms of predicting individual bank insolvency, the empirical approach typically used in developed countries has been to use a combination of micro factors, summarised in the CAMEL framework – Capital, Assets, Management, Earnings and Liquidity. Poor balance sheets (non-performing loans), poor profitability, balance-sheet mismatches, low liquidity, weak governance and excessive risk taking have been found to lead to vulnerabilities and banking distress. Because bank runs occur more often in developing countries – as market solutions to temporary liquidity problems do not work as well, and deposit insurance is not always credible – interbank market and other institutional structures have been important factors to consider in these countries.

Also in developing countries, shocks to interest rates, foreign exchange, stock prices, or an economic slowdown and recession can create individual bank distress. Legacies can also be important. Often a bank's inherited weak balance sheet will appear during or after financial liberalisation. This is true with other reforms as well. For example, in many transition economies, pre-transition banks suffered from having to allocate resources to state-owned enterprises. These surfaced only when the corporate and banking sectors were being reformed.

The theory of banking system insolvency begins from the theory of individual bank distress. Chari and Jagannathan (1988) provide an extension of the Diamond–Dybvig model to explain banking panics. They posit that banking panics result from the misinterpretation by uninformed depositors of liquidity withdrawal shocks as being withdrawals caused by pessimistic information on bank assets. Jacklin and Bhattacharya (1988) further distinguish between pure panics and information-based bank runs by emphasising the source of bank runs as the role played by interim private information about bank loans and asset payoffs. Both models can be interpreted to imply that a single bank run causes a system-wide banking crisis. Another version is that bank runs systematically relate to events that change the perception of depositors' risk – such as extreme seasonal fluctuations (see Miron, 1985), unexpected failure of a large (typically financial) corporation, and major cyclical downturns (see Gorton, 1988). Mishkin (1996) provides a broader framework on the role of asymmetric information in financial crises in developing countries.

Another propagation mechanism is contagion through interbank deposits. Spillovers of individual banking distress can affect the entire banking system via interbank lending. Factors such as the size of the financial institution and the functioning of interbank and other financial markets will determine the likelihood of contagion. In this respect, banks in emerging markets are more at risk. In term of theoretical models, Allen and Gale (2000) show that, to protect themselves against liquidity preference shocks, banks hold interbank claims with each other that are interregional in nature. However, this opens the possibility of a small liquidity preference shock in one bank or region to spread throughout the economy. Another propagation mechanism, suggested by Diamond and Rajan (forthcoming), assumes that banks have a common pool of liquidity. Bank failures can cause aggregate liquidity shortages, which can lead to the failure of other banks, thus making a total meltdown possible even without any informational or contractual links between banks.

The micro factors that can be important determinants for banking system distress refer to the quality of a country's entire institutional framework. Poor market discipline due to moral hazard or limited disclosure, a weak corporate governance framework, excessive deposit insurance and poor supervision can determine the degree of information asymmetries, quality of bank management and the build-up of vulnerabilities, which in turn can trigger banking system crises.

At the system level, macroeconomic factors – shocks to interest rates, foreign-exchange devaluations, commodity shocks, economic slowdowns and capital outflows – can also be important determinants of crises. Banking crises can be triggered by sudden capital outflows as shown by Calvo, Leiderman and Reinhart (1994). Foreign currency exposures by banks and their subsequent issuance of foreign-currency-denominated domestic loans can make banks vulnerable to external shocks (Chinn and Kletzer, 2000). System-wide problems can include legacies, which become public with or after financial liberalisation. Finally, there are many cases when poor early intervention drives a small degree of distress into a major banking crisis. For example, *ad hoc* policy approaches can cause confusion among depositors, trigger further runs and lead to a full-scale financial crisis. These causes have been reviewed in many papers, most notably World Bank, 2001.

HOW TO PREVENT AND LIMIT FINANCIAL CRISES

An understanding of currency and banking crises and their causes can help policy makers to reduce the chance of their occurrence. The policy elements necessary to achieve this reduction have been much discussed in the debate over international financial architecture over the past few years. These include better macroeconomic management, including fiscal and exchange rate management, which will help reduce the risks of unsustainable exchange rates and currency crises. Changes to the international financial system itself may help prevent liquidity crises from becoming crises in solvency. For a review of these broader design issues of the international financial architecture, refer to Fischer (2002).

The debate on international financial architecture has also led to new guidance on improving the way the financial sector functions. The elements include a drive for better regulation and supervision, although one must realise the regulatory and supervisory limits in weak institutional environments, as in many developing countries (as highlighted by Barth, Caprio and Levine, 2003). Increasingly private-sector mechanisms for monitoring are considered to be more useful for financial-sector stability and efficiency. Increasing knowledge in banking system transparency by way of greater shareholdings of foreign banks and other financial institutions is one example. And it will remain important to apply some limits to bank operations, such as limits on maturity mismatches, portfolio composition, foreign-exchange exposure and asset growth.

An important but often overlooked dimension to systemic bank crises is that their output losses, fiscal and other costs can be controlled. What has become general best-practice advice on managing a banking crisis can limit costs:

❑ intervene early and address problems comprehensively and credibly;
❑ structure and manage the recaps adequately;
❑ do not close banks without alternative financial intermediation mechanisms in place; and
❑ complement banks with corporate restructuring.

This best-practice advice also involves proactive policies, such as supporting core, good elements of the financial sector by providing financial support to healthy banks, or at least banks with intrinsic franchise value, and having some adequately designed lender-of-last-resort facility. Possibly some support to corporations is needed, such as help for small and medium-size firms in the form of working-capital financing or, more generally, support for trade finance.

Many countries do not follow best-practice policies, however, making small banking crises grow systemic and become very costly. Honohan and Klingebiel (2002) show that poor early crisis management can add from 35% to 75% of the cross-country variation in fiscal costs of crisis. Most costly are the provisions of open-ended liquidity support to insolvent financial institutions; the issuance of an unlimited guarantee of financial institutions' liabilities, not limited to just deposits; and the policy of regulatory forbearance and repeated recapitalisations. If a country pursues best-practice policies, crisis cost would be only 0.98% of GDP, whereas with bad policies, cost would be 62.6% of GDP. Importantly, the analysis shows that the effects on economic growth of these bad policies is limited or even perverse; that is, these policies hardly enhance economic growth, or perhaps even retard it. This suggests that these policies, especially the blanket guarantee, are largely government transfers – from some taxpayers to other, privileged taxpayers. As such, systemic banking crises are very much a function of the policies adopted and the political economy.

Countries should expect and be prepared for future financial crises. A vigilant monitoring of vulnerabilities and financial exposures is needed to limit both the risk of financial crisis and the impact an actual crisis will have. This can take the form of frequent financial stability assessments using well-designed analytic and forecasting frameworks, including the early-warning systems presented in the rest of this volume. Some degree of contingency crisis planning can also be useful, particularly on how to react to the first sign of an incipient banking crisis, as that often determines whether or not a more systemic crisis results. Most importantly, however, countries need to continually enhance their overall incentive framework so that private-sector financial institutions and corporations are willing and able to manage their financial risks properly. This requires good macroeconomic management, including proper exchange-rate management and ensuring that all three pillars for achieving a solid financial and corporate sector are in place: private capital for backing up financial institutions and corporations, and providing adequate incentives for risk management; an active market role in monitoring and disciplining financial institutions and corporations; and the official sector in its role of supervising financial institutions.

REFERENCES

Aghion, P., P. Bacchetta and A. Banerjee, 2000, "A Simple Model of Monetary Policy and Currency Crises", *European Economic Review*, **44(4–6)**, pp. 728–38.

Akerlof, G., and P. Romer, 1993, "Looting the Economic Underworld of Bankruptcy for Profit", *Brookings Papers on Economic Activity*, **2**, pp. 1–73.

Allen, F., and D. Gale, 2000, "Financial Contagion", *Journal of Political Economy*, **108(1)**, pp. 1–33.

Barth, J. R., G. Caprio Jr, and R. Levine, 2003, "Bank Regulation and Supervision: What Works Best?", *Journal of Financial Intermediation*, **13(2)**, pp. 205–48.

Blanchard, O., and M. Watson, 1982, "Bubbles, Rational Expectations and Financial Markets", in Paul Wachtel (ed), *Crises in the Economic and Financial Structure* (Lexington: Lexington Books).

Burnside, C., M. Eichenbaum and S. Rebelo, 2001, "Prospective Deficits and the Asian Currency Crisis", *Journal of Political Economy*, **109(6)**, pp. 1155–97.

Caballero, R. J., and A. Krishnamurthy, 2001, "International and Domestic Collateral Constraints in a Model of Emerging Market Crises", *Journal of Monetary Economics*, **48(3)**, pp. 513–48.

Calvo, G., L. Leiderman, and C. Reinhart, 1994, "Capital Flows and Macroeconomic Management: Tequila Lessons", *International Journal of Finance and Economics*, **1(3)**, pp. 207–24.

Chang, R., and A. Velasco, 2001, "A Model of Financial Crises in Emerging Markets", *Quarterly Journal of Economics*, **116(2)**, pp. 489–517.

Chari, V., and R. Jagannathan, 1988, "Banking Panics, Information, and Rational Expectations Equilibrium", *Journal of Finance*, **43(3)**, pp. 749–61.

Chen, Y., 1999, "Banking Panics: The Role of the First-Come, First-Served Rule and Information Externalities", *Journal of Political Economy*, **107(5)**, pp. 946–68.

Chinn, M., and K. Kletzer, 2000, "International Capital Inflows, Domestic Financial Intermediation and Financial Crises Under Imperfect Information", NBER Working Paper number 7902, National Bureau for Economic Research, Cambridge MA, September.

Diamond, D. W., and P. H. Dybvig, 1983, "Bank Runs, Deposit Insurance, and Liquidity", *Journal of Political Economy*, **91(3)**, 401–19.

Diamond, D. W., and R. G. Rajan, forthcoming. "Liquidity Shortages and Banking Crises", *Journal of Finance*.

Dooley, M. P., 2000, "A Model of Crises in Emerging Markets", *Economic Journal*, **110**, pp. 256–72.

Fischer, S., 2002, "Financial Crises and the Reform of the International Financial System", NBER Working Paper number 9297, pp. 1–51, National Bureau for Economic Research, Cambridge MA, October.

Flood, R. P., and P. M. Garber, 1984, "Collapsing Exchange-Rate Regimes: Some Linear Examples", *Journal of International Economics*, **17**, pp. 1–13.

Gorton, G., 1988, "Banking Panics and Business Cycles", *Oxford Economic Papers*, **40(3)**, pp. 221–55.

Honohan, P., and D. Klingebiel, 2002, "Controlling Fiscal Costs of Banking Crises", in D. Klingebiel and L. Laeven (eds), "Managing the Real and Fiscal Effects of Banking Crises", World Bank Discussion Paper number 428, pp. 5–29 (Washington, DC: World Bank), January.

Jacklin, C. J., and S. Bhattacharya, 1988, "Distinguishing Panics and Information-based Bank Runs: Welfare and Policy Implications", *Journal of Political Economy (US)*, **96**, pp. 568–92.

Johnson, S., *et al*, 2000, "Corporate Governance in the Asian Financial Crisis", *Journal of Financial Economics*, **58(4)**, pp. 141–86.

Kindleberger, C., 1978, *Manias, Panics and Crashes: A History of Financial Crises* (New York: Basic Books).

Krueger, A. O., 2002, *A New Approach to Sovereign Debt Restructuring* (Washington, DC: International Monetary Fund).

Krugman, P., 1979, "A Model of Balance-of-Payments Crises", *Journal of Money, Credit, and Banking*, **11(3)**, pp. 311–25.

Krugman, P., 1997, "Are Currency Crises Self-Fulfilling?", *NBER Macroeconomics Annual* (Cambridge, MA: MIT Press), pp. 345–78

Krugman, P., 1998, "What Happened to Asia?", mimeo, URL: web.mit.edu/krugman/www/

Krugman, P., 1999, "Balance Sheets, the Transfer Problem, and Financial Crises", in P. Isard, A. Razin and A. K. Rose (eds), *International Finance and Financial Crises: Essays in Honor of Robert P. Flood Jr* (Dordrecht: Kluwer Academic Publishers).

Miller, M., and L. Zhang, 2000, "Sovereign Liquidity Crises: The Strategic Case for a Payments Standstill", *Economic Journal*, **110(460)**, pp. 335–62.

Miron, J., 1985, "Financial Panics, the Sensitivity of the Nominal Interest Rate and the Founding of the Fed", *American Economic Review*, **76(1)**, pp. 125–40.

Mishkin, F., 1996, "Understanding Financial Crises: A Developing Country Perspective", NBER Working Paper number 5600, National Bureau for Economic Research, Cambridge, MA, May.

Obstfeld, M., 1986, "Rational and Self-Fulfilling Balance of Payments Crises", *American Economic Review*, **76(1)**, pp. 72–81.

Obstfeld, M., 1996, "Models of Currency Crises with Self-Fulfilling Features", *European Economic Review*, **40(3–5)**, pp. 1037–47.

Sachs, J., 1994a, "Russia's Struggle with Stabilization: Conceptual Issues and Evidence", in M. Bruno and B. Pleskovic (eds), *Proceedings of the Annual Conference on Development Economics* (Washington, DC: World Bank), pp. 57–80.

Sachs, J., 1994b, "Beyond Bretton Woods: A New Blueprint", *The Economist*, **333**, 1–7 October, pp. 23, 25, 27.

Salant, S., and D. Henderson, 1978, "Market Anticipation of Government Policy and the Price of Gold", *Journal of Political Economy*, **86**, pp. 627–48.

World Bank, 2001, *Finance for Growth: Policy Choices in a Volatile World* (Washington, DC).

2

Currency and Debt Crises: A Review of the Early Warning Systems*

Alessio Ciarlone, Giorgio Trebeschi

Banca d'Italia

INTRODUCTION

Emerging-market economies have experienced many financial crises, driven by such factors as poorly developed financial systems, volatility of macroeconomic policies, a weak banking sector, high dependence on external flows, and uncertain growth prospects. These financial crises have had disruptive effects on the economies in question, causing contraction of GDP, rise in unemployment rates, social unrest, limited ability to access international capital markets, and widespread contagion.

For all of these reasons, both the academic and the official sector have felt the importance of developing models that can not only identify weaknesses and vulnerability in emerging-market economies, but also send timely and correct signals about the onset of a financial crisis, the so-called early warning systems (EWS).

Most of the EWS models developed so far have tried to signal the onset of currency and banking crises, both individually or jointly determined (twin-crises).[1] Even if these models show mixed results in terms of forecasting accuracy, they nonetheless offer a systematic and objective method of predicting this type of crisis and are widely used in international financial institutions (IFIs) as well as in the largest private investment banks.

*We would like to thank our colleague Antonello Fanna for his helpful comments and for the continuous intellectual and moral support. The usual disclaimers apply.

Until now, however, little work has been done on "debt" crises, which can be broadly defined as forms of default or reneging of the terms of domestic or external obligations. In our opinion, developing an EWS for debt crises is extremely useful, since in the very recent past emerging-market economies have shown a tendency to abandon pegged exchange rates and move towards more flexible regimes. Thus, speculative attacks to the exchange rate may no longer be a central worry. Moreover, emerging-market economies have shown a tendency to prefer bond issuance, both domestically and internationally, as a means of fulfilling their financing needs. The period from 1994 onwards has been characterised by large sovereign and corporate defaults or debt-servicing difficulties on foreign currency-denominated bonds.

Currency and debt crises may be generated by common factors, such as unfavourable macroeconomic developments, a deterioration in external financing conditions (such as a sudden reduction in capital flows or a sharp increase in their cost) or an increase in the extent of international investors' risk aversion. From this point of view, therefore, studying the determinants of a currency crisis may shed some light on the potential difficulties facing a country when servicing its external debt. Some models do, in fact, conclude that currency crises in developing countries are closely linked to the probability of sovereign defaults, in the sense that a currency crisis increases the probability of fiscal distress (see Goldstein, Kaminsky and Reinhart, 2000; Reinhart, 2002).

Notwithstanding the previous considerations, currency and debt crises do remain quite distinct events, in fact:

❑ the two types of crises are explained by two different sets of independent variables: measures of real exchange-rate overvaluation, external imbalances, foreign exchange reserves and export growth are good explanatory variables for currency crises; debt crises, instead, might be better explained by economic factors that measure the weight of domestic and/or external debt, the amount of debt service obligations or the ability of a country to generate sufficient resources to meet these obligations promptly;

❑ the two types of crises are not perfectly correlated, as shown in Sy (2003), in the sense that it is possible to have a currency crisis that is not associated with a debt crisis, as it is conceivable that a country may fall into arrears or may default on its external debt without any major disruption in the exchange rate, as happened in Pakistan in 1999; and

❑ it is not clear what the causal relationship should be: in fact, one could expect a sharp depreciation of the exchange rate as a response to an excessively high growth of the external debt or a rapidly worsening scenario for the country's financing needs; under such a scenario, investors might not trust the government's ability to face its external obligations any more and might start selling off assets denominated in that particular currency.

This chapter is organised as follows: the next section briefly describes EWS models for currency crises; the following section is dedicated to a more comprehensive review of EWS models for debt crises; and the last section suggests how to improve upon the empirical definition of debt crisis for future EWS research.

EWS FOR CURRENCY CRISES

Standard EWS models apply statistical and econometric procedures to forecast the likelihood of a financial crisis, defined in a pre-determined way, over a given time horizon. An EWS, therefore, requires both a precise definition of what a financial crisis is and a mechanism for generating predictions; the latter includes a set of supposedly relevant factors and a systematic method to obtain prediction from these variables.

An important categorisation among the various models developed in the last 10 years is based on the particular econometric methodology used to assess the role played by the different macroeconomic and financial variables in determining the main elements of vulnerability and the onset of a financial crisis. Two main econometric approaches have been used: non-parametric methods based on the so-called "signal approach" and parametric estimations based on probit-logit regressions for limited dependent variables.

According to the signal (or indicator) approach, the pre-crisis average level (or the growth rate) of a variable supposed to be significant in determining a financial crisis is compared to the value for a tranquil period. If the variable behaved differently before a crisis, an extreme value might provide a warning signal. The question as to what the "optimal" extreme value should be is solved by minimising the "noise-to-signal" ratio, ie, by comparing the percentage of crises correctly predicted against the percentage of false signals. Once the most significant variables have been identified, a composite leading indicator can be built as a weighted average of the individual signals. This procedure has the advantage of pointing out, in a relatively easy and immediate way, which macroeconomic and financial variables are more significant in rushing an economy into a crisis. It is therefore useful for those analysts who are primarily interested in finding the main elements of vulnerability, regardless of calculating exact probabilities. The seminal paper in this category of models is undoubtedly the one written by Kaminsky, Lizondo and Reinhart (1998). Another important contribution is the paper by Berg and Pattillo (1998).

In the limited dependent variable probit/logit models, the crisis indicator is still constructed as a binary variable, as in the signal approach, but now the explanatory variables are entered in linear fashion. The logit and probit techniques ensure that the predicted outcome always lies between zero and one. In the context of EWS, therefore, the estimated result might be interpreted as the probability of a financial crisis. Notwithstanding its easily understandable outcome, this approach is not faultless. The first practical problem lies in the fact that, by nature, the number of crises is limited, resulting in few "ones" and many "zeros" and in poor estimation results; a second flaw stems from the fact that the interpretation of the coefficients as "marginal" effects is not so straightforward; lastly, these models do not take into account the existence of non-linear relationships among explanatory variables. The seminal paper in this category of models is undoubtedly the one written by Frankel and Rose (1996). The use of a multinomial logit model has been suggested by Bussiere and Fratzscher (2002).

A problem that is common to both the "signal" and the logit/probit approach deals with the evaluation of their respective predictive performances: in general, the out-of-sample predictive ability is not as accurate as the in-sample performance. A detailed discussion of this topic can be found in Berg, Borensztein and Pattillo (2004).

Along with the two approaches outlined so far, many other econometric specifications have been developed in order to discover the causes of financial crises, even if they did not have the same success: Abiad (2003) suggests a Markov switching approach, Nag and Mitra (1999) use an artificial neural network, Blejer and Schumacher (1998) recommend a value-at-risk (VAR) approach, Zhang (2001) proposes an autoregressive conditional hazard model, Krkoska (2001) estimates a restricted VAR.

EWS FOR DEBT CRISES: A SURVEY OF THE LITERATURE

The literature on the empirical models that look for the determinants of a debt crisis is quite small compared with the large body of theoretical and empirical work that has been produced on the factors behind currency or banking crises.

Our objective here is to give a general overview of the attempts to identify the causes of the process that might make it increasingly difficult for a country to repay its domestic or external obligations, to the point where the country itself is forced to declare a moratorium.

A necessary classification is between models that are based on the evolution of a particular set of macroeconomic variables, as the main factors leading to the build-up of a crisis, and models that extract information from financial data and market prices for widely traded financial instruments such as sovereign bonds or, more recently, credit default swaps (CDSs).

Models based on macroeconomic variables

The first attempt to develop an EWS for debt crises is the analysis by Detragiache and Spilimbergo (2001), whose objective is to show how the levels of some important macroeconomic factors might determine the occurrence of debt repayment problems.

Their starting point is the recognition that the crises in Mexico and East Asia highlighted the role played by external liquidity, especially when there is a "sudden stop" in the flows of capital towards emerging-market economies. Many observers, in fact, noticed that both Mexico's and the Asian countries' balance sheets showed a significant maturity mismatch, ie, their short-term external liabilities were not matched by foreign assets with the same characteristics. The model corresponds with the theoretical and empirical literature that highlights the role played by international illiquidity in determining a financial crisis (see Chang and Velasco, 1998; Radelet and Sachs, 1998).

From a theoretical point of view, the relationship between liquidity variables and financial crises has been modelled through self-fulfilling creditors runs (see Chang and Velasco, 1998): when the amount of debt that a country has to "roll over" is small enough, the "bad" equilibrium disappears and there is no crisis. Thus, measures of external liquidity could be correlated with financial crises and, for this reason, they ought to be carefully monitored by policymakers.

The objective of the authors, therefore, is to find support for the theoretical relationship between liquidity variables and financial crises and to improve upon the existing empirical evidence. Previous models, in fact, received quite mixed results, mainly because they tried to measure the significance of liquidity factors in the context of currency, rather than debt, crises. Instead, Detragiache and Spilimbergo's analysis predominantly focuses on this type of event, making their paper a seminal contribution to the topic.

The occurrence of debt crisis is defined as a situation in which the country either has sizeable arrears of principal or interest on external obligations or there is debt restructuring or rescheduling with commercial creditors. Through the means of a classical probit analysis, the authors find that liquidity variables, among others, are indeed highly significant and have the right signs, meaning that the less liquid a country the more likely a debt crisis. An important policy implication is that monitoring the components of external liquidity could give very useful insights on the probabilities of entering into a debt crisis.[2]

Catao and Sutton's analysis (2002) is different from Detragiache and Spilimbergo's contribution in several respects. First of all, while the latter focuses on a more general problem of a country experiencing a "liquidity crisis", which does not necessarily have to end with a moratorium on debt payments, Catao and Sutton's contribution attempts to shed some light on the determinants of outright defaults. From this point of view, their crisis classification is based more on anecdotal evidence than on a formal quantitative approach. Moreover, in their analysis, only government debt counts, while this is not the case in Detragiache and Spilimbergo's study, where public- and private-sector repayments difficulties were mingled.

Another innovation lies in the fact that Catao and Sutton propose the introduction of a new set of explanatory variables, linked to the historical volatility of some macroeconomic aggregates that, in their opinion, could boost the low predictive performance of Detragiache and Spilimbergo's model. In this respect, Catao and Sutton's contribution is in line with that body of theoretical literature according to which the volatility of macroeconomic variables, especially that induced by economic policy variations, might play an important role in explaining the optimal decision of a country to default on its debt obligation (see Eaton and Gersovitz, 1981; Eaton, Gersovitz and Stiglitz, 1986).

According to Catao and Sutton's view, a first source of macroeconomic volatility can be identified in the unpredictable movement of the terms of trade: their variations are deemed to have an adverse effect on both debt-servicing capacity and sovereign risk, through their impact on fiscal revenues and the real exchange rate. Behind this "externally induced" volatility, the authors underscore the role played by fiscal and monetary policies, as well as the degree of capital controls, in influencing the repayment capacities of an emerging-market economy. In fact, the estimated coefficients of the "policy-induced" volatility are all positive and statistically significant, meaning that countries characterised by greater volatility and unpredictable and inconsistent macroeconomic policies are more prone to default episodes.

Manasse, Roubini and Schimmelpfennig (2003) improve upon both of the preceding models in several ways. The objective of their analysis seems to be more in line with Catao and Sutton's approach, since they try to identify a set of macroeconomic variables that could explain the occurrence of a "sovereign" debt crisis, meaning that private-sector repayment difficulties are netted out from the analysis. Nonetheless, there is an element that makes their model more similar to Detragiache and Spilimbergo's contribution: the dependent variable is the occurrence not just of an outright sovereign default, but of a more general debt crisis, which might encompass "liquidity" and "roll-over" problems as well, identified by large non-concessional financial assistance from the IMF.

The starting set of potential regressors comprises something in the region of 47 macroeconomic variables, which are classified in six different groups according to their nature; by means of a multiple-stage strategy the authors are able to pick up only those variables that represent "best performers".[3] As expected, the macroeconomic variables that turn out to be significant in determining the probability of running into a debt crisis of the "default" or the "liquidity" type can be drawn from the set of usual suspects. That is, those that measure the weight of external indebtedness, the flow of financial resources that have to be destined to debt repayments, the revenue-generating capacities of a country, the volatility of domestic economic policies or the changes in international financial conditions.[4]

A shortcoming of all the preceding empirical studies is that none of them take into account the evolution of important financial variables, such as the spread between the yield of an emerging-market bond and the return on similar bonds issued in an advanced economy.

In the light of this consideration, Pescatori and Sy (2003) show that the definition of debt crisis based only on the occurrence of a sovereign default (as in Catao and Sutton), or of arrears on external obligations towards commercial creditors (as in Detragiache and Spilimbergo), or on the occurrence of large IMF financial assistance (as in Manasse, Roubini and Schimmelpfennig), proves to be too restrictive and less effective as an early warning signal of financial distress. Instead, such an event might be easily identified by a market-based indicator obtained simply by looking at the evolution of spreads, or prices, on the secondary market for emerging-market bonds. In this setting a crisis is reported to occur when the spread goes above a given threshold.

The estimation results seem to show that the in-sample predictive performances of their market-based definition are much better than those resulting from a characterisation solely based on sovereign defaults. The out-of-sample comparisons seem to point to the same conclusion.

The importance given to financial market data places Pescatori and Sy's paper between the models solely based on macroeconomic variables and the models based on risky market instruments. In fact, while the methodology used by the authors is the conventional logit regression analysis used in other macro-based models, the emphasis on bond spreads brings their approach closer to the market-based models outlined below.

Models based on risky market instruments

The literature on the valuation of risky market instruments has developed in two main streams: the structural-model approach and the reduced-form approach.

In the structural approach the focus is on trying to model the process that drives asset prices and determining in this way the probability of default on risky market instruments. The first paper in the field utilises the *option theory approach* (or the contingent claims analysis), initially presented in the seminal article by Black and Scholes (1973) and subsequently elaborated by Merton (1974, 1977). This idea, which was originally applied just to corporate debt obligations, has been recently expanded to take into account the case of sovereign entities as well. According to Black and Scholes, shares in a company can be thought of as a call option on the assets of the company itself, with strike equal to the face value of the outstanding debt: ie, shareholders can exercise the option, repay the bondholders and keep the difference between asset and debt value. Default would occur if, at maturity, asset value were below the value of the outstanding debt. Once the process that drives asset value is known, it is possible to determine the probability of default using Black and Scholes' formula.

Gray, Merton and Bodie (2003) and Gapen *et al* (2004) develop a similar framework that applies the contingent claims analysis to a country's economy as a whole. In the simplest version of their models, they identify three sectors: the corporate, the financial and the public. These are viewed as interconnected portfolios of assets, liabilities and contingent claims: for example, all of the corporate sector debt corresponds to bank loans and can be thought of as the sum of risk-free debt plus a short position in a put option on corporate assets. The implicit option materialising as an asset for one sector, and as a liability for another, can make it easier for a problem arising in one sector to spread around the economy as a whole.

The contingent claim analysis can shed some light on sovereign debt sustainability, defined by macroeconomists as a "situation in which a sovereign borrower is expected to continue servicing its debt obligation without default or restructuring and without unrealistically large adjustments to the internal and external balance". In order to carry out the analysis, one has to compare the value of sovereign assets with the default barrier, both expressed in foreign currency. The sovereign assets include foreign-currency reserves and a net "fiscal asset" that is determined by discounting the expected stream of net future primary fiscal surpluses, while the default barrier is determined by the default-free value of foreign debt: a sovereign would default when the asset value hit the default barrier. Once the total asset value and its volatility has been estimated, it is possible, in a similar way to the case of corporate debt, to determine the probability of default for the sovereign or, alternatively, a threshold for the spread above which sovereign default is highly likely to occur.[5] The framework depicted in Gray, Merton and Bodie can help in analysing financial crises in a broad range of situations, not just focusing on government: joint currency, banking and debt crises can be explained by means of the linkages between sectors and by the implicit guarantee the government gives to the banking sector.

The second stream of work relating to the evaluation of the probability of default for risky financial instruments refers to the *reduced-form approach*. According to this approach, and under the hypothesis that financial markets are efficient and sufficiently liquid, the difference in value between a risky and a risk-free asset is determined by the expected loss from holding the risky asset. In this setting, a default can be thought of as an event driven by a random process, whose characteristics can be inferred directly from market data. At any time, in fact, the expected loss can be disentangled into a probability of default and a recovery rate in the case of such an event.

The reduced-form approach can be found in a number of studies, such as Jarrow, Lando and Turnbull (1997), Lando (1998), Duffie and Singleton (1999), Merrick (2001) and Andritzky (2003). The simplest version of these models, as in Jarrow, Lando and Turnbull (1997), can be applied to a defaultable zero coupon. Let $H(t, T)$ be the price at time t of a risk-free zero coupon bond with maturity T (for example, a US Treasury bill) and $V_i(t, T)$ the price of a defaultable zero coupon bond with the same characteristics (for example, an emerging-market bond issued by country i). The following relations apply for the price of the two bonds:

$$V_i(t,T) = H(t,T) \cdot \left\{ \left[1 - p_i(t,T) \right] + R \cdot p_i(t,T) \right\} \qquad (1)$$

where $p_i(t, T)$ is the risk neutral probability of default at time t over the period from t to T and R is the recovery rate in case of default.

Equation (1) can be generalised to other types of bonds: for example, a coupon bond can be thought of as a collection of zero coupon bonds. Using annual compounding, the value of the risky coupon bond would be:

$$V_t = \sum_{i=1}^{N} c_{t_i} \cdot (1 + r_{t_i})^{-t_i} \cdot \left[P_{t_i} + R \cdot p_{t_i} \right] \qquad (2)$$

where time goes from t_1 to t_N; c_{t_i} and r_{t_i} are, respectively, the cashflow and the risk-free interest rate at time t_i; p_{t_i} is the default probability between t_{i-1} and t_i; P_{t_i} is the probability of surviving up to period t_i and R is the recovery rate.

The striking growth of emerging bond markets over the past 10 years provides sufficiently liquid markets for analysts to extract information from available prices. For instance, Merrick (2001) uses a cross-section of five outstanding Russian Federation and five Republic of Argentina US dollar eurobonds to extract both the implied recovery ratio and the risk-neutral default probability term structure during the August 1998 Russian default crisis.[6] The need to estimate the recovery ratio stems from the consideration that in the case of sovereigns, as opposed to corporate bonds, there is not a long recovery-rate history available, as default events are indeed quite unusual among the former.[7] One should also consider that, as opposed to the case of corporations, there is not a bankruptcy code for sovereigns, and governments have usually nothing more to lose than their reputation.[8]

Using a pricing model for risky bonds that is similar to those depicted in Equation (2), Merrick finds that:

❑ the pre-crisis average implied recovery rate for Russia is lower than the level estimated on historic data for US corporate or for Brady plan restructured sovereign debt (27.3% as opposed to something ranging between 40 and 70%);
❑ the implied risk-neutral default probability increased sharply a week before the default announcement and continued to increase thereafter;

❑ the implied recovery rate was reasonably steady before the restructuring announcement and decreased sharply after, from an average of 27.3 to 10.3%; and

❑ the contagion from the Russian crisis spread to the market for Argentinian bonds as an upward revision of the implied default probability rather than as a change in the recovery rate.

Andritzky (2003) applies a similar framework to study the behaviour of nine liquid Argentine US dollar eurobonds between 8 June, 2000 and 6 May, 2002. His findings point out that default parameters jump significantly during the period. In particular, implied recovery values are well above 50% at the beginning of 2001, after the augmentation of the standby credit with the IMF, and drop to less than 30% at the end of 2001. Implied probability of default appears to be strongly negatively correlated with the implied recovery rate during times of stress.

More recently, with the increasing expansion and importance of the credit derivatives market, new models have been developed that take into account information given by the prices of those instruments.[9]

The credit derivative market and the cash market are clearly closely related: one should expect that, without frictions in the market, the spread on sovereign bonds would be equal to the premium paid by the protection buyer in a CDS contract with the same maturity (see Duffie, 1999; Hull and White, 2000).

However, the presence of market frictions and some features of the CDS contracts imply that a positive default swap basis is usually observed, where the basis is defined as the difference between the CDS and the bond spreads. One important factor is the relative liquidity in the CDS and cash markets. For sovereign issuers, in fact, the bond market tends to be more liquid than the CDS market, hence the existence of a positive basis during normal trading time. Nonetheless, traders usually report that, during periods of distress, price discovery and liquidity migrate to the CDS market, as the demand for protection is driven by investors with long positions in bonds who need to hedge their portfolio, and by hedge funds that find it more straightforward to buy protection than to borrow and go short on bonds.

There is anecdotal evidence that, due to the disruption in the clearing mechanism of the cash market after 11 September, 2001, price discovery migrated to the credit derivative markets. Chan Lau and Kim (2004) find mixed evidence regarding which market dominates the price discovery process for emerging sovereigns, whether it is the bond or the CDS market. On the one hand, they find that during the period from March 2001 to May 2003 the CDS market led the price discovery process in Russia and Colombia while, on the other hand, the two markets were equally important in Brazil and Bulgaria.

A new strand of literature is being developed that uses CDSs to construct early warning indicators of financial distress.

Chan Lau (2003) makes use of the CDS pricing model of Duffie (1999) to obtain the "maximum recovery rate" compatible with observed prices, and computes the related probability of default. The idea is that, as the value of a swap is conventionally zero at inception of the contract, the "premium leg", ie, the present value of future payments made by the protection buyer, should be equal to the "default leg", ie, the present value of the payment the protection seller has to make in the event of default. Using data on Argentinian CDSs, Lau extracts the maximum recovery rate, defined as the upper bound of feasible recovery rates given the term structure of spreads.[10]

The most important results of the analysis suggest that the correlation between the one-year forward probability of default and the maximum recovery rate implied by the term structure of spreads was positive during normal periods and declined steadily from July 2001 ahead of the December default. This suggests that CDSs can be used to construct early warning indicators of debt default.

CONCLUSION: DEBT CRISIS DEFINITION FOR EWS RESEARCH

The review of the economic literature on the determinants of a debt crisis has shown that one of the primary concerns of researchers is to define just what constitutes a debt crisis. The actual problem is that, in reality, such crises may take on different forms, ranging from an outright default declared by an insolvent country on part or all of the stock of external or public debt, to more general debt-servicing difficulties determined more by illiquidity than by insolvency. Each of the models we have reviewed in the previous pages, nonetheless, takes into account just one aspect of this multifaceted event.

According to Detragiache and Spilimbergo (2001), a "debt crisis" is defined as a situation in which either or both of the following conditions occur:

❏ the country has arrears of principal or interest on external obligations towards commercial creditors (banks or bondholders) that add up to more than 5% of the total commercial debt outstanding; and/or
❏ there is a debt restructuring or rescheduling agreement with commercial creditors on either sovereign or private debt.

The length of a "debt crisis" will be determined by the number of years during which the arrears fall above the 5% threshold, while it will be considered concluded only when this limit is not exceeded; nonetheless, if a new crisis begins within four years of the preceding one, it is not considered a new episode but a continuation of the previous event.[11]

On the other hand, Catao and Sutton's crisis classification is quite different, since it is based more on anecdotal evidence than on a formal quantitative approach. Crisis end points are, in fact, taken from Beim and Calomiris (2001); crisis start points are also from here, but complemented by information from Lindert and Morton (1989) and IMF country-desks.[12]

In Manasse, Roubini and Schimmelpfennig the identification of a crisis event is again based on a more formal quantitative approach. In their model a country is considered to be in a debt crisis if:

❏ it is classified as being in default by Standard and Poor's;
❏ it receives large non-concessional financial assistance from the IMF's Financial Department, where large is defined as access in excess of 100% of the quota.[13]

The second condition allows for all these cases in which an incipient debt crisis of the liquidity type has been avoided only thanks to a large financial support from official creditors.[14]

Finally, Pescatori and Sy give another definition of the occurrence of a debt crisis, which is characterised as that event when one or both of the following conditions apply:

❏ there is an outright default of the country, as identified by Standard & Poor's;[15] and/or

❑ the secondary market bond spread is higher than a critical threshold, which is set by the authors at 1,000 basis points.[16]

An initial general suggestion stemming from the previous reflections is that an analyst should take into account the fact that a "debt crisis" cannot be equated solely with the cases in which a sovereign declares a *moratorium* on the entire stock, or part, of its public and/or external debt. The very recent past has witnessed many events in which outright default has been prevented by large aid packages provided by the IFIs (eg, Turkey in 2001 and Brazil in 2002) or by restructuring agreements finalised with the private sector (eg, Uruguay in 2002), as respectively pointed out by Manasse, Roubini and Schimmelpfennig, and Detragiache and Spilimbergo.

Nonetheless, even a combined use of these definitions might turn out to be insufficient to give a clear picture of what a debt crisis is: it should take into account that all the previous potential indicators (default, restructuring/rescheduling, large aid packages from the IFIs) represent just the conclusion of a process that evolves through time and is characterised by the presence of mounting problems in honouring debt payments. These increasing debt-servicing difficulties might well be signalled by the accumulation of interest or principal arrears (as in Detragiache and Spilimbergo) or by a worsening of the market evaluation of a country's credit-worthiness, as measured by an increasing spread over US or euro-denominated bonds (as in Pescatori and Sy).

Any future research on EWS for debt crises should therefore take into account the complexity posed by the definition of what "debt crises" really are and combine the different aspects analysed in the papers reviewed in this section. Given the growing importance of emerging financial markets, the macro-based models should be complemented with information on market expectations extracted from bond spreads as well as from CDSs, as recognised by the IMF itself (2002).

---

1   A currency crisis can be defined as a speculative attack on the exchange rate resulting in a sharp devaluation, or depreciation in the case of a flexible regime, of the currency (if successful) or in a large outflow of reserves, accompanied by a sharp increase in interest rates (if unsuccessful). A banking crisis can be defined as actual or potential bank runs or failures to induce banks to suspend internal convertibility of their liabilities or which compel the government to intervene by extending assistance on a large scale.

2   The liquidity variables used in the model are: (1) debt service due (principal maturing in the year plus interest payments on debt with original maturity of more than one year), (2) short-term debt (debt with an original maturity of less than one year), (3) the stock of international reserves at year end.

3   The six groups are: external debt variables, public debt variables, variables from the IMF early warning system of currency crises, other macroeconomic variables, fiscal variables and political economy variables.

4   The macroeconomic variables that turned out to be significant are: total external debt to GDP; short-term debt (on a residual maturity basis) to reserves; external debt service to reserves; current account balance to GDP; trade openness; US treasury bill rate; real GDP growth; inflation volatility; high inflation; years of presidential elections.

5   Volatility of the asset value can be determined by several factors, the most important of which are uncertainty about the fiscal outlook for the following years or uncertainty about the outlook for the exchange rate.

6   Reduced-form models usually pin down risk-neutral probability. If investors are risk-averse they require a risk premium; therefore implied risk-neutral default probability might be greater than the true probability of default.

7   Altman and Eberhart (1994) and Altman, Cooke and Kishore (1999) give a detailed default recovery history for US corporate bonds.

8   As a benchmark one can look at Beloreshki (2003) for an overview of countries that completed their Brady plan restructuring after 1989.

9   Packer and Suthiphongchai (2003) offer a comprehensive overview of the sovereign credit default swap market.

10 The dataset comprises daily mid-point quotes of CDS spreads with maturities 1, 2, 3, 5, 7 and 10 years for Argentina from 3 August 1998 to 12 December 2001 and daily data on US dollar swaps. The implied probability of default associated with a maximum recovery rate is the highest feasible default probability, hence a conservative estimate for the true probability of default.

11 Using this definition, Detragiache and Spilimbergo identify 54 debt crises that seem to have been concentrated in the early 1980s.

12 By these means Catao and Sutton identify 19 default events in their final sample.

13 Not only has the loan to be approved, but also a financial disbursement has to be actually made during the first year of the programme.

14 Manasse et al identify 31 crisis events for 37 emerging-market economies in the period 1971–2001.

15 Standard & Poor's defines default as the failure to meet a principal or interest payment on the due date. In the case of a sovereign issuer, this happens when scheduled debt is not paid or when an exchange offer of new debt contains less favourable terms than the original issue.

16 It is a common view that market participants regard sovereign bond spread above 1,000 basis points as a signal of a greater probability of default. This common view is corroborated by extreme value theory and kernel density estimation that the authors carry out in their analysis.

REFERENCES

Abiad, A., 2003, "Early Warning Systems: A Survey and a Regime Switching Approach", IMF Working Paper number 03/32.

Altman, E. I., D. Cooke, and V. Kishore, 1999, "Defaults and Return on High Yield Bonds: Analysis Through 1998 and Default Outlook for 1999–2001", New York University Salomon Center, January.

Altman, E. I., and A. C. Eberhart, 1994, "Do Seniority Provisions Protect Bondholders' Investments?", *Journal of Portfolio Management*, **4**, pp. 67–75.

Andritzky, J., 2003, "Implied Default Probabilities and Default Recovery Ratios: An Analysis of the Argentine Crisis 2000–2002", University of St Gallen, available via the internet at URL: http://www.vfs.unizh.ch/papers.htm.

Beloreshki, T., 2003, "Default and Recovery Rates in Emerging Markets", in F. Fabozzi (ed), *Professional Perspectives on Fixed Income Portfolio Management*, vol **3** (New York: John Wiley and Sons).

Beim, D. O., and C. W. Calomiris, 2001, *Emerging Financial Markets* (New York: McGraw-Hill Irwin).

Berg, A., and C. Pattillo, 1998, "Are Currency Crises Predictable? A Test", IMF Staff Papers **46(2)**, pp. 107–38.

Berg, A., E. Borensztein, and C. Pattillo, 2004, "Assessing Early-Warning Systems: How Have They Worked in Practice?", IMF Working Paper Number WP 04/52.

Black, F., and M. Scholes, 1973, "The Pricing of Options and Corporate Liabilities", *Journal of Political Economy*, **(3)**, pp. 637–59.

Blejer, M., and L. Schumacher, 1998, "Central Bank Vulnerability and the Credibility of Commitments: a Value at Risk Approach to Currency Crises", IMF Working Paper Number WP 98/65.

Bussier, M., and M. Fratzscher, 2002, "Towards a New Early Warning System of Financial Crises", European Central Bank Working Paper Number 145.

Catao, L., and B. Sutton, 2002, "Sovereign Defaults: The Role of Volatility", IMF Working Paper Number WP 02/149.

Chan Lau, J. A., 2003, "Anticipating Credit Events Using Credit Default Swaps, with an Application to Sovereign Debt Crises", IMF Working Paper Number WP 03/106.

Chan Lau, J. A., and Y. S. Kim, 2004, "Equity Prices, Credit Default Swaps and Bond Spreads in Emerging Markets", IMF Working Paper Number WP 04/27.

Chang, R., and A. Velasco, 1998, "The Asian Liquidity Crisis", Working Paper No. 98–11, Federal Reserve Bank of Atlanta.

Chang, R., Velasco A., 2000, "Banks, Debt Maturity and Financial Crises", *Journal of International Economics*, **1(51)**, pp. 169–94.

Detragiache, E., and A. Spilimbergo, 2001, "Crises and Liquidity: Evidence and Interpretation", IMF Working Paper Number WP 01/2.

Duffie, D., 1999, "Credit Swap Valuation", *Financial Analysts Journal*, pp. 73–87, January/February.

Duffie, D., and K. Singleton, 1999, "Modeling Term Structures of Defaultable Bonds", *Review of Financial Studies* **(12)**, pp. 687–720.

Eaton, J., and M. Gersovitz, 1981, "Debt with Potential Repudiation: Theoretical and Empirical Analysis", *Review of Economics and Statistics*, **48**, pp. 284–309.

Eaton, J., M. Gersovitz, and J. E. Stiglitz, 1986, "The Pure Theory of Country Risk", *European Economic Review*, **30**, pp. 481–513.

Frankel, J. A., and A. K. Rose, 1996, "Currency Crashes in Emerging Markets: An Empirical Treatment", *Journal of International Economics*, **41(3–4)**, pp. 351–66.

Gapen, M. T., *et al*, 2004, "The Contingent Claims Approach to Corporate Vulnerability Analysis: Estimating Default Risk and Economy-Wide Risk Transfer", IMF Working Paper Number WP 04/121.

Goldstein, M., G. L. Kaminsky, and C. M. Reinhart, 2000, "Assessing Financial Vulnerability, an Early Warning System for Emerging Markets", Institute for International Economics, June.

Gray, D. F., R. C. Merton, and Z. Bodie, 2003, "A New Framework for Analyzing and Managing Macrofinancial Risks", MfRisk Working Paper Number 1, available at URL: http://www.moodys-mfrisk.com.

Hull, J., and A. White, 2000, "Valuing Credit Default Swaps I: No Counterpart Default Risk", *Journal of Derivatives*, **(8)**, pp. 29–40.

IMF, 2002, "Early Warning System Models: The Next Step Forward", *Global Financial Stability Report*, March.

Jarrow, R., D. Lando, and S. Turnbull, 1997, "A Markov Model for Term Structure of Credit Risk Spread", *Review of Financial Studies*, **(10)**, pp. 481–523.

Kaminsky, G. L., S. Lizondo, and C. M. Reinhart, 1998, "Leading Indicators of Currency Crises", *IMF Staff Papers*, **88(2)**, pp. 1–48.

Krkoska, L., 2001, "Assessing Macroeconomic Vulnerability in Central Europe", *Post Communist Economies*, **13(1)**, pp. 41–55.

Lando, D., 1998, "Cox Processes and Credit–Risky Securities", *Review of Derivatives Research*, **(2)**, pp. 99–120.

Lindert, P. H., and P. J. Morton, 1989, "How Sovereign Debt Has Worked", in J. Sachs (ed), *Developing Country Debt and Economic Performance* (Chicago: Chicago University Press).

Manasse, P., N. Roubini, and A. Schimmelpfennig, 2003, "Predicting Sovereign Debt Crises", IMF Working Paper Number WP 03/221.

Merrick, J. J., 2001, "Crisis Dynamics of Implied Default Recovery Ratios: Evidence from Russia and Argentina", *Journal of Banking & Finance*, **(25)**, pp. 1921–39.

Merton, R. C., 1974, "On the Pricing of Corporate Debt: the Risk Structure of Interest Rates", *Journal of Finance*, **(29)**, pp. 449–70.

Merton, R. C., 1977, "An Analytic Derivation of the Cost of Loan Guarantees and Deposit Insurance: An Application of Modern Option Pricing Theory", *Journal of Banking and Finance*, **1**, pp. 3–11.

Nag, A., and A. Mitra, 1999, "Neural Networks and Early Warning Indicators of Currency Crises", Reserve Bank of India Occasional Papers, **20(2)**, pp. 183–222.

Packer, F., and C. Suthiphongchai, 2003, "Sovereign Credit Default Swaps", *BIS Quarterly Review*, December.

Pescatori, A., and A. N. R. Sy, 2003, "Debt Crises and the Development of International Capital Markets", IMF Working Paper Number WP 04/44.

Radelet, S., and J. D. Sachs, 1998, "The East Asian Financial Crisis: Diagnosis, Remedies, Prospects", *Brooking Papers on Economic Activity*, **1**, pp. 1–90.

Reinhart, C., 2002, "Default, Currency Crises and Sovereign Credit Ratings", NBER Working Paper Series, number 8738.

Sachs, J. D., Velasco, A., Tornell, A., 1996, "Financial Crises in Emerging Markets: The Lessons from 1995", *Brookings Paper on Economic Activity*, No. 1, pp. 147–215.

Sy, A. N. R., 2003, "Rating the Rating Agencies: Anticipating Currency Crises or Debt Crises?", IMF Working Paper Number WP 03/122.

Zhang, Z., 2001, "Speculative Attacks in the Asian Crisis", IMF Working Paper Number WP 189/01.

3

New Developments in Country Risk: The New Anatomy of Crises, Rising Public Debt Burdens, and Basel II*

Khalid Sheikh, Peter Heijmans

ABN AMRO

INTRODUCTION

The modest objective of this chapter is to stimulate discussion on some key links between country risk and developments in strengthening the global financial architecture.

The New Basel Capital Accord aims to improve risk management practice by financial institutions, thereby contributing to the solvency and stability of the global financial system. Unfortunately, this noble goal has added a new dimension to country risk that could trigger a strong volatility in economic activity, which could actually cause country risk events.

The phenomenon whereby financial sector deregulation and new financial instruments could act as a powerful amplifying factor in business cycles, and consequently play an important role in enhancing the severity and length of a downturn, or even trigger a country crisis, was a key lesson learned from the events of the late 1990s.

In what follows, we consider how the nature of emerging market crises has changed, and explain the new anatomy of today's (and

---

*The ideas reflected in this chapter are those of the authors and do not necessarily reflect those of ABN AMRO.

tomorrow's) crises. We then discuss the phenomenon of rising public debt levels, and identify the main explanations behind the recent developments, and present some near-term prospects. Finally, in the context of these global trends, we ask whether the New Basel Capital Accord might have some unintended effects. However, we are aware that currently some of these issues are being addressed by the Basel Committee.

THE CHANGING NATURE OF FINANCIAL CRISES

The first major shocks to the stability of the international regime of private foreign investment were felt with the Russian Socialist Revolution of 1917, which brought about the nationalisation of foreign and domestic investment. Similar events took place decades later, with revolutionary transformations in China, Eastern Europe and Egypt. Classified as "strategic", natural-resource exploration infrastructure was expropriated in Mexico (1938) and Iran (1951). In 1971, assets of the British Petroleum Exploratory company (Libya), Ltd, were expropriated by the Libyan authorities. In the 1980s, Tiananmen Square in China changed what had been considered a safe environment for foreign investment, bringing about US$10 billion in uninsured losses. The drug war in previously stable Colombia has had a similar effect. A number of emerging market economies suffered severe currency crises and systemic banking crises in the last two decades. While most of the 1990s have been characterised by an expansion in private infrastructure investment demand and supply, economic and political crises occurred in Asia, Latin America and Eastern Europe since 1994. The crises involved real losses, dramatically increased investors' perception of market risk and increased their awareness of the need for adequate political risk management.

Country risk is still a reality. It has become an even greater reality with the Argentinean crisis in 2000, where the Argentineans redefined the internationally accepted rules of engagement and negotiations.

Four types of country crisis have plagued emerging economies. Each of the different crises can come in its pure form, but in recent years they often arrive in combination. The underlying triggers of these crises are likely to operate simultaneously in the foreign-exchange market, market for bank assets, and sovereign debt paper.

At the risk of gross analytical oversimplification, the typology of crises can be thought of as: currency crises, fiscal crises, banking crises and geopolitical crises. Each of the crises can be triggered by any of the following.

❏ An exogenous shock to markets that causes market participants to revalue the ability of sovereigns and local commercial banks to adhere to inter-temporal obligations.

❏ An exhaustion of borrowing limits.

❏ Self-fulfilling prophecy. Market participants rationally expect a certain type of policy to be implemented to counter a deteriorating situation, but, as the impact of the policy is not immediate, they start to panic, and this panic creates a crisis.

❏ An inadvertent policy shock. Policy reform in one segment of the economy creates an adverse effect in another segment of the economy. Suppose, for instance, a government that is borrowing at very low domestic interest rates decides to integrate into world financial markets. As a consequence, the terms of borrowing become harsher, which can trigger a fiscal crisis.

The magnitude of these crises, duration, time to resolve and, more importantly, transfer mechanisms has changed in the course of the last two decades. Table 1 illustrates the pattern and costs of major banking crises that took place in the 1990s, based on research from the World Bank.

WHAT LESSONS HAVE WE LEARNED FROM PAST CRISES?

First, we have learned to be wary of regulatory reform. The drive to a new financial architecture in conjunction with strong economic forces has pushed many emerging economies too early and too quickly into a more integrated world, without the necessary preparation. Indeed, many of the crisis-afflicted countries were in an intermediate stage of financial reform and did not have appropriate policies and institutional frameworks in place to mitigate the risks associated with volatile and liquid global financial markets.

Second, we have learned that our misunderstanding of country risk can make crises worse. Emerging countries in the same region and with similar economic structures were perceived by investors as "equal" and consequently incurred the same risks, suggesting either contagion or spillover effects, or both. Partially as a consequence

Table 1 Patterns of major banking crises, various countries

Country	Crisis year	Fiscal cost (share of GDP)	Peak non-performing loans (share of total loans)	Real change in GDP	Change in exchange rate	Peak real interest rate	Decline in real asset prices
Finland	1992	11.0	13	-4.6	-5.5	14.3	-34.6
Indonesia	1998	50.0	65–75	-15.4	-57.5	3.3	-78.5
Korea, Rep of	1998	37.0	30–40	-10.6	-28.8	21.6	-45.9
Malaysia	1998	16.4	25–35	-12.7	-13.9	5.3	-79.9
Mexico	1995	19.3	30	-6.2	-39.8	24.7	-53.3
Philippines	1998	0.5	20	-0.8	-13.0	6.3	-67.2
Sweden	1991	4.0	18	-3.3	1.0	79.2	-6.8
Thailand	1998	32.8	33	-5.4	-13.7	17.2	-77.4

Source: Claessens, Klingebiel and Laeven (2002).

of this clumsy response by lenders, a number of traditional risks resurfaced in the wake of crises (transfer and convertibility risks, expropriation and currency volatility), albeit to a different extent.

Third, in terms of crisis recovery, we have learned that we must be cautious about seeking one single solution. It would be more appropriate to work on an *ad hoc* basis – hence the role and mechanics of the restructuring bodies (Paris Club/London Club) should be reappraised.

Fourth, we have learned that our traditional ways of perceiving and analysing country risk may no longer be valid. A classic definition of country risk is transfer and inconvertibility risk, arising from the possibility that the borrower may not be able to secure foreign exchange to service its external debt, even though its own accounts are healthy. However, the Asian crisis exemplified that this definition was too rigid and did not capture market developments sufficiently. The trigger for the country crises then was macroeconomic and structural fragility.

Many researchers and international financial organisations have given insights into the crisis transmission mechanisms. This can briefly be described as the fact that corporations and banks who had financed their needs through the international capital markets and did not hedge their positions, and found themselves unable to secure normal financing domestically when interest rates went up to mitigate FX volatility. As a consequence, banks and corporations were more exposed to exchange rate and interest rate risks. This resulted in the deterioration of banks' bad loan portfolios, which led to many collapses in this sector.

The importance of this notion is that, from an analytical perspective, it became clear that the then-used models of country risk were outmoded as they focused merely on the developments of the external sector (the early-warning models gave the highest weight to criteria such as debt to GDP, FX reserves to imports and FX volatility).

Fifth, we learned that we needed to enhance rating models and develop early-warning indicators, which could not only flag upcoming crises but also model the crisis transmission mechanism more effectively. These steps are part of the effort to move away from the popular way of characterising country risk as an absolute risk. Instead, country risk should be described in terms of a probability distribution over future outcomes, while measuring the value of unexpected or expected losses at a specific point in time. Analytical tools should look through the business cycle.

Overall, the historical record of country risk events and international financial responses raised the following questions:

- ❑ Do market participants (banks, export credit agencies, pension funds, multilaterals) have a clear notion of the evolution of risks?
- ❑ How do country risks correlate to the soundness of cyclical policy changes (business cycles) and vulnerabilities in the domestic financial sector?
- ❑ Why are we not able to signal the occurrence of these risks in an early stage, so we can formulate pre-emptive policies?

THE NEW TRENDS DRIVING COUNTRY RISKS

Prior to 1990, infrastructure services and trade were generally believed to be a public good with governments being responsible for providing these services. But insufficient investments, growing pressures on government budgets and a general concern about inefficient service provision by the responsible public-sector entities resulted in a turnaround of this situation in a large number of emerging economies.

Over the last decade, the private sector has become a key player in providing financing for these services. This is due to a number of simultaneous developments such as the lowering of global trade and investment barriers, and the fall in communications and transport costs. Also, privatisation and financial deregulation have led to a strong political and economic performance in emerging economies.[1] This economic performance has been led by rapid export expansion and supported by substantial capital inflows.[2]

So, the template of the 1980s, where the official community had a clear framework of the roles of public and private entities, and where moral persuasion by governments forced regulated financial institutions to roll-over loans and extend new credit lines – thereby avoiding or allowing recovery from crises – has a very limited applicability today. In today's world (where debt capital flows are overwhelmingly private – from private lenders to private borrowers) considerations relate more to markets, mechanics to restore market confidence, and – to a lesser extent – to individual borrowers and lenders.

The numerous technological, accounting and regulatory changes in the last 15 years have had a dramatic impact on the behaviour of the players involved, and consequently introduced a number of trends which have country risk implications.

❑ Closer linkages between domestic and international markets, and within and across countries, have meant that sovereigns no longer dominate international borrowing. This has also increased interdependency and contagion risk.

❑ Utilisation of more complex structures and a range of new financial instruments to obtain needed finance has increased the spectrum of choices enormously, but has also introduced new types of risk. The complexity is also illustrated by the growing involvement of the Export Credit Agencies and multilateral organisations in covering and mitigating the different types of country risk.[3]

❑ Growing short term capital flows have increased the likelihood of balance-of-payments (BoP) volatility.

❑ The profile and composition of external debt has changed. Debt is no longer heavily concentrated among relatively homogenous international banks, but is now held by a diverse group of financiers. These financiers may be focussed on rates of return and their fiduciary responsibilities to their shareholders, and have little concern about a long-term lending relationship with a sovereign, making them less willing to take a long-term perspective when problems arise.

❑ There has been a substantial rise in the perceived risk by investors and lenders to infrastructure projects and trade finance, with macroeconomic developments threatening project viability and the reliability of long-term governmental commitments becoming questionable.

❑ There is an ongoing shift in economic gravity to the larger emerging markets, which are in the midst of their transition both politically and economically.

The implications of these changes have been significant, as we have witnessed eight financial crises within six years and nearly a quarter of a trillion US dollars in debt, resulting in risk being shifted from the balance sheets of private sector financiers to official ledgers.[4] Crises also unfold more rapidly, more deeply and with greater complexity. To our understanding, in addition to the trends mentioned above, the underlying causes of this are: a sharp reversal in foreign capital flows, especially in the short term; violent political and economic swings; blanket guarantees by the International Monetary Fund (which eliminate investor's risk and introduce moral hazard); and contagion and poor national balance sheets and weak domestic banking systems.

THE ANATOMY OF A MODERN FINANCIAL CRISIS

Traditional country risk analysis has often been based on the examination of "flow" variables, such as the current account and the fiscal balance of the government, and the country's "aggregate external balance sheet", such as total external liabilities and assets of the country. But financial crises since the mid-1990s have clearly demonstrated that it is equally important to look inside the economy, and to examine the "stock" variables and balance sheet weaknesses of the country's key economic sectors, such as the government, the banking sector and the corporate sector. The information of a country's aggregate domestic and external balance sheet can usefully show the potential vulnerability to sudden stops and reversals in external capital flows, but they are often insufficient for examining the origin and the anatomy of such flow reversals. Information about sectoral balance sheets is useful, if it is available in time to identify vulnerabilities. In practice, however, in-depth analysis of sectoral balance sheet vulnerabilities can only be made available with significant time lags.

Figure 1 shows the anatomy of a modern major financial crisis, illustrating it as a kind of self-reinforcing ("snowballing") cycle. The insight presented here is not new, but is based on the so-called "balance sheet approach", which has gained interest in the academic literature in recent years.[5] The balance-sheet framework has drawn attention to the fact that financial crises can emerge from weaknesses in banks' balance sheets, from vulnerabilities in corporate or household balance sheets, and also from problems and vulnerabilities in government-sector balance sheets. The framework usefully helps to explain how financial problems in one sector can transfer into other sectors in the economy, eventually triggering an external balance-of-payments crisis. Weaknesses in the balance sheets of the sectors concerned often relate to maturity and currency mismatches, heavy reliance on debt financing, and solvency problems, which hinder a

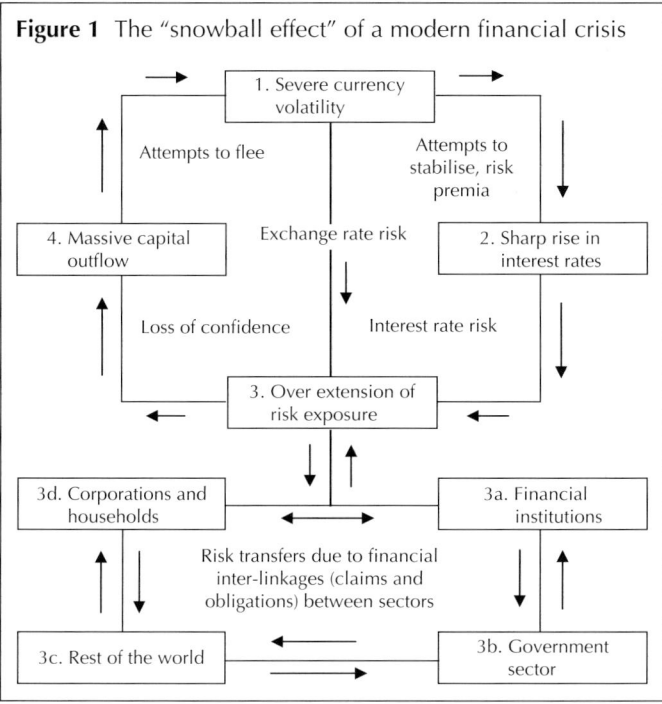

Figure 1 The "snowball effect" of a modern financial crisis

sector's ability to service its debt in the face of a shock. Maturity and currency mismatches create exposure to market risks, such as exchange-rate and interest-rate risk, which can eventually lead to solvency problems, where assets are insufficient to cover the liabilities, including those originating from contingent liabilities.

A financial crisis occurs when a shock exposes the vulnerability of one sector or more in the economy and a sharp decline in demand occurs for financial assets of the sectors concerned. For example, investors and creditors can abruptly lose confidence in the government's ability to service its debt obligations, in the corporation's ability to repay loans or in the bank's ability to pay out all deposits. The resulting capital outflow then leads to increasing balance-sheet problems, which can cascade from one sector into other – even relatively healthy sectors – as a result of the financial interlinkages between the different sectors (claims and obligations).

The balance-sheet problems not only cascade from one sector into another, but they also increase in the process due to capital outflow, exchange-rate volatility and rising interest rates – indicated by the four elements in the upper half of Figure 1. As foreign investors pull out of a country, the exchange rate comes under pressure. Interest rates then increase because investors now require a higher risk premium, or because monetary authorities may try to slow the capital outflows with a tightening of interest-rate monetary policy. If banks and corporations borrowed extensively in foreign currency, as has often been the case in emerging-market economies, a sharp fall in the exchange rate implies that their debt obligations increase sharply in local currency, so that a relatively high-debt position can quickly become an unmanageable-debt position. Furthermore, the rise in interest rates means that the companies and the banks face increasing costs. Thus, a fall in the exchange rate can lead to increasing problems if banks and corporations have exposed themselves to interest-rate and foreign-exchange risk through extensive foreign borrowing at floating rates in US dollars or euros. A collapse in the exchange rate in combination with the investor's panic can thus lead to a kind of "snowballing cycle".

It is important to stress that a financial crisis can originate from every point in Figure 1. For example, countries with large amounts of foreign currency debt in the corporate and banking sector, such as Thailand and Indonesia (1997) and Russia (1998), experienced severe financial distress as a sharp currency devaluation intensified corporate and banking crises, which required large government interventions. Subsequently, the financial position of the government worsened, further reinforcing the currency crisis. Argentina (2001–02) is a recent case where a decline in government-sector assets triggered default on domestic and foreign debt, resulting in actions leading to a severe banking and currency crisis. Brazil has sizeable foreign-currency-linked and local-currency debt. In 2002, political and economic uncertainty caused an increase in the spreads on public debt, which was accompanied by a substantial devaluation.

The banking sector often plays a crucial role in the transmission process of the balance-sheet problems. For example, concerns about the central government's ability to service its debt obligations (perhaps because foreign investors lose confidence, and demand a higher risk premium), can diminish the confidence in the local banks holding this government debt and may lead to a depositor run. Also, a sharp depreciation in the exchange rate, in combination with an unhedged foreign-exchange exposure in the corporate sector, can quickly lead to deterioration in the confidence in the banks that have lent to that corporate sector. A depositor run can take place by withdrawing of cross-border lending by foreign investors, or the withdrawal of deposits by domestic residents.

Another conclusion that can be drawn from the recent financial crises is that local banks' balance-sheet problems can eventually end up with the government, due to increased liabilities – and support – as a result of implicit or explicit government guarantees, but these problems do not always materialise directly in the form of a government debt default.

RISING PUBLIC DEBT

Despite the benign environment for emerging markets and improvements in macroeconomic fundamentals in recent years, emerging-markets public debt still increased for a large number of emerging-market economies over the past five years. Although the experiences have diverged across countries, the broad picture is that Latin America and the emerging market economies in Asia have seen quite large increases in their public-debt stock, largely because of the impact of financial crises. In contrast, the public-debt burden declined in most countries in Emerging Europe, as countries were in a state of transition and governments implemented fiscal reforms to qualify for accession to the European Union. Indeed, those European governments that had high debt burdens in 1998 (Russia, Bulgaria and Ukraine) experienced impressive reductions in their total public-debt stock. In the Middle East and North Africa, the public-debt stock also declined, but it remains at relatively elevated levels (see Figure 2).

What are the main explanations behind the developments in emerging-markets public debt? Broadly speaking, public-debt changes are influenced by the primary (non-interest) balance of the government, GDP growth and "other factors". The last component actually captures a wide range of factors, including interest-rate changes, exchange-rate depreciations, fiscal costs arising from the resolution of banking-sector crises, receipts from privatisation deals and debt reductions because of sovereign debt restructurings.

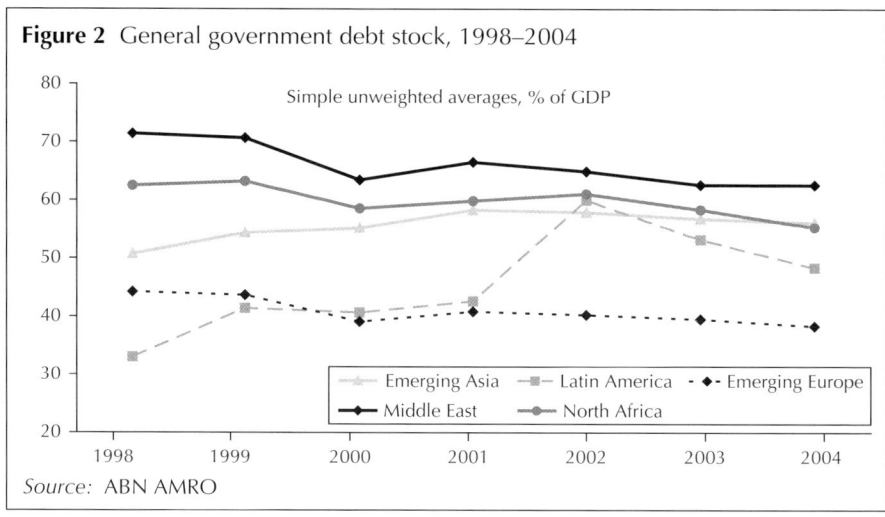

Figure 2 General government debt stock, 1998–2004

Source: ABN AMRO

Figure 3 and Table 2 highlight the changes in the debt stock by using a simple debt dynamics equation.[6]

In Latin America, Emerging Asia and the Middle East, the increase in the public-debt burden can apparently largely be explained by the "other" factor. Gross fiscal costs of emerging markets' banking crises were estimated to be more than 15% of GDP in Indonesia, Korea, Malaysia and Turkey. There have also been sizeable costs of pubic support to financial sectors in China and in the Philippines. Exchange-rate effects added substantially to the debt-to-GDP ratio in Brazil and Turkey and in Russia (mostly in 1998 and 1999). Economic growth generally supported the public-debt dynamics. The broad picture is also that the primary government balances (difference between revenues and expenditures, interest payments excluded) were often insufficient to significantly reduce the debt-to-GDP ratios.

Looking at near-term economic forecasts for 2004 and 2005, one sees that most emerging-market economies are envisaged to run primary (non-interest) surpluses consistent with what is required to stabilise or to reduce the debt-to-GDP ratio below 2003 levels (see Figure 4).[7] A number of governments in emerging-market economies are indeed making efforts to improve their fiscal position, and macroeconomic fundamentals have also been improving substantially across a broad range of emerging-markets countries.

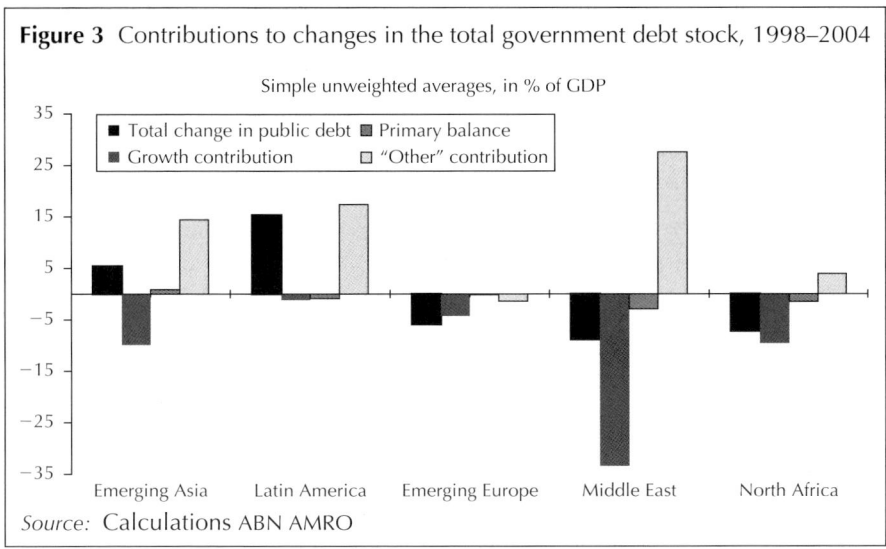

Figure 3 Contributions to changes in the total government debt stock, 1998–2004

Simple unweighted averages, in % of GDP

■ Total change in public debt ■ Primary balance
■ Growth contribution ☐ "Other" contribution

Emerging Asia   Latin America   Emerging Europe   Middle East   North Africa

Source: Calculations ABN AMRO

This has also been reflected in an impressive tightening in emerging-markets government debt spreads since the end of 2002.

Broadly speaking, the macroeconomic environment and sectoral infrastructure in many countries has also improved over recent years. Foreign direct investment of European and US banks and investment funds has brought capital to emerging markets' banks and accelerated the pace of structural reforms. This has deepened globalisation of the world financial sector and has promoted best practices in banking supervision and risk management. Also, the corporate sectors in Emerging Asia that were hit by the major crisis have significantly deleveraged and reduced their overcapacity over the past several years.

We should, however, not forget that history tends to repeat itself. Vulnerabilities, maturity mismatches and currency mismatches in corporate, banks and public sectors are still a reality. Although an improvement in creditworthiness is seen by the major rating agencies, many banking systems remain vulnerable to shocks. The Chinese banking system, with its high levels of NPLs, is generally seen as the greatest system that is vulnerable to future stress.

The last time that government debt traded at today's comfortable levels was also in 1998. Just as was the case in 1998, today's emerging-markets debt rally is now supported by the abundant

Table 2 Government debt dynamics in selected emerging markets economies, 1998–2004

	Brazil	China	Mexico	Turkey	South Korea	Philippines	Hungary	India
Debt-to-GDP 1998	42.2	13.5	24.5	41.7	13.9	66.6	62.3	51.2
Debt dynamics derived from:								
GDP growth	−3.3	−8.1	−1.9	−0.6	−2.5	−8.1	−5.3	−6.7
Primary balance	−3.1	2.4	−2.3	−4.1	−1.2	−0.7	−0.1	0.3
Other factors	18.7	23.7	3.1	38.5	18.2	21.4	1.4	21.1
Total change	12.3	18.0	−1.0	33.8	14.5	12.7	−4.0	14.8
Debt-to-GDP 2004	54.5	31.4	23.5	75.5	28.4	79.3	58.3	66.0

Source: Calculations ABN AMRO

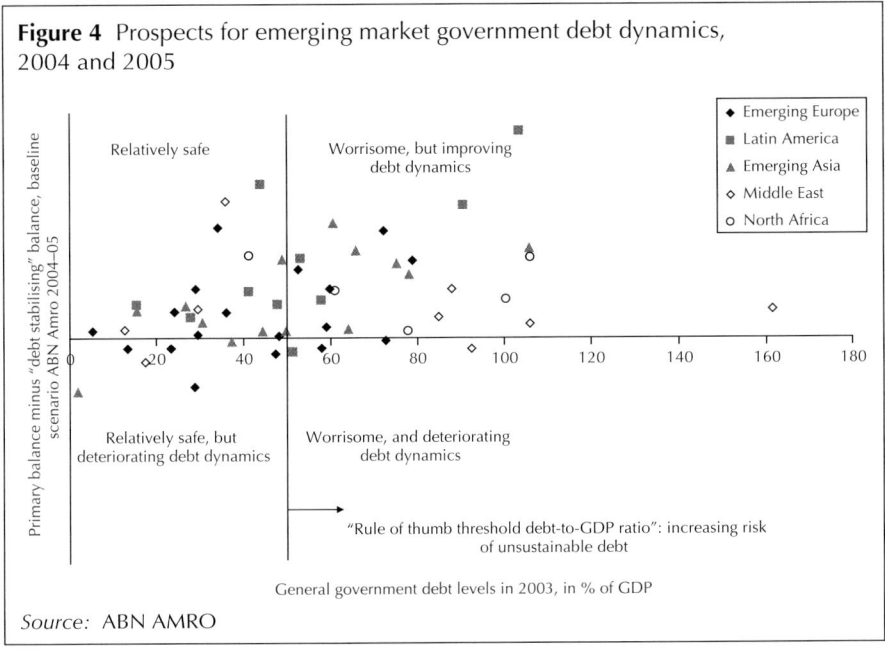

Figure 4 Prospects for emerging market government debt dynamics, 2004 and 2005

Source: ABN AMRO

global liquidity in the markets. Interest rates are relatively low, and are stimulating investors to seek for yield and to step into risky waters. Whatever the policy accomplishments that were made in the past several years, can one really say that emerging-markets public debt would be traded at today's low spreads without the abundant global liquidity? Without searching for yield, would investors really be unconcerned by the still high levels of public debt and the precarious composition of the debt stock in a number of countries?

BASEL II AND COUNTRY RISK

The most important lesson learned since the birth of macroeconomics in the 1930s is that intended stabilisation may result in unintended destabilisation. Does this axlso hold for the New Basel Capital Accord?

Many academics and bankers have voiced their concerns in this regard.[8] They argue that the implementation of the New Capital Accord could decrease bank lending to emerging markets and accentuate pro-cyclicality. This is because the Accord costs of implementation create an increased fiscal burden, as huge investments for implementation and upgrading human capital are required, which has the effect of making it more expensive to lend to emerging borrowers. As a consequence, a large percentage of emerging economies will no longer be able to access international bank lending on terms likely to be acceptable. The impact is likely to be felt most severely in the lowest rated countries – the very countries in most need of such access.

The third quantitative impact study done by all commercial banks on the initiative of the Basel Committee seems to underscore this, as it clearly indicated that internationally operating banks following the (A)IRB approach will have to step up their economic capital requirements dramatically for high-risk borrowers.[9] So banks will start asking themselves, "What is the risk my bank can take, what are the constraints my bank has, and what is my cost of capital?" This notion that such questions, and not client demands, will drive bank business decisions, will have an impact on finance and other cross-border services.

With respect to the issue of pro-cyclicality of lending, the main concern is that cyclicality will increase further for speculative-grade developing countries, and therefore their vulnerability to developmentally costly currency crises will rise. Especially, in an economic downturn, the amplifying effect of the asymmetry of information between borrowers and lenders is the greatest. Even though some pro-cyclicality is inevitable as a result of cross-border lending, regulatory measures should not aggravate it.

Under an internal ratings standard, the Basel II Accord encourages the development of sound internal systems for risk evaluation, since only banks complying with strict methodological and disclosure standards will be allowed to use these ratings as a basis for determining the regulatory capital requirement. Notwithstanding this very positive incentive to meet the new Accord, one could argue that at the same time it provides potentially perverse incentives for banks to develop new ways to evade the intended consequences of the proposed regulations. Additional opportunities for risk arbitrage exist under an internal ratings standard, because risk weights are based on banks' private information rather than on external, verifiable records. A major problem facing the supervisors is to check the truthfulness of estimates of probabilities of default. There are great difficulties already for the banks themselves to translate their own ratings into probabilities of default. Essentially, each bank must develop data similar to "mortality rate tables" that are applied in the corporate bond markets for bonds with different ratings. Input data for many years are needed to obtain estimates of mortality rates for all rating-categories over the lifetime of loans. Thus innovation to rating systems – and one would hope that innovations occur – make it more difficult both for banks and supervisors to gather the required data. The additional opportunities for risk arbitrage under an internal ratings standard are created by the scope for "gaming and manipulation" of ratings. Banks generally have access to private credit risk-relevant information that can be excluded from the system for risk-weighting presented to the supervisory authority.

One type of "gaming and manipulation" would occur if a bank uses its private information to place relatively high-risk and high-return credits in a lower risk bucket. For example, if the foundation approach is used, then the probability of default reported to the supervisory authority can be made to differ from the bank's true estimate. The latter probability may have been updated by the bank based on information that is not available to supervisors. If the probabilities of default are based on a more refined credit scoring system that has been deemed acceptable by regulators, then private information within the bank would make manipulation of the credit scores prior to translation into probabilities of default possible.

Another issue of concern is the treatment of sovereigns under the New Capital Accord, and the unlevel playing field that the current proposal creates. Large foreign banks (which will mostly use the IRB approach) will be facing higher capital charges for low-credit-quality transactions than their local peers who, in principle, operate under the standardised approach.

In addition, local supervisors could develop an environment of rules (to apply lower risk weights to certain assets) that will be beneficial for local banks. Hence it could be argued that internationally operating banks will shy away from the "emerging" markets as they are characterised by, for example: inappropriate accounting standards and reporting systems; improper classification of non-performing loans and deficient legal and judicial frameworks; an inability to enforce supervisory actions; and high concentrations of asset ownership – both financial and real – that renders the potential equity market small and uncompetitive. Under these conditions, capital ratios cannot perform their supervisory role of containing excessive risk-taking activities by banks. This is because supervisors have difficulty in determining whether shareholders' wealth is really at risk when they supply equity capital, which is, in turn, because shareholders can finance their stake with a loan from a related party, which may even be a non-financial corporation, and hence outside the regulators' purview. As there are no capital markets available to validate the "real" value of capital as distinct from its accounting value, capital standards simply do not work.

The impact of the new Basel proposals is even broader, as it will indirectly influence other financial intermediators and regulators, which are involved in financing emerging markets and within emerging economies themselves.

The structure of regulation can also affect the dynamics of financial cycles. A regulatory system built around minimum capital requirements might contribute to stability, but under certain circumstances exacerbate economic downturns. This is because widespread losses might cause banks to cut back lending to comply with the minimum requirement, to avoid damage to reputation and other costs.

CONCLUDING REMARKS

The continuing efforts of global integration bring new opportunities as well as new inequalities that need to be anticipated and for which we must find answers in a more coherent and balanced way. Greater integration means the potential for greater conflict as well as convergence, as the ties that bind can also chafe. We must define new roles for all stakeholders and make further progress on crisis prevention.

In this respect, it will be important for emerging market governments and supervisors to invest substantial efforts into a broad reform process in order to create an environment that is investor-friendly – especially in times of crisis – and that allows the country to benefit from new, and more efficient, investments. The pace of consolidation in the financial sector in emerging economies could either amplify or mitigate systemic risk. One side of the coin is that consolidation leads to a smaller number of larger and more complex entities. These organisations are faced with an increased operational complexity. They will become more difficult for creditors to understand – and it will surely become difficult to liquidate them in an orderly fashion in case of severe distress. The flip side of the coin, however, is that due to a better diversification of risk, and closer scrutiny by regulators and creditors, larger entities may be better equipped to weather storms.

Failure to do so will almost invariably result in frustrated investors, lengthy delays in new projects and the loss of resources spent in the preparation process of projects and finally, more country events.

1   A key example is Hungary 1994 where the change in privatisation policy led to a huge increase of proceeds US$5 billion, which supported the government to avoid a balance-of-payments-crisis and hence default.

2   Net capital flows to emerging markets rose strongly up to 1996. It should be noted that private capital flows remain focused on a select number of countries. FDI flows to the top ten recipient emerging economies constitute around 80% of the total in 2001.

3   The amount of new investments insured by Berne Union members increased five times from US$3 billion in 1982 to US$15 billion in 1996. Total (investment insurance) exposure of Berne Union members grew from US£15 billion in 1982 to US$43 billion in 1996. Whereas total business grew by US$39 billion over the same horizon to US$422 billion.

4   The large bailout packages granted by the IMF to Mexico (US$50 billion) 1995, Thailand (US$17 billion) Indonesia (US$34 billion) Korea (US$57 billion) 1997, Russia (US$16 billion) Brazil (US$42 billion) 1998, Turkey (US$10 billion) Argentina (US$20 billion) 2001 and Brazil (US$30 billion) 2002.

5   This paragraph draws upon: Borio (2004), Allen *et al* (2002), Gray, Merton and Bodie, (2003) and Beim and Calomiris (2001).

6   The outcomes are broadly speaking consistent with analysis of IMF (2003). However, we looked at a slightly different time-frame, and may have included other countries in the analysis.

7   Based on the interest rate, the level of GDP growth and the debt-to-GDP ratio, one can compute the primary (non-interest) balance that would achieve a debt-to-GDP ratio that is stable. If the actual (or forecasted) primary balance is less than the "debt-stabilising" primary balance, current fiscal policy implies an increasing debt-to-GDP ratio. The figures in graph 3 are computed using the average (forecasted) primary (non-interest) balance, the average (implied) interest rates on government debt, growth rates and debt-to-GDP ratio for 2004–05, and the debt-to-GDP ratio for 2003.

8   Griffith-Jones (2003), Mulder and Sheikh (2003), Griffith-Jones and Spratt (2001) and Rojas-Suarez (2001).

9   According to a recent investigation from IIF, the current version of the New Accord would result in a rise of more than 100% of the risk weighting on sovereign credits to emerging markets, relative to what is currently held.

BIBLIOGRAPHY

Allen, M., C. Rosenberg, C. Keller, B. Setser, and N. Roubini, 2002, "A Balance Sheet Approach to Financial Crisis", International Monetary Fund (IMF), Working Paper 02/210, Policy and Review Department.

Beim, D., and C. Calomiris, 2001, *Emerging Financial Markets* (London: McGraw-Hill).

Borio, C., 2004, "Market Distress and Vanishing Liquidity: Anatomy and Policy Options", Bank of International Settlements (BIS), Working paper No 158, Monetary and Economic Department.

Claessens, S., D. Klingebiel, and L. Laeven, 2002, "Financial Restructuring in Banking and Corporate Sectors", in D. Klingebiel, and L. Laeven (eds), "Managing the Real and Fiscal Effects of Banking Crises", World Bank Discussion Paper, No. 428, Washington DC.

Gray, D., R. Merton, and Z. Bodie, 2003, "A New Framework for Analyzing and Managing Macrofinancial Risks of an Economy", Moodys Working Paper 1-03.

Griffith-Jones, S., and S. Spratt, 2001, "The Pro-Cyclical Effects of the New Basle Accord", in J. J. Teunissen (ed), *New Challenges of Crisis Prevention* (The Hague: Fondad).

Griffith-Jones, S., 2003, "How to Prevent the New Basle Accord Harming Developing Countries, Institute of Development Studies", Paper presented at the WADMO Conference/General Assembly in Geneva.

International Monetary Fund, 2003, "World Economic Outlook, Public Debt in Emerging Markets", Chapter III, *Public Debt in Emerging Markets: Is it too high?*, Washington DC, September.

Rojas-Suarez, L., 2001, "Can International Capital Standards Strengthen Banks In Emerging Markets?", Institute for International Economics (IIE) Working Paper 01 (10).

Mulder, H., and K. Sheikh, 2003/2004, "Banks, Trade Finance and Financial Distress: What Can Commercial Banks Do to Support Emerging Economies in Times of Financial Distress", forthcoming paper.

4

Assessing State Stability and Political Risk in Emerging Markets

Preston Keat, Alexander J. Motyl

Eurasia Group

POLITICS MATTER IN EMERGING MARKETS

In recent years emerging-market investors have increasingly recognised that politics can matter at least as much as economic fundamentals. Governments that have the capacity to meet sovereign debt obligations may simply not have the political will to do so (eg, Russia, 1998). Market interpretations of political developments and tensions generate volatility in foreign exchange, bond and equities markets (eg, Brazil, Turkey, 2002–3) and changes in relative levels of social and political stability can lead investors to re-evaluate their strategies (eg, Venezuela and Russia, 2004).

As the relevance of political factors has become more apparent to investors, so has the general lack of comprehensive and systematic tools for evaluating them. In this chapter we outline the development and selected applications of Eurasia Group's analytical framework for measuring political stability and risk. Cases include the index's application to the 1998 financial crisis in Russia, and the market reaction to Lula's rise in Brazil.

The DESIX framework for measuring state stability

The Deutsche Bank Eurasia Group Stability Index (DESIX) is a research product of Eurasia Group, a New York-based firm specialising in political risk. By systematically tracking a variety of factors that constitute stability, DESIX serves as a comparative framework for identifying trends within and between countries as well as for anticipating the likelihood of crises.

Figure 1 DESIX variables

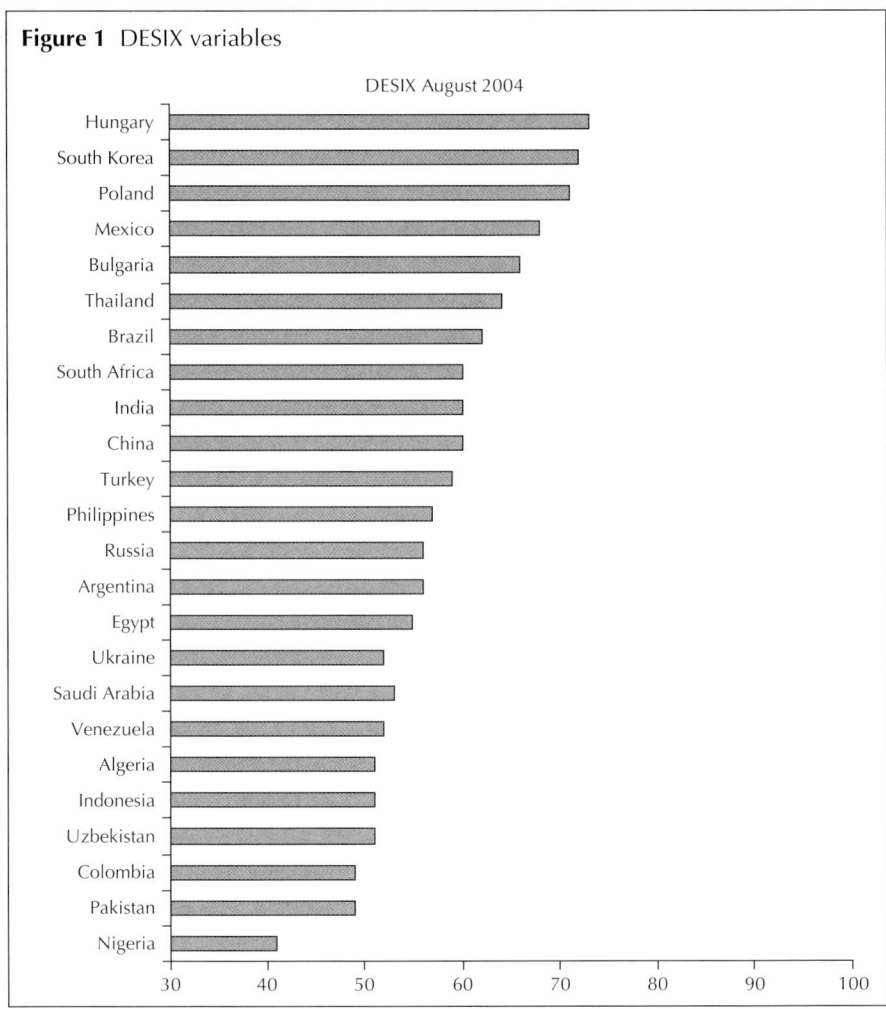

DESIX August 2004

The DESIX defines stability in terms of its conceptual opposite, instability – or *proneness to crisis*. Unstable states are, thus, prone to and most likely to experience crises; stable states are not prone to and least likely to experience crises. The DESIX defines crises as major systemic dislocations that threaten the survival of governments, regimes or states. Crises include, but are not confined to, such system-level phenomena as revolutions, rebellions, civil wars and regime breakdowns. Risk, as potential exposure to crisis, is highest in low-stability states and lowest in high-stability states.

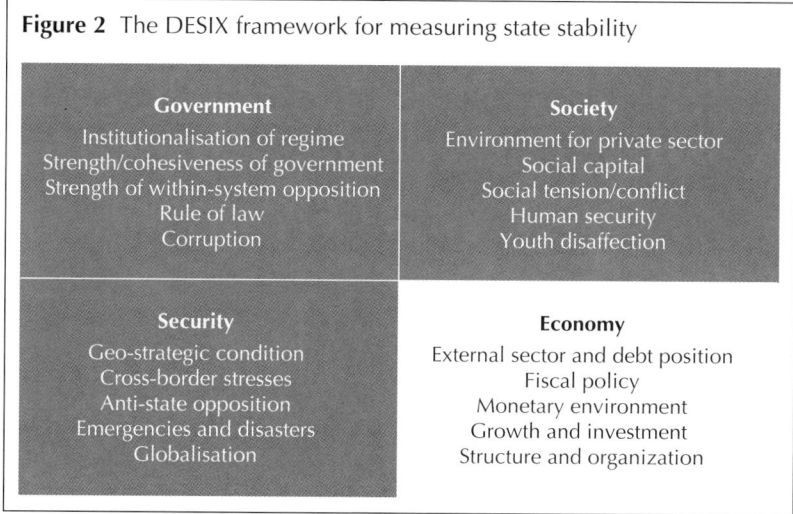

Figure 2 The DESIX framework for measuring state stability

Government	Society
Institutionalisation of regime Strength/cohesiveness of government Strength of within-system opposition Rule of law Corruption	Environment for private sector Social capital Social tension/conflict Human security Youth disaffection
Security	**Economy**
Geo-strategic condition Cross-border stresses Anti-state opposition Emergencies and disasters Globalisation	External sector and debt position Fiscal policy Monetary environment Growth and investment Structure and organization

DESIX RATINGS

The DESIX generates stability ratings based on 20 variables derived from academic theories of revolution, rebellion, civil war and regime breakdown. Because the index is agnostic about the validity of these theories, it aggregates the values associated with the variables they generate and transforms the resulting aggregate value into a measure of the overall robustness of a country's institutions and thus of a country's stability – or non-proneness to crisis.

Each DESIX variable consists of discrete institutional and temporal indicators. Institutional indicators capture the institutional fundamentals of individual variables and constitute the core of stability; temporal indicators capture changes in policy and other events that, if sustained, may herald changes in institutional fundamentals. Both institutional and temporal indicators are assigned scores reflective of their differential impact on stability – the former on a scale of 0 to 100, the latter on a scale of –30 to +30 of the institutional score.

DESIX composite ratings – as the sums of all twenty institutional and temporal ratings – are expressed on a scale of 0–100, with higher numbers corresponding to higher country stability. Composite stability ratings are broken down into the following subcategories:

❏ maximum stability (81–100);
❏ high stability (61–80);

❑ moderate stability (41–60);
❑ low stability (21–40); and
❑ minimum stability (0–20).

The higher a country's stability rating, the less prone it is to crises and the lower the risk. The lower a country's stability rating, the more prone it is to crises and the greater the risk.

DESIX composite ratings – which are the simple sums of the values assigned to all 20 variables – thus provide a uniform basis for comparing countries synchronically and diachronically, identifying broad institutional trends and inductively suggesting likely outcomes. The index thereby serves as an approximate cross-country comparative measure of the overall proneness of states and governments to crisis. As an approximate measure, the scores capture significant differences only if numerical differentials – between country A at time t and time $t + 1$ or between country A and country B at time t – exceed at least five points.

Because sustained changes in policy and recurrent events translate into institutional change, medium- to long-term divergences between institutional and temporal scores will translate into upward or downward adjustments of the former. As a result, such divergences portend either growing or declining proneness to crisis.

DESIX VARIABLES

DESIX variables are constructed in a three-step procedure involving movement from the broadly theoretical to the more narrowly conceptual – theoretical derivation, empirical plausibility and concept formation.

1) Step 1 involves distilling sets of theoretically salient factors from the four broad paradigms underlying theories of revolution, rebellion, civil war and regime breakdown.

❑ the *structure-based paradigm* isolates the sources of crisis in the contradictions generated by political, economic and social relations and institutions within states and between and among states. Central to this paradigm are a state's regime – democratic, authoritarian or some hybrid – the degree to which the regime is institutionalised and therefore rests on broadly accepted patterns of behaviour, the extent to which legal norms guide institutional processes, the quality of a state's political, military and economic relations with its neighbours, and the structure and organisation of its economy.

❑ the *group-based paradigm* isolates the sources of crisis in the conflicting interests between and among nations, classes, races and other population segments on the one hand, and between them and the political authorities on the other. Central to this paradigm are the overall political, legal and economic environment within which private-sector associations exist, the capacity of and resources available to groups to pursue their interests and the degree to which groups are antagonistic and their relations are conflictual and, thus, potentially destabilising.

❑ the *elite-based paradigm* isolates the sources of crisis in the actions of opposition leaders and vanguard parties, movements and revolutionary groups intent on mobilising constituencies in the pursuit of anti-state and antigovernment ends. Central to this paradigm are, on the one hand, the relative strength of the government – the ruling leader or leaders and the ruling party or parties, regardless of regime type – the within-system opposition consisting of elites opposed to radical change, and the anti-state opposition committed to fundamental change, and, on the other, the political, social and economic policies that serve as bones of contention among the three actors.

❑ the *perception-based paradigm* isolates the sources of crisis in the beliefs, feelings, resentments, ideologies, and emotions that motivate elites and groups to turn against existing authority structures. Central to this paradigm are phenomena – such as corruption, the quality of life, unexpected stresses, emergencies and disasters, modernisation and globalisation – that disrupt established forms of behaviour, appear to threaten livelihoods, and thereby generate outrage, anger, frustration and illegitimacy.

Although the four paradigms are rooted in different assumptions about the nature of reality and therefore represent fundamentally different approaches to social science in general and to crisis phenomena in particular, the empirical variables they generate are not incompatible with one another. Indeed, it is perfectly normal practice for analysts working within any one paradigm to be fully aware of the *empirical* importance of the variables associated with the others, even if, as is likely, they dispute the *theoretical* validity of the other paradigms. As a result, every social science theory of crisis incorporates, at some level and to some degree, the variables that all four paradigms generate. Individual theories differ, therefore, not so much in their choice of variables as in their ordering of variables. Thus, structural theories place primary emphasis on the interplay of relations and institutions, while relegating groups, elites, and perceptions to a secondary position within the theoretical account. In contrast, agent-oriented theories will subordinate structures and institutions to elites and perceptions.

2) Step 2 surveys expert studies of actual revolutions, rebellions, civil wars, regime breakdowns and other systemic dislocations to determine whether the factors produced by Step 1 are empirically plausible as well as theoretically salient. For instance, a closer look at such disparate events as the Russian Revolution of 1917, the breakdown of Weimar Germany's democratic regime in the early 1930s and the ongoing armed conflict between Israelis and Palestinians reveals that all four paradigmatically derived sets of factors figure prominently in theoretical and empirical accounts of these events.

3) Step 3 involves actual concept formation – that is, the formal conceptualisation of DESIX variables as clearly defined and bounded concepts. Concept formation entails making variables conceptually coherent and amenable to some form of quantitative and/or qualitative measurement. Establishing conceptual coherence entails ensuring that variables are internally coherent, encompassing only those defining characteristics that complement one another and therefore produce a tight "fit". Establishing operationalisibility involves ensuring that the defining characteristics of variables are at a sufficiently high level of specification so as to permit quantitative measurement or minimally controversial qualitative assessment. The upshot of this three-step process is the generation of 20 conceptually bounded variables.

POLITICS AND SOVEREIGN CREDIT RISK ASSESSMENT – RUSSIA 1998

Traditional sovereign credit risk analysis focuses principally on assessing a country's ability to meet its debt obligations.

Sovereign risk ratings typically incorporate the following explanatory factors:

❑ per capita income;
❑ GDP growth;
❑ inflation;
❑ fiscal balance;
❑ external balance;
❑ external debt;
❑ economic development; and
❑ default history.

One of the lessons of Russia's default in 1998 was that the ability to pay (as determined by the above criteria) was no guarantee for investors, and that politically driven decisions were central to understanding the government's non-payment. This failure on the part of economists and risk analysts highlighted the fact that, if political stability is incorporated in these models at all, it is typically based on *ad hoc* and non-systematic assessments.

THE STABILITY INDEX AND THE CRISIS

After years of economic crisis, the Russian economy seemed to have turned the corner by 1997. The growth in GDP for the year was minimal – just short of 1% – but even such anaemic growth was cause for optimism after seven consecutive years of economic contraction. Although structural flaws and imbalances in the economy were still evident, the government of Prime Minister Viktor Chernomyrdin had developed a reputation for being moderately (if not consistently) reformist, and it could point to some tangible achievements, most notably the reduction of the annual inflation rate to single digits. This visible progress led observers and investors to minimise the growing political and economic tensions in the country – even after they became starkly apparent with the dismissal of the Chernomyrdin government by President Boris Yeltsin in March 1998.

Chernomyrdin's successor Sergei Kiriyenko, a 35-year-old who lacked experience at the senior levels of government, formed a government with a technocratic bent and sought to build on the reforms of his predecessor. However, whatever its intentions, the Kiriyenko government failed to make major progress due to a range of constraints: the hostility of the State Duma towards his administration; a sharp decline in world oil prices; and the distraction of an ill and increasingly erratic President Yeltsin. The government proved unable to address its unsustainable fiscal deficit and debt burden, resulting by August 1998 in default and devaluation.

Below, we describe some of the most critical driving forces behind Russia's August 1998 financial crisis and express them in Figure 3 in terms of the most appropriate stability index variables.

WEAK POLITICAL LEADERSHIP

Although the powerful executive branch of government often has a determining effect on political outcomes in Russia, where the parliament is clearly subordinate to the president, the left-leaning Duma was frequently able to obstruct the Kremlin and government's reform plans, particularly during President Yeltsin's second term in office. While Yeltsin did wield the enormous personal political power of the presidency, his brief but frequent disappearances from public life, including an almost one-month sick leave in late 1997 and early 1998, created the public perception that Yeltsin was simply not in control of the government. His approval ratings during this period were almost consistently in the single digits.

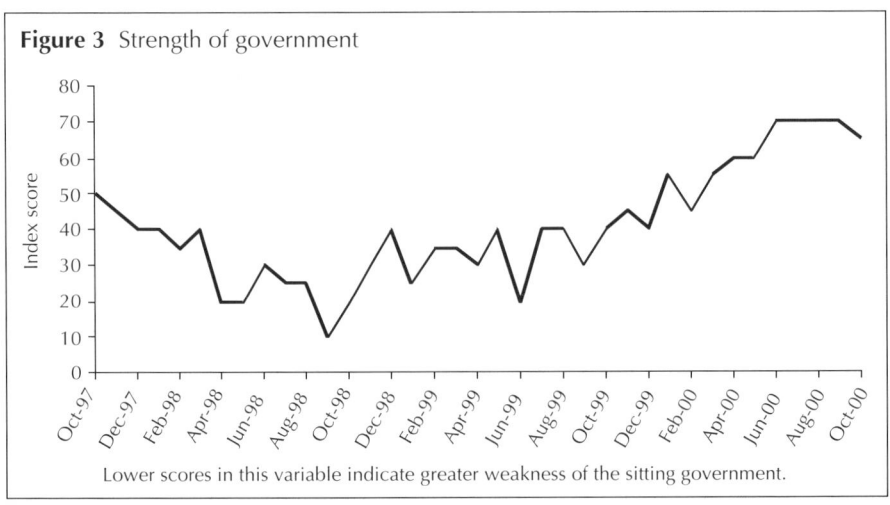

Figure 3 Strength of government

Lower scores in this variable indicate greater weakness of the sitting government.

In the run-up to the 1998 financial crisis, there was an obvious lack of clarity on who was in charge of economic policy. In November 1997 Yeltsin sacked Finance Minister Anatoly Chubais, who retained the post of deputy prime minister, replacing him with Mikhail Zadornov. And when Chubais negotiated a US$2 billion emergency loan from four international investment banks in December 1997 to support the ruble and cover the outstanding US$1.6 billion in wage arrears to the public sector, the Duma lambasted the move, and Zadornov cast doubt on Chubais's authority to negotiate the deal on behalf of the government. Although Prime Minister Chernomyrdin's own influence over key ministries seemed to be rising, or perhaps even because of this, Yeltsin sacked him in March. There were several changes in government officials with economic portfolios, including the finance minister, head of privatisation, head of the tax committee and the negotiator with international financial institutions. A pro-tracted battle with the Duma ensued over Kiriyenko's nomination for prime minister in March and April, with his approval finally arriving on 24 April. During this time (March–April 1998), there was little if any cooperation with the Duma on structural or economic reform through the spring and summer of that year, a factor that increased Russia's debt burden even further (due to rising yields).

ABSENCE OF POLITICAL CONSENSUS

The Duma, which was dominated by the Communist Party, was generally unresponsive to the government's initiatives on tax and

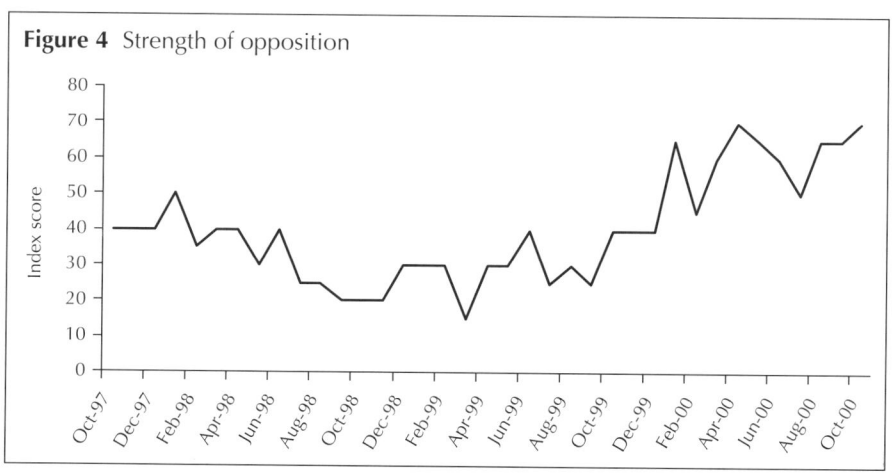

Figure 4 Strength of opposition

land reform and cutting spending in the 1998 budget. In November 1997, the Duma rejected both the government-proposed tax code, overturning its initial approval from June, and the government's proposal to form a joint working group on a compromise tax code. Two months later, Yeltsin vetoed two tax laws prepared by the government and approved by the Duma. The Duma finally adopted the 1998 budget in its fourth and final reading in March 1998. Revenue and spending targets were not changed as requested by the government, but an amendment was added allowing the government to cut expenditures in the event of revenue shortfalls. Overall, the protracted 1998 budget debate was characterised by a lack of cooperation between the executive and legislative branches.

In March, Prime Minister Kiriyenko proposed reducing spending by about US$6 billion but his plans failed. As negotiations between Russia and the IMF over a possible additional US$10–15-billion aid package continued in the summer, the government brought up another major spending cut of US$9.9 billion, entailing the reduction of the number of state employees, transferring more responsibility to regional authorities, reducing subsidies for industry, agriculture and transportation, and decreasing the tax burden on industry while increasing tax collection from individuals. The Duma approved some of the proposals, but the new pension fund law and several revenue-generating tax laws were blocked.

The government's efforts in July 1998 to take on the biggest tax evader, Gazprom, caused outrage in the Duma, and it subsequently stopped working on the government's anti-crisis programme. The Duma also opposed the US$14.8-billion bailout package agreed with the IMF, World Bank and Japan due to concerns that it was conditioned on the dissolution of Gazprom and Unified Energy Systems.

PUBLIC ANGER AND HARDSHIP

In 1997 and 1998 there were nationwide strikes in the agriculture and energy sectors, the two largest areas of economic activity, as well as by medical emergency personnel, teachers and miners because of wage arrears and other economic hardships. Wage arrears improved in the first two months of 1998 only because of an emergency loan from several foreign banks that Chubais secured in late 1997 rather than from improved tax collection. Regional authorities were also accused of misappropriating wage arrears funds. The largest

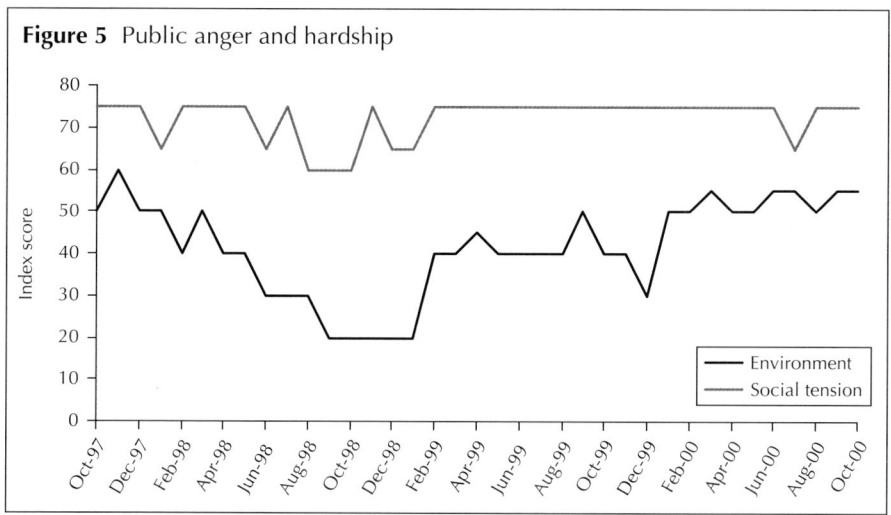

Figure 5 Public anger and hardship

nationwide demonstration before the financial crisis, numbering in the hundreds of thousands, came on 9 April, when the government failed to settle wage arrears with civil servants. A key turning point came when striking miners and energy sector workers began demanding Yeltsin's resignation starting in May 1998 – adding for the first time political demands to their economic demands.

INCOHERENT MONETARY POLICY

In early 1998, the Central Bank of Russia tried to implement a strong ruble policy to prevent ruble devaluation at the expense of higher interest rates and cut interest rates to please international credit agencies. The augmented interest rates – up to 42% on January, down to 30% in March, up again to 150% in May – complicated the overturn of the existing GKO stock (eventually making it impossible) and strained industry and banking sectors. Continued efforts to prop up the ruble depleted reserves – including a US$1.5 billion decrease in last two weeks of May. The attractiveness of high-yield GKOs decreased direct investment into industry, while government spending exacerbated the budget deficit. As a result, the 1997–8 fall in world oil prices, which lowered tax collections from the oil and gas companies and increased scheduled debt service for 1998, had to be covered by external borrowing and/or reduction of international reserves.

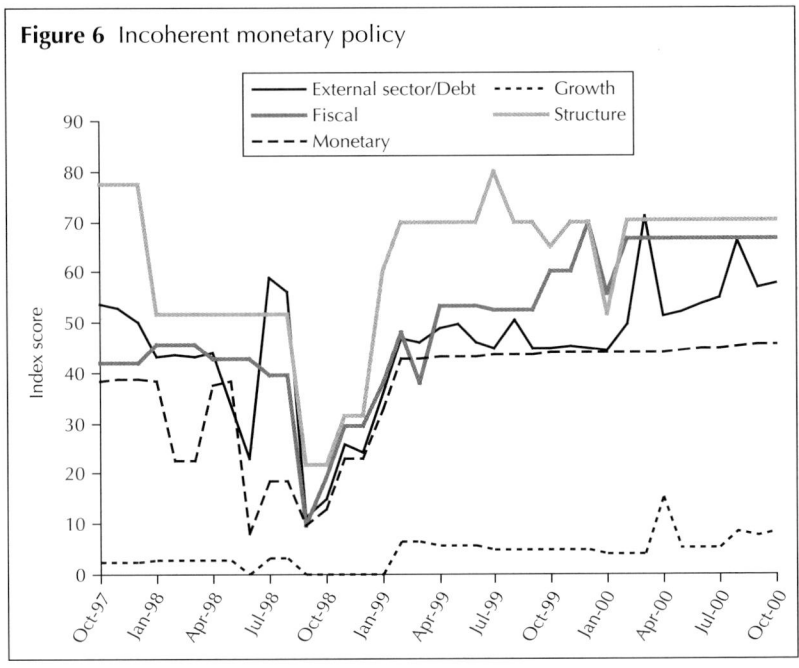

Figure 6 Incoherent monetary policy

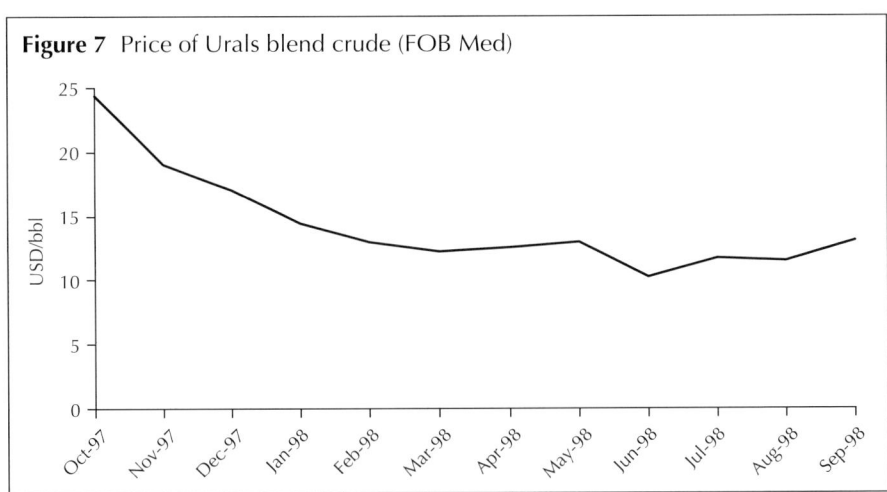

Figure 7 Price of Urals blend crude (FOB Med)

OBSTACLES TO FISCAL DISCIPLINE

Post-Soviet Russia inherited an unsustainably broad social welfare system, a legacy of state support for industry and investment – made necessary by the irrational and wasteful structure of industry – and a tax system based on confiscating and redistributing what surpluses were generated in some production sectors. Failing to implement a market-based taxation and social safety net and to reduce the state presence in the economy, the Russian government chronically failed to contain spending in the 1990s. The fiscal deficit as a percentage of GDP fell below 5% only one time between 1989 and 1998 (in 1995).

The most important obstacles to fiscal discipline were the country's dismal economic performance, inefficient tax collection and communist opposition to tightening fiscal policy and streamlining taxation. The government consistently presented budgets that included unrealistic projections of GDP growth and revenues from taxes; the result was deficits that routinely exceed budgeted levels as tax targets fell below expectations. Under conditions of low or falling oil prices, upon which the budget relies heavily for revenues, fiscal discipline became even more difficult.

Summary: don't underestimate the political dimension

Ex post, a range of economic factors have been linked to the Russian financial crisis. But in the lead up to the default and devaluation almost no economists advising market participants were warning about an impending collapse. To those who were focused on the politics of economic policymaking, however, the situation looked much worse. A number of stability index indicators were suggesting that investors should proceed with great caution in Russia – that politics and society need to be considered alongside the traditional models of credit risk.

FINANCIAL MARKET RISK IN BRAZIL – THE LULA OVERREACTION

As the prospects of a Lula (Luis Inacio Lula da Silva) victory in presidential elections grew in the late spring of 2002, the value of Brazilian bonds and currency fell dramatically. The perception in markets was that Lula, the leader of the leftist Workers Party (PT), might undermine Brazil's standing in international markets. In previous electoral campaigns he had sharply criticised the behaviour of international financial institutions such as the IMF, and there was a persistent fear among financial analysts that his economic team would not be up to the task of managing Brazil's

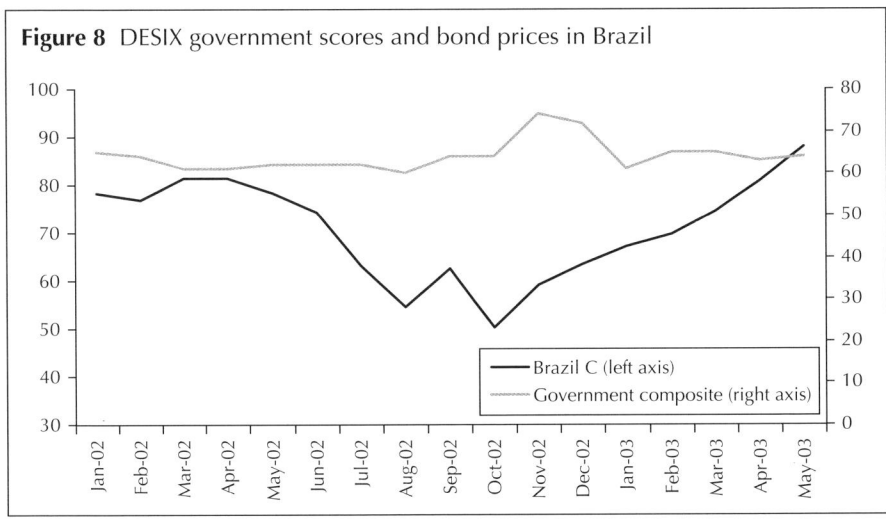

Figure 8 DESIX government scores and bond prices in Brazil

finances and ongoing marketisation. In short, investors felt that a politically driven market crisis was a real possibility if Lula won.

Throughout the downturn in Brazilian markets, DESIX political scores for Brazil were suggesting that in fact the country remained very stable, and that a Lula victory could even enhance political stability. The data reflected the facts that (a) Lula had an inclusive and conciliatory electoral strategy, and (b) a PT victory would increase the institutionalisation, and hence stability, of Brazil's democracy by enfranchising a large sector of the electorate who had never been represented in government. While markets plunged based on political fears, the underlying political story was relatively benign. Lula won, and moved swiftly to send market-calming signals about his macroeconomic policy intentions. By spring 2003, Brazilian bonds had staged a dramatic recovery (see Figure 8).

5

Country Risk Components, the Cost of Capital, and Returns in Emerging Markets

Campbell R. Harvey*

Duke University

INTRODUCTION

What is country risk and how should it impact global investment strategies? I explore the information in Political Risk Services' International Country Risk Guide (ICRG). These measures include political risk, economic risk and financial risk. The ICRG also reports a measure of composite risk, which is a simple function of the three base indices. In contrast to previous work, I also explore the components of each of the three categories.

The first part of my analysis investigates the link between these country risk measures and some more standard measures of risk. I investigate whether there is a correlation between a country's beta versus the MSCI world index and country risk ratings. While beta is a standard risk measure for integrated capital markets, many have found the world beta model inadequate to characterise risk in emerging markets. As an alternative, I also investigate the relation between the country risk measure and equity volatility. In the final part of the first section, I consider return skewness and its relation to country risk.

*Campbell R. Harvey is also at the National Bureau of Economic Research, Cambridge, MA. I appreciate the help of Jie Yang's valuable research assistance and the comments of Sam Wilkin.

In the next section, I explore whether the risk indices contain information about future expected returns. This analysis is conducted in two ways. First, I form a portfolio of countries with low-risk ratings (more risky) and a portfolio of countries with high-risk ratings (less risky). I find that there is, indeed, information about expected equity returns in these measures. However, the information is useful only for trading strategies involving emerging markets.

The trading strategies are based on historical returns. In the final part of the chapter, I examine the relation between country risk measures and the implied cost of capital. The implied cost of capital is the discount rate that makes a company's expected cashflows (based on analysts' forecasts of earnings) exactly equal the current stock price. Hence, the implied cost of capital is based on *ex ante* rather than historical data. There is a significant relation between the country risk and the implied cost of capital, which is consistent with the results of the trading strategies. Again, the relation is significant only for emerging markets.

MEASURING COUNTRY RISK

There are many services that measure country risk. The research of Erb, Harvey and Viskanta (1996) details the correlation between the different measures (which includes Moody's, Standard & Poor's, *Institutional Investor* and Political Risk Services' International Country Risk Guide (ICRG)). In this chapter, I concentrate on the ICRG data. Indeed, Erb, Harvey and Viskanta show that the ICRG data, which are available on a monthly frequency, are able to predict changes in the *Institutional Investor* measure, which is available only semiannually.

INTERNATIONAL COUNTRY RISK GUIDE

ICRG compiles monthly data on a variety of political, financial and economic risk factors to calculate risk indices in each of these categories as well as a composite risk index. Five financial, twelve political and five economic factors are used. Each factor is assigned a numerical rating within a specified range. The specified allowable range for each factor reflects the weight attributed to that factor. A higher score indicates lesser risk.

Political risk assessment scores are based on subjective staff analysis of available information. Economic risk assessment scores are based upon objective analysis of quantitative data, and financial risk assessment scores are based upon analysis of a mix of quantitative and qualitative information.

Calculation of the three individual indices is simply a matter of summing up the point scores for each factor within each risk category. The composite rating is a linear combination of the three individual indices' point scores. Note that the political risk measure (100 points) is given twice the weight of financial and economic risk (50 points each). ICRG, as well as many of the other providers, think of country risk as being composed of two primary components: ability to pay and willingness to pay. Political risk is associated with a willingness to pay while financial and economic risks are associated with an ability to pay.

The specific factors taken into account for each risk index are detailed in Table 1. While previous research has examined the information in the broad categories (ie, political, economic and financial), one of the goals of this chapter is to examine the information in the components of each of these categories. For example, how important is law and order in the political-risk-versus-investment profile?

VARIATION IN RISK MEASURES

My analysis focuses on more than 100 countries. I segment the countries into three groups: *all* countries, *developed* countries and *emerging*. In the financial analysis, I will reduce the number of countries by focusing only on those with equity markets.

Figure 1 presents time-series graphs of the equally weighted risk indices for three groups over the January 1984–July 2004 period. The equally weighted measures for the developed countries (Panel A) exhibit remarkably little variation through time. The ICRG financial and economic measures remain about the same throughout the sample.[1] The analysis for the emerging countries and all countries (Panels B and C) is different. Generally, all of the risk rating measures increase over the sample. Obviously, the increase in rating for the "all countries" sample is driven by the emerging markets.

MEAN REVERSION OF RISK RATINGS

The cross-sectional behaviour of the risk measures is explored in Figure 2. I graph the January 1984 risk level against the change in the

Table 1 Critical factors in the ICRG rating system

Factor	Points	Percentage of individual index	Percentage of composite	Label
Political				
Government stability	12	12	6	P1
Socioeconomic conditions	12	12	6	P2
Investment profile	12	12	6	P3
Internal conflict	12	12	6	P4
External conflict	12	12	6	P5
Corruption	6	6	3	P6
Military in politics	6	6	3	P7
Religion in politics	6	6	3	P8
Law and order	6	6	3	P9
Ethnic tensions	6	6	3	P10
Democratic accountability	6	6	3	P11
Bureaucracy quality	4	4	2	P12
Total political points	100	100	50	
Financial				
Foreign debt as a percentage of GDP	10	20	5	F1
Foreign debt service as a percentage of exports of goods	10	20	5	F3
and current account as a percentage of exports of goods and services	15	30	7.5	F4
Net international liquidity as months of import cover	5	10	2.5	F5
Exchange rate stability	10	20	5	F2
Total financial points	50	100	25	
Economic				
GDP per head	5	10	2.5	E1
Real GDP growth	10	20	5	E2
Annual inflation rate	10	20	5	E3
Budget balance as a percentage of GDP	10	20	5	E4
Current account as a percentage of GDP	15	30	7.5	E5
Total economic points	50	100	25	
Overall points	200		100	

risk level up to July 2004. There appears to be cross-sectional mean reversion in the risk measures. Those countries that began with a very low risk rating tend to improve. Those countries with a high rating have remained at the high level or have slightly deteriorated.

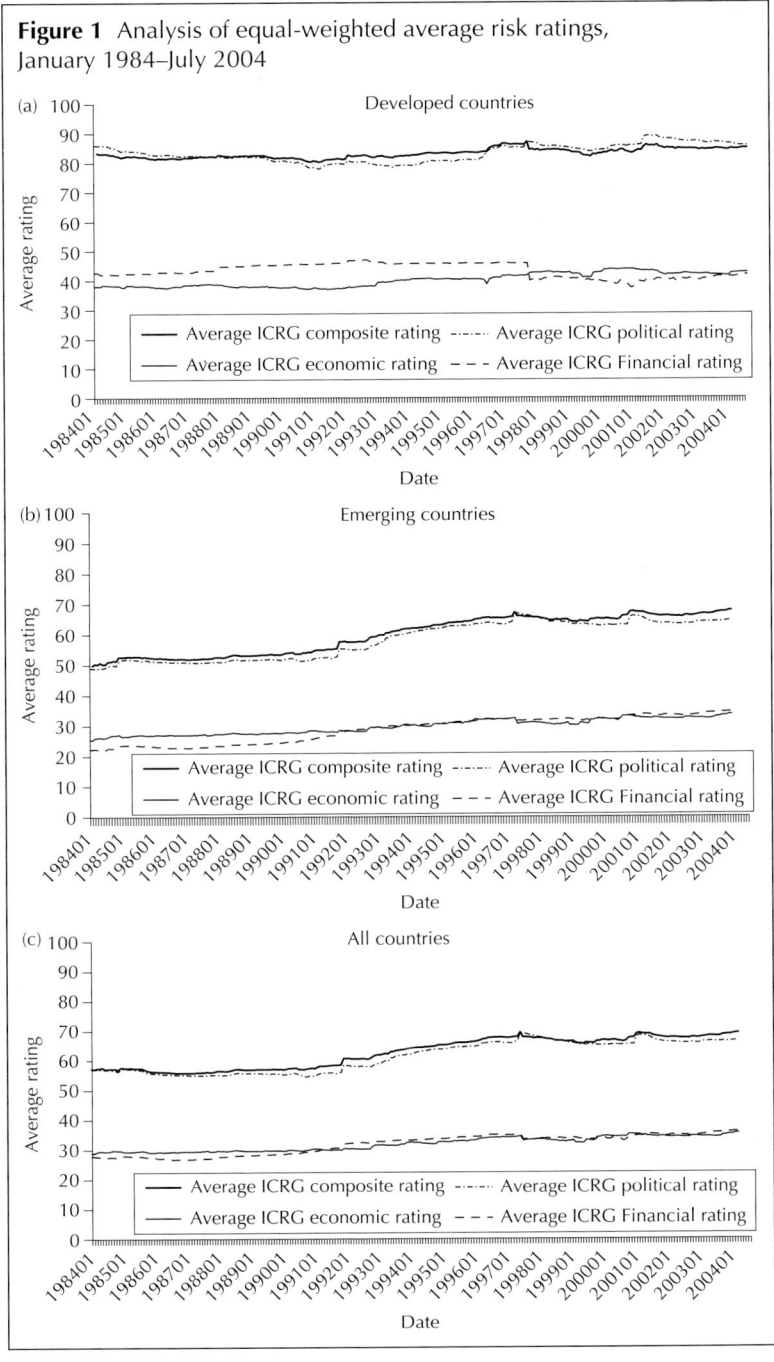

Figure 1 Analysis of equal-weighted average risk ratings, January 1984–July 2004

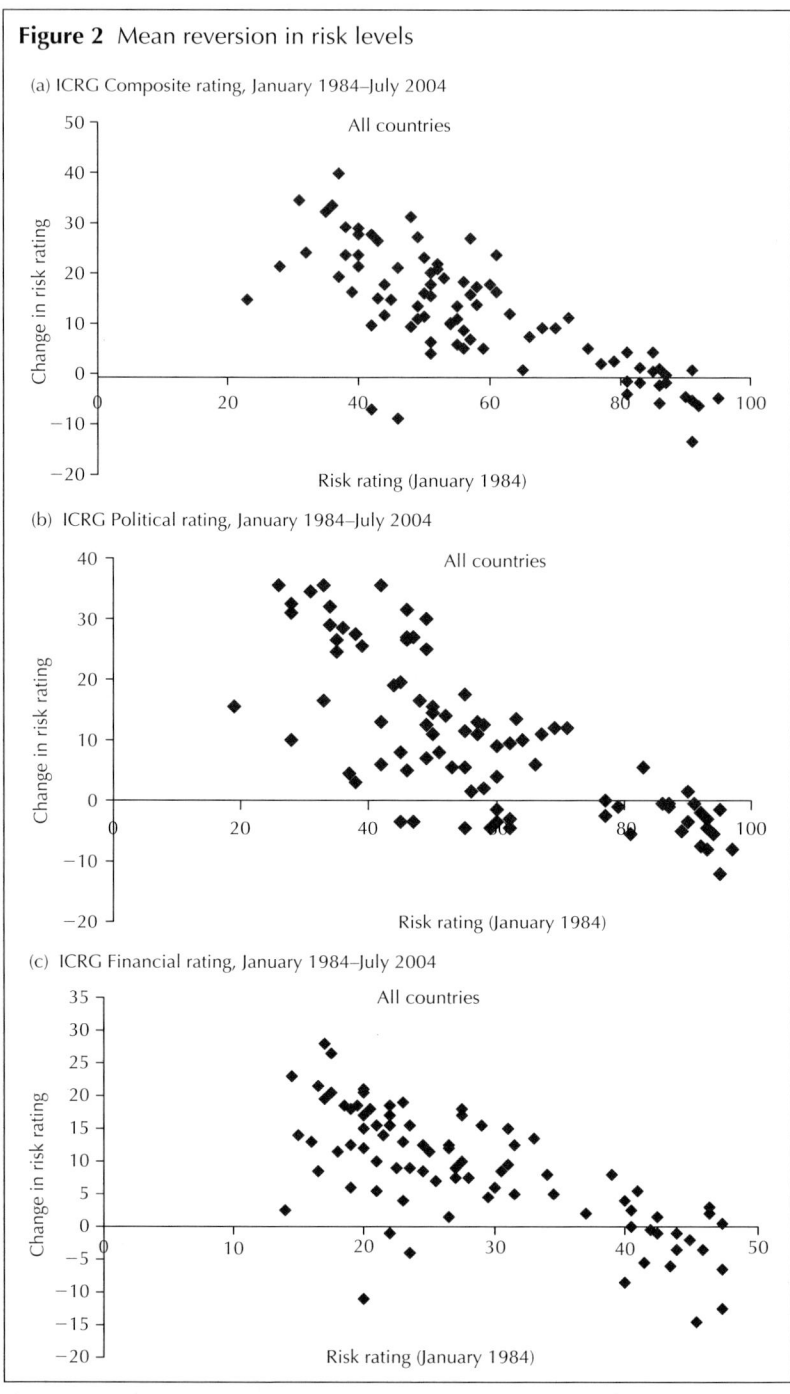

Figure 2 Mean reversion in risk levels

(a) ICRG Composite rating, January 1984–July 2004

(b) ICRG Political rating, January 1984–July 2004

(c) ICRG Financial rating, January 1984–July 2004

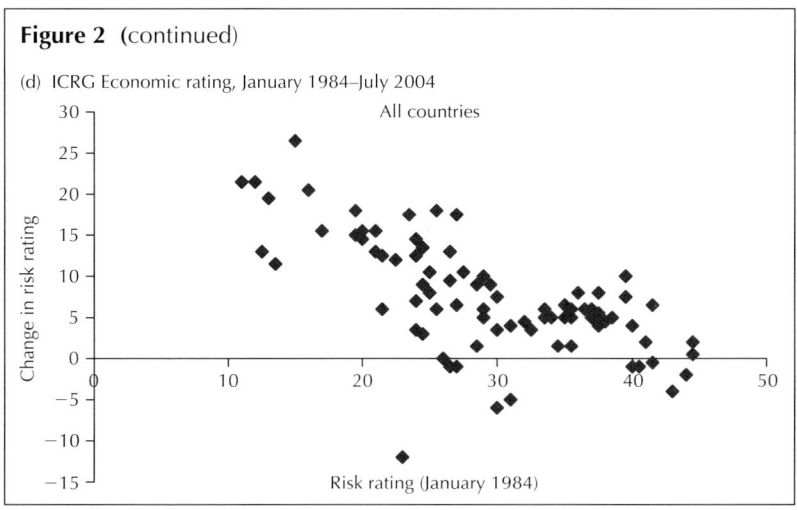

Figure 2 (continued)

(d) ICRG Economic rating, January 1984–July 2004

The cross-sectional behaviour of ratings is further explored in Figure 3. In panel A, I consider the change in the financial, economic, political and composite ratings for emerging, developed, countries with equity markets and all countries. It is clear from this graph that there has been minimal change in the ratings for developed countries – most of the improvement has occurred in emerging markets.

The next three panels of Figure 3 examine the components of each of three risk measures. In Panel B, it is evident that most of the improvement in the financial rating in emerging countries versus developed countries is due to improved exchange-rate stability and more favourable debt-service ratios. Panel C shows that the relative improvement over developed countries for the economic ratings is being driven by improved capital account as a percentage of GDP, improved budget balances, reduced inflation and more robust GDP growth. Panel D shows significant gains in democratic accountability, reduced external conflict and a sharp improvement in government stability in the political risk category.

COMOVEMENT OF RISK RATINGS

Table 2A details the correlation of the various risk measures. The upper triangle of the matrix reports the correlation based on changes

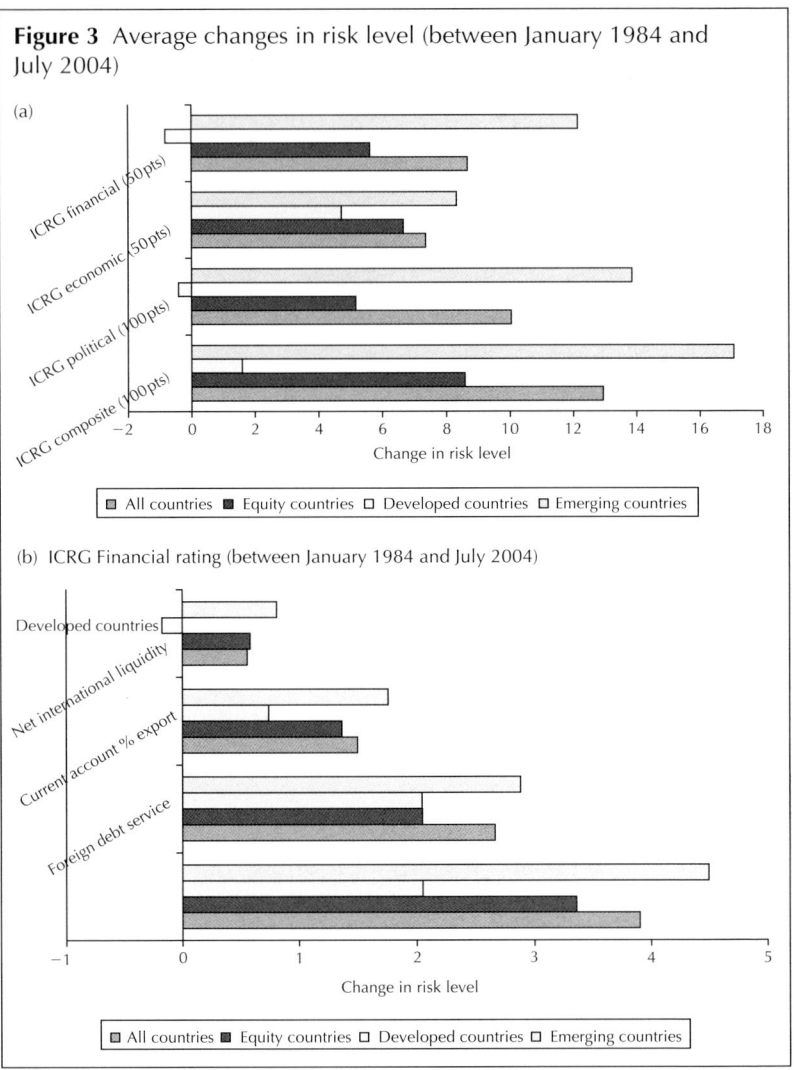

Figure 3 Average changes in risk level (between January 1984 and July 2004)

in rating and the lower triangle reports the correlation of the levels. The correlations are calculated by staking all country observations together.

The correlations are not as high as one might expect. Obviously, the correlation between the composite and the political rating is the highest because, by definition, the political rating is 50% of the composite. The highest cross-correlation of the levels of the three

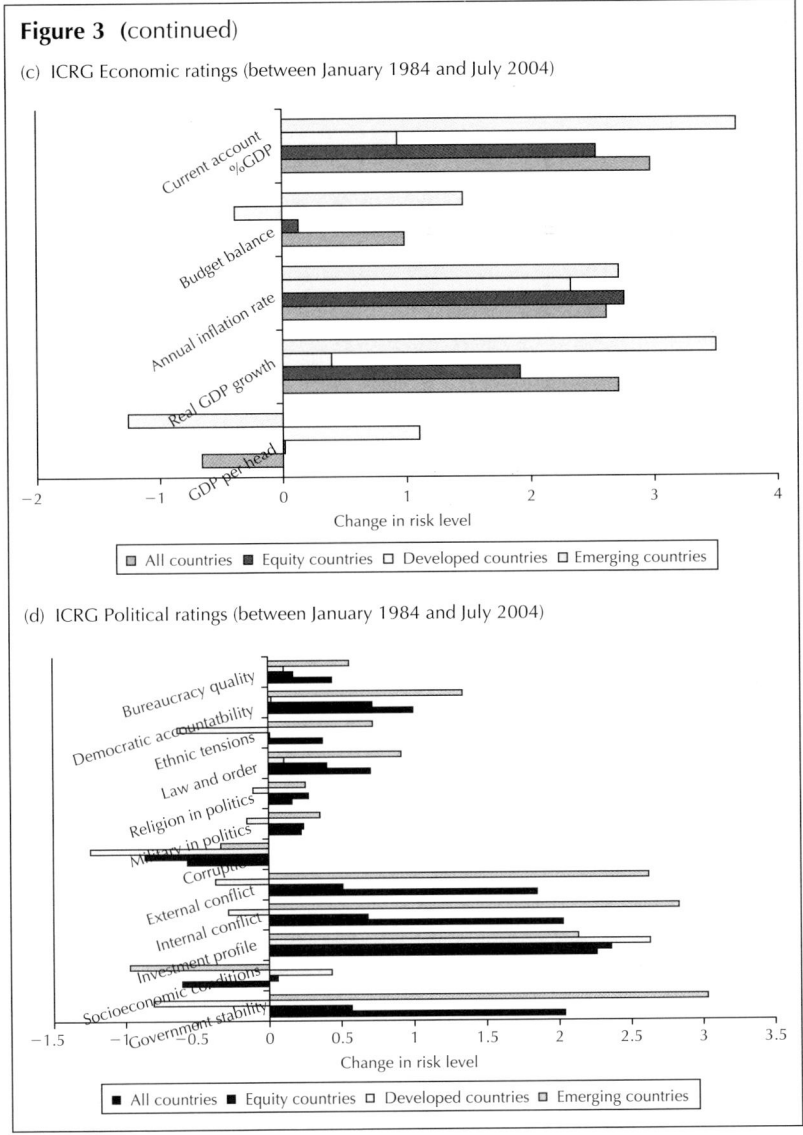

Figure 3 (continued)

(c) ICRG Economic ratings (between January 1984 and July 2004)

☐ All countries ■ Equity countries ☐ Developed countries ☐ Emerging countries

(d) ICRG Political ratings (between January 1984 and July 2004)

■ All countries ■ Equity countries ☐ Developed countries ☐ Emerging countries

ICRG components is 80%. The correlations for the changes in risk levels are all very small.

Table 2A also examines the components of each risk measure. Similar to the aggregated measures, the subcomponents show high correlations in levels and low correlations when examined as components.

Table 2A Correlations of risk measure levels and changes, monthly observations, January 1984–July 2004 (number of obs: 21821)

Source	ICRGC	ICRGP	ICRGF	ICRGE	P1	P2	P3	P4	P5	P6	P7	P8
ICRGC		0.61	0.56	0.53	0.33	0.25	0.28	0.28	0.25	0.11	0.12	0.10
ICRGP	0.95		0.12	0.03	0.54	0.34	0.46	0.47	0.41	0.18	0.20	0.17
ICRGF	0.92	0.80		0.07	0.06	0.10	0.05	0.05	0.05	0.02	0.02	0.02
ICRGE	0.83	0.67	0.75		0.02	0.04	0.02	0.01	0.01	0.00	0.01	0.00
P1	0.56	0.58	0.50	0.41		0.06	0.08	0.14	0.08	0.05	0.07	0.01
P2	0.72	0.70	0.62	0.62	0.26		0.11	0.05	0.04	0.00	0.02	0.02
P3	0.70	0.71	0.59	0.57	0.61	0.58		0.07	0.11	0.00	0.02	−0.01
P4	0.80	0.85	0.67	0.54	0.48	0.50	0.49		0.16	0.06	0.09	0.08
P5	0.63	0.67	0.56	0.40	0.34	0.32	0.37	0.63		0.02	0.06	0.04
P6	0.59	0.64	0.48	0.37	0.16	0.49	0.27	0.48	0.34		0.03	0.03
P7	0.74	0.78	0.62	0.51	0.27	0.54	0.48	0.64	0.45	0.60		0.03
P8	0.44	0.54	0.34	0.19	0.17	0.26	0.24	0.48	0.43	0.36	0.41	
P9	0.80	0.83	0.69	0.57	0.43	0.57	0.47	0.76	0.49	0.63	0.66	0.40
P10	0.58	0.64	0.49	0.33	0.34	0.36	0.31	0.64	0.44	0.40	0.46	0.43
P11	0.61	0.68	0.48	0.38	0.22	0.40	0.42	0.48	0.45	0.60	0.62	0.35
P12	0.77	0.77	0.67	0.60	0.29	0.65	0.49	0.56	0.40	0.68	0.69	0.30
F1	0.76	0.66	0.82	0.63	0.29	0.64	0.44	0.53	0.39	0.47	0.57	0.31
F2	0.68	0.59	0.73	0.56	0.59	0.36	0.60	0.50	0.39	0.21	0.38	0.22
F3	0.30	0.26	0.31	0.27	0.28	0.16	0.28	0.18	0.26	0.01	0.12	0.13
F4	0.50	0.38	0.48	0.62	0.19	0.38	0.30	0.29	0.30	0.22	0.31	0.06
F5	0.42	0.31	0.43	0.48	0.24	0.31	0.34	0.23	0.12	0.17	0.22	−0.01
E1	0.58	0.57	0.46	0.52	0.12	0.78	0.47	0.39	0.21	0.47	0.50	0.24
E2	0.52	0.48	0.49	0.48	0.70	0.26	0.71	0.35	0.26	0.06	0.23	0.11
E3	0.66	0.55	0.58	0.75	0.41	0.46	0.53	0.43	0.29	0.22	0.38	0.16
E4	0.68	0.62	0.61	0.64	0.57	0.55	0.72	0.44	0.32	0.27	0.41	0.18
E5	0.66	0.58	0.65	0.61	0.65	0.46	0.74	0.41	0.32	0.17	0.36	0.15

Table 2B Correlations of risk measure levels and changes, monthly observations, January 1984–July 2004

Source	ICRGC	ICRGP	ICRGF	ICRGE
		Averaging over countries		
ICRGC		0.61	0.54	0.55
ICRGP	0.80		0.10	0.03
ICRGF	0.70	0.39		0.07
ICRGE	0.64	0.35	0.34	
		Stacking all observations		
ICRGC		0.61	0.56	0.53
ICRGP	0.95		0.12	0.03
ICRGF	0.92	0.80		0.07
ICRGE	0.83	0.67	0.75	

P9	P10	P11	P12	F1	F2	F3	F4	F5	E1	E2	E3	E4	E5
0.16	0.15	0.13	0.05	0.28	0.29	0.14	0.29	0.10	0.20	0.28	0.21	0.28	0.33
0.27	0.25	0.24	0.09	0.09	0.04	0.01	0.00	0.01	0.17	0.21	0.02	0.23	0.24
0.02	0.02	0.02	0.01	0.44	0.61	0.08	0.17	0.08	0.05	0.09	0.02	0.11	0.19
0.01	0.01	−0.02	0.00	0.05	−0.01	0.18	0.40	0.13	0.15	0.25	0.36	0.21	0.20
0.08	0.06	0.05	0.01	0.05	0.02	0.02	0.01	0.01	0.04	0.05	0.02	0.04	0.06
0.05	0.03	0.02	0.02	0.08	0.03	0.02	0.01	0.01	0.06	0.09	0.02	0.09	0.09
0.03	0.02	0.05	−0.01	0.06	0.01	0.01	0.02	0.00	0.36	0.44	0.01	0.49	0.54
0.16	0.20	0.08	0.02	0.03	0.02	−0.01	0.02	0.00	0.01	0.02	0.01	0.01	0.01
0.08	0.08	0.04	0.00	0.05	0.01	0.00	0.01	0.01	0.03	0.03	0.00	0.04	0.03
0.07	0.06	0.05	0.04	0.01	0.01	−0.01	0.01	0.00	0.00	−0.02	0.01	−0.01	−0.02
0.08	0.06	0.09	0.02	0.02	0.00	0.01	−0.01	0.00	0.00	0.00	0.02	0.01	0.00
0.08	0.08	0.00	0.00	0.01	0.01	−0.01	−0.01	0.00	0.01	0.00	0.00	−0.01	0.01
	0.16	0.04	0.02	0.02	0.00	−0.01	0.00	0.01	0.01	0.01	0.00	0.01	0.00
0.58		0.03	0.03	0.02	0.01	0.00	0.02	0.00	−0.01	0.00	0.00	−0.01	−0.01
0.51	0.35		0.10	0.01	0.02	−0.01	0.00	0.00	0.02	0.02	−0.02	0.01	0.02
0.68	0.39	0.65		0.01	0.00	0.00	0.00	−0.01	−0.01	−0.01	−0.01	−0.02	−0.02
0.59	0.41	0.40	0.62		0.04	0.03	0.03	0.01	0.14	0.03	−0.01	0.07	0.12
0.48	0.35	0.32	0.41	0.43		0.00	0.01	0.02	−0.11	0.08	0.00	−0.03	0.01
0.17	0.09	0.16	0.18	0.19	0.24		0.05	0.01	0.01	0.00	0.03	0.01	0.02
0.27	0.20	0.26	0.39	0.41	0.23	0.14		0.00	0.01	0.02	0.01	0.03	0.14
0.28	0.23	0.17	0.28	0.34	0.31	0.01	0.28		0.00	0.02	0.02	0.01	0.00
0.48	0.28	0.36	0.60	0.59	0.18	0.09	0.32	0.26		0.20	0.00	0.45	0.46
0.32	0.19	0.22	0.24	0.26	0.65	0.29	0.18	0.26	0.08		0.07	0.40	0.45
0.45	0.24	0.29	0.45	0.43	0.57	0.21	0.32	0.30	0.31	0.48		−0.01	0.01
0.45	0.28	0.32	0.45	0.48	0.54	0.25	0.39	0.29	0.47	0.65	0.47		0.55
0.39	0.25	0.25	0.41	0.49	0.60	0.29	0.46	0.33	0.38	0.71	0.46	0.77	

Table 2B shows that stacking all country observations produces higher correlations compared with averaging correlations across the different countries. However, the "flavour" of the results remain unchanged.

PERSISTENCE OF RISK RATINGS

Table 3 shows the degree of persistence in the log changes in the risk measures and the subcomponents. I report the average auto-correlations. I present the results by all developed and emerging countries. In addition, I report the number of countries with auto-correlations that are significantly above or below zero.

For the composite, economic, political and financial meas-ures, there is very little evidence of persistence in the developed markets. Of the 26 countries, for example, only two show signi-ficant autocorrelation in the changes in the political risk ratings.

Table 3 Persistence of risk measures, first-order autocorrelations of log rating changes, monthly observations, January 1984–July 2004

Source	All countries						Developed countries						Emerging countries					
	No. obs	Avg.	No. sig above	No. sig below	Min.	Max.	No. obs	Avg.	No. sig above	No. sig below	Min.	Max.	No. obs	Avg.	No. sig above	No. sig below	Min.	Max.
ICRGC	145	−0.03	3	5	−0.50	0.28	26	−0.09	1	0	−0.27	0.15	119	−0.02	3	4	−0.50	0.28
ICRGP	145	0.03	4	2	−0.48	0.33	26	0.01	1	1	−0.16	0.21	119	0.04	4	2	−0.48	0.33
ICRGF	145	−0.05	3	3	−0.49	0.23	26	−0.11	1	0	−0.28	0.14	119	−0.04	3	4	−0.49	0.23
ICRGE	145	−0.09	2	6	−0.50	0.22	26	−0.16	0	1	−0.40	0.03	119	−0.07	2	5	−0.50	0.22
P1	145	−0.02	2	3	−0.40	0.41	26	−0.03	1	1	−0.21	0.16	119	−0.02	2	3	−0.40	0.41
P2	145	−0.01	3	6	−0.39	0.17	26	−0.02	1	1	−0.17	0.12	119	−0.01	3	4	−0.39	0.17
P3	145	−0.02	2	7	−0.42	0.18	26	−0.01	1	1	−0.14	0.11	119	−0.02	2	7	−0.42	0.18
P4	143	−0.02	5	5	−0.37	0.50	25	−0.03	2	1	−0.33	0.20	118	−0.02	3	4	−0.37	0.50
P5	143	−0.02	5	8	−0.42	0.30	26	−0.04	0	2	−0.42	0.08	110	−0.01	5	6	−0.39	0.30
P6	135	−0.02	12	8	−0.37	0.15	25	−0.01	1	1	−0.24	0.00	110	−0.02	11	7	−0.37	0.15
P7	106	−0.02	42	5	−0.50	0.47	11	−0.09	15	2	−0.50	0.00	95	−0.02	27	4	−0.46	0.47
P8	108	−0.02	40	5	−0.50	0.44	17	−0.04	9	1	−0.25	0.00	91	−0.01	31	5	−0.50	0.44
P9	122	−0.01	27	5	−0.49	0.33	16	0.00	11	1	−0.35	0.26	106	−0.01	15	5	−0.49	0.33
P10	127	−0.03	19	8	−0.50	0.31	24	−0.03	2	1	−0.50	0.00	103	−0.03	17	8	−0.39	0.31
P11	130	−0.04	15	10	−0.50	0.15	17	−0.06	9	1	−0.50	0.00	113	−0.03	6	8	−0.50	0.15
P12	100	−0.02	46	6	−0.58	0.25	14	−0.09	12	1	−0.58	0.00	86	−0.01	35	3	−0.50	0.25
F1	144	0.00	5	5	−0.42	0.49	26	−0.01	1	1	−0.42	0.49	118	0.00	4	3	−0.35	0.41
F2	145	−0.09	3	3	−0.52	0.54	26	−0.19	0	0	−0.42	0.10	119	−0.07	2	5	−0.52	0.54
F3	137	−0.03	8	7	−0.49	0.07	25	−0.03	1	2	−0.19	0.00	112	−0.03	7	7	−0.49	0.07
F4	144	−0.05	1	11	−0.50	0.10	26	−0.12	0	1	−0.44	0.04	118	−0.04	1	5	−0.50	0.10
F5	125	−0.09	21	7	−0.48	0.22	26	−0.17	0	1	−0.44	0.00	99	−0.08	21	5	−0.48	0.22
E1	142	−0.04	5	5	−0.48	0.21	26	0.01	0	1	−0.35	0.17	116	−0.06	4	4	−0.48	0.21
E2	145	0.00	3	5	−0.42	0.39	26	−0.03	0	1	−0.25	0.10	119	0.01	2	4	−0.42	0.39
E3	142	−0.04	5	7	−0.43	0.26	26	−0.08	0	2	−0.43	0.04	116	−0.03	5	5	−0.41	0.26
E4	145	−0.10	1	9	−0.60	0.21	26	−0.10	0	1	−0.41	0.16	119	−0.10	1	8	−0.60	0.21
E5	145	−0.07	1	7	−0.54	0.36	26	−0.05	1	1	−0.35	0.17	119	−0.07	1	6	−0.54	0.36

Note: Significance at 95% based on 2 standard deviations.

The emerging markets present a similar story. Of the 119 countries, only six show significant changes in the political risk ratings – about what one would expect by random chance.

While changes in the political, economic and financial ratings are generally unpredictable, the story changes when the components are examined. Many of these components are quite stable. A long string of zeros often induces significant autocorrelations. It is best to interpret this as persistence in the component risk levels.

RISK RATINGS AND RETURNS

Table 4 provides a correlation analysis of the ratings with mean returns, volatility, beta and skewness. In this table, I examine only countries with equity markets. First, I examine the beta, which is calculated against the Morgan Stanley Capital International World Index. The correlation of the composite risk measure and beta is positive and is 0.16 in the all-country sample. In addition, the positive correlation is driven by the emerging markets in the sample. The sign of the correlation is exactly the opposite of what one would expect (low-rated countries that are presumably risky have the lowest beta risk). Figure 4 graphs the betas against the average risk measures. This positive relation is largely due to the fact that a number emerging markets have very low betas with respect to the world market portfolio (see Harvey, 1995).

Panels A–D show the developed markets. The relation between betas and ratings is flat for all but the two countries with the lowest ratings. Panels E–H show the emerging markets. While the relation is weak, some of the lowest-rated countries have lower betas. The picture in Figure 4 contrasts with a similar graph in Erb, Harvey and Viskanta (1996), which showed a much sharper positive relation between beta and rating. The reason is simple. Over the past 10 years, these emerging markets have become more integrated with world capital markets. With increased integration, their betas with respect to the world tend to increase (see Bekaert and Harvey, 2000) and hence flatten out the slopes in Panels E–H.

Figure 5 shows that there is a sharp negative correlation between volatility and the risk measures. This closely squares with intuition. The lowest- (highest-) rated countries have the highest (lowest) equity return volatility. This volatility is robust across all

Table 4 Sample-period correlation between average risk measures and price moments

Risk measures	All countries				Developed countries				Emerging countries			
	Geometric return	Volatility	Skewness	Beta – MSCI world	Geometric return	Volatility	Skewness	Beta – MSCI world	Geometric return	Volatility	Skewness	Beta – MSCI world
ICRGC	0.25	−0.55	−0.38	0.16	0.15	−0.52	−0.45	0.07	−0.12	−0.28	−0.15	0.16
ICRGP	0.34	−0.48	−0.34	0.17	0.13	−0.50	−0.39	−0.03	0.11	−0.15	−0.08	0.21
ICRGF	0.17	−0.56	−0.41	0.17	0.18	−0.52	−0.47	0.18	−0.28	−0.33	−0.21	0.14
ICRGE	0.05	−0.58	−0.37	0.08	0.13	−0.33	−0.40	0.22	−0.41	−0.40	−0.18	−0.01
P1	0.10	−0.42	−0.36	0.02	0.19	−0.44	−0.41	0.02	−0.19	−0.26	−0.18	−0.04
P2	0.07	−0.62	−0.36	0.02	0.05	−0.56	−0.46	−0.06	−0.38	−0.44	−0.11	−0.06
P3	0.21	−0.62	−0.38	0.07	0.29	−0.61	0.40	0.05	−0.18	−0.45	−0.20	0.00
P4	0.27	−0.27	−0.18	0.23	0.06	−0.20	−0.17	−0.06	0.09	0.06	0.06	0.30
P5	0.41	−0.16	−0.09	0.24	0.17	−0.46	−0.20	−0.05	0.40	0.18	0.18	0.36
P6	0.33	−0.52	−0.35	0.11	0.00	−0.19	−0.33	0.04	0.11	−0.28	−0.13	0.07
P7	0.44	−0.44	−0.37	0.20	0.08	−0.47	−0.37	0.02	0.32	−0.08	−0.20	0.23
P8	0.41	−0.18	−0.23	0.27	0.25	−0.06	−0.05	−0.02	0.32	0.06	−0.14	0.32
P9	0.30	−0.42	−0.29	0.14	0.07	−0.52	−0.55	0.00	0.02	−0.02	0.08	0.13
P10	0.22	−0.25	0.03	−0.07	0.04	0.02	0.16	−0.06	0.13	−0.13	0.14	−0.13
P11	0.32	−0.41	−0.39	0.13	0.01	−0.65	−0.50	−0.07	0.19	−0.02	−0.10	0.17
P12	0.20	−0.57	−0.48	0.10	−0.07	−0.72	−0.71	0.10	−0.32	−0.29	−0.30	0.02
F1	0.18	−0.56	−0.40	0.12	0.29	−0.53	−0.38	0.08	−0.16	−0.34	−0.22	0.08
F2	0.23	−0.59	−0.37	0.06	0.17	−0.59	−0.43	−0.04	−0.19	−0.38	−0.13	−0.01
F3	−0.16	−0.25	−0.38	0.04	−0.05	−0.53	−0.44	−0.06	−0.21	−0.33	−0.41	0.08
F4	−0.09	−0.13	−0.25	0.22	−0.12	−0.55	−0.30	0.07	−0.18	0.06	−0.19	0.40
F5	−0.10	−0.24	0.02	−0.16	−0.14	0.06	0.05	0.01	0.02	−0.27	0.07	−0.23
E1	0.34	−0.51	−0.33	0.15	0.25	−0.62	−0.52	0.21	−0.41	−0.12	−0.01	0.11
E2	0.00	−0.59	−0.38	0.02	0.17	−0.57	−0.43	0.05	−0.50	−0.47	−0.19	−0.06
E3	−0.04	−0.70	−0.32	−0.15	0.24	−0.53	−0.39	0.10	−0.13	−0.58	−0.33	−0.33
E4	0.21	−0.56	−0.37	0.07	0.07	−0.42	−0.41	0.05	−0.18	−0.39	−0.14	0.00
E5	0.19	−0.33	−0.35	0.28	0.26	−0.43	−0.36	0.27	−0.18	0.02	−0.14	0.32

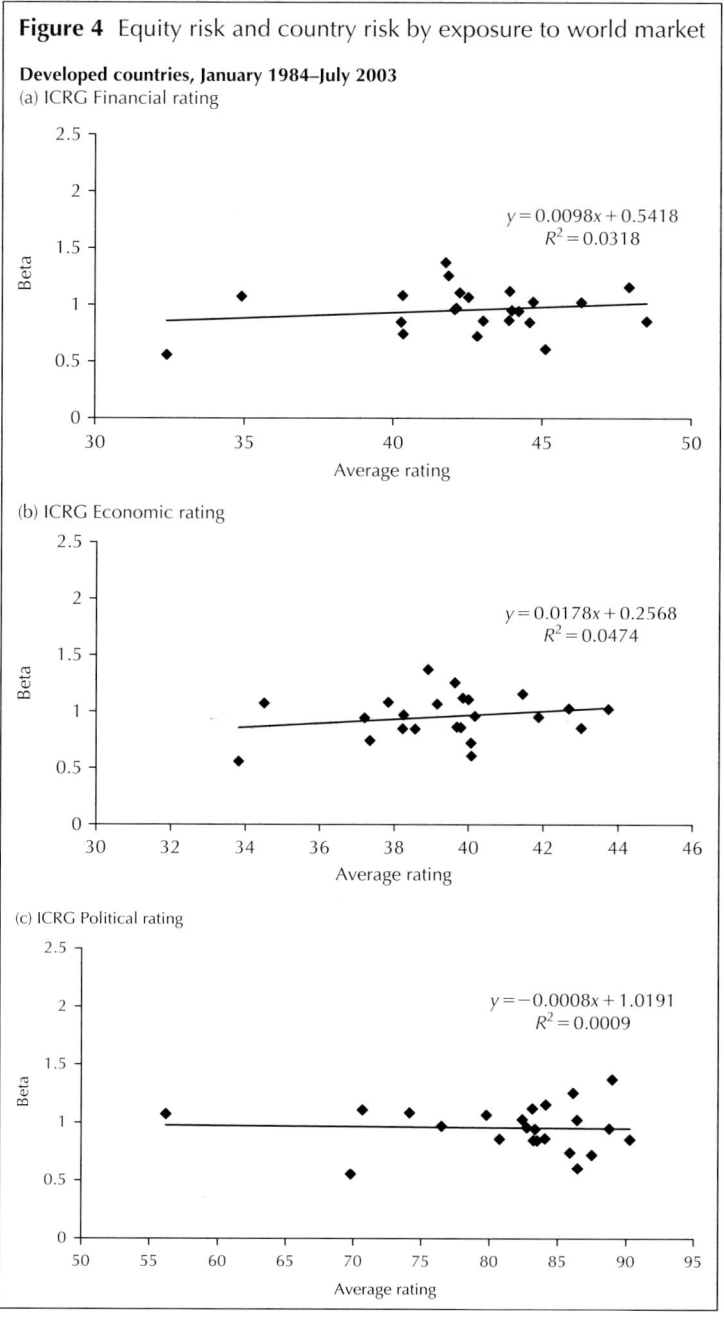

Figure 4 Equity risk and country risk by exposure to world market

Developed countries, January 1984–July 2003
(a) ICRG Financial rating

$y = 0.0098x + 0.5418$
$R^2 = 0.0318$

(b) ICRG Economic rating

$y = 0.0178x + 0.2568$
$R^2 = 0.0474$

(c) ICRG Political rating

$y = -0.0008x + 1.0191$
$R^2 = 0.0009$

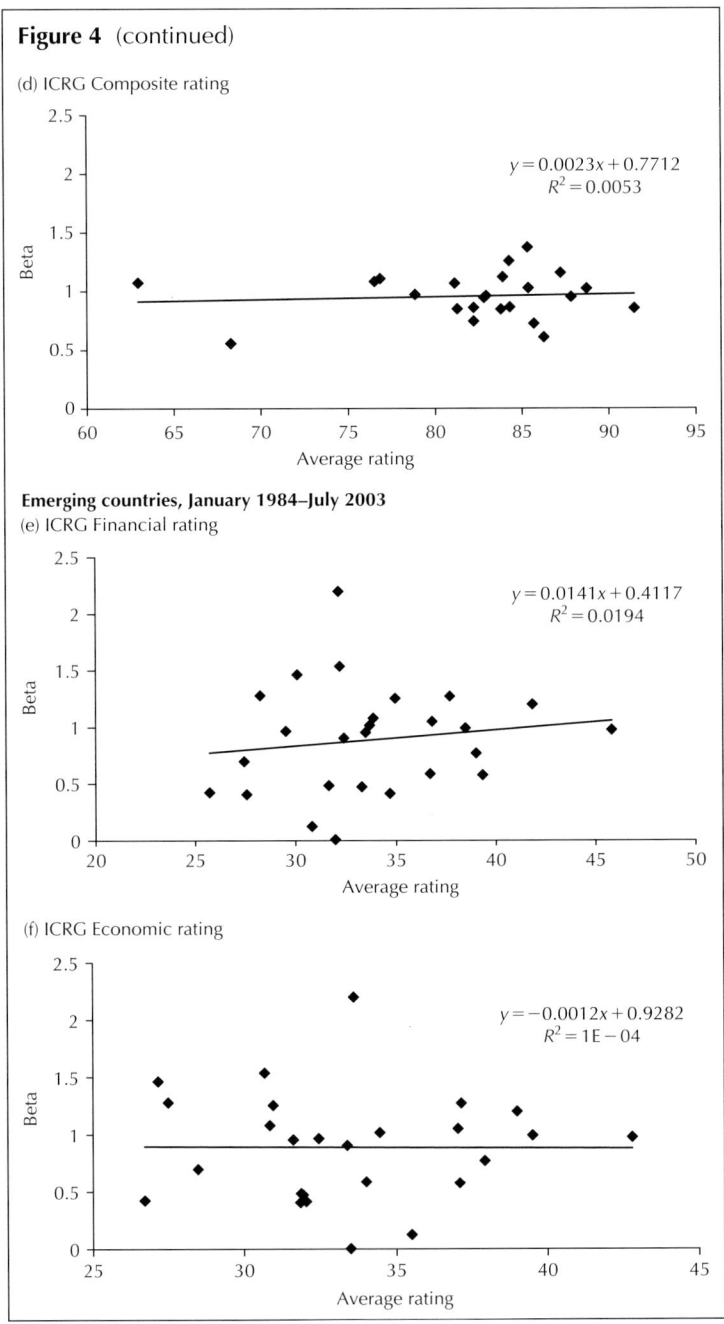

Figure 4 (continued)

(d) ICRG Composite rating

$y = 0.0023x + 0.7712$
$R^2 = 0.0053$

Emerging countries, January 1984–July 2003
(e) ICRG Financial rating

$y = 0.0141x + 0.4117$
$R^2 = 0.0194$

(f) ICRG Economic rating

$y = -0.0012x + 0.9282$
$R^2 = 1E - 04$

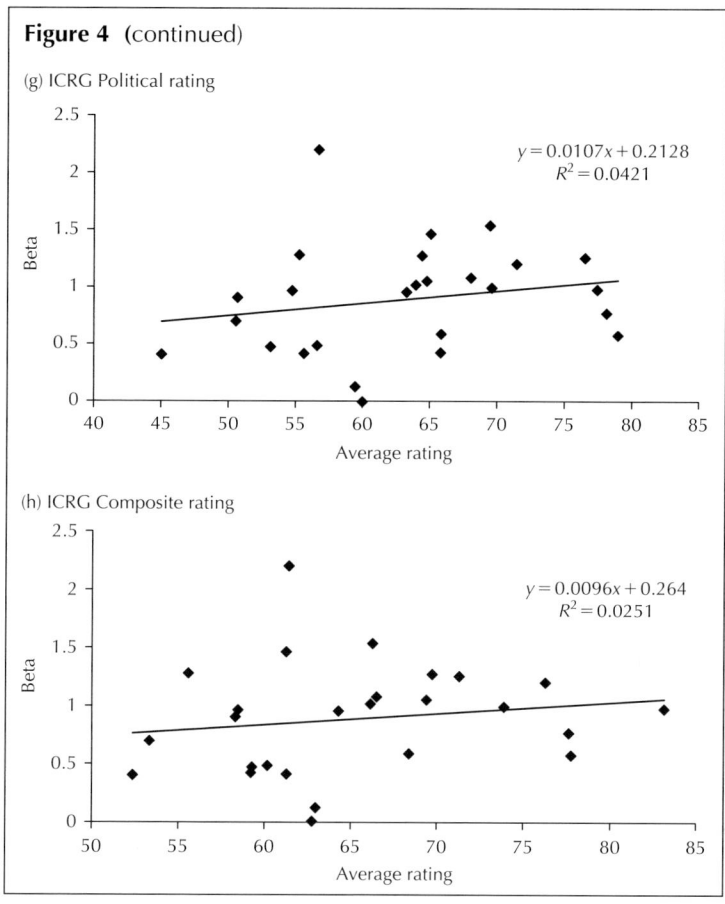

Figure 4 (continued)

(g) ICRG Political rating

$y = 0.0107x + 0.2128$
$R^2 = 0.0421$

(h) ICRG Composite rating

$y = 0.0096x + 0.264$
$R^2 = 0.0251$

risk measures. I observe a negative relation for developed markets in Panels A–D and emerging markets in Panels E–H.

Figure 6 explores the relation between return skewness and risk ratings. High-risk countries might experience big upside or downside risk that manifests itself in skewness. I find that there is generally a negative relation between the risk ratings and skew. The lowest-rated countries have the most potential for a big positive surprise. Interestingly, this relation is robust across both developed (Panels A–D) and emerging (Panels E–H) markets. However, the relation with skewness presents something of a puzzle. Markets with positive skew should have low expected returns – investors like positive skew and should bid up prices, thereby lowering expected

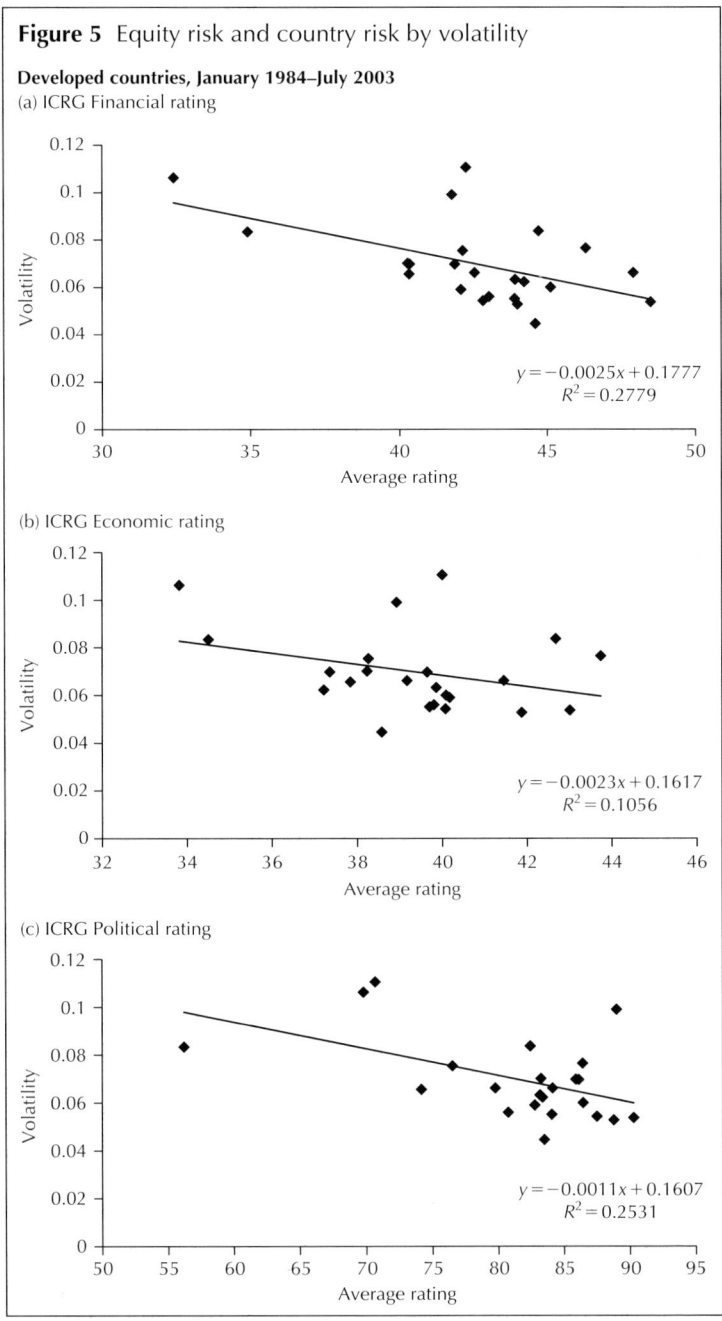

Figure 5 Equity risk and country risk by volatility

Developed countries, January 1984–July 2003
(a) ICRG Financial rating

$y = -0.0025x + 0.1777$
$R^2 = 0.2779$

(b) ICRG Economic rating

$y = -0.0023x + 0.1617$
$R^2 = 0.1056$

(c) ICRG Political rating

$y = -0.0011x + 0.1607$
$R^2 = 0.2531$

Figure 5 (continued)

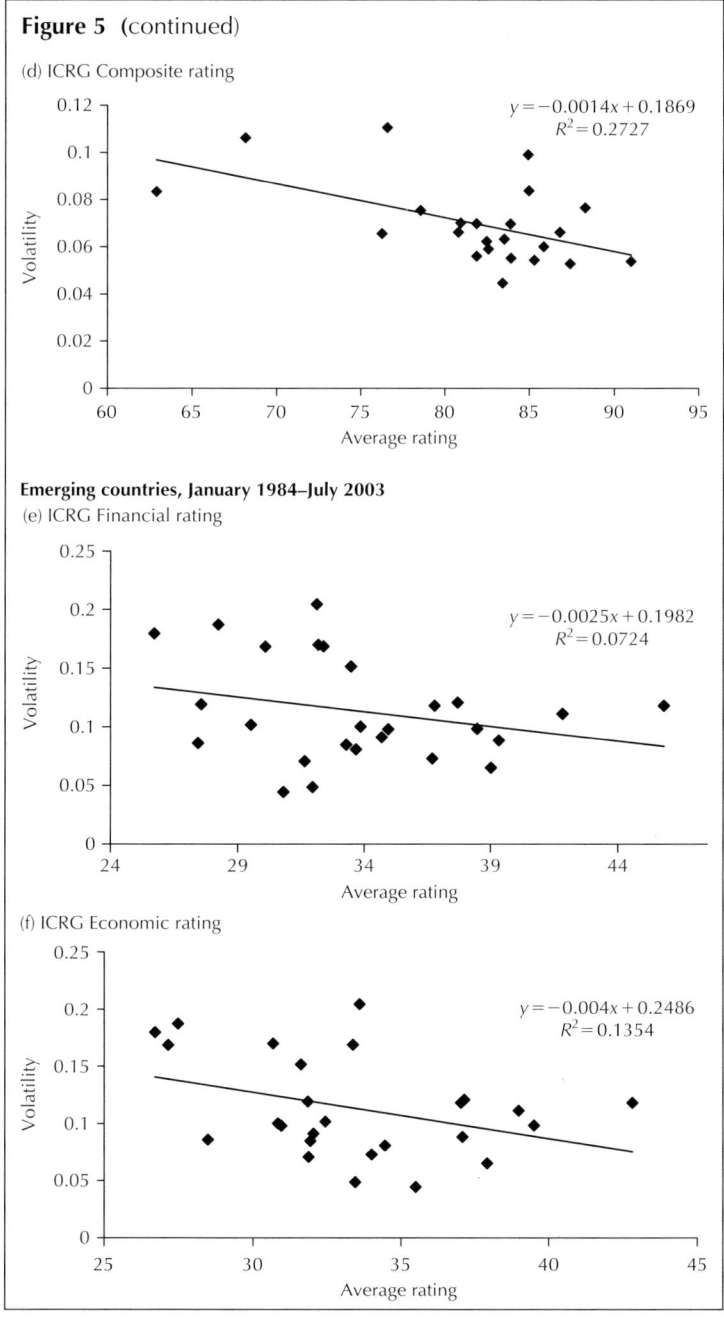

(d) ICRG Composite rating

$y = -0.0014x + 0.1869$
$R^2 = 0.2727$

Emerging countries, January 1984–July 2003

(e) ICRG Financial rating

$y = -0.0025x + 0.1982$
$R^2 = 0.0724$

(f) ICRG Economic rating

$y = -0.004x + 0.2486$
$R^2 = 0.1354$

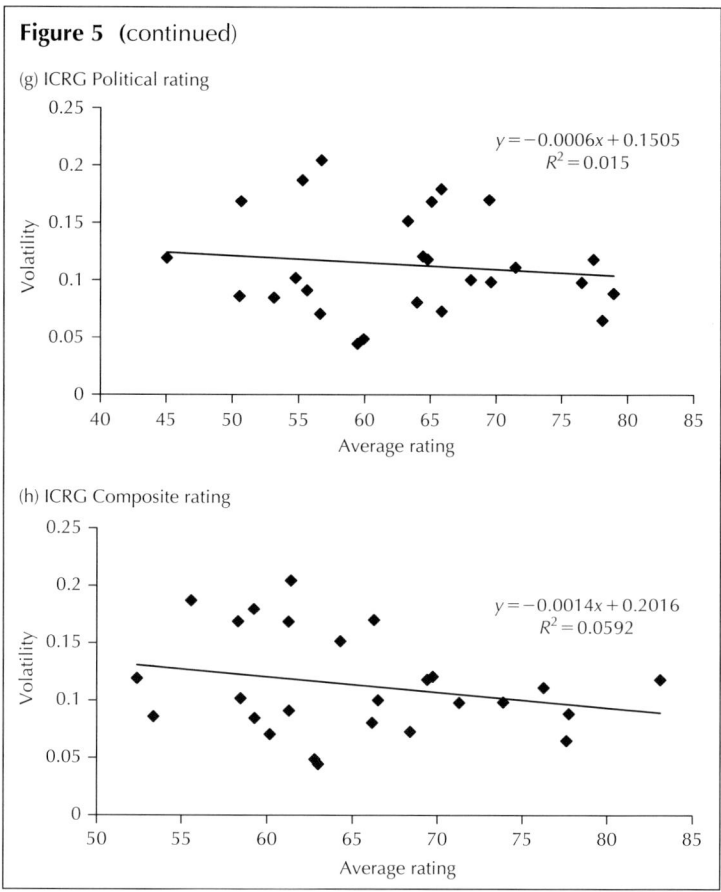

Figure 5 (continued)

(g) ICRG Political rating

$y = -0.0006x + 0.1505$
$R^2 = 0.015$

(h) ICRG Composite rating

$y = -0.0014x + 0.2016$
$R^2 = 0.0592$

returns. But this is not what I observe. The lower-rated countries have both higher expected returns and positive skewness. Nevertheless, there are two important caveats. First, the negative relation in Panels A–D for the developed countries is influenced by a few lower rated countries. Second, the relation in Panels E–H for the emerging markets while negative is only weakly negative.

WHAT TYPE OF RISK IS PRICED?

Table 4 suggests that there is a relation between average return and average rating. One way to analyse this relation is to form a portfolio strategy based on ratings changes. One version of this strategy

Figure 6 Equity risk and country risk by skewness

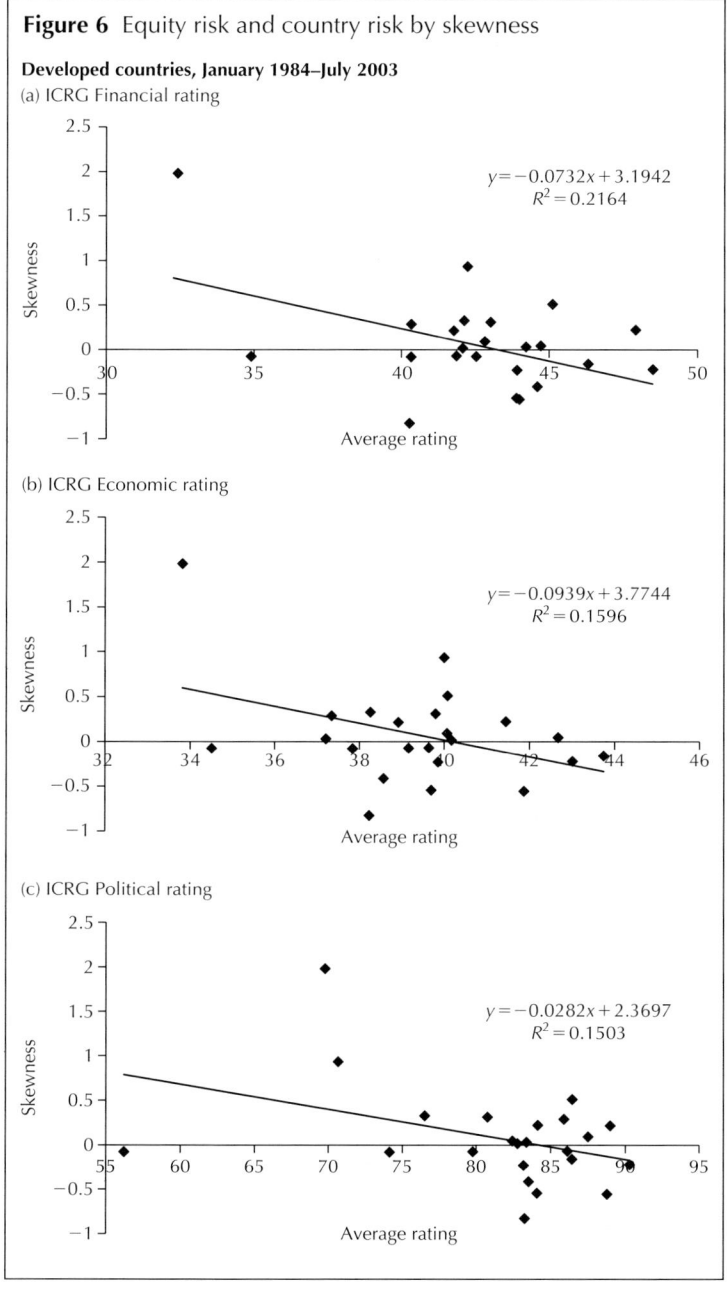

Developed countries, January 1984–July 2003
(a) ICRG Financial rating

$y = -0.0732x + 3.1942$
$R^2 = 0.2164$

(b) ICRG Economic rating

$y = -0.0939x + 3.7744$
$R^2 = 0.1596$

(c) ICRG Political rating

$y = -0.0282x + 2.3697$
$R^2 = 0.1503$

Figure 6 (continued)

(d) ICRG Composite rating

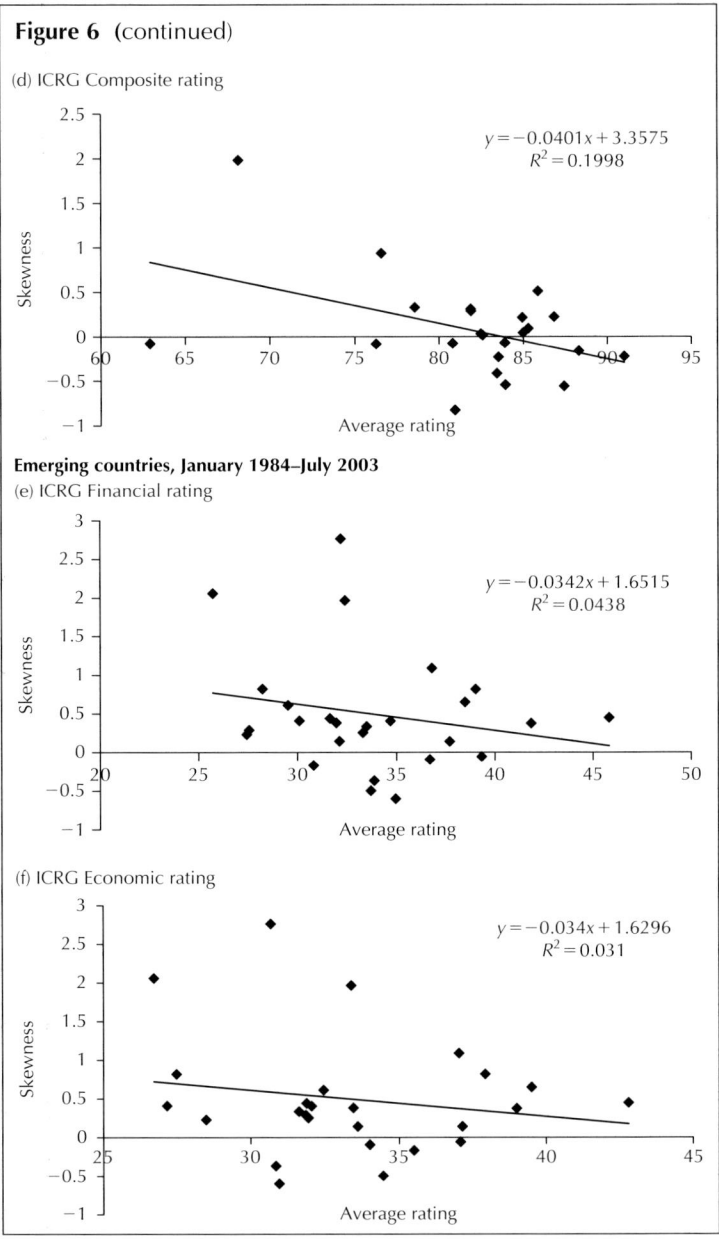

Emerging countries, January 1984–July 2003

(e) ICRG Financial rating

(f) ICRG Economic rating

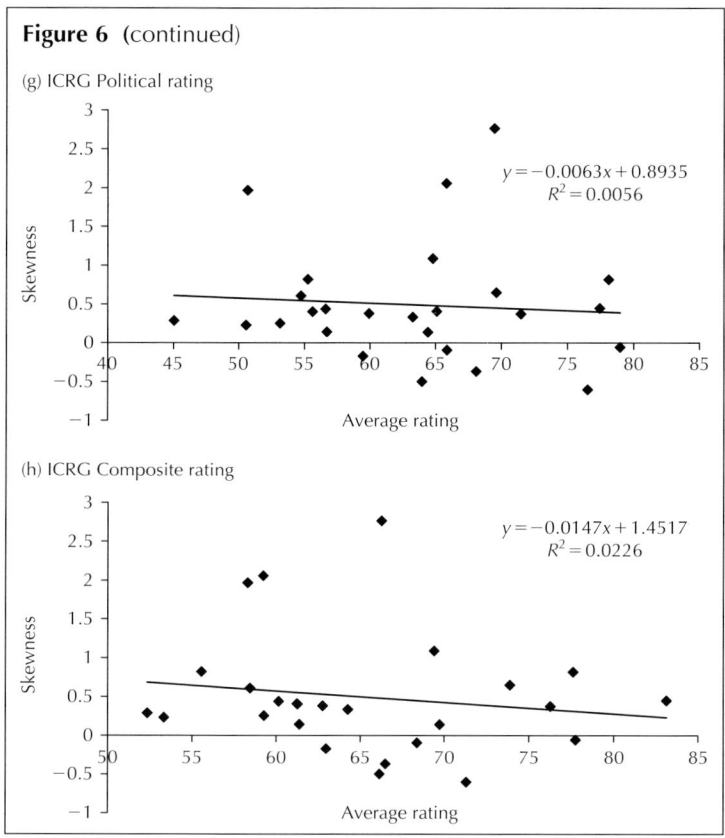

Figure 6 (continued)

(g) ICRG Political rating

$y=-0.0063x+0.8935$
$R^2=0.0056$

(h) ICRG Composite rating

$y=-0.0147x+1.4517$
$R^2=0.0226$

is analysed in Diamonte, Liew and Stevens (1996). They form two portfolios: upgrade and downgrade based on the ICRG political risk measure. Importantly, their strategy is *ex post* rather than *ex ante*. That is, their strategy is investable only if you knew in advance what next month's rating would be.

For the analysis in Table 5, I form three portfolios based on ratings levels: low, medium and high. The portfolios are rebalanced every six months. Based on the sort, I hold the portfolio for the *next* month and then resort. My method is predictive because the portfolios are formed based on past information.[2] As with other tables, I consider all, developed and emerging, countries for the portfolio strategies. I consider the broad country risk categories as well as subcomponents.

Table 5 Low, medium, high rating portfolio strategy, January 1984–July 2004

Sample	Low rating			Medium rating			High rating			Low-High rating		
	Monthly portfolio return (%)	Std. dev. (%)	MSCI world beta	Portfolio return	Std. dev. (%)	MSCI world beta	Monthly portfolio return (%)	Std. dev.	MSCI world beta	Monthly portfolio return (%)	Std. dev. (%)	MSCI world beta
Predictive rating and portfolio performance												
All countries												
ICRGC	1.36	11.53	0.80	1.09	9.23	0.95	0.96	6.82	0.96	0.41	4.71	−0.15
ICRGP	1.36	11.12	0.81	0.99	9.84	0.95	1.03	6.64	0.95	0.33	4.48	−0.14
ICRGF	1.55	11.30	0.81	1.03	8.81	0.95	0.89	7.45	0.96	0.66	3.85	−0.15
ICRGE	1.62	11.52	0.86	0.84	8.52	0.88	0.97	7.52	0.97	0.65	4.01	−0.10
P1	1.50	10.19	0.91	1.08	9.15	0.91	0.81	8.17	0.89	0.68	2.02	0.02
P2	1.22	10.94	0.86	1.23	8.86	0.91	0.91	7.74	0.94	0.31	3.20	−0.08
P3	1.44	10.88	0.88	1.04	8.84	0.90	0.92	7.82	0.93	0.51	3.06	−0.05
P4	1.23	10.34	0.80	1.22	9.51	0.95	0.91	7.69	0.96	0.32	2.65	−0.16
P5	0.98	9.79	0.81	1.27	9.37	0.93	1.05	8.35	0.97	−0.07	1.44	−0.17
P6	1.11	11.15	0.82	1.11	9.24	0.93	1.10	7.18	0.96	0.01	3.98	−0.15
P7	1.14	11.12	0.80	1.04	9.22	0.94	1.14	7.22	0.97	0.00	3.90	−0.18
P8	1.03	10.04	0.81	1.12	9.18	0.95	1.15	8.29	0.95	−0.12	1.75	−0.14
P9	1.14	10.99	0.81	0.99	9.79	0.97	1.17	6.80	0.93	−0.04	4.19	−0.11
P10	1.16	10.02	0.89	1.00	8.63	0.92	1.16	8.83	0.90	0.00	1.19	0.00
P11	1.28	10.76	0.85	0.99	9.58	0.89	1.06	7.22	0.97	0.22	3.54	−0.12
P12	1.33	11.25	0.80	0.94	9.80	0.95	1.08	6.55	0.96	0.25	4.71	−0.16
F1	1.45	11.24	0.83	0.94	9.07	0.93	1.03	7.25	0.96	0.41	3.99	−0.13
F2	1.69	10.55	0.87	0.84	9.24	0.92	0.95	7.76	0.92	0.74	2.79	−0.06
F3	1.43	9.87	0.88	1.15	8.76	0.89	0.76	8.85	0.94	0.67	1.02	−0.06
F4	0.91	9.95	0.80	1.06	8.81	9.90	1.31	8.73	1.01	−0.40	1.22	−0.21
F5	1.36	9.92	0.93	1.03	8.45	0.93	0.98	9.10	0.87	0.38	0.82	0.06
E1	1.09	10.70	0.85	1.21	9.25	0.92	1.03	7.59	0.95	0.06	3.11	−0.09
E2	1.63	10.08	0.88	1.01	8.82	0.92	0.80	8.59	0.91	0.83	1.49	−0.03
E3	1.69	11.67	0.92	0.87	8.45	0.86	0.91	8.45	0.93	0.77	4.22	−0.01

E4	1.45	10.65	0.87	1.09	8.91	0.90	0.87	7.98	0.93	0.58	2.67	-0.06
E5	1.16	10.21	0.85	1.12	8.96	0.08	1.05	8.34	0.98	0.10	1.87	-0.12
Developed countries												
ICRGC	0.64	8.82	0.96	1.40	7.80	0.95	0.98	6.49	0.96	-0.34	2.33	0.01
ICRGP	1.41	8.84	1.02	1.29	7.82	0.95	0.99	6.50	0.95	0.41	2.34	0.07
ICRGF	0.70	8.30	0.81	1.17	7.36	1.02	1.10	6.55	0.95	-0.41	1.74	-0.14
ICRGE	1.50	8.95	0.85	1.03	7.01	0.96	1.08	6.71	0.97	0.42	2.24	-0.12
P1	1.28	7.41	0.95	1.13	6.89	0.95	0.93	6.78	0.96	0.35	0.63	-0.01
P2	1.36	7.96	0.95	1.18	7.16	0.97	0.97	6.61	0.95	0.39	1.34	0.00
P3	0.93	7.85	0.96	1.10	6.94	0.95	1.13	6.99	0.96	-0.21	1.15	0.00
P4	1.29	7.68	0.99	1.03	6.96	0.94	1.09	6.86	0.96	0.20	0.83	0.03
P5	1.33	7.92	0.95	1.12	6.91	0.96	0.97	6.65	0.96	0.36	1.27	-0.01
P6	0.92	7.45	0.98	1.06	7.20	0.95	1.11	6.83	0.95	-0.19	0.62	0.03
P7	1.17	9.30	0.98	1.17	7.08	0.94	1.04	6.72	0.96	0.13	2.59	0.02
P8	0.93	7.27	0.99	1.14	6.72	0.92	1.09	7.09	0.97	-0.16	0.18	0.02
P9	0.91	9.11	0.85	1.15	7.46	1.00	1.07	6.58	0.94	-0.15	2.53	-0.09
P10	1.14	7.09	0.97	0.88	6.71	0.94	1.22	7.14	0.96	-0.08	-0.05	0.01
P11	1.34	9.49	0.99	0.85	6.78	0.94	1.14	6.57	0.95	0.20	2.93	0.04
P12	1.10	9.83	0.84	1.12	7.97	0.97	1.07	6.40	0.95	0.03	3.43	-0.11
F1	1.19	8.75	0.92	0.95	7.32	0.98	1.14	6.50	0.95	0.05	2.24	-0.03
F2	1.02	7.49	0.99	1.08	7.39	0.96	1.11	6.57	0.94	-0.09	0.92	0.04
F3	1.04	7.25	0.96	1.34	6.69	0.93	0.88	7.01	0.97	0.16	0.25	-0.01
F4	0.87	7.68	0.88	0.88	6.89	0.95	1.35	6.67	1.00	-0.47	1.01	-0.11
F5	0.99	6.70	0.96	1.03	6.93	0.95	1.25	7.26	0.96	-0.26	-0.56	0.00
E1	0.95	7.99	0.95	1.23	7.11	0.94	1.04	6.66	0.96	-0.10	1.33	-0.02
E2	0.80	7.38	0.95	1.03	6.90	0.96	1.04	6.78	0.96	-0.53	0.60	-0.01
E3	1.56	8.90	0.88	1.05	7.20	0.97	1.07	6.57	0.96	0.49	2.32	-0.08
E4	1.00	7.85	0.97	1.32	6.94	0.96	0.97	6.69	0.95	0.04	1.16	0.02
E5	0.71	7.67	0.91	1.27	6.86	0.95	1.13	6.75	0.98	-0.42	0.92	-0.07
Emerging countries												
ICRGC	1.41	11.73	0.79	0.78	10.28	0.95	0.65	10.78	0.95	0.77	0.95	-0.16
ICRGP	1.35	11.33	0.79	0.75	11.05	0.95	2.09	9.22	0.94	-0.74	2.11	-0.15
ICRGF	1.76	11.80	0.81	0.87	10.05	0.89	-0.05	11.39	1.61	1.81	0.41	-0.21

Table 5 (continued)

Sample	Low rating			Medium rating			High rating			Low-high rating		
	Monthly portfolio return (%)	Std. dev. (%)	MSCI world beta	Portfolio return (%)	Std. dev. (%)	MSCI world beta	Monthly portfolio return (%)	Std. dev. (%)	MSCI world beta	Monthly portfolio return (%)	Std. dev. (%)	MSCI world beta
ICRGE	1.64	11.82	0.86	0.51	10.26	0.80	0.49	10.36	0.96	1.14	1.46	-0.10
P1	1.70	11.92	0.88	1.01	11.28	0.88	0.64	9.98	0.80	1.07	1.93	0.08
P2	1.18	11.65	0.84	1.32	10.60	0.84	0.73	10.72	0.93	0.44	0.93	-0.08
P3	1.69	11.95	0.85	0.96	10.58	0.86	0.35	10.27	0.86	1.33	1.69	-0.01
P4	1.22	10.86	0.76	1.45	11.70	0.96	-0.15	10.91	0.98	1.37	-0.05	-0.21
P5	0.78	10.54	0.75	1.44	11.57	0.91	1.26	11.77	1.01	-0.49	-1.23	-0.26
P6	1.13	11.43	0.80	1.17	11.06	0.91	0.98	9.60	1.04	0.15	1.83	-0.24
P7	1.13	11.29	0.78	0.87	11.02	0.94	2.01	10.75	1.07	-0.88	0.54	-0.29
P8	1.06	10.78	0.76	1.10	12.08	0.98	1.29	10.74	0.92	-0.23	0.04	-0.15
P9	1.16	11.16	0.81	0.81	11.58	0.95	2.45	8.84	0.77	-1.30	2.31	0.04
P10	1.17	11.32	0.86	1.17	10.61	0.90	1.01	11.54	0.80	0.16	-0.22	0.06
P11	1.26	11.04	0.82	1.13	11.31	0.86	0.47	11.14	1.06	0.80	-0.11	-0.24
P12	1.34	11.34	0.80	0.76	11.07	0.93	1.29	8.98	1.10	0.05	2.36	-0.31
F1	1.51	11.69	0.81	0.92	10.40	0.88	0.45	11.01	1.00	1.06	0.68	-0.19
F2	1.98	11.44	0.83	0.51	10.93	0.89	0.53	10.79	0.87	1.45	0.66	-0.04
F3	2.08	12.42	0.81	0.90	10.92	0.84	0.63	10.27	0.92	1.44	2.15	-0.12
F4	0.93	11.14	0.76	1.28	10.59	0.85	1.23	11.88	1.03	-0.30	-0.73	-0.27
F5	1.76	11.81	0.91	1.04	10.85	0.89	0.71	10.64	0.78	1.06	1.17	0.12
E1	1.14	11.39	0.83	1.19	10.98	0.89	0.97	10.77	0.88	0.17	0.61	-0.06
E2	2.51	11.77	0.84	0.98	10.81	0.87	0.14	10.72	0.86	2.37	1.06	-0.02
E3	1.70	12.04	0.93	0.61	9.72	0.75	0.03	10.84	0.83	1.67	1.20	0.09
E4	1.68	11.67	0.84	0.79	10.64	0.86	0.62	10.84	0.90	1.06	0.84	-0.06
E5	1.48	11.36	0.83	0.95	10.64	0.82	0.95	11.56	0.97	0.59	-0.20	-0.14

I report summary statistics (mean, standard deviation and beta with respect to the MSCI world) for each of the three categories (low, medium and high) as well as summary statistics for the hedge portfolio (long position in low-ratings portfolio and a short position in the high-ratings countries). If the country risk measures are priced, I would expect to see a positive return in the hedge portfolio. That is, if the high risk (low rating) is rewarded then I should see the high-risk portfolio produce a greater return than the low-risk portfolio.

I start with the developed countries. There is little evidence that the country risk measures are priced in developed markets. Indeed, the hedge portfolio average return is slightly negative for the ICRG composite risk measure. Looking across the components and sub-components, I see that there is little evidence that any of these risk measures commands a premium. This evidence is consistent with the low cross-country variation in country risk in developed markets being a diversifiable type of risk for investors.

The emerging markets present a much different picture of the importance of country risk. The composite, financial and economic risk ratings produce large average hedge portfolio returns. The hedge portfolios based on the financial and economic risk measures produce average annual returns exceeding 13% per annum (the mean returns in the table are monthly returns). The composite produces a more modest 9% per annum return. The reason that the composite produces a lower return is the negative return associated with the political risk variable.

This is where the analysis of components becomes useful. Not all the categories of political risk produce negative hedge returns. The drivers of the negative returns are P5, P7, P8 and P9, which represent external conflict, military in politics, religion in politics, and law and order. There are three components, P1, P3, and P4 (government stability, investment profile, and internal conflict) that produce hedge returns of more than 12% per year.

One might think that the positive returns are simply a result of high beta risk in the hedge portfolio. The results in Table 5 suggest that this is not the case. For the emerging markets, the betas are *negative* for each of the economic, financial and political categories. As a result, the "alphas" or risk-adjusted hedge returns would be even greater than what is presented in the table.

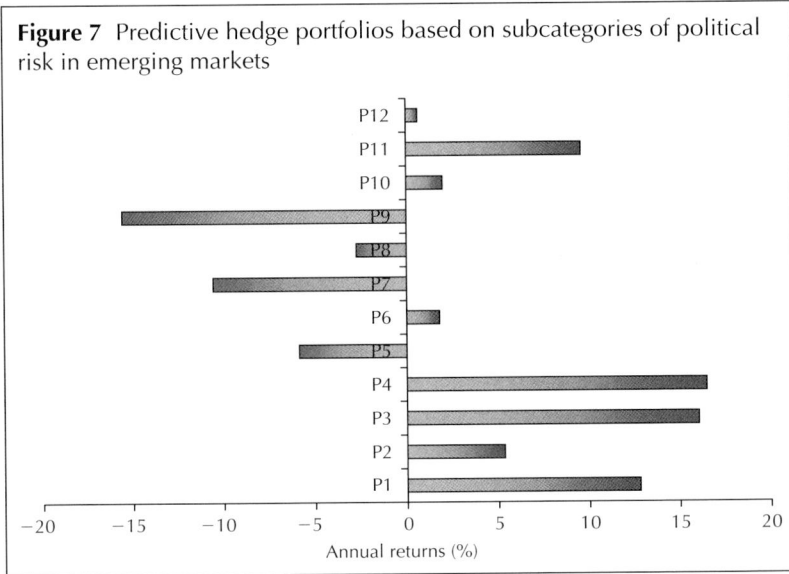

Figure 7 Predictive hedge portfolios based on subcategories of political risk in emerging markets

The evidence in Table 5 suggests that country risk is priced – but only in emerging markets. This evidence is consistent with Bekaert and Harvey's (1995, 2000) analysis of the factors that impact expected returns in integrated and segmented markets.

COUNTRY RISK AND THE COST OF CAPITAL

The hedge portfolio evidence in Table 5 suggests that country risk is an important driver of expected returns in emerging markets – but the analysis is based on past returns. Unfortunately, it is difficult to measure expected returns. Hail and Leuz (2004) calculate implied costs of capital for a number of companies in emerging and developed markets. They aggregate the costs of capital to the country level. This provides an interesting, independent sample to test some of the results in Table 5.

One can think of the implied cost of capital in terms of a dividend discount model. In this model, the stock price is equal to the future dividends discounted by the cost of capital. The implied-cost-of-capital model uses earnings forecasts to determine the future dividends. Given that I know the current stock price, I solve for the cost of capital, ie, the discount rate that matches the present value of the dividends with the current stock price. This is very

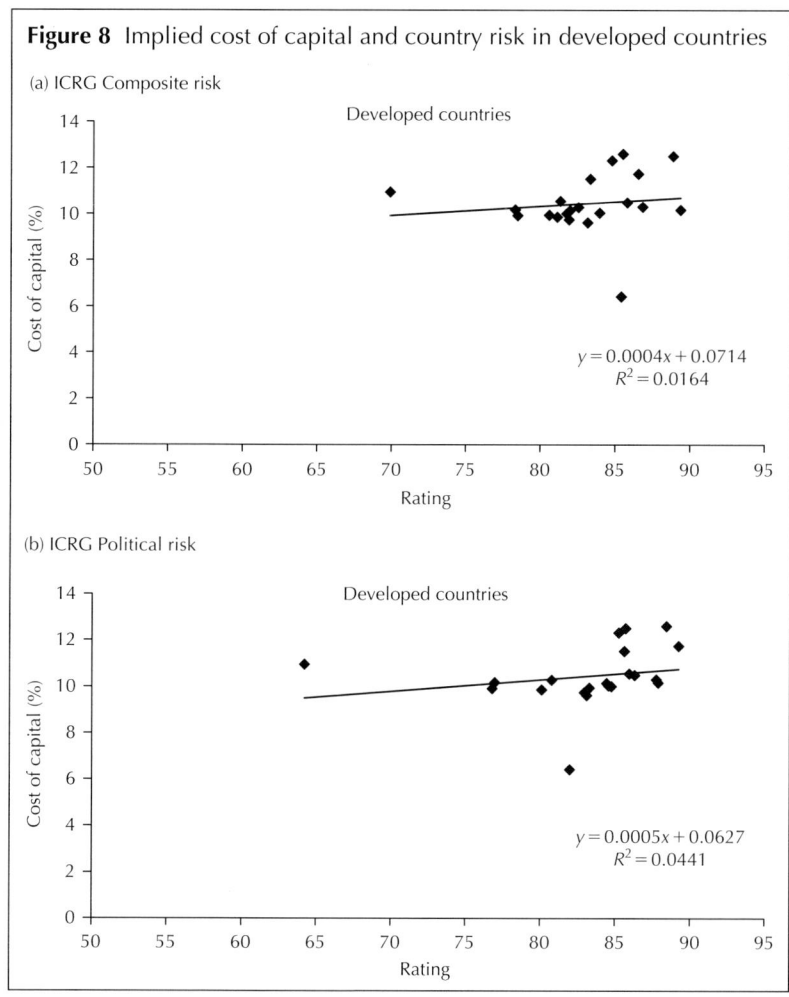

Figure 8 Implied cost of capital and country risk in developed countries

(a) ICRG Composite risk

(b) ICRG Political risk

similar to a yield to maturity. Given that I know the bond coupon and the current bond price, the yield to maturity is the discount rate that turns the present value of the coupons and final principal exactly into today's bond price.

Figures 8A and 8B examine the cross-sectional relation between the implied costs of capital and the composite and political risk ratings in developed markets. Consistent with the analysis in Table 5, there is no significant relation between the risk measures and the expected returns.

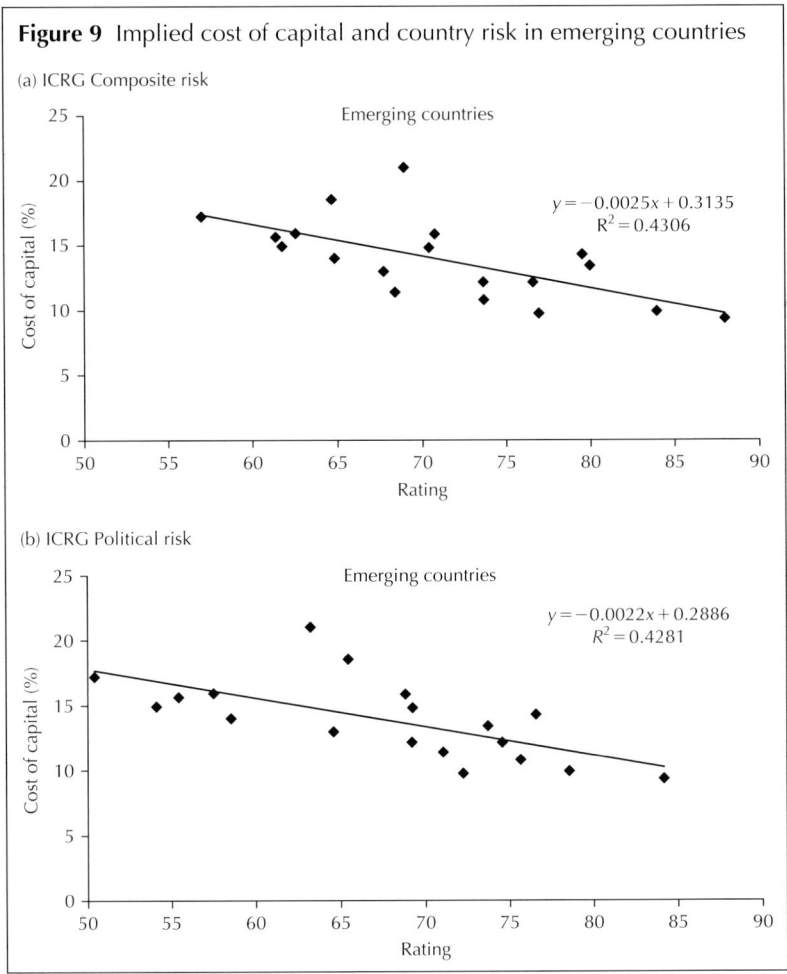

Figure 9 Implied cost of capital and country risk in emerging countries

(a) ICRG Composite risk

(b) ICRG Political risk

Figures 9A and 9B focus on the emerging markets. For these countries, there is a highly significant negative relation between the risk measures and the implied cost of capital. Lower ratings (higher risk) are associated with higher expected returns. This corroborates my analysis in Table 5 that country risk is important for emerging markets.

CONCLUSIONS
The goal of the research presented in this chapter is to explore the economic content of country risk measures and their components.

I focused on the monthly political, financial, economic and composite risk ratings from the ICRG. My analysis suggests that there is considerable information contained in the ICRG composite, financial and economic ratings, and their components. For example, when I form portfolios based on the risk ratings, I find abnormal returns in the range of 10% per year.

I present new results based on the components of the risk measures. For example, trading strategies based on the aggregate political risk rating can be improved by looking at the 12 components of the political risk rating.

Finally, I present evidence that the country risk measures are most useful for the analysis of emerging rather than developed markets. This is consistent with developed markets being fully integrated into world capital markets. For investors concentrating their portfolio in developed markets, fluctuations in country risk can be "diversified" away and this is the reason that the country risk measures do not command a premium. The story is different in emerging markets. These markets are rarely fully integrated and investors face non-diversifiable risk. For emerging markets, country risk is rewarded. I document this by showing that trading strategies that load up on higher country risk (but controlling for beta risk) command higher returns. To strengthen my case, I show there is a strong correlation between country risk and expected returns in emerging markets using implied costs of capital based on forecasted earnings in these markets.

Overall, country risk is rewarded in emerging markets. However, not all country risks are rewarded equally. This analysis has particular implications for calculating the costs of capital for direct investment in emerging markets – as well as implications for portfolio investments in emerging markets.

---

1 Notice a drop in the ICRG Financial rating in September 1997. This is a result of a reorganisation of the components. A smaller drop is evident in the ICRG Composite on the same date.

2 An alternative approach, pursued in Erb, Harvey and Viskanta (1996), is to form portfolios based on past changes in the ratings. This strategy is also predictive – but does not take the level of the rating into account.

REFERENCES

Bekaert, G., and C. R. Harvey, 1995, "Time-Varying World Market Integration", *Journal of Finance*, pp. 403–44.

Bekaert, G., and C. R. Harvey, 2000, "Foreign Speculators and Emerging Equity Markets", with Geert Bekaert, *Journal of Finance*, pp. 565–613.

Diamonte, R., J. M. Liew, and R. L. Stevens, 1996, "Political Risk in Emerging and Developed Markets", *Financial Analysts Journal*, **52**, pp. 71–6, May/June.

Erb, C., C. R. Harvey, and T. Viskanta, 1996, "Political Risk, Financial Risk and Economic Risk", *Financial Analysts Journal*, **52**, pp. 28–46, November/December.

Hail, L., and C. Leuz, 2004, "International Differences in the Cost of Equity Capital: Do Legal Institutions and Securities Regulation Matter?" Working Paper, University of Pennsylvania.

Harvey, C. R., 1995, "Predictable Risk and Returns in Emerging Markets", *Review of Financial Studies*, pp. 773–816.

6

The Private Sector Component of Country Risk

Carl F. Adams

eStandards Forum

Most country risk assessments do not directly consider the soundness of business practices in the private sector of the country in question. Instead, country risk analyses tend to focus on political, economic and similar factors. This is an unfortunate oversight. Experiences from around the world, including recent commercial and financial crises, demonstrate that countries with seemingly stable political systems and sound economic fundamentals can suddenly melt down as the result of unsound or poor business practices by the private sector. These troublesome business practices are in every instance the result of limitations on market economy, a hijacking of basic enterprise, the lack of transparency, lax (or non-existent) regulatory and supervisory oversight and the broad deficiency of country codes and standards for business arrangements from global best practice. In short, flawed business practices by the private sector are the result of a breakdown or weakness in the minimum infrastructure necessary for a market economy and profitable enterprise.

As a functional role for all actors in a country's economy, the private sector deserves fullest consideration as the determinant of country risk. The private sector in a country is not simply the victim of public policy, political expediency or government ambitions. It is in most cases, in fact, a driver of such official sector behaviours. Although country risk assessments pay great attention to the consequences of country events on commercial and financial order, the private sector itself is not often identified as a shaper of country risk.

This chapter argues that a proper evaluation of the private sector is a crucial component of country risk assessment. We describe a method for assessing this private sector component as a structured and organised review of a country's compliance with international regulatory standards. We conclude that the soundness of private-sector business practices influences country risk by defining the state of development or quality of conditions in the country's market infrastructure that is suitable for transparent, fair market-economy operations. This soundness of a country's local business practices is determined in part by the local standards and codes that are enfranchised by regulatory oversight and supervision. Therefore, an analysis of local commercial and financial standards as they affect private-sector business practices is a crucial part of any country risk assessment. To the extent that local codes and standards for business practices comply with global best practices, private enterprise will benefit from greater wealth expansion with less country risk.

THE PRIVATE SECTOR'S STRONG INFLUENCE ON COUNTRY RISK

The private sector thus exerts a strong influence on country risk in several ways and at various levels. Through price discovery, the business practices will reflect changing values and priorities of the society and will accordingly dictate the necessary policy agendas for governance of the country, hopefully in an accurate and sensitive, timely manner. If the market economy signals are clear and transparent, there is a great likelihood that public policy will be appropriately responsive within available means, and country risk levels will decline. If the market economy signals are not clear or are not appropriately addressed, stress will rise and country risk will increase. Similarly, even if market economy forces are operating and are correctly understood, any frustrated or incomplete sense of private-sector enterprise will increase country risk. The business activities in pursuit of profitable economic gains will quickly create political risks if they are not transparent, if they are perceived to be unfair, if they are dominated by crony alliances or are revealed to be driven by access to information that is not fairly or evenly available to all market players.

DEFINING AN UNHEALTHY PRIVATE SECTOR
AS COUNTRY RISK

As well described and fairly represented by the other chapters in this book, the topic of country risk is reasonably and logically approached from many disciplines and schools of thought. All of the arts, sciences and humanity studies offer genuine value and contributions to a useful understanding of country risk, including sovereign risk. The most significant (but not an exhaustive list of) approaches to country risk include studies of economics, political science, history, sociology, law, religion, archaeology, geography, demographics and statistical sciences.

The traditional conceptual frameworks for assessing country risk focus on the commercial and financial consequences of events in a country for business, for government, for consumers and for external trade. This is the emphasis of country risk studies by *economics*. Conceptual frameworks organised around civic institutions, political process, governance, policy implementation, and multinational diplomacy – including relationships and treaties among societies – are of course the country risk perspective of *political science. History* offers the country risk topic a framework of both military and civil outlines for analysis; *legal studies* provide comparative law analysis as a very useful and powerful way to look at country risks; and *religious philosophy* and *cultural assessments* provide favourable and further insight for discrimination among countries of the risks likely to occur with influence for social, political and economic order.

A consideration of the influence on country risk by conditions for the private sector offers no conflict with any traditional approach or conceptual framework from the several established country risk disciplines. In fact, a view of the situations for the private sector in a country is only fully valued when each of the academic areas listed above (economics, political science, history and so forth) is considered. The multidisciplinary concepts used to consider the private sector as a component of country risk does require explicit definitions and stated assumptions for coherence and consistency.

In this chapter we describe country risk to mean unhealthy private-sector conditions or unsound business practices in a country. In general, when we refer to an "unhealthy" private sector, or "unsound" business practices – factors that indicate the private sector is a danger to country risk – we mean:

> An unhealthy or unsound business practice is the occurrence of any event in a country jurisdiction that (1) destroys, interrupts, diminishes, or confiscates economic value – a reduction of or move away from the market economy. Unhealthy or unsound practices also include any event in the country that (2) restricts access to the benefits and free use of economic value – interference with a positive trend for entrepreneurial pursuits in the country.

"Country" is defined as a societal jurisdiction of sovereign authority, oversight and identity – usually of a nation, but also applicable for subnational or regional jurisdictions as established by law, custom or enforceable agreement among members of the society.

Proper context for this private-sector component of country risk requires the further elaboration of two assumptions. First, by "private sector", we mean the commercially productive operating agents of a country jurisdiction, whether owned by the government or by non-government entities. Private sector is defined as all enterprise within a country that engages in the growth and cultivation of wealth and economic value as its primary role and function. The growth and cultivation of wealth, however, must be accomplished and sustained by principles of free, or relatively free, forces of supply and demand for the output of the enterprise. Free forces of supply and demand must also form discovery of "prices for value" with settlement and clearance of an exchange of ownership for such value. This means that for any enterprise where output price and value are set by forces other than reasonably transparent supply and demand – by fiat of some controlling agent, including monopolies or oligopolies – such enterprise is excluded for our discussion here from the definition of private sector. It does mean, however, that a sovereign or government-owned enterprise operating in a commercial way and within the operating limits of market prices is included in our concept of "private sector".

The second assumption as context of our definition of this component of country risk is that private enterprise is only commercially viable when it operates under entrepreneurial assumptions of the market economy. This means that private sector enterprise survives and prospers only if its output is valued more than its costs of production – and that both output valuation and accounting for costs of production are determined by market discovery rather than by political, social or governmental sovereign discretion. These two concepts for the private sector, market economy and private enterprise, frame the definition of country risk expressed here and establish our assumptions for exploring and expanding the role of the private sector in overall country risk.

Regardless of how one defines "country risk", an essential and highly influential component of country risk definition is the action and behaviour of private enterprise. Practical, microeconomic and explicit activities and procedures of the private-sector players in commercial order shape the real risks of country jurisdictions – *de facto* and *de jure*. Social forbearance of the country for various behaviours and procedures clearly and routinely define the unique political risk of each country. Over time, in the context of relationships with other countries, social forbearance distinguishes greater or lesser country risk among country jurisdictions. Paying attention to the country conditions that enhance or degrade market economy and private enterprise, we suggest, is a valuable methodology for assessing country risk.

DETERMINING THE HEALTH OF THE PRIVATE SECTOR

"Market economy" means that the reasonably free forces of supply and demand operate sufficiently to discover what has value in the country and at what price. If there is a market economy operating or at least trending towards operation, then the existence of "enterprise", entrepreneurial spirit in the country – the pursuit of marginal economic gains over economic costs of activities under transparent and fair market rules of order – can and will sustain any country at low or declining risks. The soundness of private-sector business practices, both commercial and financial, must be assessed on these twin characteristics: market economy and progressive enterprise.

Are market economy and private enterprise proper and positive conditions for the private-sector component of country risk? Every country exists on a philosophical and political spectrum between extremes of total freedom and total central dictatorship and control. History demonstrates social successes for countries all along this continuum over time. But, as the world enters the 21st century, complex influences are in play such as globalisation, information and communications technology development, fuller awareness of demographics, the natural and biological environments, gender- social- and human-rights awareness, the ethical issues of religious/cultural dynamics and the political expressions and consequences from all of these forces. However, there are a few generalisations for country risk assessments that can be made and respected by most philosophical and political opinions regarding the health of the private sector.

First, a market economy (where free or reasonably free forces of supply and demand operate to transparently discover prices and values) is generally and broadly more desirable and is better regarded by most objective country risk criteria. Even communist, centrally controlled or transitional economy jurisdictions such as China, Russia, India, Vietnam, Cuba and North Korea are now exhibiting defined moves towards market economy. In most cases, these countries are actually permitting official recognition of private enterprise to blossom.

Second, given the good favour for country risk that promotes a market economy, it is widely held by informed opinion that private enterprise – the non-public, non-government commercial players in a market economy – should be encouraged, promoted and held accountable for the best, productive cultivation of wealth on which the entire society (country) finds benefit and success. The suggestion here is that public-sector, or "state", enterprises have inferior and inappropriate resources to lead the wealth-creation process by market-economy standards. The private sector is therefore regarded as a country's more natural "farmer of wealth in the society" – a better actor among economic sectors for creation of wealth.

Further, there is current and credible evidence that the reasonable division of labour among economic sectors favours a market-economy model and the wealth-production role of private enterprise. In this model both the public and private sectors are motivated by cycles of greed and fear. Country risk analysis benefits from an assessment of the humility among "divisions of labour" for individuals in the public sector versus private-sector egos. Compensation and rewards behaviour is a good metric for this analysis in any country. Likewise, public-sector fear versus private-sector greed also offers a dynamic and creative way to consider country risk as it is driven by the interactions of the two forces exerted between the two sectors.

Business practices of the private sector establish a fault line for country risk where the behaviours of greed and fear converge. Like moveable, massive tectonic plates these behaviours of greed and fear exhibited by the private sector and public sector are the source of country risk. Business practices in a country showcase the special need to consider the private sector as a component of country risk. A simple, four-quadrant table of drivers for both the private sector (as we define it here in very broad terms of market economy and private enterprise) and the public sector helps elaborate or enlighten country risk and offers useful comment on the dynamic and cyclical nature of the motivational forces – greed and fear.

The private sector's up-cycle of greed is its natural pursuit of profit, wealth expansion, high returns and appreciation of value. Such greed-driven cycles are by nature held in check with the private-enterprise fears of failure – as in default, bankruptcy, loss of liquidity, decline of value or outright restriction/loss of ownership and control of economic values. The public sector's up-cycle of greed (potentially but not necessarily out of synch with the cycles of greed and fear for the private sector) is similarly evidenced by

Figure 1 Dynamic drivers of country risk

	Greed	Fear
Public sector	Power, Influence, Control, Status, Sovereign dominion	Impotence, Loss of office, Loss of control, REGIME CHANGE, War, Loss of "face"
Private sector	Wealth gains, Full yields, High returns, PROFITS, Value appreciation	Default, Bankruptcy, Reorganisation, Liquidation, Loss of value, Loss of ownership/control

quest for power, control of governance, enhanced status and ultimately the exercise of sovereign dominion in the jurisdiction (country). This public-sector pursuit of greed, of course, is held in check by fear: perceptions of impotence, loss of official status, reduced control and influence on matters of state, or ultimate loss of face through regime change, war or dramatic natural destructive forces. For country risk analysis, it is useful to use this dynamic quadrant of fear and greed for both the private and public sectors as a gauge for "hedging" commercial exploits (and the boundaries of ethics and moral behaviour) with political and governance excess. It is quite instructive in any country analysis to assess how ascendancy of greed – by either the private sector or the public sector – may be held in healthy balance by the forces of greed and fear of the two sectors. For example, one might posit that unbridled capitalism in any country (private-sector greed) can be "hedged" with evidence of public-sector fear or the stimulus of potential public-sector fear. Alternatively, public-sector greed may be hedged if there is evidence of private-sector fear or its likely development.

The private-sector component of country risk looks in general at the necessary but not sufficient conditions for market economy and private enterprise to prosper. At a high level, country conditions must afford minimal preconditions or qualitative factors for the private sector's function and success. Those conditions, in order of priority, are physical security, health/education/welfare and then human rights. Security means importantly the ability to feel reasonably secure for life and limb in normal daily conduct or activity – clean water/air, subsistence food, safe passage and mobility to engage in economic activity, with some reasonable and prevailing order to protect person and property. These are obvious essentials for private enterprise. The preconditions of health, education and welfare are the necessary conditions for enterprising agents to commercially operate as opposed to just surviving and in conditions conducive to growing wealth with benefits from such value cultivations. The human-rights precondition is open to many cultural and sociopolitical interpretations (as the current world order demonstrates) but it is nonetheless essential for respect of human persons, for the environment in which societies operate and for the diversity of the creative world order and the interactions among country jurisdictions.

In short, this means that a country's business practices, regulatory standards and supervisory framework are crucial determinants of the "health" of the private sector – and, therefore, of the private-sector component of country risk. As a gauge of country risk it is useful to remind ourselves here that preconditions of culture and ethics in many countries result in divergent and various situations for making money (private-sector drivers) and making policy (public-sector drivers). The very good news for country risk analysis is that much work has been done and more is in active development to measure and assess these preconditions for market economy and private enterprise. Somewhat bothersome, however, is that most work thus far to assess the preconditions is from the public sector and nongovernmental organisations (NGOs). There are relatively few efforts to date by the private sector to quantify or measure preconditions for the market economy and private enterprise.

ASSESSING THE PRIVATE-SECTOR COMPONENT OF COUNTRY RISK

A formal and organised checklist for successful enhancement of market economy and private enterprise is available and in full working order for country risk analysis. As a consequence of the cycles of country crises and initiatives by the global standard-setting authorities in dealing with them over the post-World War One period, topics and best practices are identified as "conditions precedents" for well-working private sectors. The significant caveat and qualifier is that, despite the creation of such standards and codes for best practice, there is no global sovereign enforcer to regulate compliance by any country with the benchmarks – other than enlightened self-interest and negative international public opinions of countries that do not comply. Both enlightened self-interest and greater public opinion awareness are enhanced enforcers of country best practices due to globalisation's technology boon and the rapid expansions of Internet communications and technology.

Further handicapping the formal requirements for country codes and standards is, to be sure, the changing, dynamic nature of the standards and principles underlying them. Each crisis and scandal creates suggestions of new codes and standards, new or altered underlying principles, or some new proponent of authority to add certainty and clarifications for the way the country conducts "best practices". The experiences in South Korea in 1997, Russia and Long Term Capital Management (LTCM) in 1998, the Enron and energy-sector meltdowns, Argentina's sovereign default in 2001, WorldCom's demise and the equity market bubble in technology values, investment research scandals, accounting and audit policy conflicts, Mexico, Brazil, and Turkey with the IMF on numerous occasions, Basel II capital standards implementations, mutual fund trading practices, Parmelat's fraud and bankruptcy, pension plan fragilities, and insurance brokerage arrangements – these and many other experiences suggest a long and growing list of episodes showcasing the dynamic tableaux for country codes and recommended standards for "best practice".

A FRAMEWORK FOR ASSESSING REGULATORY STANDARDS

Duly noting such caveats, then, where are we now regarding our country risk needs for assessing country compliance with codes and standards that at the least describe country-specific conditions for the private sector? Two levels of organised assistance are currently available. First, the global standard-setting authorities, prompted by the episodes and scandals of international affairs during the 1990s, have established high-level standards and codes for country best practices. These codes and standards are for financial market order and define an acceptable, minimum infrastructure for strongest encouragement of market economy and private enterprise.

The 12 global standards and codes are organised into three broad areas:

❑ macroeconomic policy and data transparency;
❑ institutional and market infrastructure; and
❑ financial regulation and supervision.

Ten issuing authorities formulated key standards for each of the 12 standards. These authorities and others continue today in the formulation and refinement of standards from these broad areas. The areas of significance for global codes and standards, the 12 specific standards, the issuing bodies and the original dates of formulation are shown in Table 1. This summarises the breadth and scope of these measures for the infrastructure necessary to enhance market economy and private enterprise in any country. As a simple guideline or rule, when either public policy or enterprise executive management steps around or away from compliance with any of these 12 standards and their underlying principles, country risk increases.

Country risk assessments of the private-sector conditions will at a minimum need to start with assessments of country compliance with each of these 12 codes and standards – to the extent that such assessments may be found and are provided by qualified, reliable and preferably independent sources. The good news is that, in real measure, such assessments are indeed increasingly available. Many reputable and independent assessments for most of the 12 codes and standards are provided by UN Group institutions, especially the World Bank and the International Monetary Fund (IMF). The other standards-setting global authorities to some extent offer some assessments for some countries. Professional associations, NGOs, academic institutions, accounting consultancies, international rating agencies, law firms, government development and trade promotion agencies, and a few private sector institutions or their associations also provide some assessments of country compliance with these benchmarks. The somewhat discouraging news is that the collection and assembly of country compliance assessments is time-consuming, awkward and expensive. The rigor of consistency in assessments and the ease of consistent comparisons among countries and among the 12 different standards are also very uneven at this time.

An initial and coherent initiative to assemble competent assessments of 83 countries' compliance with each of the 12 global codes and standards is freely available to the market and all country risk analysts. The eStandards Forum of the Financial Standards Foundation, based in New York and privately funded by its founders, provides an organised, public collection of public assessments of country compliance with the global codes and standards.[1]

As an illustrative sample of the organisation and display of the eStandards Forum Web site content, Table 2 shows a sample of eight countries assessed for each of the 12 global standards and codes using the eStandards Forum compliance categories: Full Compliance, Compliance in Progress, Standards Enacted, Intent to Adopt Standards Declared, No Compliance, and No Assessments

Table 1 Key codes and standards for sound financial systems

Area		Key standards	Issuing body	Dates formulated
Macroeconomic Policy & Data Transparency				
1	Monetary and financial policy transparency	Code of Good Practices on Transparency in Monetary and Financial Policies	International Monetary Fund	1999
2	Fiscal policy transparency	Code of Good Practices in Fiscal Transparency	International Monetary Fund	1998
3	Data dissemination	Special Data Dissemination Standard (SDDS)/General Data Dissemination System (GDDS)[a]	International Monetary Fund	1996/1997
Institutional & Market Infrastructure				
4	Insolvency & creditor rights	Principles & Guidelines for Effective Insolvency Regimes and Creditor Rights Systems	World Bank	2001
5	Corporate governance	Principles of Corporate Governance	OECD	1999
6	Accounting	International Accounting Standards[b]	International Accounting Standards Committee (IASC)[c]	Since 1974
7	Auditing	International Standards on Auditing (ISA)	International Federation of Accountants (IFAC)[c]	
8	Payment & settlement	Core Principles for Systemically Important Payment Systems/	Committee on Payment & Settlement Systems (CPSS)/	2001

compliance. Country risk analysis will be directly expanded by such developments.

❑ finally, as the world changes – politically, socially, technologically, economically – there will continue to be valuation changes driving the private sector's component of country risk, and this is evident in the *alterations in risk versus rewards* – as chasing yields and changing risks.

More investors will use regulatory standards as a country risk indicator

To bring all of this together for country risk, one must remember the quiet, quaint but indisputable commercial power of investors. Investors possess an ability to change public-sector behaviour (in the greed-versus-fear cycle) by *valuation* or pricing for risk in countries based on assessments of compliance with global codes and standards. The practice of charging higher, risk-premium values for more risky, less supportive conditions for market economy and private enterprise in a country is called *risk mining* for profits and avoiding loss. The alternative but similar process for investors in any country is to discount or reduce the risk-premium valuations for less risky, more supportive conditions for market economy and private enterprise in a country.

Risk mining as a practice of investors is an age-old phenomenon but for country risk is in the very earliest of days. Risk mining experience with globalisation clearly shows real value for risk management and for country risk pursuits. Already a body of research evidence is accumulating for sceptical countries that compliance with global standards and codes pays off in economic wealth creation results. World Bank, IMF and expanding academic research support the value to countries in compliance with the benchmarks for best practices for the support of the private sector. Increased and better foreign direct investment (FDI) in a country, better public bond ratings, improved and more modern bank credit qualifications, plus enhanced and expanded development of local markets for local savings and repatriation of offshore wealth through remittances and unofficial flows is a bounty already for countries well scored on compliance with infrastructure enhancing market economy and private enterprise.

It is noteworthy and very encouraging to see *financing for development* spreading as a valid concept among public-sector interests in the very poorest countries. Private-sector enterprise ensuing from opportunities created by this development trend will enhance growth opportunities and lower political risks for many countries – as the research evidence already suggests it will.

Such trends as risk mining by the private sector and financing for development by the public sector will further spur and expand the use of third-party assessments and audits of risk and compliance with global codes and standards. The increased use of such audits and assessments will build private-sector willingness to provide such services, for a reasonable but fair fee, and will expand country risk metric capabilities. Already we may list numerous and exciting innovative programmes showcasing the progress of development finance: the United Nation's Financing for Development and Millennium Challenge programmes for poverty reduction, the US government's Millennium Challenge Corporation, the UK's FIRST Initiative, and many more.

Investors will take into account more types of capital flow when they assess country risk

A special value for country risk assessments using the components of private-sector influence is the clear but expansive move to consider and include capital flows in addition to official flows, portfolio investments and banking loan extensions. Globalisation assures observers that not only financial investment and portfolio flows management are at issue: all capital flows are included in this private-sector component of country risk, including:

❏ FDI – the real value flows into commercial expansion efforts;
❏ remittances across borders by the private sector actors in all countries;
❏ insurance and reinsurance flows, both via vendor policies and by self-insurance and reinsurance activities within a single enterprise;
❏ unofficial transfers and transactions of the "black markets" operating everywhere and every day without regard for – but determined by – official policies and institutions; and
❏ intracompany transfers and service contracts.

All flows of funds are critical components of private-sector activities for discerning country risk, both in developing countries and more significantly among developed sovereign jurisdictions. Thus there is positive benefit for country risk from the broader focus on market discipline. The private-sector practices, via innovative financial products such as derivatives, off-balance-sheet and bankruptcy-remote vehicles, and the more aggressive quantitative modelling of financial relationships in and with the private sector, are especially revealing and beneficial for country risk analysis. Compelling evidence of this development is the formal observation and analysis of the private sector of the capital markets in ongoing work by the International Capital Markets Department of the IMF and its Financial Stability Surveys. Country risk analysts should expect more of such scrutiny of the private sector by formal research and be assured that there is much qualitative and quantitative value for country risk in such content.

Media focus on country risk will promote codes and standards evaluations

Current media and news focus on political risks, macroeconomic global developments and consequential public policy choices and debates provide a rich content from the private sector's component contribution to country risk. The reality of the US role in the world as an economic system, as a military consideration, and as a political actor has changed since the demise of the former Soviet Union as a superpower. This reality changed even further after the terrorist attacks on the US in 2001. Clearly the media and popular publicity from these changes influence the private sector. The US changes and global events set in motion the, now very different, world order for global valuations. These valuations are different not only in the US but also in the entire non-US world. The consequences for the private sector and the new globalisation rules by which it opportunistically manoeuvres continue to evolve with no clear-cut signal of who and where the winners will align and how or why current players might lose out. The reactions by private-sector forces to US influences will have many dimensions and defy a simple survey. Military/industrial resources will not soon be eliminated, although technology and information/data and intelligence capabilities will remain a priority.

Countries where the market economy and private enterprise have a support can participate fully even if their recent legacy is unattractive or flawed. The private sector in many countries – not only the industrially advanced or large economic centres – can and will participate. Biological cycles and natural environmental issues continue to hold high global value, and education/research stands high on the agenda for growth priorities and country risk. Policy choices in all countries (note the greed/fear cycle dynamics) must and will factor in the capabilities of private-sector advantages even though competition in the public and private sectors is an unkind and unforgiving force for vested interests. Coping with the US as a single superpower further emphasises the need for country risk analysis to give private-sector components – market economy and private enterprise – first-order influence on the assessments and their meaning for risk taking and risk rewards at the country level.

Executive management will focus more on country compliance with global codes and standards

Private-sector executive management issues for market economy and private enterprise are steeped in tough, strategic options because of the complex global macroeconomic and political risks. Coping with all the global changes in the political order and macroeconomic transitions gives no executive an easy or enviable assignment for sustaining the enterprise viability and success. Recent scandals and public scrutiny of executive compensation merely heighten the degree of difficulty for private-sector executive management. Again, the four-quadrant picture of greed and fear dynamics between private- and public-sector players – by country and among countries – offers a useful guide for political risk interpretations. The realignments of interests among sources and uses of financial savings, the demise of established values in the commercial and financial sectors at the hands of technology – either from new technology innovations or from innovative services for existing established technology – and the erosion of traditional loyalties by the ageing cycle, demographics, migrations and the shrinkage of time and distances are all reality for executive leaders of the private sector. It is no wonder that market economy and private enterprise remain the hallmarks of private-sector readings for country risk with all of these issues pressing on management to compete, survive and succeed.

Public policy management (regulators, tax assessors, government planners – elected officials and dictators alike) also face an untested and unpredictable array of choices on the global wave of uncertainty. Regulation and supervision of all exposures to country risk issues of the market economy and private enterprise goals is a daunting task. This is more so when the forces confronting private-sector executives are translated into actions over which the public sector must exert fiduciary and oversight responsibility composure. Regulators and the public sector as a result now exert increased intrusion on the activities of the private sector, with Basel II and international accounting conventions just two obvious recent examples. Such regulation and supervision in a changing global order heightens country risk, of course, and makes strategy for private-sector executive management very challenging. This leads to private-sector decisions or actions that in turn confirm or undermine the public-sector policy initiatives – the power of risk mining for example or financing for development – and will directly affect country risk.

Assessments of the "private-sector component" will be integrated with other types of country risk metrics

Risk-management techniques in this volatile environment offer useful metrics for conditions promoting the market economy and private enterprise. Popular current risk-management methodologies, for example, include credit modelling, "value at risk" tracking for market risk, numerous market signals from prices, spreads, ratios and trigger events or collateral management mitigation techniques for risk off-set, statistical models of products and market strategies, scenario constructions with stress testing, official policy observations, rating agency analytics, and various media scores. For country risk, all of these private-sector metrics of risk behaviour become significant and provide a more sophisticated language appropriate for country discrimination.

Like all other areas of risk management, the increased use of quantitative metrics and descriptive tools is cast versus fundamental analysis and judgements. There is no reason to debate whether one methodology is better than the other. Clearly, both quantitative analytics and traditional fundamental qualitative experiences are essential for good country risk assessment. The disciplines of quantitative tools describing both private- and public-sector conditions serve an irrefutable purpose, lending order and rational logic to the messy analytics of country risk. Numbers and modelling formulas are reliable and are therefore very useful for descriptions of complex valuations in an equally complex world market. But models are only as good and as effective as the assumptions and numbers fed into them. That is why the experience of fundamental and traditional disciplines (many of the academic disciplines of country risk as we listed in the beginning) remains essential. The behaviour of private enterprise is complex. The discovery of prices (value) in any country includes an assessment that fully considers options contracts for future valuation and creative derivatives of cash and traditional pricing market values. This price-discovery process is not only for financial services. Such practices are also part of the country risk taking and rewards found in the market economy and private enterprise in all country jurisdictions.

The private-sector component of country risk continues to expand and will increase awareness of the common sense in judging market economy and private-enterprise conditions by country and even at subnational sovereign jurisdictions. This trend will provide additional sources of information from which country risk metrics can ensue. Future authorities for standards and probable sources of independent, credible assessments of market economy and private enterprise as a component of country risk will come from several thought-leadership centres. Some of them include private-enterprise associations, public-sector lobbyists, industry trade groups, corporate governance and directors' services. Creative assessments may also come from banks, investment banks, insurers, consultants, public policy leaders, academics and international and multinational institutions such as the Bank for International Settlements. The US Securities and Exchange Commission, the Federal Reserve Bank System, the UK's Financial Services Authority and more recent oversight institutions such as the US Public Companies Accounting Oversight Board will surely offer further suggestions for country codes and standards of best practice, as will legal counsellors, accountants, and experienced auditors. These authorities and centres of global experience are fully expected to add further competence and quality to the assessments of conditions promoting market economy and private enterprise by country.

CONCLUSION

Assessments of the country conditions that promote and enhance the market economy and private enterprise are powerful and persuasive aspects of country risk. Assessments of country compliance with global codes and standards of best practice suggest current and future metrics for the evaluations of the private sector's influence on, and its direct contributions to, country risk. Better conditions for market economy and progressive enterprise in any country reduce country risk and boost transparent, real wealth growth. To provide complete and thorough assessments of country risk, then, analysis must include full and responsible assessments of the private sector's condition and its overall contribution to all risks in the jurisdiction.

---

1 Country risk analysts are encouraged to examine the extensive information freely available at http://www.eStandardsForum.com.

7

Four Experts Discuss the Science and Art of Country Analysis

Sam Wilkin

Countryrisk.com

The previous chapters in this section offered a range of views on the factors that must be considered for successful country analysis, including state stability, the health of the private sector, and variables related to currency and banking crises. The chapters in the next section demonstrate the application of such principles, to Brazil, Russia, China and Turkey.

The contributors to this volume represent diverse perspectives, including academia, banking, insurance, multilateral institutions, and regulators. But the scope of professionals with an interest in, and insight into, country analysis is even broader. This chapter records interviews I conducted with four respected country analysts representing Wall Street, academia, the intelligence community, and a human rights pressure group.* The topic is "the science and art of country analysis", broadly conceived.

The interviewees
Joyce Chang is global head of the Foreign Exchange, Emerging Markets and Commodities strategy groups at JP Morgan. Ms Chang could, if she wished, stake a claim to being the world's top emerging-markets analyst. *Institutional Investor* has named her the number-one emerging-markets strategist for the past seven consecutive

---

*Sam Wilkin wishes to thank David Hale and Christian Stracke for their invaluable advice and assistance regarding the content and conduct of these interviews.

years. She is also a repeat winner of the top spot in *Euromoney* and *Latin Finance*'s "Research Olympics" surveys. Prior to joining JPMorgan Chase, Ms Chang was a managing director at Merrill Lynch and Salomon Brothers.

Carl Ford, Executive Vice President of Cassidy & Associates, was head of the US State Department's Bureau of Intelligence and Research (INR) until 2003. The Senate Intelligence Committee's "otherwise scathing" report on intelligence failures in Iraq "not only spared this bureau from most of its harsh criticisms" but endorsed INR for the accuracy of its analysis, according to the *International Herald Tribune*. INR accurately predicted that Turkey might not allow US troops to cross its territory, challenged the view that Iraq was reconstituting its nuclear weapons programme, and warned of postwar political and economic turmoil. Prior to heading INR, Mr Ford served at the Defense Intelligence Agency (DIA) and the CIA.

Arvind Ganesan is the director of the Business and Human Rights Program at Human Rights Watch. He is involved in research, advocacy, and policy development on issues involving business and human rights with a primary focus on the energy industry. Mr Ganesan has authored and co-authored three books, covering child labour in India, the killing of street children in India and, most recently, *The Enron Corporation: Corporate Complicity in Human Rights Violations*.

Marvin Zonis is professor emeritus of international political economy at the Graduate School of Business at the University of Chicago. He is a noted pundit on issues of political instability, particularly in the Middle East, and has testified before committees of the US Congress and appeared on television programmes from *Nightline* to *Oprah*. He is also an adviser to business on emerging-markets investing. His books include *The Kimchi Matters: Global Business and Local Politics*, *The Eastern European Opportunity* and *Majestic Failure: The Fall of the Shah*.

The interviews
WILKIN: Let's begin at the beginning. How did you get into the country analysis business? Mr Ford?

FORD: Well, I'd always been interested in international affairs, but a tour in Vietnam in the mid-sixties certainly got my attention about how important China was. So I went back – I had only two years of college at that point, I was in the army – I went back to school and changed to Asian studies and got a graduate degree in East Asian studies. I started studying Chinese and other Asian histories, political science, sociology, anthropology.

After my graduate degree I went back into the army, but branch-transferred from infantry to military intelligence. After another tour in Vietnam, I found myself as an analyst on China military at DIA [the Defense Intelligence Agency]. When I was at DIA I was recruited to join the CIA as an analyst. I switched over and resigned my regular army commission, in order to take the position at CIA. I loved my 10 years in the army, but I decided that if I was going to be in intelligence it was better to be on the first team. The first team in the military is infantry, armour and artillery. Intelligence was important but it was clearly second team. In the CIA it was the main business. From my first assignment at DIA – which was in 1971 – I have had a succession of jobs focused on country or regional analysis of Asia and more recently the Middle East and other parts of the world.

ZONIS: I became interested in international relations because I grew up in a family of immigrants. And every Saturday and Sunday we would go to one grandmother or grandfather or the other, and that side of the family would sit around the table and talk about what was going on in the old country, and how they left. There were all these stories, which seemed to me then wildly romantic, escaping by sleighs in the middle of winter covered with furs, and racing to Romania to escape the Bolsheviks.

So between my junior and senior year in high school I applied to be an exchange student with the American Field Service. And because they thought the name "Zonis" was a Greek name, they sent me to Athens. I had a marvellously exciting, stimulating summer living with a Greek family. In those days Athens was incredible: it was a sleepy town overshadowed by the ruins of antiquity; it was shepherds grazing their flocks in the Parthenon, which you could just walk right up to and nobody was there.

And what got me interested in country analysis was I remember reading – and being electrified by reading – Adam Smith: *An*

Inquiry into the Causes of the Wealth of Nations. And it started me questioning why everybody isn't rich, and what were the attributes, and what did the countries do, that did get rich? And I've always found that to be an absolutely fascinating question, because I've never thought it took particular genius to get rich: you just had to do a few things right. And I was so interested in what were those things and why did some countries do them right and others not.

CHANG: For me it was a happy accident. I had been going to graduate school at Princeton, doing development economics, and Salomon Brothers advertised for an intern in 1990 to focus on emerging markets.

At that point there was no such thing as emerging-markets research. But Salomon Brothers had an emerging-markets desk – called a less-developed-country trading desk – beginning in 1984. For an investment bank they had an incredibly strong and good early call on emerging markets. Most other banks had their genesis in this market as commercial bank lenders to emerging markets countries and ended up subsequently owning the defaulted loans of emerging markets borrowers. Salomon was able to be much more opportunistic because they were not the original lender. So they had a less-developed-country desk, where they had been trading and making markets in the interbank loans.

But Brady bonds and global bonds, didn't exist in 1990. And at that point everyone was talking about whether inter-bank loans could develop into a global market, and whether the Brady plan [to securitise emerging market debts] would work. Because, remember, when the Brady plan was first proposed, a lot of people were very sceptical.

I ended up starting as an intern at a point in time when the market was just developing. And so a lot of the first things I wrote were the first sort of frameworks for doing sovereign risk assessment because nobody else had a research group. And then when I graduated Salomon ended up hiring me full time. Even then everyone thought that my focus would be the inaugural "Yankee" bonds that were coming to market for the Asian issuers. Nobody really thought that Latin America and emerging Europe would be the focus. And so when I was hired full time I initially had a huge hybrid of different issuers – including covering the province of

Ontario. People did not think emerging markets debt would become a universe that would rival the size of US high-yield.

WILKIN: How about in the human rights field?

GANESAN: Well, keep in mind that, traditionally, human rights groups don't do what you'd call "country analysis". We would look at very discrete aspects of what a government does, you know – investigating how they deal with prisons or how the police functions or how the military functions.

But in our work on business and human rights – and I would say this also applies to another part of our programme, and that is labour rights and trade – we're starting to see more and more how a number of different country factors are impacting the human rights situation. This started particularly when we were looking at the oil industry, where the industry and the commodity play such a dramatic role in the political economy of governance. We started taking a – well, I wouldn't say a much different view than traditional human rights work, but we definitely started looking at it in a different way.

For example, in our work on Angola, a lot of what we've been looking at is how the government uses oil money, and what are the drivers behind that. And obviously a lot of it's misspent and mismanaged. But it's also led us to look at various things that we wouldn't have otherwise looked at – Angola's indebtedness, and how they exist on the money, and what their priorities are. And how all this has an impact on human rights, and how, conversely, their desire to maintain certain types of political control affects how they engage in economic activity as well.

So what we found in cases like that in other parts of the world is that the political economy has a human rights component. And increasingly we say that the way a government functions in large part has a major impact on human rights, but not necessarily in a traditional sense. So I think from our standpoint it was really a kind of evolution based on where our work was going.

WILKIN: OK. Still on the subject of origins, let me ask: who were the greatest influences on how you understand the world – on the approach you take to country analysis?

CHANG: I was hired by a former professor named John Purcell in corporate bond research at Salomon Brothers. He was in charge of that group. And he had a very interesting background for a guy on Wall Street. He had worked at – I think it was at Banker's Trust, during the debt crisis. But before that he was a professor of political science, mostly specialising in Latin politics at UCLA. John was actually looking for someone with a background that was more centred on political risk. He thought that was most important for understanding emerging markets risk – somebody who had a background that could sort of bridge the political and economic risk assessment.

I thought his way of analysing the political and institutional dimensions of emerging markets was something that was really missing from Wall Street. He had a profound impact on my deciding to do work on Wall Street rather than going back to work overseas in emerging markets (I had previously worked for USAID in the Philippines, Jordan and India). He focused on the way decisions are made in countries, and the strength of institutions, whether they have democratic processes that are transparent and work well and can ensure continuity of policies. That was pretty unusual; the standard background was a PhD economist, or somebody from the official creditor [eg, IMF, World Bank] side.

FORD: Well, I would have to say that Dr George Lensen – head of the Asian studies programme at Florida State where I went to school – was a particularly important influence. He had served in the military in World War Two in China, as a Japan specialist, and so his experiences and his understanding of Asia were not just out of a book. It was very much real-life experience, something like I thought I wanted to do.

He also had interesting approaches and ideas about how to do analysis and research. His seminars were very much hands on – we actually had to get our hands dirty in terms of obtaining original materials, and spend a lot of time thinking about how to go about analysing countries and problems and issues.

Then when I went to DIA there was a lady there, Eva Watkins, who had been covering the Chinese army since the late 1940s. And she was legendary at DIA. She was very intent on keeping data.

She had an office full of files where she had kept track of things for 20 years. So, if you wanted to find something out, all you had to do was to go into her files. And you could look up things in an organised way that would help you deal with problems in 1971, 1972, 1973. And so this notion of how important it was to deal with details and evidence and databases and having raw materials to work from was very important.

If you showed an interest in China military and were willing to work, she was great, taking young analysts under her wing and guiding them through her databases and her experiences. She would give you a sense of how she did what she did that was almost an apprentice programme for myself and several other analysts. I appreciate that and I learned so much from it. Without it I don't know where I'd have been.

GANESAN: For me it wasn't a person that shaped my thinking, it was an event. It was my experiences working in countries like India and Angola. I did a book on the Enron project in India, the human rights implications of it. And in the course of doing that research – this was nine years ago – I learned about all the other controversies around the project and how the government was approaching it and a wide range of things. [Enron's Dhabol project, an immense power plant in India, ultimately failed due to disputes with the Indian government.]

And that really was the first experience where I started looking at a much larger picture. On why things were happening the way they were, and how that ultimately contributed to human rights abuses. That gave the indication into how to look at, say, economic activity – a specific investment project in this case – and understand the factors that ultimately lead to human rights violations.

ZONIS: I remember the tremendously powerful effect that reading Hobbes had on me, *The Leviathan*, which I read as an undergraduate. This argument that without "the leviathan" [the state] life was "nasty, brutal and short". And I guess that hit home when I got to the Middle East because I thought of how powerful the constraining behaviour of states were that kept people in line. And so I've always thought – even before it became popular, in recent years – that governments are more important in market economies than most people seem to think. Because without governments to constrain people we wouldn't have a market economy at all.

But even more crucial was my schooling. After college I went to the Harvard Business School for a year and decided it wasn't for me. And then I went to get a PhD in political science and lived in Iran to do dissertation research for about two and a half years. Then I came to the University of Chicago to teach Middle Eastern studies, and I was using the skills that I had learned at the Harvard Business School and MIT – in other words, the combination of economics and political science.

But eventually I came to the realisation that this wasn't getting me where I needed to get, and it was because there were emotional issues that were so powerful in the Middle East. I didn't know very much about analysing or thinking about emotional issues. So I applied to the American Psychoanalytic Association, for permission to be trained as a psychoanalyst, which was a big deal then because they only wanted MDs to be trained as analysts. I did get the permission and I spent about eight years at the Chicago Institute for Psychoanalysis – the mainline, Freudian institute where you lie on the couch and free-associate. And so then I brought to the study of countries, and the question of why some are rich and some are poor, those three disciplines – economics, politics, and psychology. And I think that's been an extremely important part of the way I think about the world.

WILKIN: Let me change the topic a bit. The profession of country analysis is known for its blunders. Failures of prediction – missing the fall of the USSR and that sort of thing. Presumably there are some common mistakes that lead to these failures.

CHANG: In my field the most common source of errors is becoming fixated on one indicator. In this case, the balance of payments. There's a whole debate in this industry, about whether the current account deficit is the leading indicator, or whether you should concentrate on fiscal indicators? If you look at just the balance of payments and current account, you miss a lot. Argentina, that was a fiscal crisis – an unstable fiscal scenario. The framework that we use looks at a country's cashflow.

We also look closely at the monetary and foreign exchange rate policies in addition to that. Pegged currency regimes have been the root cause of a lot of emerging markets crises. And currency mismatches. If you have a pegged currency and fall off the peg and have mostly US dollar-denominated liabilities, you just get hit due to the currency mismatch. There are a number of patterns that are just classic causes of emerging-markets crises, and that's one. Not just the balance of payments.

GANESAN: Having too narrow a focus is certainly a problem. I think most companies do assess political risk. But "political risk" tends to mean figuring out who in the government you need to talk to, to get things done. Or thinking of coups and wars and things like that.

But the issue is, if there are inherent problems with the government – say widespread corruption or mismanagement, or widespread human rights abuses, or what I would label "poor governance" as a whole – that tends to foreshadow pretty serious risks for investment in a country. It's not simply because of instability. It's also things like creeping nationalisation and bad economic decision making that ultimately impacts industry. You see this around the world. Where governments are really unresponsive to their citizens there is at some point an effect on the economic health of the country. Whether it's because corruption undermines the rule of law and the whole system. Or because, as a result of mismanaging so much money, the government just takes a more predatory approach to business and tries to extract revenue in any way possible, because it has misspent or failed to collect what it would normally get through taxes.

You have to do this on a local level. Take the case of India, which is a democracy and has a pretty vibrant court system. The courts work, but their judgements are not uniformly enforced. Whereas you might have nationwide weaknesses in many cases, in a diverse place like India you can have very localised weaknesses. Like the judiciary and law enforcement in some states. In India, they may do a good job elsewhere, but you still have fundamental weaknesses, just on a smaller geographic scale.

The other thing companies miss in their risk assessments is to really take a good look at themselves. Because that is a huge part of political risk. I tend to believe that the companies that have really bad controversies – well, that's a pretty good red flag that there's a general management problem. You can look at management as such and see that, not only are they getting into human rights problems, they're quite capable of getting into other problems that could undermine the company as well.

You know Enron is a good example of that. If you look at the reasons why they had so many problems in India, and you extrapolate why they had so many financial problems and ultimately collapsed, there are a lot of parallels. The lack of accountability, oversight and real standards – all considered less important than the aggressive pursuit of short-term gain. So I now tend to look at human rights risk as a governance risk. Not just governance of countries, but also corporate governance. And this risk is a very good indicator of potentially serious investment risks as well. And I don't think the human rights world or the financial community has fully articulated that.

WILKIN: What about in the intelligence community?

FORD: Well, I think there is a certain mindset that leads to errors in analysis. I think what's happened in recent years, not just at the CIA, but throughout the intelligence community, is that analysts have been encouraged to focus on current intelligence – a focus on the news and what happened yesterday. That's current intelligence. Even though that's an extremely important part of intelligence, it really isn't analysis. It's a very passive sort of exercise in which you're prompted to think about the problem in terms of what came in last night, and comparing that with other recent items.

Analysis really starts first with "What's the question?" It's more in-depth. You start by asking and designing a question and a research strategy for answering it – that is often the really hard part. There's plenty of information out there, but how do you find out the important pieces? How do you know it's important? How do you look for it? How do you put it together?

When I first started, less than a fourth of the analysts did current intelligence. The other three-fourths, or more, did research that supported current intelligence. Today it's more like 90% do current intelligence and 10% do something else, and you pay a penalty for that. If you don't have people questioning conventional wisdom – if you don't have people going back, and seeing if what happened last year was what we really what we thought it was, and reporting that to people, to say, "By the way, we were wrong six months ago and this is why you ought to know that" – if you don't have people creating knowledge, other than the big dots that sort of stick out and are picked up in current intelligence, you're going to make mistakes. You're not going to see things. You're not going to be able to deal with very ordinary problems like weapons of mass destruction in Iraq.

That failure had very much to do with the fact that people focus so much on current intelligence. They either didn't or couldn't go back and ask key questions about, for example, "Is what's happening now similar, different or the same as Saddam's weapons-of-mass-destruction programmes during the first Gulf War?" Of course we know a lot about that now. But no one went back and asked or compared and contrasted the differences between the two areas. I can't guarantee that we would have found anything. I'm greatly disturbed that we didn't even try. We didn't ask those in-depth, analysis-type questions.

ZONIS: Keep in mind that country analysis is also really, really hard. There are so many variables which we cannot predict. And one of the things that makes country analysis such a stimulating and marvellous thing to think about is because it is so unwieldy. There are so many unpredictable variables that there are constant surprises, both on the upside and on the downside. And so it's a very tough thing to do.

The other reason I think there are a lot of errors made in country analysis is that people who study any particular country intensively tend to fall in love with that country. You see it in so many different ways. For example, when we send a US ambassador out into the field to represent the US with any particular country, it is sometimes the case that the ambassador ends up representing that country and its interests to the United States of America. He becomes the interlocutor who brings to Washington what that country wants and why they ought to get what they want. So that's another reason. It's very tough to maintain your ruthless objectivity when studying a country.

Having said all this, it doesn't mean that it's not worth doing, because the exercise – even though it might turn out to be wrong – helps to generate systematic, coherent thinking about countries. While it may generate the wrong prediction, it's very tough to ask that all predictions should be right.

WILKIN: So what, then, is the key to successful country analysis? How do you avoid the pitfalls? What do you look for?

FORD: Two things are crucial – evidence, and expertise. Let me talk about evidence first. I always believe that evidence speaks a lot louder than opinion. That doesn't mean that evidence is always accurate, a fact, true. It does mean that you had a rigorous look at what data is available, and based on that evidence you made certain inferences or predictions. And if anyone doubts the veracity of what you say they can go back and check it. Opinions are hard to go back and check.

What I always tell young analysts is that senior officials really don't care what you think. They don't want a wise-man approach – "I think, I believe". If you go in and say, "Mr President, based on my work at CIA, I believe..." you get thrown out of the office. But if you go in and say, "Mr President, I've looked at this problem, here's the evidence I've put together, and based on that, this is what is happening..." – and if you've done your homework well – he'll say, "Good job." Even to a rookie. So that evidence gives people credibility, evidence shows rigor, evidence shows that you're thinking.

Gathering evidence is also a learning process. That's the other thing that's crucial to good analysis: expertise. A country is something that you have to spend a lifetime studying. If you always think about it in the macro sense it's very hard. You really have to start answering a few questions, you get a little bit more knowledgeable, you get a little bit more expert, and over time you accumulate knowledge and experience that can't be obtained in any other way. You can't read it in a book; you've got to do it.

Those are skills that I learned as a young analyst at both DIA and CIA – as much as anything, as an apprentice. Virtually everyone that I knew there had more than five years' experience and most had fifteen or twenty. These days, the average years of experience of analysts working in the CIA is less than five years. The only place left that has a lot of experience is INR, where it's fifteen years.

That is truly alarming, because expertise is crucial. There really is no substitute for smart, experienced people. People who have "been there, done that". People who have made their share of mistakes, their share of breakthroughs, but have had a considerable period of time to think about their country or their particular problem, whether it be weapons of mass destruction or terrorism or whatever the issue might be.

Unfortunately, if the system doesn't encourage and develop experts, if it doesn't help train them, then pretty soon you've got a whole lot of very smart generalists, and very few experts, and I think that's where we're at right now. In today's intelligence world each time you get promoted you get a different job. You move on to something else in the agency. We have made it very difficult for our supervisors to be anything other than administrators. They were promoted, not because they were expert on the subject that they were going to be supervising, but because they are a very capable person.

ZONIS: I absolutely agree about the need for expertise. Good country analysis takes a very deep familiarity with a country. One can do country analysis just knowing a few variables, and trying to apply a few variables to country. You can get somewhere with that, it's not a worthless exercise. But I think that, to the extent that the knowledge is deeper and the touch is more tactile, I think one can do a better job of understanding the variables, and how they might play out. Which again is not to say – it's not necessarily the case – that if you have a deep familiarity you're going to be right.

CHANG: I don't thing there's a single good formula for good country analysis. But I think it's key to spend a lot of time on the political risk and understanding the country's fiscal management. It's critical to have a very integrated approach beyond looking at numbers. We spend a lot of time on the ground trying to understand the institutional framework for a country. Somebody can say the numbers look great but that often doesn't capture a lot of the story in emerging markets.

One crucial factor is the predictability of policy. To get at that, you have to look at how they handle transitions. Do they have a history of transparent and orderly elections and fair elections – which a lot of emerging-markets countries still don't have. Is there an independent central bank, which ensures continuity of policy. Is there a stable core of government officials who are entrenched in the system, so that even if you change the top levels there is a sense of continuity?

In a lot of emerging-markets countries, new governments have been able to come to power after a crisis and dismantle all institutions without popular protest since the outgoing government was very unpopular. This was the case for Menem in Argentina, Fujimori in Peru and Putin in Russia. Everybody loved them in the first term, each was overwhelmingly re-elected for a second term, but then makes terrible mistakes in the second term. This is what happened in Fujimori and in Menem's second terms, and I think for Putin right now, the concentration of power around him is a growing problem. You need to have a mature system that allows a diversity of opinion, and has some checks and balances.

Take Argentina. [As early as 1999, Chang's research team accurately forecast that Argentina was headed for a crisis.] In Argentina we saw a number of alarming trends. Basically they had a fiscal situation that was not sustainable and there was no way to rectify this situation because of their co-participation formula between the central and local governments. Fiscal mismanagement and the deteriorating trend in debt dynamics, exacerbated by messy politics, provided the best forewarning of the crisis. The balance of payments and size of the current account deficit were less relevant sources of the country's crisis.

If you look at certain ratios, for instance how much revenue a country collects, Argentina had one of the worst tax collection ratios. The crisis was multidimensional. Growth, and revenue generation capacity and debt-to-exports were much lower than the same ratios for Brazil.

Still, a lot of people still said, "Well, Argentina's a much better credit." But the fact that they had no countervailing political parties – no credible opposition parties – everybody said was positive, but it really wasn't. Political reform did not follow economic reform in Argentina. In Brazil, there are far more diverse and credible parties. The PT [the Worker's Party, an opposition party] had held local office in many governments for years. That means when people start to wonder, "What happens when the opposition takes office?" – well, in Brazil, the PT had a very long tradition of being in government in a lot of large states.

Argentina was much more personality-driven. Too much of the political system centered on Menem and his ability to provide goods in exchange for favours. Once the privatization proceeds were exhausted, the power of the executive branch was severely weakened. In Argentina, it was more about Cavallo and Menem's personalities and less about the process. Investors got caught up in listening to the smoothest and most polished technocrats. People would say, "Oh, but Argentina has Cavallo. Cavallo's back, so it'll be fine." Or, "It's Menem and Menem completely transformed that country." And in his first term he did. But he also dismantled a lot of institutions. So it was too much personality-driven and not about institutionalising a process. And this became unsustainable. Argentina's last chance was an ill-fated zero-deficit strategy in an attempt to regain market credibility. I think that Argentina was a case of the perfect storm.

GANESAN: I agree it's crucial to take a broad view of a country. I think you're looking at three aspects with regard to political risk. First, you're trying to assess transparency and accountability – both financially and behaviourally – of the government. Second, you're assessing whether the government is really abusive or corrupt. And third, whether the institutions within the state really function to the degree that they can exercise a level of oversight – perform their regulatory functions neutrally and adequately – or if they even exist.

These are all interrelated. Typically, if the state – or if the government – is really abusive towards its population, that's a pretty good indication that the judiciary is not independent or does not function properly. And if you see that dynamic playing out that should be a red flag for investment because that creates an investment risk.

For example, look at oil companies in Nigeria. Over time the state was weak and ruled by successive dictatorships. And the oil industry did not try to maintain standards. It was for the most part silent about what the government was doing – it had joint-venture partnerships with the government and it seemed to be going OK.

But as the government became less responsive to its population, more autocratic and more corrupt, the system around where the companies were operating degenerated. The rule of law degenerated. There were repressive tactics by the military including in guarding the oil installations. And the population of the country didn't see the benefits, the economic benefits. The population didn't see the government as what it should be – as an independent arbiter in disputes between a company and the population, like in an environmental case, for example. The Nigerian government didn't do that and took a predatory approach to its own population – whether cracking down on protests, or not enforcing environmental laws, or stealing the money that was coming from the oil-drilling activities.

So what you got was an increasingly disenfranchised population that ultimately started going after the oil industry directly. And now as that situation has been allowed to fester and develop over decades you've got virtual chaos. You have armed groups operating in these areas, often attacking oil industry personnel and installations. Some companies rhetorically are trying to be much more responsible. And there is an elected government in place. But the situation's deteriorated so far that there's no easy fixes. I mean, due to the violence, companies are being forced to declare political *force majeure*.

WILKIN: Presumably, in a country like Nigeria, that was a dictatorship, it's often hard to see these things coming. The country is closed. If you don't have access to classified sources, where do you get information?

GANESAN: I think the human rights community has an advantage there. We end up looking at a lot of primary sources, sources that most people just don't look at. Take the CIA, for example, or take a company, or take a government. If they want to know what's going on in a country, they're going to talk to other intelligence people. Or to other companies operating in that country. Or to the military and police.

But the people we talk to are usually the victims of the military and police. So, while we talk to officials, we also get a completely different perspective on what's going on. You see things from a number of different levels. When you talk to a government, you see the policy. You see how they're trying to implement it. But you don't see what actually happens, how effective it is, what the impacts are. And that's something that, traditionally, human rights groups and other groups just started with. It's kind of a top-down versus a bottom-up approach.

So I recommend reading our reports, or the Amnesty reports, on a country. I also recommend the full annual Article IV reports the IMF does on every country annually – where they assess the economy on a range of different levels.

CHANG: In our case we actually go to the countries a lot. We take investors there. We think people really do need to see the countries to understand them.

We talk to a lot of officials. We talk through medium-term issues, and look at the dialogue they have with investors, and see if they have the ability to attract investment. If they are under a large IMF agreement we look to see if they have a framework in place that will attract private capital flows, as well as official creditor flows. Do they have a debt-management team that understands liability management, reserve management?

But we talk to a lot of different people and I think that's the key. We talk to former government officials who've gone back to academia. Independent economists, members of congress. When we were looking at Brazil we talked to different people who were in the Worker's Party and different political parties. For emerging-markets countries which are in very different stages of evolution, the key is to have a very diverse base of contacts to draw points of view from.

WILKIN: Is there any country or region that's really up on your radar screen right now? The next boom – or the next crisis?

ZONIS: I am very interested in China. And it's such an interesting and important country, not only because it's the world's most populous country, but because it's the largest recipient of foreign direct investment, one of the world's fastest-growing economies for over twenty years. And I've been there a few times over the last couple of decades – I mean, I always say to people, "It's the only place in the world where you can just sit down on a street corner and watch economic development happening."

But this pace of growth is also unsustainable in my judgement. And I've been saying it's unsustainable for the past three or four years. I'm watching with intense interest because if it is not sustained sufficiently – it doesn't have to get sustained at the present level, but economic growth has to be substantial – the vast urbanisation is going to result in people having difficulty finding work, finding income, finding food, and there's likely to be political instability, political violence in China. China has all the characteristics of countries that tend to have political violence following economic difficulty. So it seems to me that it's the most interesting country in the world right now.

GANESAN: I think there are some emerging oil producers that are at a major crossroads. I would say Azerbaijan, Equatorial Guinea, Angola to a great degree, and maybe Georgia. They all have very poor historical records on human rights. And they're all just starting to boom, just starting to get investment. Angola is already seeing a major windfall and it's going to increase. Equatorial Guinea is seeing a major windfall. And Azerbaijan is on the cusp of it. Georgia, as a transit state, will be benefiting from that income as well.

And for all of those – the fundamental question is, will this wall of money entrench and enrich already questionable governments, or will it, through international pressure and companies adhering to high standards, lead to a level of openness and accountability that ultimately will be beneficial to the country? There's nothing inherent about foreign investment and oil revenues that says this will be good for these countries. There have actually been a number of studies that show oil producing countries end up with worse governance. These countries are at a crossroads – will they develop and prosper, or will they end up like Nigeria, with disastrous governance, instability and huge investment risks?

The way I would look at it is that industry and governments – and a lot depends on the government within a country, but also outside governments – are equally important. Because if you're going to see improvements everybody has to be on the same page in terms of what they're asking for.

CHANG: I'm not too worried about country risk right now. When you look at what's going to cause a crisis, it's often the currency regime. You know you had nineteen countries that went from fixed to floating rate over the last few years and only four have moved in the other direction. And they're very isolated cases. Like in Ecuador with dollarisation. The currency pegs are gone which had been at the epicentre of most crises. With this catalyst for crises gone, you do sort of transform the nature of emerging markets.

What you have now is that technical analysis is playing much more of a role in the dynamics of the emerging markets. The more investment-grade it becomes, the more that a lot of other technical and industry factors, influences from other global markets, developments in the local markets themselves, start to matter. It's less about sovereign and country risk than it is about technical analysis as the markets change. Country factors, politics and that kind of thing aren't driving it as much any more.

WILKIN: Are you happy or sad about that?

CHANG: Well, I think it's very good that emerging markets are maturing. Finding ways to finance themselves locally. I mean, it's one component of looking at a market that's constantly evolving. The world is changing. It's not happy or sad thing.

Section 2

Country Risk Cases

8

Building a Stress-Test Scenario for Country Risk: The Case of Turkey*

Luigi Ruggerone

Banca Intesa

"How did you go bankrupt?"
"Well, gradually, and then suddenly!"

– Jay McInerney, *Bright Lights, Big City*

INTRODUCTION

One of the main concerns of risk managers and regulators around the world is stress testing. This expression is widely used in the risk literature and in risk managers' everyday life to mean the understanding and analysing of the possible latent risks on a trading book deriving from extreme variations in market prices (eg, interest rates, exchange rates, equity prices, etc), and/or from significant changes in the structure of the correlation among assets within the same portfolio. More recently, mainly as a result of the Asian and Argentinian crises, stress testing has been gaining momentum with regulators particularly concerned with the vulnerability of domestic and international financial systems to sudden and unexpected default episodes; changes in international interest rates; stricter accounting rules; or macroeconomic policies in general. Thus, stress testing is being increasingly applied with a macroeconomic focus, in addition to the traditional portfolio focus, where stress testing

*All the interesting parts of this chapter have greatly benefited from suggestions by and discussions with Vittorio Conti, Mauro Maccarinelli, Cino Molajoni and the editor Sam Wilkin. The rest is the author's. The views expressed here are those of the author only and should never be referred to as those of Banca Intesa.

originated. But this is not the whole story.[1] Country risk managers in private financial or industrial institutions are also increasingly involved in constructing stress-test scenarios for country risk that can be used to gauge the impact on sovereigns in a wide range of situations, spanning from FDI and proprietary M&A to periodical country limits revision within the bank's credit policy.

The aim of this chapter is to provide a general guide to why and how a stress-test scenario for country risk can be helpful in contributing to the corporate decisions within a multinational bank or industrial company. This chapter is organised as follows: the first section revises the reasons why a stress test analysis for country risk can be of great use within a private institution. The next section briefly analyses the methodological evolution of country risk assessment, and the following section examines how a stress test can be constructed by discussing the identification of relevant variables to be shocked. The section after that provides an example of a stress test and the final section concludes.

WHY CONDUCT A COUNTRY RISK STRESS TEST?

While not yet very popular among traditional commercial bankers, stress testing for country risk can become a very powerful tool in the hands of higher management and boards of directors. There are two main reasons for constructing a stress test: first, to measure possible changes in the value and risk of a loan portfolio due to country factors (this kind of stress test can also be useful for setting and reviewing country exposure limits); second, to measure the potential impacts of country factors on a new, major investment – whether M&A or greenfield.

Defining country risk for stress testing

In order to make a country risk stress test meaningful, a broader definition of country risk must be used. By the expression *country risk*, not only do we consider the likelihood that the country, ie, the sovereign, will not be in the position, for whatever reason, to honour its foreign obligations, but we also embed all those direct and indirect risk factors that originate from macroeconomic policy *latu sensu*. That is, political choices and country-specific structural factors that can impair the capability (or the willingness) to pay of potentially any debtor located within the boundaries of that very country.[2]

A good example of this is the public utility sector in Argentina. After the announcement of partial default on external debt by newly elected President Adolfo Rodriguez Saà on 23 December, 2001, the Argentinian convertibility law, fixing the parity of the domestic peso to the US dollar (US$), ceased to be in effect as of 6 January, 2002. On that date, a dual exchange rate regime was introduced, one fixed at 1.40 pesos to the US$ for foreign trade, and the other determined by the forces of the free market that quickly took the exchange rate up to 4 pesos to 1 US$ by the end of March 2002. In order to mitigate the inflationary effects of a 40% devaluation of the official exchange rate for the peso, and to limit the impact of the crisis on households and small business, the government froze public service tariffs and prohibited any indexations through the Public Emergency Law number 25,561 and the Decree number 293/02.[3] These latter measures *de facto* imposed an enormous financial burden on the utilities sector, which, in the years of the convertibility law – characterised by very low inflation, even deflation – had been issuing huge amounts of hard currency debt, counting on the stability and credibility of the currency peg and benefiting from tariffs often indexed to higher US inflation. This dual exchange rate, combined with the freezing of the tariffs, proved to be unsustainable for the companies in the Argentinian public utility sector and pushed them to default on their debts.

As it should be apparent from this extreme example of Argentina's utilities, building appropriate scenarios that stress-test the ability of countries to withstand shocks and/or macroeconomic and financial measures implemented to fend off endemic or epidemic crises should be perceived as crucial issues in managing country risk.

Stress-testing a loan portfolio

We present here a very simple example that shows how a country default credit VAR can be computed and how this estimate of the credit VAR reacts to changes in the country risk assessment.

In order to keep things as simple as possible, we make some basic assumptions, and then suggest ways to further enrich and make the analysis more realistic:

1. Bank XYZ has a portfolio of three commercial loans of €100 million each, extended to three sovereigns, country Red (R), country

Green (G) and country White (W), whose ratings, and relative one-year default probability, are, respectively, BBB/0.24%; BB/1.08%; B/5.94%.[4]

2. The recovery rate on the loans in case of default is the same in all three cases and is equal to 40%, ie, the loss given default (LGD) is equal to $(1 - 0.4)$ for each of the loans in the portfolio.

3. The default probability is distributed as a binomial, ie, ours is a two-state world: default and no-default.

Thanks to the simplifying assumptions we made, and indicating with p the probability of default, it is straightforward to compute the expected loss (EL) and the unexpected loss (UL), given by, respectively:[5]

$$EL = p \times LGD \times Exposure$$
$$UL = \sqrt{p \times (1-p)} \times LGD \times Exposure$$

At this stage, in order to obtain an estimate of the $VAR^{99.9\%}$ comparable to the normal distribution, all we have to do is to multiply our UL by 3.08. The exposure to country risk of a bank XYZ's loans portfolio, and the VAR generated by this kind of risk, can then be summarised as in Table 1.

Suppose now that the country risk unit of Bank XYZ runs a stress-test scenario whose output turns out to be a substantial stability, over the next 12 months, for countries R and W, while, as far as country G is concerned, it will be subject to particular strains that are likely to cause a deterioration of the country's rating to B. Should this deterioration of country risk actually materialise, through the augmented default probability, there would be an

Table 1 Loan portfolio: from nominal exposure to VAR

Country	Exposure (€million)	Rating	LGD	p	EL	UL	$VAR^{99.9\%}$ (€million)
R	100	BBB	0.6	0.24%	0.144	2.94	9.04
G	100	BB	0.6	1.08%	0.648	6.20	19.1
W	100	B	0.6	5.94%	3.564	14.18	43.7
Total	300						71.84

immediate impact on the existing portfolio of loans, whose country default credit VAR would increase from €71.84 million to €96.4 million. This could have interesting implications at the operational level in the bank. Suppose, for instance, that bank XYZ has a policy of keeping its country default credit VAR below the €80 million threshold level that would obviously have been breeched in the case of country G's credit merit deterioration. Thus, in the case of bank XYZ, a stress-test scenario for country risk would probably trigger a strategy of reallocation of risks by either selling part of the loans in the market or by seeking country risk protection, in order to keep the credit VAR below the limit imposed by the risk appetite indicated by the relevant corporate decision makers.

There are obviously various other ways by which stress testing for country risk can impact on an existing loans portfolio even in our very simplified country default credit VAR model. One might consider, for instance, adjusting recovery rates, which can differ a lot depending upon the attitude of the governments towards foreign investors or upon the type of underlying contract.[6] Indeed, there is widespread consensus, supported also by empirical evidence, that commercial loans bear normally a much higher recovery rate than, for example, financial operations that tend to finance the working capital of banks or corporates located in emerging countries.

Admittedly the example given here, while effective in conveying the relevant ideas about stress testing for country risk and its impact on an existing portfolio, is somewhat simplistic. However, there are ample margins to make the analysis more sophisticated: by moving towards a more sophisticated distribution function for default probabilities, by allowing for some form of correlation among countries and by accounting for a sort of transition matrix that captures the probability that a country's rating migrates, over the considered time horizon, from one rating class to another.

Stress-testing an overseas investment

When the issue in question is a new overseas investment, country factors may impact the bank or company that is investing abroad, in a potentially risky country, through many channels. Hence the challenge in this type of stress testing is to consider all the impacts that country factors can have on the investment value.

First of all, assuming that the target company is quoted on the country's stock exchange, the investment in the company is exposed to the swings of the domestic equity market. There is ample evidence, especially for those emerging countries where capital liberalisation has reached a high level, that the volatility of their equity markets is much higher than that observed in more mature environments. There is likewise evidence that such higher volatility is determined, among many other things, by the variation in the credit rating of the country and the inflows and outflows of foreign capital that is either attracted or repelled as a consequence of political, economic or structural changes in the country under scrutiny.[7] Thus, on embarking in an equity or greenfield investment in an emerging country, the stakeholders take the risk of having the value of their newly acquired asset slashed by an adverse movement in the country's credit rating, or in the investors' sentiment towards the country where the new investment is based. It is worth stressing that adverse dynamics of the asset's value, induced by a deterioration of the country risk that triggers a sudden and huge outflow of capital, can take the form either of a slump in the equity market capitalisation or of a deep loss of value of the domestic currency, or, more probably, a combination of the two.[8,9] It should then be clear that a stress-test analysis that can highlight and provide an estimate of those factors that may induce, over a reasonable time horizon (typically 3–5 years), a deterioration in the country risk, should be one of the most important tools to be used in any important investment decision.

Second, a deterioration in country risk that drags down also the credit merit of banks, financial institutions and the corporate sector of the country determines an upward shift in the cost of capital that has to be borne when tapping the international financial markets. Thus, if the participation in the new venture abroad is only a first step that has to be followed by further investments to enhance productivity, then it is wise to run a country risk stress test in order to have a more precise idea about the extra financial cost that the company may incur in the future, should a deterioration in country risk materialise.

The third transmission channel of country risk dynamics on to assets' value that we discuss in this section applies mainly, if not exclusively, to those institutions such as banks and insurance companies whose portfolio is almost entirely made up of sovereign or quasi-sovereign bonds. It is worth stressing that often the port-folio composition of banks and insurance companies in many emerging countries is not the result of an optimisation process that seeks to maximise the return given a certain risk, but rather a forced choice induced by political pressures and by the lack of valid alternative domestic assets. This is the case in all those coun-tries, such as Slovakia, Turkey, Croatia and Peru, in which the restructuring of virtually defaulted sectors of the economy – mainly the banking sector – has been financed by huge issues of long-term bonds backed by a government guarantee and "sold" to domestic banks, insurance companies and institutional investors. Under these circumstances, any portfolio valuation, be it static or dynamic, of these domestic financial institutions is tantamount to the static or dynamic evaluation of the creditworthiness of the ultimate guarantor: the sovereign. Again, constructing a stress-test scenario that enables us to gauge the possible future path of sover-eign creditworthiness provides a crucial input for the decision process as a whole and for the pricing, when a binding offer for the equity stake has to be made.

ASSESSING COUNTRY RISK FOR STRESS TESTING

Before we start tackling the issue of how to build a stress test for country risk, it is worth elaborating on what are the determinants of the "value" of a country and how these determinants can be affected by economic, financial and political changes that ultimately affect a country's creditworthiness.

Macroeconomic models and their failings

Traditionally, a country's creditworthiness is analysed through the lense of macroeconomics, whose focus is on a dynamic comparison of income and expenditure flows at the aggregate level. In this framework, a country's financial soundness is gauged through an analysis and a forecast of how much income, through taxes and exports, a country can generate, and how much expenditure it has to face, in the form of public expenditure, interest and principal repayments. Macroeconomic flows are certainly a crucial set of variables to look at when assessing country risk. However, as the Asian crisis exemplified, where financial mismatches and explicit and implicit bail-out costs played a crucial role in pushing some countries into default, it is necessary to widen the scope of analysis in order to have a better country risk assessment.[10] First of all, for a fairly wide set of emerging countries, there is a liquid and efficient secondary market where sovereign bonds and credit default swaps (CDSs) on sovereign bonds are priced and exchanged. This means that there is some information to be extracted from prices and spreads, and their respective volatilities, about the sovereign risk assessment that international investors make day in and day out while trading in the international financial markets. Second, there are countries where, due to history, tradition or political factors, the government guarantees explicit or, more frequently, implicit transfers to the banking and/or the corporate sector. The government thus reduces the default probability of domestic banks and industries, but burdens the state accounts with potential future costs and losses that can threaten the economic and financial stability of the country. What makes the picture even more difficult to embed into a model is the fact that there is ample theoretical and empirical evidence that these "political factors" – ie, implicit guarantees, among other things – and their changes in the course of time (due to, for instance, elections, *coups d'état*, emergence of dictators, changes in the political economy and so on) affect the country's financial and economic stability in a highly non-linear way.[11] The co-existence of macroeconomic flows, market prices for sovereign debt and evident non-linearity in the relationship between most of the variables involved has induced some country risk researches to venture, with some success, into the Merton-based methodology, applying concepts borrowed from contingent claims analysis (CCA) to analyse sovereign and country risk.

Contingent claims analysis[12]

CCA, originally applied to firms, can be adapted to countries. Its basic assumption is that assets issued by any financial entity are volatile and that the claims on those volatile assets bear some kind of risk that depends upon the seniority or priority of the claims themselves. The total value of an entity financed through debt and equity $V(t)$ is the sum of equity $E(t)$ and debt $D(t)$ and is equal to total assets $A(t)$ plus reserves $R(t)$. As assets are stochastic – usually in the literature they are modelled through a Brownian motion – they can decline below the face value of the debt plus accrued interest, the default barrier (DB), where there is default for the financial entity. Thus, holders of the junior claims, ie, equity, have, at time T, a contingent claim on the residual assets, once debt has been paid. This means that they get either the difference between $A(T)$ and DB, or nothing at all. Furthermore, the value of risky debt at T, ie, $D(T)$, is the minimum between $A(T)$ and DB, which is tantamount to saying that it is equal to DB less the maximum between the difference between DB and $A(T)$, and nothing at all. Putting everything in a more formalised way, we have:

$$V(T) = A(T) + R(T) = E(T) + D(T)$$
$$= \max[A(T) - \text{DB}, 0] + \text{DB} - \max[\text{DB} - A(T), 0]$$

You will immediately recognise that the first term on the right-hand side of the final equation is a call option, while the last one is a put option. Thus, the value of the financial entity at time T – be it a company or a country – is the sum of a call option plus the default free value of the debt issued – DB – less a put option. Using the Black–Scholes formula, it is possible to find a solution for the value of both the call and the put options. The latter, for instance, is given by:[13]

$$P = \text{DB}e^{-rT}N(-d_2) - AN(-d_1)$$

Where DB and A have already been defined above, $N(*)$ is the cumulative distribution function for a standard normal variable, r is the risk-free rate of interest and, defining σ_A the standard deviation of returns on the asset:

$$d_1 = \frac{\ln\left(\dfrac{A}{\text{DB}}\right) + \left(r + \dfrac{1}{2}\sigma_A^2\right)T}{\sigma_A\sqrt{T}} \; ; \quad d_2 = d_1 - \sigma_A\sqrt{T}$$

Note that d_2 is defined as the risk-neutral distance to default and its cumulative distribution is the risk-neutral probability of default.

What needs to be done, at this stage, is to estimate the values of the elements in the equations (eg, the assets, their returns and volatility, the DB, the reserves, etc) in order to find the "value" of the financial entity.[14] When the financial entity to be evaluated is a country the assets include:

❑ currency reserves;
❑ present discounted value of fiscal and other revenues;
❑ equity in public assets;[15] and
❑ exclusive right to issue money (seigniorage).[16]

As to the liabilities we have:

❑ present discounted value of public expenditures;
❑ local-currency debt;
❑ foreign-currency debt;
❑ financial guarantees (explicit and implicit); and
❑ monetary base.[17]

Any variations in any of the assets and/or liabilities indicated above would have a non-linear impact on the value of the options and on the level of DB and, ultimately, on the value of the country itself. For instance, if a country strengthens its fiscal position by reducing future expenditures and improving its fiscal revenues, this, in the CCA model, would be reflected in an improved value of the country, that is, a lower country risk. By the same token, a newly appointed government that extends wider guarantees to the corporate or the banking sector would be reflected, in this framework, by an increase in the liabilities, in the DB and, consequently, in a worsening of the country's credit merit. Furthermore, any event that triggers an outflow of foreign capital from the country ultimately causes a depreciation of the local currency, a loss of reserves and an increase in the local currency level of foreign denominated debt, thus weakening the financial position of the country as it is reflected in the model described here.

What has briefly been presented in this section shows that, by the use of a CCA model, it is possible to construct a stress-test scenario. This can be achieved by modifying the values of assets and liabilities of a country according to the analyst's view about issues such as:

❑ future fiscal position;
❑ vulnerability to financial panic and currency crisis;
❑ attitude of the government towards the private sector;
❑ exploitation of seigniorage.[18]

The impact of such a macro financial stress-test scenario on the country's economic and financial strength can then be evaluated. Going further ahead, this line of reasoning leads to the utilisation of "Greeks" to assess a country's vulnerability.[19] One can interpret the value of the put option in the CCA model presented here as the present value of the EL. Since the value of the put option depends, in a non-linear way, upon the value and the volatility of the sovereign assets, by calculating the first and the second derivatives of the option value with respect to assets – delta and gamma, respectively – and the first derivative with respect to volatility – vega – one can further assess the vulnerability of a country's creditworthiness.

HOW TO BUILD A STRESS TEST FOR COUNTRY RISK

Subsequently, as we have a complete toolkit to start building a stress-test scenario for country risk, we can actually outline the various phases that a country risk manager has to go through in producing a meaningful stress test exercise.

Set the time horizon

As a stress-test scenario is essentially, at the beginning of the process, a forecast of the future evolution of some macroeconomic and market variables, it is crucial to decide the time horizon upon which the analyst wishes to span. Typically, macroeconomic and market forecasts become less and less accurate as they refer to instants of time that are further away in the future. In the case of stress-test scenarios for country risk the usual time horizon spans over one year, even if, when it comes to assessing the creditworthiness of a country for an M&A operation, the exercise requires one to formulate a scenario that looks, at least, three to five years into the future.

Identify the variables

Once the time horizon has been defined, it is necessary to identify the economic, financial and market variables that need to be shocked to produce a meaningful stress-test scenario for country risk. It goes without saying that the best way to start a scenario analysis like this is to gather a variety of economic, financial, political and anecdotal information about the country under scrutiny.[20] This intelligence activity of information gathering should provide the country risk manager with a precise view about the vulnerabilities of a country and about the dimension of the shocks with which to hit the macro-economic system in order to obtain a reasonable stress-test scenario.

Standard variables
As a general rule, when analysing emerging countries, macroeconomic flows are often a very good starting point. There is ample availability from various sources of forecasts and projections of countries' reserves, net fiscal position, level of domestic and foreign debt, principal and interest payments schedule, and monetary base that can be used as an input for devising a meaningful scenario with which to assess the future financial solidity of a country.[21]

Country-specific variables
In addition to these standard macroeconomic variables, it is some-times necessary to consider other transmission channels through which a shock can feed and impact the creditworthiness of a coun-try. Most of these channels are country-specific; that is why a deep and direct knowledge of the country under scrutiny is a prerequisite for good country risk management. We have already noted the role that implicit bail-outs in favour of the banking sector had in driving some East Asian countries over the edge of financial collapse; how-ever, other sources of potential instability exist. Think, for instance, of the pivotal financial and economic role that the export of oil, gas and other oil-related products has for countries such as Mexico, Russia and Venezuela – and these are just a few of the emerging oil-exporter countries that are also big debtor countries, and that have recently come through full-blown, or nearly full-blown, crises. In assessing each of these countries' present and future credit merit, a country risk manager cannot overlook the importance that the future price of oil and oil-related products can have on the fiscal and export revenues and, ultimately, on the country's assets.

Another channel through which a country's creditworthiness can seriously be impaired is the foreign exchange. In general, due to their lower reliance on equity and their small corporate sectors, emerging markets are more sensitive to increases in the level of foreign-currency-linked debt, than in the level of equity indices. Domestic currency depreciation can indeed raise the credit risk of those countries, for instance Brazil and Turkey, whose debt is largely denominated in foreign currency. Thus, a sound knowledge of the structure and composition of foreign debt is an important priority when building a stress-test scenario in order to identify whether the future dynamics of the exchange rate can play an important role in determining the credit risk related to the country under scrutiny.

Another country-specific feature of some emerging markets that should not be overlooked when building a stress-test scenario for country risk is the duration of domestic-currency-denominated debt. In some cases, and Brazil and Turkey are again a good example, the duration of the local currency debt is so short that the cost of its service reacts almost instantaneously to any variation in domestic rates induced by monetary policy. Thus, in periods characterised by uncertainty and concerns about currency depreciation, any reaction of the central bank in attempting to protect the currency from excessive depreciation by raising short-term rates can end up weighing on the domestic debt, thus impacting negatively on the country's financial solidity.

Once a list of variables that identify and capture any potential vulnerability of the country has been carefully prepared, it is necessary to identify, quantify and calibrate the shocks with which to hit the variables. As a stress test should highlight the impact of extreme but still plausible events, it is always wise to refer to past history in constructing a vector of shocks with which to hit the variables considered relevant for the country whose credit merit is to be assessed. Of course, as every financial or banking crisis exemplifies, history does not necessarily repeat itself, and it is often useful to use some "imagination" and produce stress-test scenarios that embed exceptional, but still plausible, shocks.

AN EXAMPLE OF A STRESS-TEST SCENARIO: TURKEY
Turkey is an extremely interesting example in many respects. From a country risk manager's perspective, the country represents a splendid example of a very resilient economy, capable of recording impressive growth rates over a long time span in the presence of extreme inflation, and characterised at times by financial crises, sharp and fast depreciation of the exchange rate and a political environment always on the borderline between the Middle East and Western Europe. All these elements make Turkey a perfect candidate for an exercise of stress-test scenario for country risk, as

there are so many macroeconomic, financial and political variables that can be subject to sudden changes, which can have a remarkable impact on the country's credit merit.

We reproduce here a stress-test scenario for Turkey that was actually performed in spring 2004 at Banca Intesa Risk Management, thus all the figures described refer to those available in the second quarter of 2004, and the shocks with which the system was hit apply to those figures. This exercise bears some interest in many respects: on one side it is an actual stress-test scenario taken directly from our recent past experience; on the other we can actually check *ex post* whether the results produced by this exercise have been confirmed by the evolution of Turkish risk. Finally, the period in which the stress test was run was characterised by a good deal of uncertainty regarding both the chances of Turkey's starting negotiations for EU entry, and the US Fed's monetary policy and the actual risk appetite of institutional investors for emerging countries.[22]

Mapping the risks

We started by producing a "map" of risks for Turkey, trying to consider and embed in our exercise all the possible economic, financial and political vulnerabilities of the country. At that time, considering the available figures and the political and economic debate within and outside the country, we came up with the following map of risks for Turkey:

❑ **Global risks:** The sheer size of the public debt (75% of GDP in 2003) and the overvaluation of the Turkish lire (TRL), coupled with a widening current account, make Turkey extremely vulnerable to a deterioration of the appetite for emerging markets triggered by higher rates in the US. Even more so, if one thinks that 45% of Turkish debt is indexed to the US$.

❑ **Political risks:** The fate of AKP-led government seems to depend largely on the EU decision about accession negotiations for Turkey. A delay in the EU decision, expected by the end of 2004, could force Turkey into a political crisis that could scare away international investors. By the same token, admission to negotiations would catalyse further investors' appetite.

❑ **Policy risks:** It will not be easy for the Turkish government to deliver, over the next five to ten years, a steady annual growth of

4–5% and a primary surplus of 6.5% of GDP. That is, conditions necessary to guarantee future financial stability for Turkey. Furthermore, the announced plan to remove six zeros from the TRL and to adopt an explicit inflation target could backfire in an environment characterised by exchange-rate volatility and fiscal slippage.

❑ **Transition risks:** Even if Turkey joins the EU, no EU funds are likely to reach Turkey before 2013. Given the still huge dependence of Turkey upon foreign aid (US$8.5 billion in September 2003 from the US government), will the country go along the path out of US influence and into the European Union?

At the time of mapping, there was wide empirical evidence that the above concerns were certainly not out of place. By looking at the private and public sectors' external debt service, it became clear that the peak of external debt servicing would occur for Turkey in 2006, when more than US$20 billion will have to be repaid by the general government.[23] Given the still remarkable growth rate of Turkey and its huge dependence upon oil imports, there was – and still is – a concrete chance that, in order to keep under control the growing current account gap, in two years' time the exchange rate might be devalued in comparison to its level in the second quarter of 2004. This would cause an increase, in domestic currency terms, of the debt-repayment burden that may trigger a balance-of-payments crisis. Such an event would have devastating effects on Turkey, as the country was, and still is, one of the largest debtors vis-à-vis the IMF. The loans extended by the IMF to Turkey were, last spring, almost 16 times the value of the country quota in the Fund. The number is all the more impressive when compared to the position of the Fund towards other indebted countries such as Brazil (six times its quota), Argentina (five times) and Indonesia (slightly more than three times). This means that, should the Turkish situation suddenly deteriorate from a balance-of-payments point of view, it would be extremely difficult for the Fund to provide extra help.

Alternative scenarios
With this map of risks in mind, we proceeded by constructing three scenarios. The first one was simply an extension in the future of the trend that the country had been following since the beginning of

2002, characterised by solid GDP growth, rapidly declining inflation, productivity growth, a strengthening domestic currency and a gradually looser monetary policy.[24] We also drew two alternative scenarios: one intermediate (mildly pessimistic) and another as worst-case scenario. The intermediate scenario was characterised by a depreciation of the TRL against the US$ by around 15% to offset the growing external imbalance; an attempt to limit and slow the slippage of the domestic currency through an increase in short-term rates to a level of 25%; a sale of US$ reserves in the range of 10% of the total country reserves; and an overall stability of the equity market, signalling a limited loss of confidence from international investors in the country. The worst-case scenario, designed to mimic and replicate a crisis deeper than that of 1998 (but milder than that of 2001, which led to the abandonment of a currency board agreement) was characterised by a domestic currency breeching the psychological threshold of 2,000,000 against the US$; domestic short-term rates spiking to 60%; the use of reserves to defend the currency by more than 15% and a stock market losing some 30% of its value, on the back of decreasing international confidence towards the country. It is worth stressing that, in designing these scenarios, we did not devise any shocks on the fiscal front, as we believed that the driver of a possible, sudden crisis would almost certainly come from the forex and/or domestic rates channel(s).

The technical instrument used to assess and evaluate quantitatively the impact of these two scenarios on Turkey's country risk was Moody's MfRisk. This is a software program based on a contingent-claim model applied to sovereign and country risk very similar to that described earlier (see "Assessing country risk for stress testing"). By inputting our scenario into Moody's MfRisk model we obtained, among many others, the results in Table 2.

Table 2 Alternative scenarios: comparing sovereign risk

	Market scenario	Intermediate scenario	Worst-case scenario
Probability of default (sovereign)	2.6%	3.2%	3.9%
1-Year CDS spread (basis points)	212	261	312
5-Year CDS spread (basis points)	493	545	597
Equity volatility of banking sector	34.9%	40.7%	70%

Interpretation of results in Table 2

The table enables us to describe and elaborate on the last part of a stress-test scenario: the interpretation of results. It is worth emphasising that there are a few significant things that Table 2 does tell us, but there are many others that it would be inappropriate to infer from the results given by the scenario analysis. The first important thing that the table tells us is that, even in a very unfavourable state of the world, the country should not be pushed beyond the DB. Rather, the probability of default would increase to a level very close to 4%, which can be approximately associated to a rating class of B+, in Standard & Poor's terms, or B1 using Moody's taxonomy, as opposed to a current market scenario consistent with a BB- or Ba3 rating, respectively.[25] This means that, should things turn out to be bad for the country under scrutiny, it would be likely to be downgraded by at least one notch with respect to the "current market scenario". Such a downgrading would obviously be consistent with a higher spread on sovereign CDS. What the second and third rows of the table tell us is that, in case the intermediate or the worst-case scenario materialises, we should account for an increase in the equilibrium yield differential between local sovereign foreign denominated paper and risk-free bonds of similar maturity. This has important implications for the evaluation of a portfolio of long-term sovereign bonds in the hands of a local bank, or a local insurance company or pension fund, because, in the case of sovereign spread deterioration, the analyst should apply a higher discount rate, which would ultimately imply a fall in the actual value of the bonds portfolio under scrutiny. However, what the table does not tell us is how the sovereign spreads on various maturities reach their estimated equilibrium value as indicated in the table. It is very reasonable to assume that, in case of a sharp deterioration of the current account, coupled with increasing short-term domestic rates and local currency depreciation, sovereign spreads may well overshoot for a while their long run equilibrium value.[26] Thus, the results of our stress-test scenario should be interpreted as a steady-state description consistent with the realisation of the scenario(s), but which have nothing to say about the dynamics that characterise the transition from the previous steady state. Finally, the last row in the table provides an estimate of the equity volatility of the banking sector in each of the three scenarios. As is well known, volatility means risk, so it should not come as a surprise that volatility increases with the degree of sovereign risk deterioration and reaches the peak (70%) in the worst-case scenario. This kind of estimate is particularly useful when the stress-test scenario is run within a project of FDI into a listed company, whose market value can be subject to events that affect country risk.

CONCLUSIONS AND OPEN ISSUES

The analysis and the exercise in this chapter show the importance, both from a theoretical and a practical point of view, of designing, running and interpreting a stress test for country risk. Our main concern here has been to underline the operational importance of designing an appropriate stress test for country risk that can be of great use in the risk management within a financial institution.

At this stage it seems also important to mention that remaining issues exist that will have to be tackled by future research and analysis.

The first issue that requires consideration is correlation. The variables and the model we have presented and then used to assess the impact of various scenarios on sovereign and country risk focus exclusively on one country at a time. This does not mean that we do not recognise the crucial importance that correlation, spillover effects and contagion can have in driving the dynamics of sovereign and country risk. However, while the theoretical and empirical literature on contagion is by now very wide, there still seems to be a lack of efficient instruments for practitioners to use in order to quantitatively assess the degree of country risk contagion.[27] Another serious limit to our analysis is the lack of any views and/or information about the possible overshooting of market spreads – ie, risk perception – that normally goes hand in hand with any significant changes in the global economic and financial environment and that is driven by the "animal spirits" of international investors.[28] This is, in our view, a very serious limit, as the deepest deteriorations in country risk, which have ultimately led to full-blown defaults, seem to have often been induced by the emergence of self-fulfilling expectations that pushed the economic and financial system beyond the DB.

1 In the jargon of economists this would be deemed *scenario analysis*. However, as it will become clearer in this chapter, scenario analysis is only the first step of a stress test that provides, as an output, the effects of the scenario on the creditworthiness of the country and or the sovereign.

2 For a discussion on this issue, see Ruggerone (2003).

3 For a timeline of selected events in Argentina between 1991 and 2002, see Appendix IX in IMF (2004).

4 The default probabilities used in this paragraph are taken from Table 7.1 in Bouchet, Clark and Groslambert (2003), who use Standard & Poor's figures.

5 In particular, notice that, in case of binomial distribution, the standard deviation is given by $\sigma = \sqrt{p(1-p)}$. For an explanation of this approach, see also Chapter 4 in Saunders (1999).

6 See http://rru.worldbank.org/DoingBusiness/ExploreTopics/ClosingBusiness/CompareAll. aspx?direction=desc&sort=3, on which the World Bank publishes a very interesting table that summarises, among other figures, the findings in terms of country-specific recovery rates of the research project "Efficiency in Bankruptcy". You can use these country-specific recovery rates to calculate a country default credit VAR by using the appropriate recovery rate for each country in your portfolio.

7 For a wider and deeper discussion of these issues, see Chapter IV, Volatility of private capital flows to emerging markets in IMF (2003).

8 As equity investments are typically recorded in the balance sheets of Western companies in hard currency, any loss of value of the emerging market's currency implies a loss of value in hard-currency terms.

9 Note that a large depreciation of the local currency weighs also on the future income stream of dividends that can in turn affect the current value of the target company.

10 The literature on the Asian crisis is boundless; however, for insightful analyses see Corsetti, Pesenti and Roubini (1999), Krugman (1998), or Radelet and Sachs (1999).

11 Interesting examples of empirical evidence about this non linearity are Brewer and Rivoli (1997) and Manasse, Roubini and Schimmelpfennig (2003). As to a theoretical model that highlights a non-linear relationship between political factors and the risk of a financial crisis see Femminis and Ruggerone (2004).

12 The main reference here is Gray, Merton and Bodie (2003), and also Gray (2002), whose notation is used in this paragraph. Also Chapter 7 in Bouchet, Clark and Groslambert (2003) provides useful insights into a Merton-based methodology for country risk assessment.

13 See Hull (1993).

14 Such an estimation is certainly not easy, particularly for a sovereign; however, Chapter 7 in Bouchet, Clark and Groslambert (2003) suggests a way of estimating the value of a country's assets and its volatility by use of macroeconomic and market data.

15 In some emerging countries this can be a very important item. Think, for instance, to the property of 37% of Gazprom in the hands of the Russian government, or PDVSA owned by the government of Venezuela.

16 For a theoretical and empirical analysis of the exploitation of seigniorage in emerging countries, see Ruggerone (1996) and Easterly and Vieira da Cunha (1994), respectively.

17 Base money is a liability in the presence of perfect capital mobility, as holders of domestic money can exchange local currency into foreign currency, reducing the level of hard-currency reserves of the central bank. In the extreme case of a currency board agreement – like Argentina until December 2001 – holders of local currency have in their hands a call option on the hard-currency reserves held by the monetary authority.

18 It is interesting to note that the monopolistic *right* to print money is an asset for the government/central bank, but, when this right is actually and materially exploited and the base money increases, this turns – and rightly so – into a liability.

19 In a recent work, Gray and Pipatanagul (2004) use the "Greeks" to measure the change in value of the options in the CCA model due to a change in the assets' value and in the assets' volatility. This is an alternative, very effective way to run a stress-test scenario for country risk.

20 We once read, but we forget where, that "country risk is an art". Knowing anecdotes and combining them with quantitative variables to come out with a good country risk assessment certainly needs some artistic inclination.

21 As for sources, in our professional experience we can think, for instance, of the Economist Intelligence Unit Country Data, Bloomberg, World Market Research and of various websites of governments and ministries, but this list is certainly not exhaustive.

22 See the sovereign spread of the index EMBI Global Constrained calculated by JP Morgan, which, between the end of April 2004 and 11 May, jumped from 481 to more than 550 basis points, reflecting a sharp decrease in emerging sovereign risk appetite from market participants.

23 Turkish Treasury figures published at the end of April 2004.

24 Just to give a flavour of this, at the beginning of 2002 inflation was at 73.2%, while at the end of 2003 it was slightly above 18%. As to GDP growth, in the 1990s it was, on average, 4.1%, while in the first quarter of 2004 it was 4.6%.

25 The experienced reader will notice here that we are stretching our argument a bit. In fact we are mapping our estimated sovereign probability of default into a ranking of ratings that are presumably calculated using a rather different model than the one employed here. However, although this practice would not be acceptable from a formal point of view, our hands-on experience suggests that it proves to be very effective from an empirical perspective. In reality, as the "market scenario" has been the "true" one so far, Turkey has indeed been upgraded, consistent with our mapping of the model predictions into the ratings.

26 Sovereign spreads on bonds or CDS are a market variable subject to investors' expectations, thus, as the seminal paper of Dornbush (1976) explains in very clear terms, it does happen that market variables subject to expectations may jump above their new post-shock long-term equilibrium before gradually converging to it.

27 See, for instance, the World Bank website dedicated to contagion of financial crises: http://www1.worldbank.org/economicpolicy/managing%20volatility/contagion/.

28 See Keynes (1936).

REFERENCES

Altman, E. I., J. B. Caouette, and P. Narayanan, 1998, *Managing Credit Risk: The new great financial challenge* (New York: John Wiley & Sons).

Bouchet, M. H., E. Clark, and B. Groslambert, 2003, *Country Risk Assessment: A guide to global investment strategy* (New York: John Wiley & Sons).

Brewer, T., P. and Rivoli, 1997, "Political Instability and Country Risk", *Global Finance Journal*, 8, pp. 309–21.

Corsetti, G., P. Pesenti, and N. Roubini, 1999, " 'Paper Tigers?' A model of the Asian crisis", *European Economic Review*, 43, pp. 1211–36.

Dornbush, R., 1976, "Expectations and Exchange Rate Dynamics", *Journal of Political Economy*, 84, pp. 1161–76.

Easterly, W., and P. Vieira da Cunha, 1994, "Financing the storm: Macroeconomics Crisis in Russia", *Economics of Transition*, 2(4), pp. 443–65.

Femminis, G., and L. Ruggerone, 2004, "Bailouts and Bank Runs in a Model of Crony Capitalism", *Contributions to Macroeconomics*, 4(1), http://www.bepress.com/bejm/contributions/vol4/iss1/art11.

Gray, D., 2002, "Macro Finance: The Bigger Picture; Risk Management for Investors", *Risk,* June.

Gray, D. F., R. C. Merton, and Z. Bodie, 2003, "A New Framework Analysing and Managing Macrofinancial Risks of an Economy", MfRisk Working Paper 1-03.

Gray, D. F., and T. Pipatanagul, 2004, "New Sovereign Risk Indicators: Using the 'Greeks' as a Sensitivity Measures of Sovereign Risk", Moody's MfRisk Research and Commentary, Available through subscription at URL: http://www.moodys-mfrisk.com.

Hull, J., 1993, Options, Futures and Other Derivative Securities (New Jersey: Prentice Hall).

IMF, 2003, "Global Financial Stability Report: Market Developments and Issues", September.

IMF, 2004, "Report on the Evaluation of the Role of the IMF in Argentina, 1991–2001", Independent Evaluation Office, June.

Jones, M. T., P. Hilbers, and G. Slack, 2004, "Stress Testing Financial Systems: What to Do When the Governor Calls", IMF Working Paper number 127, July.

Keynes, J. M., 1936, The general theory of employment, interest and money.

Krugman, P., 1998, "Bubble, Boom, Crash: Theoretical Notes on Asia's Crisis", mimeo (Cambridge, MA: MIT).

Manasse, P., N. Roubini, and A. Schimmelpfennig, 2003, "Predicting Sovereign Debt Crises", IMF Working Paper number 221, November.

Radelet, S., and J. Sachs, 1998, "The Onset of the East Asian Financial Crisis", mimeo (Harvard: HIID).

Ruggerone, L., 1996, "Unemployment and Inflationary Finance Dynamics at the Early Stages of Transition", *Economic Journal,* **106**, pp. 483–94.

Ruggerone, L., 2003, "Il rischio paese: metodi di valutazione e di mitigazione per banche e imprese", Collana Ricerche, Servizio Studi e Ricerche Banca Intesa, forthcoming in Spanish in *Boletín Informativo Techint,* Buenos Aires; also available at URL: http://www.bancaintesa.it/repository/files/Research/Macroeconomia/Collana%20ricerche/R2003-04.pdf.

Saunders, A., 1999, *Credit Risk Measurement: New Approaches to Value at Risk and Other Paradigms* (New York: John Wiley & Sons).

9

Domestic and External Political Factors and Country Risk: The Case of China

Therese Feng

Fitch Ratings

Sovereign political risk in the People's Republic of China (PRC) is unique in reflecting the demands on, and challenges to, an authoritarian regime that has been created by unprecedented economic, social and cultural change over the past three decades. No other country in modern history has experienced a transformation of such rapidity, depth or scale as China is undergoing. Since 1980, real GDP growth of 8% per year has lifted 200 million people out of poverty and more than doubled average per capita income. The economy has undergone a wholesale makeover in moving from a centrally controlled system dominated by state-owned enterprises to a market-oriented one that is increasingly powered by vibrant private enterprises. In the space of a generation more than 20% of the 1 billion-plus populace moved from the country to the city. Increasingly confident foreign policy is reflected in China's rising contributions to regional security and economic integration, and China itself has transformed from a society largely closed to the West, to one that is grappling with the dislocations engendered by rapid industrialisation, increasing openness and globalisation.

Fitch Ratings has rated China since 1999 and, as of October 2004, assigned ratings of A– and A respectively to China's long-term foreign and local currency ratings. China's formidable strengths are counterbalanced by equally striking weaknesses. Huge foreign-exchange reserves support a robust external liquidity position, sustained by trade gains that have raised China's share of world merchandise exports from 3.0% to 5.9% in eight years. These strengths are offset by acute weaknesses of a fragile banking system still saddled with substantial bad loans, weak finances among many state-owned enterprises, and rising quasi-fiscal liabilities of local governments. At the time of writing, the state also faced macroeconomic policy challenges generated in part by a difficult policy mix of crude and incomplete monetary controls, a fixed exchange rate, largely state-dictated investment, rising needs for social entitlement and the difficult link between state enterprise and banking sector reform.

In many ways political risk in China has appeared to figure more as a second-order concern, given the monolithic control of the Chinese Communist Party (CCP) and the much more pressing issues posed by evolution to a market economy. Especially after the 1989 Tiananmen Square incident, the party has appeared almost static, with few real challenges to its authority. Yet the CCP and governing framework have actually evolved in response to external and internal developments. In 2003–4 the party faced several unusual challenges arising from political succession, SARS and rising political activism in Hong Kong and Taiwan.

This chapter looks at the evolution of sovereign political risk in China. It assesses how political risk has changed over time, and identifies key pressures and risks to the current leadership. In particular, it focuses on recent developments in Taiwan and Hong Kong, which are providing new unanticipated challenges on the periphery. Finally, it evaluates what these developments could augur for China's future political transformation.

SOVEREIGN POLITICAL RISK FACTORS

Assessing political factors of sovereign risk requires the consideration of both static and dynamic aspects of a country's governing institutions, the domestic political and business environment, and geopolitical relations.

The most basic assessment of static factors considers the stability and legitimacy of political institutions, which reflects the degree of popular representation, existence of checks and balances among branches of government, effectiveness of governance, and transparency of decision-making. The proliferation of outlets for popular dissent, such as a free press and deep civil institutions, can diffuse challenges to a regime. Conversely, marginalisation of a large portion of the populace, mounting income disparities or racial divisions can prove destabilising. Relations with neighbouring countries are key to the risk of war and external security concerns, which can also impose a significant burden on public finances or deter investment.

The most fundamental dynamic factor to be assessed is the degree to which leadership succession is peaceful and predictable. In authoritarian states, power that is highly concentrated in individuals, informal rather than institutionalised power relations and low political transparency can lead to unanticipated and drastic changes in leadership. These may be preceded or followed by periods of political conflict or social instability, and major policy changes or reversals.

Preserving authority can also be a particular challenge for authoritarian systems given weak legitimacy, the reliance on coercion for popular compliance, highly centralised decision-making and a reliance on personal rather than institutional power. This is even more so for a regime that needs to maintain relevance in the midst of rapid socioeconomic change. Pressures from within (such as rising corruption or income inequality), or from without (such as democratisation in surrounding states), or increased access to information that increases popular awareness of the failings of the regime, can amplify the challenges to a regime. Where a country is undergoing rapid transformation, the willingness of leadership to undertake appropriate political change and the capacity of political institutions to evolve takes on particular importance.

China's changing domestic political risk factors

China is a true outlier as one of the highest-rated sovereigns with an authoritarian political regime. The system is a party-state in which the CCP remains the sole legitimate political entity, is interwoven into all other institutions and makes policy for virtually all realms of action. In this centralised system local power is still largely derived from grants by the centre. Local elections have been held for 20 years, yet popular representation is extremely limited in light of a still high degree of party control of electoral processes, the prohibition on organised political groups, and lack of strong popular representative institutions. At the upper levels, power is still largely identified with individuals and their informal networks, rather than embodied in institutions with offsetting checks and balances. The Chinese media are increasingly vibrant, yet the party still controls content. Official tolerance of an individual's right to think and advocate critical ideas has greatly increased, but discussions of the role of the party and changes to government remain taboo. Relative to similarly rated countries with more representative political systems, this political environment implies a somewhat higher level of political risk on the basis of: (1) political uncertainty associated with leadership change; (2) the greater associated potential for abrupt policy change and its less favourable implications for macroeconomic performance; (3) challenges to political stability and, by inference, regime durability arising from the absence of official channels for dissent; and (4) shallow institutions for sustaining the rule of law.

Over the last 30 years the leadership has tried to contain political risk by fostering high economic growth to counteract emerging political demands and by undertaking limited reform that would provide greater resilience to the authoritarian regime.[1] Political change has been discontinuous, yet the political climate has significantly evolved. During the 1980s the pace of political liberalisation was profound. After the ravages of the 1966–76 Cultural Revolution, Premier Deng Xiao-ping attempted to rebuild legitimacy for the party by decisively turning away from Maoist thought and the destructive cycle of directed political campaigns, while gradually opening up to Western ideas and influences. Within the party, top officials conducted substantial political debates and undertook a series of bold experiments to strengthen the legislature and legal system, allow growth of civil society and to introduce village elections. Political experimentation occurred in the context of broad-based growth aided by internal economic reforms and a gradual opening up to the world economy. During this period a range of party leaders called for the separation of party and government, and of the party and enterprise, as well as for introducing democratic practices within the CCP.

Following Tiananmen, however, systemic political change has been sharply constrained, although limited political experimentation has continued. During Tiananmen, widespread pro-democracy demonstrations evinced the political alienation of a sizeable portion of the urban population. These protests had the potential to undermine the fundamental legitimacy of the leadership, and by extension the party. No other single event in the post-Mao period has posed such a high risk to the state. The state's violent ending of the mass protest demonstrated the leadership's determination to maintain authoritarian rule even at a high cost. For the party these events underlined the necessity of eradicating any independent organisations with the potential to challenge the state or disrupt social stability, and created the template for harsh regime responses to subsequent challenges such as the suppression of the Chinese Democratic Party in 1998–9 and the Falun Gong religious movement in 1999 (see Nathan, 2003).

Tiananmen was also decisive in ending any incipient movement towards democratic reform on the part of the leadership. During the 1990s, what political reform did occur was primarily externally driven, top down and incremental (see Fewsmith, 2004). In 1992, Premier Deng Xiao-ping's famous southern tour relaunched the economic reform agenda, allowing the government to regain much of the popular support it had lost in 1989 (see de Lisle, 2004). Rapid growth promoted the development of an economic elite dependent on political largesse and largely unwilling to challenge the existing political system. Growth also relieved some of the pressure on the ruling elite to undertake reform while providing the state with more resources to co-opt challenges to its power. China resorted to an assertive nationalism to counter the direct international pressure for human rights and democracy that globalisation posed, in an active push against western ideas.

Despite the appearance of political stasis, the increasing institutionalisation of leadership succession has been one of the most important reforms undertaken. By the 1990s the party had already begun to implement norms of institutionalisation at the highest levels, including term limits for party officials, mandatory retirement at age 70 and restraints on nepotism (see Li, 2002; Nathan, 2003). The clearest recent evidence of the realisation of institutionalisation has been the peaceful and orderly leadership succession from the third generation of leadership, led by Jiang Zemin, to the fourth generation, headed by Hu Jintao, in 2002–4. This process has also represented probably the single most important recent event helping to moderate China's political risk.

This transition was unprecedented in that Hu had been anointed as successor more than 10 years ago, yet neither the senior guard of retired elders nor the military intervened in succession during the interim.[2] Hu's accession reflected the implementation of rules for personnel promotion, namely that cadres were selected on the basis of meritocracy (administrative skills, technical knowledge and educational background), rather than personal fealty; and the selection of leadership was less factionalised. Because of the resulting political balance in different party factions and absence of a single dominant figure, China's new leaders have a greater orientation towards collective decision-making, which tends to produce greater continuity in policy. Jiang's resignation from his last official post in late 2004 effectively completed the power transfer, reducing uncertainty over the consolidation of Hu's political control and concerns over policy coordination and implementation.

The party is also attempting to bolster popular legitimacy and foster higher accountability. It has promoted greater inclusiveness in calling to admit private entrepreneurs. Under Hu, the leadership is striving to become more representative of people who have been marginalised by the economic transformation (without encouraging such interests to organise politically). The 900 million rural dwellers and increasing number of migrant urban jobseekers are high on the CCP's agenda, which is increasingly focused on the potential social stability fuelled by increasing unhappiness over low rural incomes, rising unemployment and widespread corruption. There are moves to promote a greater collective accountability of the top leaders and to shift away from elitism within the party. The leadership is also attempting to make government and the party more open and responsive to wider social interests, by encouraging greater consultation and public participation as well as independent expert input into government decision making. At the level of the individual, ideological diversity remains limited, but a greater official tolerance for and even emphasis of the primacy of protecting citizen rights (the right to know, the right of due process) based on Chinese laws has emerged, particularly in response to the initial mishandling of the 2003 SARS epidemic.

Rising challenges
Yet the leadership faces enormous internal challenges. Corruption, conservatively estimated by the Chinese press to consume 3–4% of GDP annually, has the potential to undermine the legitimacy of

local government and, by implication, public support for party and regime legitimacy. Such abuses stem from the state's extensive involvement in the economy as well as in the underdevelopment or breakdown of mechanisms for monitoring and political account-ability (see Pei, 2002a and 2002b). Though it is unlikely to directly destabilise the government while economic growth obscures some of the more egregious ills, systemic risks of instability can rise if there is a failure to curb widespread abuse.

Corruption also has the potential to exacerbate other problems troubling the Chinese state, including rising economic inequality and the declining quality of local governance. Although China's GINI coefficient of 40.3 (see World Bank, 2004) is not the highest in Asia, rapid growth in coastal and urban areas has opened up an income gap estimated at 5–6 times that of the rural interior (see Qiu Xiaohua, 2002). A growing population of have-nots and econom-ically marginalised households has been generated by economic restructuring, which has meant a forcible end to not only guaran-teed employment but also the provision of medical care, pensions, and schooling. Some 44 million employees have been taken off the state payroll, yet the rate of re-employment within the private sec-tor, while poorly documented, has been falling (see Dreyer, 2004). Urban poverty is growing given the weakening of social insurance and a still vastly inadequate social safety net, high and rising unemployment and the emergence of jobless growth. The party's law commission reported that the incidence of protests rose by 14.4% in 2003 to 58,500, with the number of people involved in social unrest increasing by 6.6% by 3 million. These figures pre-sumably comprise:

1. small-scale protests among laid-off former state-owned enter-prise workers;
2. former state-enterprise pensioners demanding payment;
3. collective violence among rural migrants; and
4. tax riots among farmers.

However, visible urban protests have not yet posed a material threat to the regime, since they remain dispersed, lack sustained leadership and have no widespread urban support. Other issues with the potential to foster discontent include an ageing, increas-ingly gender-imbalanced and still-growing population, severe and increasing pollution, massive continuing economic dislocation and unmet demands for energy (see Dreyer, 2004).

Periphery risk factors for China

In the last five years, however, the greatest political unpredictability for China has been generated not from within but on the periphery, from jurisdictions where some degree of democratic transition has already been achieved. In Taiwan, which professes self-determination despite international recognition as a province of China, recent electoral developments have added to a sense of increasing political centrifugal momentum at the same time as bilateral economic integration with China has accelerated. In Hong Kong, a territory that reverted to Chinese sovereignty in 1997, unprecedented recent mass demonstrations in 2003–4 protesting proposed restrictions on civil liberties and too-measured progress towards direct elections took Beijing by surprise.

The nature and pace of political evolution in each area – China, Hong Kong and Taiwan – appears to be separate and uneven. Yet the uneasy linkage of highly disparate political systems has also meant developments in each jurisdiction can pose significant risks, direct or indirect, to the others. The political evolution of China influences its policy towards Taiwan and Hong Kong. Yet, just as developments in Taiwan influence the mainland, so do they affect the PRC's stance relative to Hong Kong. Over the long run, Beijing's capacity to resiliently accommodate and diplomatically respond to political change in each jurisdiction will be key to its ability to withstand inevitable peripheral challenges. At the same time, measured domestic political change may help to narrow somewhat political disparities with periphery jurisdictions in the long run. But, in this peculiar triangular arrangement, risks remain that miscalculation on anyone's part – Beijing, Hong Kong or Taipei – could prompt less measured actions, such as: forcible intervention, military action, mass protest or the declaration of independence. This would have serious implications for future political transitions in all entities.

TAIWAN

Historically the PRC has always faced challenges on its borders – separatist movements in Tibet and Xinjiang, disputes with India and the need to assure access to strategic resources and routes in the

South China Sea. But no other boundary association has posed the continuous threat of a major war over the last 55 years within a highly strained, richly ambiguous and highly nuanced relationship of coexistence. Taiwan's current status dates from 1949, when a government-in-exile was established under US auspices, in reaction to the CCP's victory on the mainland. While Taiwan asserts equal political status to China and mutually exclusive jurisdiction, China insists on a one-China policy whereby Taiwan will inevitably be absorbed into the mainland, and its right to ensure that process by force. In deference to the PRC's claims of sovereignty, few countries and international institutions recognise Taiwan as an independent state, but rather as a province of the mainland.[3] An uneasy peace is maintained across the 120-mile Taiwan Strait by virtue of the US assurance of Taiwan's defence via the 1979 Taiwan Relations Act. Some 2 million mainland Chinese migrated to Taiwan at the founding of the republic, yet generational change, intermarriage with long-term Taiwanese and greater openness to the West – as well as prohibitions on diplomatic exchanges, direct trade and travel, and direct communication on both sides – have moved much of the Taiwan populace away from straightforward identification with the mainland.

Consolidating economic ties, polarising political positions

Ongoing democratic evolution of Taiwan has posed an increasing challenge to the PRC government. In the late 1970s an informal opposition movement captured one-third of the votes in local elections and was allowed to compete in subsequent elections at both local and national levels. Beginning in the mid-1980s, the evolution of Taiwan's governing structures and its domestic political landscape have reflected recurrent constitutional reform, the designation of universal franchise for elections at all levels of government, legalisation of opposition parties, lifting of martial law, and emergence of a free press.[4] Key constitutional reforms clarified the divisions of power among branches of government, expanded democratic participation and strengthened the party system, contributing to a decline in strength of the ruling party and its legislative control.[5]

The 25-year process has been one of gradualism accompanied by stability, favoured by rapid and equitable growth, and the emergence of a sizable middle class amid profound economic transformation. Compared with China, both Taiwan's political starting point and subsequent evolution have been strikingly divergent. Unlike the CCP, the founding Kuomintang Party (KMT) did not begin from a stance of ideological opposition to democracy (see Pei, 1998). Instituting elections initially served to establish the KMT's popular legitimacy, but these then evolved into a legally sanctioned channel of competing for power. Not only did this contribute to the eventual decline in the KMT's influence: it also forced the government to open up national political institutions, such as the legislature, to direct election. Secondly, the coalescence of Taiwanese ethnic identity facilitated political mobilisation, allowing native Taiwanese to assume greater political power, culminating in the election of Chen Shui-bian of the opposition Democratic Progressive Party (DPP) to the presidency in 2000. At the same time, political discourse and Taiwanese public sentiment also moved away from the expectation of eventual reunification with the mainland (under a Taiwan government), towards greater support for democratic self-determination and in some cases advocacy of actual independence.

In spite of the profound incompatibility in the political positions of the mainland and Taiwan, rapid economic growth has proceeded in both countries within a context of relative regional stability. Even the absence of official government dialogue since 1995 has not fundamentally undermined accelerating cross-straits economic integration. Massive Taiwanese investment in the mainland has transformed the PRC into Taiwan's biggest trade partner (34.5% of exports), and production by Taiwanese-owned companies on the mainland has grown to represent two-thirds of Chinese information technology (IT) production (see Lardy, 2004). Since mid-2000 the accelerated migration of whole IT supply chains – basically original equipment manufacturing networks of suppliers and distributors – from Taiwan to Beijing, Shanghai, and mid- and south coastal China processing zones has integrated China into key areas of global IT production. China has rapidly grown to become Taiwan's primary destination for registered outward investment (53.7%), while Taiwanese companies are significant in mainland urban employment and generate an estimated 5% in mainland government revenues (see Cheng, 2004). And an estimated 1 million Taiwanese live and work on the mainland.

Questions of national sovereignty

The political risk Taiwan poses to the PRC appears to be less one of contesting China's political system or values, and more a challenge to the fundamental legitimacy of leadership as derived from a basic conviction regarding national sovereignty. For, in evaluating cross-straits risk, the importance of Taiwan to China cannot be underestimated.

In Beijing's eyes Taiwan is critically linked to a fundamental concept of national sovereignty and self-respect, as well as regime legitimacy (see Swaine, 2004). Furthermore, following the reversion of Hong Kong and Macao, Beijing regards the eventual reunification of Taiwan as the last piece of the puzzle, and as confirmation of its emergence as a great world power after its forced fragmentation by outsiders during the nineteenth century and a century of national vulnerability and perceived weakness. The PRC is less interested in direct territorial rule over the island than in avoiding the permanent loss of the island to independence, which the Beijing leadership believes would fundamentally undermine its authority. Such a development would also create an unfavourable precedent for separatist movements in Tibet, Xinjiang and Inner Mongolia. But China perceives implicit risks to its own internal stability if Taiwan were "lost" – an event that would fatally undermine the authority of Beijing leadership and the Communist Party's mandate, and potentially lead to social chaos. It believes these risks would be as great as or greater than the damages resulting from an armed conflict with Taiwan and the US. And Beijing would fight to avoid losing Taiwan if the leadership concluded that no other measures existed to halt an imminent declaration of independence, even if victory was uncertain.

A low but not insignificant risk of war

Military and strategic calculus would appear to dictate that the risk of war – that is, the likelihood that China would elect to forcibly intervene in Taiwan – is small. Historically the military superiority of both the US and Taiwan in relation to China has served as a significant deterrent. Recent assessments suggest that China remains two decades behind the US in terms of military technology and capability, although more than a decade of comprehensive military modernisation by the Chinese has profoundly narrowed the technological and capability gap between China and Taiwan. At the same time, cross-straits military confrontation would have exorbitant economic costs for China. Major casualties would include: delayed development of China's nascent IT industry – already a major contributor to GDP growth – which has been hugely dependent on Taiwanese expertise and investment; substantial disruption of Sino-American trade ties and investment; and a reduction in Chinese exports estimated at more than 14% (see Cheng Tun-jen, 2004). China would also severely damage its diplomatic ties with the US, which have improved due to joint efforts against terrorism and on China's leading role in multilateral negotiations with North Korea.

Yet, viewed through the perspective of leadership legitimacy, Taiwanese political developments in 2003–4 could pose an increasing potential direct threat to Beijing's authority, particularly if the Chinese leadership is not perceived by its people as taking a more forceful stance on Taiwan in the near term. During President Chen's first term the PRC largely turned its back on Taiwan, labelling Chen as a dangerous advocate of Taiwan independence. This strategy was one of ignoring Chen's diplomatic overtures and restricting Taiwan's diplomatic relations and participation in international forums and organisations, while encouraging bilateral trade and investment in an effort to increase the island's economic dependence on the mainland. With Sino-US relations improving after 2001, China also increasingly relied on the US to act as an intermediary to limit Taiwan activism. However, these approaches proved ineffectual in curbing what the Chinese leadership views as Taiwan's unacceptable inching towards independence.

Both the conduct of the 2003–4 presidential campaign and its unexpected result, the re-election of President Chen Shui-bian, are likely to have generated a keener sense of frustration and urgency regarding cross-straits policy on the part of Beijing. During the campaign President Chen advanced the unprecedented proposal of drafting a new constitution that would be directly approved by popular referendum in 2006 and thereby bypassing the opposition-dominated legislature. Beijing, which had maintained a hands-off stance up to that point, was taken by surprise. It viewed the proposal as an unambiguous step towards President Chen's inferred goal of permanently separating Taiwan from China. After the US pointedly warned Taipei against challenging the cross-straits status quo, President Chen proposed to hold referenda concurrent with the presidential election on largely symbolic statements regarding weapons acquisition and cross-strait negotia-tions. Subsequently, the referenda were found invalid in failing to achieve 50% voter participation. Nevertheless, the creation of a national referendum mechanism by the legislature and the actual holding of a vote were unprecedented in the history of Taiwan. Furthermore, the popular mechanism is particularly threatening to China in the suggestion of statehood implied by use of a referen-dum to resolve "national" issues and the potential creation of an avenue for democratic decision making that would circumvent existing processes.

Now, with the Taiwanese presidency "lost" and the more pro-China political opposition apparently fragmenting, China faces the unpalatable possibility that the pan-Green coalition could dominate upcoming legislative elections.[6] According to China this could enable President Chen to solidify control of the politi-cal system and move Taiwan more boldly towards independence – beginning with constitutional reform – in the remainder of his term. While this probably overstates Chen's independence ambi-tions, an outcome in which the governing party itself falls short of a legislative majority but secures a pan-Green majority in coali-tion with the Taiwan Solidarity Union (TSU) its ally over the last four years, potentially entails the greatest uncertainty for cross-straits relations and could strongly pressure China to define a harsher near-term stance. This is because the TSU could assume greater influence within the governing coalition given its swing vote position, an arrangement that would put greater pressure on the administration to adopt a more aggressive stance on Taiwan self-determination while also resisting greater economic integ-ration with China. A leading TSU figure recently stated that a three-year window of opportunity exists for the island to move for independence while China is "preoccupied" by domestic economic issues.

From the Taiwan perspective, legislative developments could support the possibility of more assertive initiatives on Taiwan iden-tity and self-determination. Perhaps as a result of Beijing's prior forbearance, there appears to be a widely held sense that PRC authorities will tolerate moves by Taiwan's leaders that are offi-cially denounced as unacceptable (see de Lisle, 2004). This opti-mism could be dangerous in encouraging moves that endanger the status quo. Conversely, if Taiwan activists conclude that the only means of securing continued autonomy in the face of the PRC's rising power and leverage is to push further towards formal independence, this strategy might be pursued even in the face of a substantial risk of conflict and a low likelihood of success.

Further out, cross-strait relations could be entering a new phase of heightened volatility and uncertainty. A clearer reading of political risk and its implication for sovereign ratings will be obtained only after 2004, when the outcomes of Taiwan and US elections are known. Nonetheless, it is likely that the terms and conditions of the cross-straits relationship and the response functions of both governments are changing, given the likelihood of rising domestic pressures on both the Chinese and Taiwanese leadership. In this increasingly sensitive situation, the potential for an escalation to armed conflict increases, as even a relatively modest shift in policy or stance risks creating the misconception that more significant changes are under way. How stable a new equilibrium is may depend increasingly on how skilfully Taiwan avoids miscalculation or Beijing resists misinterpretation.

HONG KONG

For China, the reversion of Hong Kong to the mainland under the one-country, two-systems arrangement bestows unparalleled benefits but poses no uncertain political perils as well. No other developing nation or formerly socialist regime has attempted to reintegrate a territory with such distinct political and social systems and dramatically different level of economic development. Yet Hong Kong represents perhaps the best laboratory for Beijing to figure out how to devolve authority to a local government and undertake controlled democratisation within a Chinese context. It is also potentially an intermediate stage in the mainland's political evolution. If Beijing can adroitly navigate acknowledging the democratic aspirations that exist among the Hong Kong people while pursuing political reform at a pace within Beijing's comfort zone, then the one-country, two-systems arrangement will have been proved a dazzling success. Ideally, this would also imply wholly preserving Hong Kong's strong judicial and legal institutions, and its civil liberties – and to the fullest extent possible recreating them on the mainland.

Hong Kong's Special Administrative Region (HKSAR) status

An understanding of Hong Kong's unique political status and its evolving political system is key to assessing the risks the territory poses to the mainland. Hong Kong's autonomy is guaranteed for the 50 years following 1997 within the one-country, two-systems framework, under the quasi-constitutional Basic Law that defines the territory's governing structure and relationship with China. HKSAR is vested with executive, legislative and judicial powers for territorial self-rule, while the carry-over of most laws previously in force during British rule preserve the territory's distinct status and character. Basic rights and freedoms (of speech, assembly, association, research and religious belief) are also guaranteed. The Basic Law calls for gradual political reform with the ultimate goal of universal suffrage, but it does not stipulate how or when such changes should take place.

HKSAR's political system is dominated by a powerful executive branch that is only partly counterbalanced by the Legislative Council (LegCo). Half of LegCo's 60 seats are elected by popular franchise, and the remainder by restricted franchise. Transparency of the bureaucracy is well established but accountability is diminished somewhat by an informal alliance between the government and business elite that has traditionally directed decision-making. The governing framework also lacks institutionalised outlets for dissent.

The Basic Law gives Hong Kong's Court of Final Appeal ultimate adjudication. But the Law grants the Standing Committee of the National People's Congress (NPCSC) in Beijing ultimate authority in interpreting and the sole power to amend the Basic Law. The NPCSC also has the right to invalidate laws in areas that touch upon Beijing's authority or the relationship between Beijing and Hong Kong.

Beijing has abided by the Basic Law and until recently has visibly interfered less in Hong Kong's affairs than prior to the territory's reversion to Chinese rule. China's interest in maintaining the autonomy and prosperity of Hong Kong – key to sustaining high foreign direct investment inflows, access to international capital flows and markets, and modernisation of the Chinese service sector – has been evident in its hands-off stance in economic and financial management, maintenance of rule of law and legal judgments. There have been some exceptions, primarily in the political realm, including the appointment of a replacement Provisional Legislature in 1997; the 1999 overturning by the NPCSC of a Court of Final Appeal decision on the right of abode (after the Hong Kong government appealed); and more subtle pressures on journalists to self-censor on topics of sensitivity to China or Hong Kong business interests.

Political transition in Hong Kong

Hong Kong possesses a curious mixture of many of the political institutions of a mature democracy, yet an incomplete democratic transition. One hundred and fifty-six years under British colonial rule established a strong rule of law tradition, judicial independence, press freedoms and an open market economy. Yet the political system was opened up to direct elections for local advisory institutions only in 1982 (see Pei, 1998). By then, existing social institutions and a wealthy, well-educated populace supported a stable political transition. Among the Hong Kong people, rising political mobilisation was galvanised by the prospect of 1997 and by the emergence of institutional channels for political participation. Indirect elections for the LegCo in 1985 brought into power many of the key political activists who now dominate the current democratic movement. Legislative activism during the mid-1980s introduced the notion of political accountability to the public.

While political reform slowed sharply in the wake of Tiananmen, a shift in British policy towards more overt support of democratic reforms proved important in expanding political participation. The protection of civil liberties was encoded in a Bill of Rights, the number of competitively elected LegCo seats was increased, the voting franchise enlarged, and LegCo's institutional identity enhanced. The 1990s also saw the emergence of full-fledged political parties and increased mobilisation of local intelligentsia.

Political events and risks

The risks to Hong Kong itself are clear: that the government's adherence to a "China line" or that Beijing's behind-the-scenes influence could gradually erode existing civil rights and pluralistic institutions, co-opt political interests, or slow its evolution towards a fuller democracy. But integrating HKSAR has also posed risks for the mainland. Hong Kong's free flow of ideas and porous border with China facilitate the flow of sensitive information to the mainland. As importantly, its open society and potential as a fundraising venue have raised concerns that it could be a staging ground for dissent and, furthermore, act as a springboard into the mainland. In this light Beijing has been shown to be highly sensitive to the potential for foreign support to political liberalisation within the territory.

Beijing's ultimate oversight of existing institutions assures considerable control over the pace of political reform within the territory. There is no real risk of HKSAR's being "lost" from China. But there is the potential for friction between the leadership and populace to be exacerbated when diverging opinions exist over the pace and nature of political liberalisation. Handled poorly, this could chip away at perceptions of the accountability and legitimacy of Hong Kong leadership. Poor management has the potential not only to foster increasing popular alienation with the local administration, but also to raise questions about the nature of the governing relationship between Hong Kong and Beijing.

Recent developments have shown how difficult it is for Beijing to anticipate and manage developments within an independent entity with a distinct political trajectory. In 2003–4, mass protests in Hong Kong evidenced widespread discontent with political decisions taken by the administration. During the summer of 2003 a 500,000-person demonstration against proposed "Article 23" anti-subversion and sedition legislation prompted Chinese President Hu to comment on his concern about political developments and to provide a warning that constitutional reform in the territory must be "orderly and gradual". The legislative proposals appeared largely geared to preventing violent insurrection and acts of terrorism, but potentially circumscribed individual liberties that were otherwise protected in the Basic Law. The protests also crystallised popular disaffection with Chief Executive Tung Chee-Hwa, for whom support had fallen following several years of poor economic performance and given perceptions of poor management of the SARS outbreak. Opposition to the administration was also reflected in strong gains for the Democratic Party in November 2003 local elections.

Against this backdrop the ongoing debate on Hong Kong's constitutional development had intensified, with calls for the next chief executive (CE) to be elected by universal suffrage.[7] Beijing abstained from intervention during the Article 23 demonstrations, but quickly made clear its opposition to accelerated electoral reform in Hong Kong with (a) a strident media campaign warning would-be reformers that the demands for democracy were unpatriotic;

(b) accusations of collusion between Hong Kong reformers and Taiwanese separatists; and (c) suggestions that foreign governments were involved in the push for accelerated electoral reform.

In early 2004 China's dispatch of legal scholars to the territory signalled to many its intent to direct HKSAR's political evolution more forcefully and openly, and perhaps an increasing anxiety about the potential for the democracy movement to spill over to the mainland. The NPCSC undertook an interpretation of Basic Law provisions as to selection of the CE and LegCo, as initiated by Beijing. The decision stipulated that the CE should report to the NPCSC as to the need to amend the selection, with the NPCSC making a decision in light of the "actual situation in Hong Kong and the need for gradual and orderly progress". In late April, after the CE recommended an amendment to the selection procedures, the NPCSC ruled out universal suffrage for choice of CE in 2007 and specified that the share of directly elected seats remain at 50% for the fourth term of LegCo, commencing in 2008. This effectively rules out major electoral reform until 2012. At the time of the April ruling the deputy secretary general of the NPCSC notably reiterated that "all powers of locality derive from the authorisation of the central authorities".

These decisions establish parameters within which political evolution in Hong Kong can occur. Recent developments in Taiwan appear to have left little room for Beijing's tolerance of faster political reform in Hong Kong. Yet the events in Hong Kong challenge the HKSAR government's already weak mandate and have the potential to further undermine the perceived legitimacy of the administration itself. The actual autonomy conferred under "one country, two systems" is also in question, although independence in economic and financial affairs has not been compromised and Beijing has not violated the Basic Law. It is not inconceivable that discontent with the HKSAR government could increasingly be extended towards Beijing.

High participation in the recent LegCo elections of September 2004 suggests the increasing political engagement of the populace. Yet pro-democracy parties may have seen their political leverage moderated somewhat.[8] This could imply that, for the moment, Beijing may gain a respite from popular pressures in the territory. Ideally, this would provide Chinese leadership with the opportunity to adopt a more moderate stance and constructively engage the Hong Kong democrats in collaborating on a roadmap for the territory's political evolution (see Hung and Swaine, 2004).

CONCLUSION

In the space of a generation China has transformed from an inward-looking, poor and centrally controlled economy to a market-oriented one that is dynamic, increasingly open and globally influential. In contrast, political reform has been much more measured, mediated by an authoritarian leadership that has achieved increasing resilience of the ruling framework while still curtailing the development of pluralism in both governance and civil society.

China has seen a recent diminution of political risk associated with leadership succession, through the institutionalisation of advancement and succession processes. These developments have been echoed in decision making that is more collective and less ideological, with positive implications for policymaking. Recent efforts to make the party more open and responsive to a wider range of social interests, and to enhance government accountability could also shore up governability.

The regime nonetheless faces huge challenges. Market-oriented economic reform has been key to the regime's past ability to deflect emerging political demands and maintain stability. Yet sustaining future economic dynamism will increasingly require addressing corruption, ensuring greater transparency and implementing the rule of law – and, by implication, an increasing curtailment of the CCP's power (see Pei, 2002a and 2002b). Economic restructuring and greater openness have also generated more diverse interests in Chinese society. With few political channels for representation, the potential for political alienation may be increasing, especially for those segments that have been economically marginalised.

It is not inevitable that a political transition of China's authoritarian regime will occur. Over the space of another generation it is possible to foresee China achieving a full separation of party and state; the emergence of limited pluralism; proliferation of a vibrant and relatively free press; and increasing official transparency, within the existing framework. Both recent leadership statements and internal experimentation suggest that this is a path of acceptable liberalisation, which would begin to bring its political structures and institutions more in line with existing economic and social settings, while maintaining the party's rule.

However, China's political evolution will also reflect a complex path dependence, which remains strongly sensitive to internal and external developments, and increasingly the events in Taiwan and Hong Kong. The last two years have shown that predicting and managing political developments in these autonomous jurisdictions has been especially difficult for China, perhaps because of an imperfect understanding of local popular sentiment or complex domestic political dynamics. Yet because of China's concept of national sovereignty – a unified Greater China – all three entities are yoked together in a strained linkage. Whether these highly disparate political systems will converge naturally or forcibly, or remain separate and relatively independent, will depend much on China's ability to gradually undertake political reform at home, as well as its capacity to resiliently accommodate and diplomatically respond to political change in Taiwan and Hong Kong.

1 For in-depth discussion of how resilience has been built into China's regime, see Nathan (2003).
2 Leadership succession is discussed in detail by Wu (2003). See also Nathan (2003) and Li (2002).
3 In 1945 upon its surrender Japan ceded Taiwan to the Republic of China to administer, pending transfer by treaty to Chinese sovereignty, which never formally occurred.
4 Reporters Without Borders rated Taiwan's press the third most free in Asia in 2002.
5 A good summary of Taiwan's democratic transition is provided in Pei (1998).
6 This coalition comprises the DPP, TSU and Taiwan Independence Party, made up primarily by Hoklo (Taiwanese whose families migrated before 1895), who range in view from embracing status quo to advocating lawful independence.
7 The Basic Law allows for changing the method of choosing the CE from 2007 and of selecting members for the 4th term of LegCo starting in 2008, although power to appoint the CE unambiguously remains with Beijing.
8 These comprise principally the Democratic Party, Frontier, Association for Democracy and People's Livelihood, and Article 45 Concern Group.

REFERENCES

Cheng Tun-jen, 2004, "Doing Business with China: Taiwan's Three Main Concerns", Woodrow Wilson Asia Program Special Report 118, pp. 12–18.

de Lisle, J., 2004, "Fifteen Years After Tiananmen: Persistence, Memory and Change in China", Foreign Policy Research Institute e-note, June.

Dreyer, J. T., 2004, "The Limits to China's Growth", *Orbis*, **48(2)**, pp. 233–46.

Fewsmith, J., 2004, "Elite Changes and Prospects for Reform", transcript of presentation at "The Future of Political Reform in China", Carnegie Endowment for International Peace, 29 January.

Hung, V., and M. Swaine, 2004, "Hong Kong's Legislative Elections: Implications for Democratisation in Hong Kong and U.S.–China Relations", Carnegie Endowment, URL: http://www.carnegieendowment.org/files/Hong_Kong.pdf.

Lardy, N., 2004, "The Taiwan Presidential Elections", presentation for Brookings/Center for Strategic and International Studies/US–Taiwan Business Council, 6 May.

Li, C., 2002, "China's Leadership Succession and Its Implications: Trends and Paradoxes", written testimony prepared for the US–China Security Review Commission's public hearing, September 23.

Nathan, A. J., 2003, "Authoritarian Resilience", *Journal of Democracy*, **14(1)**, pp. 6–17.

Pei, M., 1998, "Democratisation in the Greater China Region", *Access Asia*, pp. 5–40, July.

Pei, M., 2002a, "Beijing Drama: China's Governance Crisis and Bush's New Challenge", Carnegie Endowment Policy Brief, November.

Pei, M., 2002b, "China's Governance Crisis", *Foreign Affairs*, pp. 96–109, September/October.

Qiu, X., 2002, quoted in *Zhongguo Xinwen She* (China News Service, Beijing), translated in FBIS, 21 October.

Swaine, M., 2004, "Trouble in Taiwan", *Foreign Affairs*, **83(2)** (March/April), URL: http://www.foreignaffairs.org/20040301faessay83205/michael-d-swaine/trouble-in-taiwan.html.

World Bank, 2004, *World Development Indicators* (Washington, DC: World Bank).

Wu, Yu-Shan, 2003, "Jiang and After: Technocratic Rule, Generational Replacement, and Re-emergence of Gerontocracy", paper presented at the Conference on Prospects for China's Political Future: The Sixteenth Communist Party Congress of the People's Republic of China, Hoover Institution, Stanford, January 24–5.

10

Structural Weaknesses and Country Risk: The Case of Brazil

Christian Stracke

CreditSights

The last two decades have been among the most turbulent in Brazil's modern financial and economic history. A default on the public debt, a desperate period of hyperinflation, a new currency that was intended to conquer inflation but led to a painful devaluation, and, most recently, a financial panic in the months before the election of President Lula in October 2002, has led Brazilians and foreign observers to wonder when – and if – the recurring cycle of financial crises will end. The short answer to this question is that the crises could end if Brazil could significantly increase its long-term economic growth rates. From 1981 to 2003, Brazil registered compounded GDP growth of just 1.95% per year, well below the rate of growth of the labour force and far below growth rates achieved not just in Brazil's Asian peer economies but also in most developed economies. Low economic growth has had the predictable pernicious effects of keeping tax revenues – and therefore the funds to cover basic necessities such as public infrastructure, healthcare and education – on a path of substandard growth, breeding poverty and chronic unemployment, and undermining investor confidence in the government's ability to meet its commitments on the public debt.

Simply stating that low economic growth is the problem is not, however, an especially useful answer. More important is the question of what has been driving such low economic growth for so long. Brazil seems to have an answer for everyone on this question: high real interest rates, a history of hyperinflation, an inefficient tax system, a grossly wasteful public-sector social security system, a chaotic political system – all of these are factors behind Brazil's economic malaise. But lurking behind the myriad problems that afflict Brazil is the gnawing question of labour productivity, or, more precisely, the persistent lack of productivity growth in Brazil. Productivity is, after all, the driver of economic development and is therefore one of the most important cornerstones of sovereign creditworthiness over the long term. Productivity, along with population growth, drives GDP higher, and the rate of GDP growth can, if high, help to guarantee a sovereign's ability to service its liabilities, while a low GDP growth rate can confound the very best intentions to maintain a prudent fiscal stance, as the world saw all too clearly in Argentina's default and devaluation in late 2001.

Productivity is, then, both the ailment and the cure in Brazil. As long as productivity remains low, Brazil's cycle of recurring financial crises will continue, but, if Brazil can solve its decades-long productivity problem, it could also put an end to the recurring crises. This chapter begins with a review of Brazil's historical problems with generating productivity growth and then looks for some explanations behind the low, or even negative, productivity growth rates that Brazil has endured for most of the last two decades. The second part of the chapter extends our findings on Brazil's productivity to try to generate a realistic forecast for long-term GDP growth rates, and discusses what that long-term growth rate will imply for Brazil's debt sustainability. Finally, the chapter turns to the political challenge Brazil must face in order to implement far-reaching economic reforms that could create the conditions for a significant increase in its long-term productivity growth rates.

THE HISTORICAL RECORD

Productivity growth in Brazil has collapsed ever since the early 1980s, and even now is showing no signs of turning around. Between 1970 and 1979, the boom years for Brazil's economy, productivity growth rates averaged an incredible 5.2% per year as the economy was in its final stages of transformation from a largely agrarian one to the diversified economy of manufacturing, services and agriculture that it is today. Once that transformation was largely complete by the 1980s, however, the level of productivity growth collapsed, and annual change in productivity was negative at −0.2% through that lost decade. The period since 1990 has been little better. After steep declines in productivity in the early 1990s as the economy reeled under hyperinflation, productivity has recovered marginally, averaging 0.0% change since 1990 and averaging just 0.25% per year over 2001–02. Even with the relative increase in productivity growth since the collapse in the 1980s and early 1990s, productivity growth is still nowhere near what it has been in the US or even the EU, developed economies where one would expect that productivity gains would be more difficult to generate than in the still developing Brazilian economy.

To understand how productivity growth has been so low, one must consider that nearly all economic growth in Brazil since the early 1980s can be attributed to increases in the economically active population, not to investments in the stock of physical capital or in investments in human capital. Between 1981 and 2002, Brazil's economy grew by an accumulated 63% in real terms, or roughly 2.25% per year. During that same period, Brazil's economically active population – that share of the total population either working or actively seeking work – grew by a total of 67%, or roughly 2.36% per year. The labour force grew as the demographic boom of the 1950s and 1960s worked its way into the population of potential workers, and as women who were previously not considered part of the labour force increasingly began to seek work away from the home. The economy has rebounded somewhat in 2004 and growth should remain above 3.0% in 2005, but that growth is largely making up for abysmal growth rates in recent years, and has been driven in large part by export growth, not by domestic demand.

Note that the productivity data presented here are from CreditSights calculations and may be somewhat worse than other productivity estimation series available for Brazil because we use estimates on the economically active population, not simply the total working-age population as a proxy for the labour force. Using the economically active population estimates from the International Labor Organization (ILO), as we have, generates more realistic productivity data, because by simply using the working-age population and assuming constant workforce participation over time the series excludes the gradual secular increase in the female workforce participation rate that has been evident in

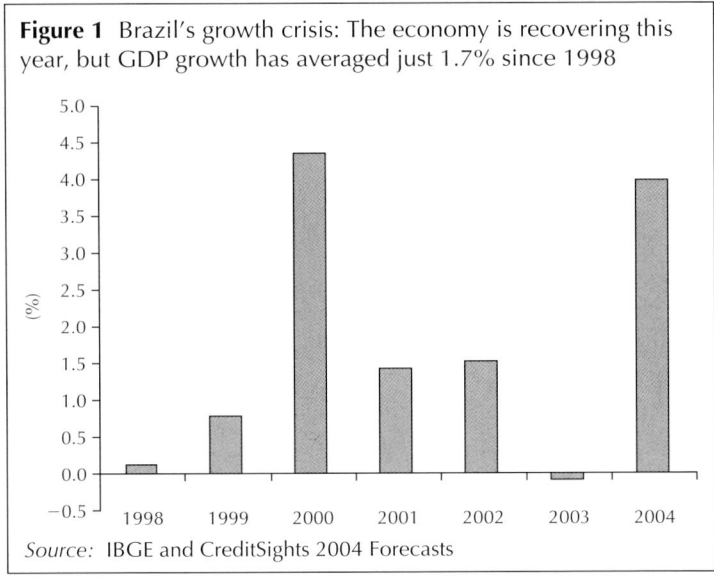

Figure 1 Brazil's growth crisis: The economy is recovering this year, but GDP growth has averaged just 1.7% since 1998

Source: IBGE and CreditSights 2004 Forecasts

most societies over the last half-century. To generate these productivity data, we have divided GDP by the economically active population as estimated by the ILO (we have interpolated points between the five-year ILO estimations), and we have assumed that the employment rate has remained constant as a share of the total labour force, and that hours worked per worker has remained constant over the span covered in this series. The assumption that hours worked has remained constant may appear controversial, but we would note that the most recent estimate for hours worked in Brazil's 2000 census shows that the average work week stood at 42.1 hours per week in 2000. Even if one assumes that the work week stood at 45 hours per week in 1965, our productivity data will have only understated productivity gains by 0.2%, with much of that understatement probably coming in the 1960s and 1970s. ILO hours worked data for Brazil begin only in 1990, but those data show little, if any, change in the work week since 1990.

The total factor productivity (TFP) mystery

Perhaps the greatest mystery in the study of productivity in Brazil is the mystery surrounding fluctuations in TFP. TFP is often considered as "true" productivity, because it reflects the efficiency with which labour utilises capital in order to generate output. Total labour productivity is essentially the combination of increases in the stock of physical capital (building roads, ports, factories and so on) plus increases in labour's efficient use of that capital stock, or TFP. TFP can be a result of technological change, and it can also stem from improved worker training. The relationship between the two sources of TFP is the subject of heated debate among growth economists, but, because technological change can often be assumed to be exogenous, especially in developing countries that often depend on technological innovations from developed countries, the segment of TFP related to education and worker training is often the subject of the most interest in development economics. In Brazil's case, unusually low spending on education should be far more of a concern for investors and for policymakers than it is, as Brazil ranks extremely low among its Latin American peers (not to mention its EM peers in Eastern Europe and East Asia) in terms of university education. Brazil's level of enrolment in university as a percentage of the eligible age group ranks alongside Honduras and El Salvador, far behind regional leaders.

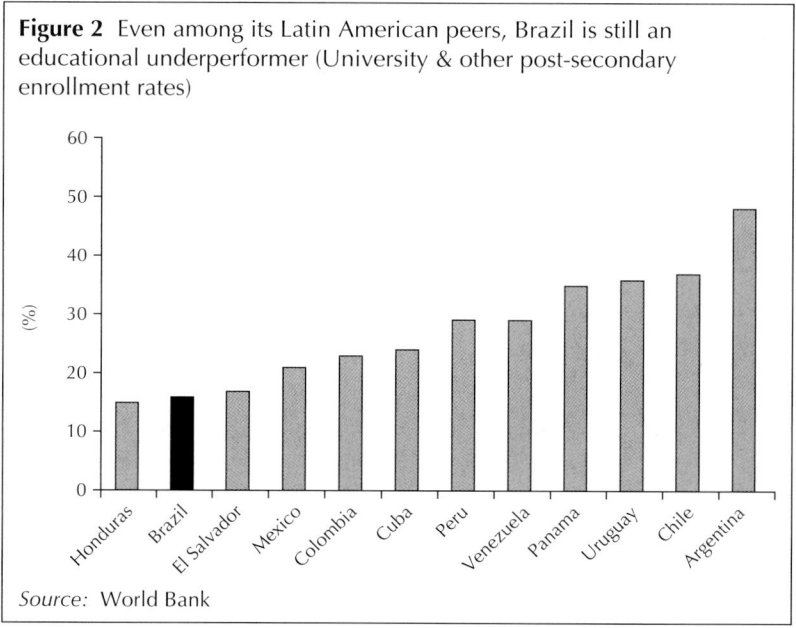

Figure 2 Even among its Latin American peers, Brazil is still an educational underperformer (University & other post-secondary enrollment rates)

Source: World Bank

A lack of investment in advanced training has meant that Brazil's record with TFP has been nothing short of disastrous over the previous several decades. In a study published by the World Bank (see Fajnzylber and Lederman, 1999), TFP was shown to have fallen in nearly all Latin American economies in the period from 1950 to 1995, including in Brazil. TFP fell by an incredible 1.3% per year during that period, suggesting that something is so amiss in Brazil's economy that labour is growing progressively less efficient in utilising the economy's capital stock, at a time when one would have expected rapid technological progress to show TFP on the rise, as it has been in most developed nations and in East Asia. The fall in TFP is by no means unique to Brazil within the region, but what is exceptional about Brazil, however, was that, whereas most Latin economies showed TFP growth during periods of "reform" (periods during which the government was liberalising the economy) and TFP declines during non-reform periods, Brazil somehow managed to exhibit lower TFP during reform periods and higher TFP during periods characterised by lack of reform. During periods of no reform, Brazil's TFP increased 1.5% per year more than (or fell 1.5% less than, depending on the year) during periods characterised by economic liberalisation.

The fact that change in TFP has been significantly worse in Brazil during periods of economic liberalisation raises serious questions about the efficacy of public policy on the problem of low or negative productivity growth. One might assume that periods of economic liberalisation have been accompanied by periods of relative fiscal austerity, as reform-minded governments have often proposed reforms as a way to emerge out of economic crises (as was the case in the Real Plan, for instance), and those crises have simultaneously demanded fiscal austerity. Fiscal austerity could mean less government spending on education, a critical component of TFP growth. More generally, it is conceivable that an interventionist public sector in Brazil has historically been instrumental in diffusing technological improvements into the economy, although such a hypothesis is clearly controversial and would require a level of microanalysis that is probably impossible given the lack of reliable historical data on the level of individual sectors of the economy.

The capital formation shortfall

Whatever the reasons for the counterintuitive disparity in TFP change between reform and no-reform periods, the chronic decline in TFP remains a depressing fact of life for Brazil. What little productivity growth there has been over the last several decades appears to have been the product of increases in the stock of physical capital: workers themselves may be less efficient in utilising physical capital, but at least there is more physical capital to work with. On this front, however, Brazil has seemingly run into a brick wall for much of the last twelve years. Between 1965 and 1989, gross capital formation (domestic plus foreign investment in the capital stock before depreciation losses) averaged 22.4% of GDP. These years of relatively high capital formation as a share of GDP were consistent with a period of relatively high productivity growth as the stock of physical capital rose: between 1965 and 1989, annual labour productivity rose by 2.6% per year, a respectable amount consistent with a fairly healthy GDP growth rate. Since 1990, however, capital formation as a share of GDP has suffered a steep decline, falling to 19.5% of GDP. The drop from 22.4% of GDP to 19.5% may not appear very significant, but, when one assumes that net capital formation (gross less depreciation) is about 12% of

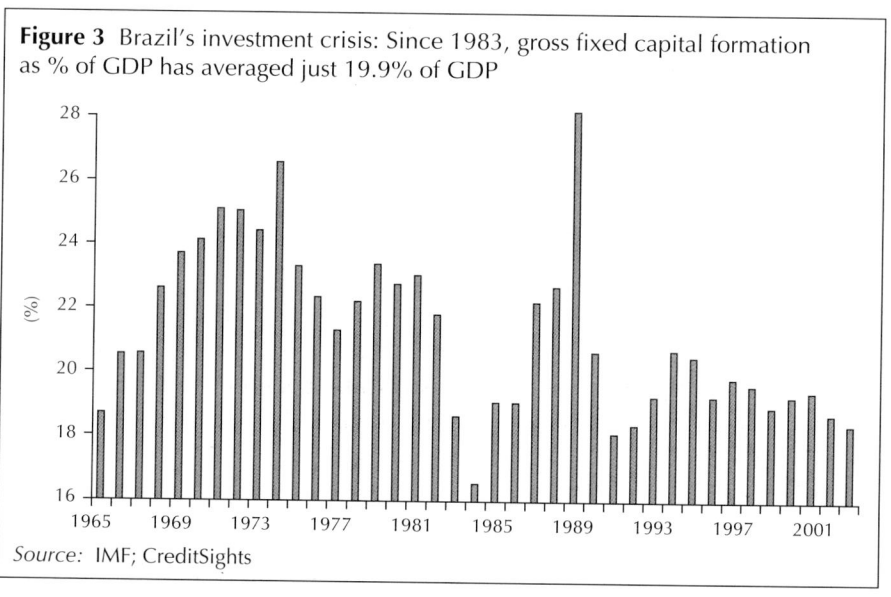

Figure 3 Brazil's investment crisis: Since 1983, gross fixed capital formation as % of GDP has averaged just 19.9% of GDP

Source: IMF; CreditSights

GDP less than the gross figure, depending on the depreciation rate assumed, the drop is much more acute than may first appear.

The steep drop in gross capital formation as a share of GDP in the 1990s and the first few years of this decade is especially troublesome given the unprecedented rise in foreign direct investment (FDI) in Brazil during the past 10 years. FDI held steady at nearly 1.0% of GDP through much of the 1970s and early 1980s, then fell precipitously during the crisis years of 1986–93. Since then, however, FDI has soared to around 5% of GDP, although a likely drop in FDI and a stronger exchange rate this year will probably push FDI/GDP closer to 4%. The increase in FDI/GDP has occurred alongside the steep drop in capital formation, leaving one to wonder how total capital formation as a share of GDP can have declined so much at a time of an unprecedented surge in foreign investment capital.

There are some possible explanations for the counterintuitive trend of higher FDI and lower capital formation, but none of the explanations are very satisfying. FDI is not exactly the same as foreign investment in physical capital; purchases of Brazilian corporations by foreign firms are counted as FDI, even though the foreign firm may commit no foreign capital towards capital formation. FDI may also be high in part because the public sector has progressively divested itself of state-owned firms, which would mean lower public-sector investment in physical capital and higher foreign investment. Still, neither of these explanations can explain the massive drop in domestic investment in capital formation. First, foreign purchases of Brazilian firms does not necessarily imply that those foreign firms will pump new cash into capital formation, but in general one would expect that capital investment would follow the initial purchase of the Brazilian firm. Second, the public sector may have divested many state-owned enterprises, but one would expect that those formerly state-owned companies would still need investments in physical capital, whether they are owned by the state, by Brazilian private sector shareholders or by foreign companies. Public-sector divestment should not have any effect on total domestic investment in capital formation.

Finding the true cause behind the drop in capital formation is not within the scope of this analysis, but we suspect that a combination of tight fiscal austerity plus an extended period of high real interest rates is to blame. The fiscal austerity that characterised the admin-istration of President Cardoso entailed often difficult contractions in public-sector investment spending, largely because investment expenditures are one of the few flexible expenditure items in the Brazilian budget. That fiscal austerity continues under the Lula gov-ernment, and if anything the use of cuts in investment spending in order to maintain high primary surpluses appears to be more pro-nounced under this government than it was under the Cardoso government, although improved tax receipts in 2004 have helped restore some of the cuts to investment spending. High real interest rates, meanwhile, make private-sector investment unrealistic, because few companies can hope to generate returns on invest-ments in physical capital sufficient to service the double-digit real interest rates that have prevailed in Brazil through most of the period since 1994. Even after the slow disinflation enjoyed since October 2002, real one-year interest rates remain above 11%. So long as the public sector remains unable to ramp up investment spend-ing, and so long as the private sector finds Brazil's real interest rates prohibitively expensive, even FDI inflows of 5% of GDP will not be enough to generate the total capital formation Brazil needs in order to drive productivity growth higher.

MODELLING THE FUTURE

The first section of this chapter established, all too depressingly, that productivity gains have been minimal in Brazil for much of the last two decades. The economy has grown as workers have entered the labour force, but worker productivity, whether through higher skills or through greater access to capital to use in production, has defied expectations and registered disappointingly low gains. In this second section, we apply our analysis of labour productivity to a long-term forecast of economic growth in Brazil. With productiv-ity growth remaining low, both because investment is insufficient and because education is lacking, our growth model forecasts a long-term GDP growth rate of just 2.3% per year through the rest of the decade and beyond. We then apply the results of the growth model to CreditSights' debt sustainability model and find, not sur-prisingly, that a growth rate of 2.3% implies a rapidly deteriorating credit profile as deficits outstrip economic growth. Finally, we dis-cuss potential remedies to the lack of growth, but none of those remedies is particularly realistic without wholesale change in public policy. Against a backdrop of chronically low potential economic growth and, ultimately, an unsustainable debt profile, Brazil must work against the clock to implement a full range of reforms in order to jump-start a long-awaited recovery in productivity growth.

The growth model

Given our understanding about the lack of productivity growth in Brazil, we have devised a GDP growth model to try to find the future path of economic growth given sluggish productivity growth. We have used the generally accepted Cobb–Douglas production function model, and where output is a function of labour and fixed capital inputs, where increases in output are determined by the elasticities of output with respect to increases in inputs. The model and the assumptions used are as follows:

$$Y = \beta_1 \times X_2^{\beta_2} \times X_3^{\beta_3}$$

Where Y = output (GDP)
X_2 = labour input (economically active population)
X_3 = capital input (stock of non-residential fixed capital)
β_2 = elasticity of output re : labour
β_3 = elasticity of output re : capital

The initial stock of fixed productive capital
In order for the production function to operate, we had to derive an estimate for the initial stock of fixed productive capital for the beginning of our data series in 1965. The lack of quality data has forced us to use developed-country averages as a proxy for the initial stock; we found that the ratio of fixed non-residential capital (essentially equipment and structures) averaged approximately 115% of GDP in the US between 1940 and 1998, and prior to the depression (during which time the K/GDP ratio soared as GDP fell) stood slightly higher at 130% of GDP. We took the 115% of GDP ratio from the US and applied it to the beginning of our time series for Brazil starting in 1965. We also found that the share of total net fixed investment going to non-residential fixed capital was relatively constant in the US at 33% of total investment.

Because of the lack of disaggregated Brazil fixed-investment data, we have assumed that a similar share of total net investment in Brazil has been directed to non-residential investment throughout our survey period.

The capital depreciation rate
After we derived an estimate for the initial stock of non-residential fixed capital, we needed to find an estimate for the depreciation rate in order to find the net increase in the capital stock, given the lack of comprehensive fixed investment data in Brazil. We have resorted again to using the experience in the relatively data-rich US to find an estimate for Brazil. The US saw 8% net depreciation through most of the era since 1929 where data are available, and we have used that 8% average in this Brazil growth model. Note that the 8% per year depreciation rate on non-residential fixed capital used in this model is close to that used in a recent Banco Central do Brasil study (see Kfoury Muinhos and Lago Alves, 2003). This study found inventory depreciation to be 8.6% and extrapolated that rate on to capital goods as well. We believe a slightly lower depreciation rate is more appropriate given the fact that non-residential structures should depreciate at a lower rate than the goods inventories the Kfoury Muinhos and Lago Alves study surveyed. Assuming an 8% depreciation rate, we find net non-residential fixed investment to have averaged just 2.7% of GDP per year during the post-Real Plan era since 1994.

TFP component
We should also note that we do not include a TFP variable in the equation, primarily because there does not appear to have been any measurable growth in TFP in Brazil since at least the late 1970s. As we discussed in the first part of this chapter, accumulated productivity growth has been essentially zero between 1978 and 2002. During this time, the stock of non-residential fixed capital has risen as a share of GDP, suggesting that TFP may have actually decreased since the late 1970s given that labour productivity (or the ratio of workers to GDP) remained stagnant while the stock of fixed capital has increased relative to GDP. For simplicity's sake, then, we simply assume that TFP is zero and is not a factor in the production function.

Slower labour force growth going forward
In building the Brazil growth model, we assume that the growth in the labour force will remain significantly slower throughout this decade than it was in the 1970s, 1980s and 1990s. The labour force grew by 3.4% per year in the 1970s, slipped to 3.2% per year in the 1980s, then slipped again to 1.9% in the 1990s. Using forecasts from the ILO, we assume that the growth rate in the labour force will average just 1.2% from 2001–10.

Continued low net investment rates
Another main assumption we use in extrapolating our model's results on to GDP growth rates between now and 2010 is that net fixed investment will remain low as a share of GDP. We take the 2.85% average annual growth rate in the stock of non-residential fixed capital between 1994 and 2002 (the post-Real Plan era) and assume that that rate prevails over the rest of the decade. This assumption is, if anything, relatively generous, given that Brazil enjoyed a windfall of foreign-investment-related fixed investment during that period. If anything, reduced foreign-investment inflows and the diminished capacity of the public sector to finance capital investment would suggest that the growth in the stock of productive fixed capital would be lower going forward. We assume, however, that the partial structural reforms introduced by President Lula will be approved to some degree, and that those reforms will help compensate for the downdraft in foreign and public-sector investment through improved domestic confidence and, potentially, higher net investment rates from the private sector.

Applying to the model our assumptions that (1) the labour force will grow by just over 1% per year and (2) that the stock of fixed capital will grow at the same rate seen since the advent of the Real Plan in 1994, we find that Brazil's GDP growth rate should average just 2.3% per year through 2010. Thereafter, the growth rate will depend on the future course of the growth in the labour supply, but if one assumes that growth in the labour force continues to decline to, say, 0.9% per year, expected GDP growth would be just 2.1% per year.

The model's results
Given the results of our production function for Brazil GDP, we find long-term potential GDP growth to be just 2.3% per year. Not

surprisingly, our model shows a very high degree of reliability, with an R-square of 0.97; because GDP (Y) is by definition a function of labour (X_1) and capital (X_2) inputs, the high R-square of the model is understandable. The 2.3% long-term GDP growth rate is derived from the assumptions outlined above, as well as a relaxed assumption: constant returns to scale. One of the most important results of our model is the fact that Brazil's economy has exhibited increasing returns to scale. In building our model, we have relaxed the assumption usually employed – following the Solow growth model for the US – that economies exhibit constant returns to scale. In other words, the Solow model and many similar growth models assume that, if the amount of both labour and capital increases by 1%, GDP will also increase by 1%. In mathematical terms, a model displaying constant returns to scale would fix the elasticity variables β_2 and β_3 where $\beta_3 = 1 - \beta_2$. If, however, $\beta_2 + \beta_3 < 1$, the economy would show decreasing returns to scale; and if $\beta_2 + \beta_3 > 1$, the economy would show increasing returns to scale.

In Brazil's case, our initial suspicion was that its economy would display decreasing returns to scale, because we guessed that structural problems in the economy would mean that increases in labour and/or capital would be inefficiently utilised. Our model, however, shows just the opposite: Brazil's economy shows increasing returns to scale, meaning that a 1% increase in inputs generates more than 1% in output. Returns to increases in fixed capital appear to be the source of Brazil's increasing returns to scale, because the model shows β_2, the elasticity of output with respect to the labour supply, to be 0.43 while β_3, the elasticity with respect to the supply of capital, is 0.62.

Implications for debt sustainability
Applying our forecast for 2.3% GDP growth to CreditSights' Brazil debt sustainability model yields, not surprisingly, a thoroughly gloomy outlook for Brazil's debt profile over the next several years. We assume a structural central government primary surplus of 2.45% of GDP, but that primary surplus is eroded over time by continued increases in the social security deficit, the trajectory of which is only partially improved by the current social security reform proposal. The social security deficit continues to grow as a percentage of GDP, both because of the limited nature of the recent

social security reform (which does not address the growing deficits in the state-subsidised private sector pension system, for instance), and because GDP will grow less quickly than is envisioned in most official projections of the social security system's future deficits. Leaving our assumptions about the path of the exchange rate and domestic interest rates unchanged, we find that the 2.3% GDP growth rate forecast effectively dooms Brazil to an unsustainable debt profile. Under the scenario where Brazil's long-term potential GDP growth rate does not change from the 2.3% we have calculated, the country's central-government-modified gross liabilities rise to 100% of GDP in 2008 and hit 150% of GDP in 2014. To state the obvious, no bondholder is going to be willing to lend to Brazil once debt/GDP rises to 100% of GDP and is on track to top 150% of GDP.

REMEDIES: ALL EYES ON INVESTMENT SPENDING

The results of our growth model and its application to our debt sustainability model are grim, to say the least, but they are by no means cast in stone. Given our assumptions on future growth in the labour force and the stock of productive fixed capital, the historical behaviour of the Brazilian economy suggests that growth will be no more than 2.3% per year. But a different set of assumptions could still put Brazil on track to more robust growth, especially if investment spending could rise and/or investment in human capital could increase.

On the first point, we would note that the fact that Brazil's economy has displayed increasing returns to fixed investment suggests that an improvement in Brazil's investment rate could have significant results in terms of economic growth. By our calculations, every 0.1% increase in the annual growth rate of the stock of non-residential fixed capital would yield a 0.06% increase in the GDP growth rate, independent of any change in the labour supply. Given that net fixed investment is depressingly low by historical standards in Brazil, a return to investment levels seen in the 1970s and 1980s could generate much higher GDP growth rates than the 2.3% per year our model predicts given our assumptions. If the annual growth rate in the stock of fixed capital were to rise from our assumed 2.85% per year to 4.9%, the level prevailing during the 1980s (the supposedly "lost" decade), GDP growth could average 3.5%, or roughly the amount by which most official debt-sustainability projections assume the economy will grow in the long term. If Brazil were somehow able to return to 1970s levels of investment (with 6.2% growth in the capital stock per year), GDP growth could average 4.3% per year.

Generating higher levels of net investment may be much easier said than done, however. The list of structural impediments to investment is too long to describe in detail in this chapter, but a few major impediments stand out. First, the problem of creditor rights appears to be a chronic disincentive to investment in Brazil. Brazil's bankruptcy law, heavily weighted in favour of the debtor, especially if that debtor is a small or medium-size firm, has made banks and other lenders increasingly wary of providing the funds necessary to finance many private-sector investments. Meaningful reform of the bankruptcy law was to have been a hallmark of the Lula presidency, but, at the time of writing, the bankruptcy reform remains with Congress, a sacrifice of the political struggle between Lula and Brazil's opposition parties.

Second, the public sector cannot be counted on as a driver of investment spending any time this decade. If Brazil is to be able to avoid default in the long term, it will, at a minimum, have to maintain a consolidated primary surplus (central government plus states, municipalities, and public companies) above 4.25% of GDP for the indefinite future. That fiscal constraint makes increased public spending on infrastructure impossible to finance through deficit spending. The public sector could alter the structure of its expenditures away from current spending (especially on government workers' wages and pensions) and towards increased capital spending, but this option seems unrealistic at best. The recent disagreement over President Lula's hesitant reform of the public-sector social security system makes wholesale change in government spending – through firing government workers, cutting real wages and implementing draconian cuts in pension spending – appear to be wishful thinking. Finally, growing deficits in the overall social security system (even after this year's reform, given the widening gap in the INSS private-sector pension system) will, if anything, tend to reduce the public sector's capacity to invest in capital projects as the decade unfolds. We discuss the deficit in the social security system in more detail below.

Third, Brazil cannot expect a windfall of foreign investment spending in the coming years, even if structural reforms provide a moderate improvement in confidence among foreign investors. For one thing, the initial wave of investments following privatisation in the 1990s is now complete. Those foreign companies that, having already upgraded a privatised company in Brazil, might consider further increasing production there will have no small number of reasons to think twice about expansion. Brazil's severe electricity shortages in 2001 have been addressed by only modest investment and slower-than-expected economic growth; any significant upswing in growth could run into the brick wall of electricity shortages all over again, and fear of brownouts will remain a compelling disincentive to investment. The seemingly arbitrary nature of Brazil's justice system will also warn potential foreign investors away from fixed investment. Already wary of judicial populism following the situation in Argentina, foreign investors may take the recent ruling in a Rio de Janeiro court that privatised telephone companies could not raise their rates according to the contractually defined formula as a sign of Argentina-style judicial despotism in Brazil. FDI in Brazil should remain around US$12 billion for the next several years, but we doubt that FDI will return to US$20 billion levels and above without considerable structural change.

TFP growth: how realistic is it?
One variable we have not included in our growth model (for reasons described above) is the potential for growth in TFP, or the efficiency with which labour utilises capital. It is incorrect to claim that there has been no TFP growth in Brazil over the last few decades – clearly, certain sectors and certain industries have enjoyed increased labour efficiencies as technology and some improved education has translated into greater TFP. On average, however, the limited TFP growth that has occurred in some sectors has been offset by no growth (or even declines) in TFP in other sectors. As poorly educated workers enter the labour force, many Brazilian workers have ended up in low-skilled or no-skilled jobs in the informal sector, where they may be even less productive in terms of contribution to total economic output than were their parents in a more agrarian Brazil a generation ago. The net effect, therefore, has been efficiencies in finance, communications, and

certain manufacturing sectors offset by inefficiencies in many service and potentially even some manufacturing sectors. Note that Brazil's official GDP data include the informal economy (to an admittedly imperfect degree), so the GDP numbers used in generating our growth model should capture the effect of growth in the informal sector.

Going forward, improvements in education (both of the young and continuing education for adults) would be needed to significantly increase labour efficiency across all sectors. Again, however, Brazil faces structural impediments to change on this front as well, primarily through the fiscal constraint. The TFP problem is thus a catch-22: Brazil cannot increase education expenditures (and thereby raise GDP growth rates) so long as the fiscal accounts remain constrained, but the fiscal accounts will remain constrained so long as economic growth (and TFP growth) is weak. Brazil may well have room for improvement in terms of the efficiency of education spending or the quality of education services given the level of spending, but such changes would take years to implement and then bear fruit. Comprehensive reform of Brazil's heavily regulated labour system could produce TFP improvements much more quickly than improved education spending, but the high level of resistance to public-sector pension reform – a reform that affects only a minority of Brazilians – suggests that meaningful labour reform is unrealistic.

In general, then, we would not assume a significant improvement in TFP growth over the next several years.

REFORM, REFORM, REFORM

Given Brazil's structural impediments to investment and falling labour-force growth, our model suggests that Brazil can count on only modest GDP growth for the foreseeable future. Modest growth is not good enough, however, for a credit with a sizeable stock of gross debt on which it is paying high – not to say extortionate – real interest rates. Without comprehensive structural changes, Brazil cannot grow itself out of its predicament, and its unsustainable debt profile will remain a road to default. Meaningful, comprehensive and timely reforms could, however, affect the long-term potential growth rate. Comprehensive social security reform – a reform that does not just slow the increase in the deficit, but eliminates it – could open the way to critical public investment in capital projects and education. Judicial and bankruptcy reform could improve creditors' rights and reduce fears of an arbitrary justice system. Labour reform could unlock potential productivity gains for a generation of underemployed workers, while reform of the Central Bank of Brazil to make it autonomous and immune from political pressures could reinforce investor confidence in monetary policy, thereby encouraging fixed investment. Some of these reforms are already making their way through Congress, although with mixed prospects. President Lula has proved to be far more supportive of economic structural reforms than many of his critics had accepted, but he seems unwilling to push too far, especially with his re-election prospects in the October 2006 vote still unclear. For meaningful reform to take effect in the next few years, President Lula will have to somehow find a way to drive politically unpopular reforms through Congress, especially through the Senate, where the opposition can usually control a working majority.

Of the many structural reforms that Brazil will need to enact in order to generate higher productivity growth, comprehensive social security reform will be the most important, but also the most controversial. President Lula has already successfully shepherded a partial social security reform through Congress, but that reform, approved in late 2003, has only slowed the growth of the deficit in Brazil's social security accounts. The deficit in Brazil's public-sector pension system is currently the biggest drain on the social security accounts, and it was the focus of the 2003 reform. But that reform, by imposing a tax on public-sector pensioners' benefits and by raising minimum retirement ages, has only stopped the public sector workers' pension system deficit from growing. The social security deficit that covers private-sector workers, where the government guarantees a minimum pension to all enrolled workers, even if their pension contributions have been insufficient to warrant the minimum benefit, has a deficit that is growing each year, with no end in sight to the increases in its deficits. By our calculations, Brazil's overall social security deficit should remain at least 5.0% of GDP for the next several years, and should grow to even higher levels if the private-sector social security deficit continues to widen.

Whether Brazil can significantly reduce its social security deficit in the years ahead could well be the deciding factor in whether Brazilian labour productivity will be able to grow at a higher rate. The 5.0% of GDP that Brazil spends on its pensioners – essentially an income transfer from current workers to retirees – is one of the heaviest social security burdens in the world. In the US, where analysts have repeatedly warned about future social security deficits, the social security system is currently in surplus and will not shift into a cashflow deficit, where benefits paid to retirees begin to total more than contributions, until late in the next decade. Most developed economies have large actuarial deficits – the total amount of benefits to be paid over the very long term less expected contributions – in their social security systems, but few have outright deficits, and few governments in the world, developed or not, must shoulder a social security deficit of the magnitude that Brazil must cover each year. The 5% of GDP that Brazil must take from taxpayers to cover retirees' benefits would, if brought to zero, provide a huge windfall of new spending on education and infrastructure, or it could be channelled into tax incentives for productivity-enhancing investments.

While the 5% of GDP that Brazil invests in its social security system each year may seem like a tempting target, a slash in pension costs is much easier said than done. President Lula has already spent a considerable amount of his limited political capital on a very partial reform of the pension system covering public sector workers; the reform, passed in late 2003, cuts the deficit by only a few tenths of a percentage point of GDP and keeps the deficit in the public-sector pension system from growing yet more in the years ahead, but even this modest reform was seen as an extraordinary political achievement given Brazil's historic inability to cut benefits. A more comprehensive reform is essentially unthinkable before the next presidential elections in October 2006, and even then a new president may find other areas in which to apply his or her post-electoral mandate. The strength of the public-sector workers' unions makes further reform of the public-sector pension system almost impossible. The state-subsidised private-sector pension system, which is now the fastest-growing portion of the overall deficit, would have to be reformed by punishing the poorest workers enrolled in the system, because it is poor workers who receive the state subsidies. Such a regressive social security reform may be less regressive than Brazil's current social security system – where current workers subsidise retirees and where educational standards suffer so that retirees can receive full benefits – but the fact that any private sector social security reform would have to be achieved on the backs of the poorest retirees makes such a reform politically unrealistic.

With comprehensive reform of fiscal spending unlikely in the next few years, Brazil's bondholders will have to look for other avenues for Brazil to achieve higher productivity growth in order ensure long-term creditworthiness. Microeconomic reform – reforms of Brazil's hidebound regulatory environment – is one area where the Lula government is trying, so far with limited success, to improve long-term growth prospects. A more efficient use of Brazil's swollen public sector could be another way to improve the long-term outlook, especially if outright spending cuts are politically untenable. While such mini-reforms would be welcome, a comprehensive shift in Brazil's long-term economic growth outlook is unlikely without a massive reform of the social security system, together with a series of tax cuts that reduce the public sector's tax take from the lofty 40% of GDP where it now stands. President Lula's government can and should be applauded for the modest reforms it has been able to push through Congress over the last two years, but much more remains to be achieved before Brazil's long-simmering productivity crisis can be brought to an end.

REFERENCES

Fajnzylber, P., and D. Lederman, 1999, "Economic Reforms and Total Factor Productivity Growth in Latin America and the Caribbean, 1950–95: An Empirical Note", World Bank Working Paper number 2114, May.

Kfoury Muinhos, M., and S. A. Lago Alves, 2003, "Medium-Size Macroeconomic Model for the Brazilian Economy", Banco Central do Brasil Working Paper number 64.

11

Assessing Operational Risk: The Case of Russia

Guy Dunn

World Markets Research Centre

Over the past decade the subject of risk analysis has moved from the peripheries of the international business decision-making process to the centre stage. This is particularly true in the financial sector, where a series of emerging-market crises throughout the 1980s and 1990s have forced regulators to ensure banks maintain a more rigorous approach to risk in order to mitigate against such losses in the future.

The clearest example of this is, of course, Basel II, which makes it a regulatory requirement for banks to demonstrate their credit, market and operational risk systems as part of their due diligence. Basel II has been criticised by some banks, who claim that it is not only onerous, but also in effect a licence to print money for the rating agencies. Whether this is true or not, the reality is that Basel II is here to stay and banks and other financial institutions are now endeavouring to ensure that their internal risk assessment processes meet the required regulatory standard.

Sovereign credit risk analysis – literally the risk that a government will default on its bonds or other debts – is central to Basel II, and tends to dominate discussions of risk analysis at banks. However, Basel II also covers what it terms market risk (effectively, exchange and interest-rate risks), as well as operational risk. These operational risks represent something of a mixed bag to banks, ranging from computer systems breaking down through to corruption, terrorism and government instability (or what is more commonly known as political and country risk).

These operational risks are much harder for banks to quantify (and therefore measure) than sovereign credit and/or market risks. The problem for the banks is that many operational risks (for example, terrorism or war) tend to be low-probability risks, but with a potentially high impact. Banks have often handled these sorts of risk by taking out political or catastrophe risk insurance – which, in essence, shifts the risk burden to the insurance companies. However, it is impossible to insure against everything and the key is to strike the right balance between spending money to mitigate or insure against the risk, and ensuring that the project or investment remains financially viable. A good operational risk system also should enable banks to make informed risk/return-based choices between different investment possibilities (eg, Pakistan or India).

Basel II makes it a regulatory requirement for banks and other financial institutions to demonstrate their operational risk-analysis capability as part of their due-diligence process. Many banks have their own internal operational risk-assessment systems in place, but the more forward-thinking banks also rely heavily on outside risk-rating companies. The main attraction of using an outside rating company is not only that they tend to be objective and independent, but they provide a useful yardstick against which to test the company's own assumptions – something that is vital in effective due diligence.

The World Markets Research Centre (WMRC) assesses both credit and operational risks on 202 countries for its clients, but it is on the latter that this chapter will be focused in order to help provide a more rounded view of the full extent of Basel II. This chapter will define what is meant by risk, look at how banking and other clients use risk, and then outline how WMRC is recalibrating its operational risk methodology to meet the requirements of our clients in an ever-changing world. Using Russia as a case study, the final section will show how this new approach to operational risk works in practice.

PITFALLS IN MANAGING OPERATIONAL RISK

Our experience of dealing with banks and other corporates on operational risk has enabled us to draw several conclusions regarding business and its attitude to risk analysis and mitigation. One of

the biggest lessons is that many corporations remain far too optimis-
tic about operational risk – even if past experience should dictate
otherwise. In practice this means that companies often plan around
the "norm" and are often ill-equipped or at least ill-prepared to
handle a shock or drastic change to this norm. Rather than assume
"it won't happen here" or "it won't happen to us", corporations
need to consider the full range and extent of threats they face when
drawing up their operational risk-mitigation strategies. It is better
to be over- than under-prepared.

A second lesson is that high-profile operational risks tend to
absorb management time and can shift attention away from the real
(but more mundane) threats to the business. Another way of
explaining this would be to say that there is too much concern about
the risk of low-probability events with horrific consequences (such
as a terrorist attack) than there is about high-probability events with
lesser consequences. The challenge for banks and other companies
is to assess the *likelihood* and *impact* of (and their *exposure* to) all such
threats when drawing up risk-mitigation procedures.

A third lesson is that all risk-management systems are by definition imperfect and that all risk managers are human and therefore
prone to errors and prejudices. Risk managers need to be prepared
to admit past mistakes and be open to constant and frequent
reassessments of the operational risks they face. Risk is a constantly
evolving issue in every country in the world and risk analysis
needs to be as objective and up-to-date as possible. An out-of-date
risk assessment is a bad risk assessment. One of the most common
mistakes companies make is to rely too heavily on the advice, feedback and opinion of in-country managers regarding the operational risk environment. Sometimes these in-country managers
can be "too close to the action" to actually see what is happening.
At other times, they may have their own (probably subconscious)
personal reasons for not facing up to the extent of the real risk –
these could range from an unwillingness to be seen as a "failure"
career-wise through to personal prejudices or even to more private
concerns regarding friends and/or family matters.

A fourth, and perhaps the most important, lesson regarding
operational risk is that risk management is, by its very nature,
defensive. Senior managers tend to notice risk management only
when something goes wrong. Successful risk management is, at

best, seen as invisible and, at worst, seen as an overreaction. The "Y2K" computer problem is a good example of this. Were unnecessary millions spent to nullify a risk that was not there at all? Or were essential millions successfully spent to avoid billions being lost if the systems had all collapsed? The same debate is found in other areas of operational risk analysis and mitigation. In the immediate aftermath of the September 11th attacks in the US, millions of extra US dollars were spent by banks and corporations on extra security and business continuity procedures. However, each month that goes by without a new attack in the US raises sceptical questions about the extent of the terrorist threat and the financial sense in spending so much money on precautions. Are the extra precautions mitigating the risk of terror or is the risk not that great after all?

A fifth and final lesson is that some industries have proved to be better at dealing with risks than others. The most frequently cited example here is the energy industry, which is – by the nature of its business – forced to operate in unstable and dangerous countries in order to gain access to oil and gas deposits. Another industry with a similarly robust approach to risk is the pharmaceutical sector. In this sector, companies have to run the "risk" of researching hundreds of different drugs for every one they have the "reward" of bringing to the market. For their part, banks have a slightly chequered history in assessing risk. On the plus side, they were the first sector to take risk assessment seriously and since then have remained at the forefront of new risk techniques and innovations. However, as we have seen with the emerging-market crises mentioned above, their risk-analysis systems have not always got it "right". Furthermore, they tend to be better at dealing with credit or market risks than operational ones. Basel II is, in effect, an attempt to address this by forcing all banks to meet what could be termed global "best practices".

A SOUND APPROACH TO OPERATIONAL RISK

Risk is different from uncertainty, which is unquantifiable. Rather, risk is an educated gamble, based on the odds.

At WMRC, we define risk and risk analysis in the following way:

> Risk is the possibility of loss resulting from a threat or event. Risk Analysis is the process of assessing risk from internal and external threats to an entity, its assets, or personnel.

When assessing operational risks, many of our banking and other clients follow a similar methodology to each other. This is best described using the following matrix

$$\text{Threat} + \text{Exposure} + \text{Impact} = \text{Risk}$$

In this matrix "Threat" means the threat assessment (for example, WMRC operational risk ratings assessing the level of terrorism or political unrest would fit in here); "Exposure" is an assessment of their company's specific vulnerability (for example, how many staff are at risk or what is the level of their investment); finally, "Impact" looks at the financial, human, security or other impact of the threat on the company. By extension, Risk is therefore an assessment of the threat to the company, the level of potential exposure and the potential cost. Once this is calculated, the company can then assess how important it is for them to mitigate that risk, and at what financial cost.

The following two examples show how this matrix could be used in practice by banks and other companies to work out their operational risk profiles.

❏ *Example one – Terrorism*: In spite of the recent media coverage generated by terrorist attacks, the threat of terrorism is generally low. An individual bank's exposure (ie, the likelihood that *they* would be targeted specifically as opposed to someone else) also is generally low. However, the impact if they were targeted is potentially enormous in terms of potential casualties, damaged property, business continuity, etc. The risk therefore needs to be properly considered because, despite the low threat of being targeted, the actual impact if they were targeted would be enormous.

❏ *Example two – ATM crime*: The threat of theft or fraud or vandalism at a bank's ATM is high. The bank's exposure is also high as they will have tens of thousands of ATMs worldwide. However, the impact is lower because the amount of money involved in individual cases is low, and stolen or copied bankcards can be quickly banned. Again, the bank needs to act properly to mitigate this risk because of its high frequency.

AN IMPROVED RATING SYSTEM FOR OPERATIONAL RISK
Operational risk is an evolving issue, not least since the events of September 11th. As a result, risk-analysis systems need to be

constantly reassessed and (if necessary) refocused to meet these new threats, as well as users' changing needs. At the same time, consistency and continuity of coverage is key to operational risk analysis and no change should be taken lightly, especially if it affects a cornerstone of the system.

In March 2004, WMRC carried out a major market-research study to enable us to understand more clearly what was deemed essential to our existing operational risk system, and which areas needed further development. The study was in two parts: an electronic survey of all our clients and a series of one-to-one detailed interviews with key clients.

Approximately 40% of WMRC's clients are from the banking, insurance and financial world, the remaining are multinational corporations, governments and universities. Of the 264 clients who completed the survey, just over 30% were in risk management, while a similar number were in a strategic planning position.

The survey results were generally consistent with our expectations. As one would expect, operational risk analysis is used to assist with strategic planning (38.6%), assessing new business opportunities (40.5%) and evaluating risks for specific projects (52.3%). One other important use (27.3%) is as an independent yardstick against which to test their own and their companies' assumptions. The biggest surprises were probably the low number who used it to evaluate insurance coverage (11.0%) and make decisions about security (14.0%).

Table 1 What is your primary use for operational risk information?

Evaluating risks for specific projects or investment	138	52.3%
Briefing senior management	120	45.5%
Assessing new business opportunities	107	40.5%
Strategic planning	102	38.6%
To give perspective to news stories and developments	92	34.8%
As an independent yardstick	72	27.3%
As a guide before overseas trips	51	19.3%
Making decisions about security	39	14.8%
For sales and/or marketing decisions	37	14.0%
Planning and evaluating insurance coverage	29	11.0%
Total	264	382.2%

Source: WMRC Client Survey, March 2004

The survey and interviews also showed that there were two factors that were deemed to be essential cornerstones of the system:

❑ *Qualitative ratings*: the fact that ratings are set by our analysts (using our qualitative operational risk methodology) on the political, economic, legal, tax, operational and security environments in each country. Qualitative ratings are preferred because they help facilitate forward-looking analysis. Using an obvious example, ratings based on quantitative data would not have helped in assessing the risk of an al-Qaida attack in Spain as prior to March 2004 no such attacks had taken place. Qualitative analysis, by contrast, would allow a rating to be set that would take into account Spain's high-profile involvement in the war in Iraq.

❑ *Fixed weightings*: the fact that the ratings for each of these six risk factors (politics – 25%, economics – 25%, legal – 15%, tax – 15%, operational – 10%, security – 10%) is weighted to enable us to calculate an overall operational risk rating for the country. This means that the overall risk score is an aggregation of these six scores, and clients welcome this objectivity. The other attraction of a fixed weighting is that it prevents an overemphasis on high-profile, but less likely threats. As an example, this enables users to keep the threat of terrorism, and its likely impact on their operations, in perspective.

The survey showed that users also value independence, consistency and frequency of coverage in operational risk analysis, as well as the ability to make easy country-to-country comparisons. However, there were two key areas where enhancements were suggested:

❑ *Improved functionality/customisation*: As a result of the survey, the functionality of our rating service was improved to allow increased customisation. This is key to a bank's use of operational risk because no two companies' risk profiles are ever the same. Users are now able to change both the ratings and weightings on our system to match their own exposure. They may wish to change the rating for an individual country, for example, if they perceive that their excellent relations with the government makes them less vulnerable to political risk. They may wish to change the weighting of a risk factor, for example, to more accurately reflect their job requirements – a chief economist may wish to increase economic risk's weighting from 25% to 50%.

❑ *Introduction of 25 new sub-risks*: The other change we made in response to the survey was to break down the six risk factors into various sub-risks. For instance, security was broken down into four weighted sub-risks (civil unrest – 20%, crime – 30%, terrorism – 30% and external security threats – 20%) each of which is now rated in a qualitative manner against new risk definitions. This is essential to good operational risk analysis for several reasons. The most important is that it allows the greater degree of risk calibration that is required under Basel II. It also again allows more refined rating. Previously, countries such as Mexico and Saudi Arabia could both be rated at a similar level for security risk. However, Mexico was rated because it had high crimes rates and a low risk of terrorism, while Saudi Arabia was rated for exactly the opposite reasons. Under the 25 sub-risk system, the real reason for the rating (terrorism or crime) is immediately seen.

Armed with these requirements, we have been able to develop a new rating system for operational risk. The following section, using Russia as a case study, outlines the key sub-risks, weightings and components of this new system. Our actual risk reports on individual countries are much more detailed than this, but it gives a flavour of our system and approach. These ratings were valid as of 1 October, 2004.

THE CASE OF RUSSIA

Table 2 Russia – Operational risk analysis

Risk	Risk weighting (%)	Sub-risk (weighting)	Sub-risk rating	Risk rating
Political Risk	25			42.2
		Institutional permanence (30%)	46	
		Government stability (20%)	33	
		Political cohesion (30%)	49	
		External political threats (20%)	32	

Table 2 (*continued*)

Risk	Risk weighting (%)	Sub-risk (weighting)	Sub-risk rating	Risk rating
Economic risk	25			46.7
		Market orientation (20%)	47	
		Policy consistency and forward planning (30%)	41	
		Diversity and resilience of economy (20%)	68	
		Macroeconomic fundamentals (30%)	32	
Legal risk	15			53.7
		Quality of legislation (25%)	36	
		Transparency of legal system (20%)	44	
		Independence/quality of judiciary (25%)	56	
		Enforcement of laws (30%)	68	
Tax risk	15			48.7
		Quality of tax laws (25%)	56	
		Corporate tax burden (40%)	37	
		Individual tax burden (15%)	31	
		Enforcement of taxes (20%)	67	
Operational risk	10			55.4
		Attitudes to foreign business (15%)	48	
		Business infrastructure (25%)	61	
		Labour quality/relations (30%)	53	
		Activism (10%)	28	
		Bureaucracy/corruption (20%)	66	
Security risk	10			63.8
		Civil unrest (20%)	46	
		Crime (30%)	69	
		Terrorism (30%)	83	
		External security threats (20%)	28	
Overall risk rating – RUSSIA				49.9 (*Medium* risk)

Key: Insignificant 0–10; Very low 10–20; Low 20–40; Medium 40–60; High 60–70; Very high 70–85; Extremely high 85–100

POLITICAL RISK (OVERALL WEIGHTING 25%)

Under political risk, we analyse the extent to which the political system facilitates the good conduct of business. A stable political system is generally cohesive and inclusive, functions well under stress and maintains its stability when faced with unexpected major challenges.

Our political risk score is calculated by rating the following four weighted criteria:

Institutional permanence (weighting 30%)

Under this sub-risk category, we assess the degree to which a country's political institutions are mature, sturdy and well established and are able to deal with its various problems with a minimum of disruption and/or coercion. The representativeness of the political system also is assessed.

Russia receives a rating of 46. Political institutions in Russia have not developed through consensus and debate, but were set in place by the victors of a series of bitter power struggles in the early 1990s. The prime example of this is the 1993 constitution, which was approved following a violent confrontation between supporters of then president Boris Yeltsin and the Soviet-era Russian parliament. This sets out a centralised federal system in which real power resides in the presidency, whose broad powers include the right to issue decrees and dissolve parliament.

By vesting so much power in the president, at the expense of parliament, this system clearly has its weaknesses. However, it does foster strong leadership and there is little likelihood of this division of power being restructured significantly in the short-to-medium term.

Government stability (weighting 20%)

Under this sub-risk category, we assess the extent to which the current government's position is secure and the administration is relatively free to drive policy initiatives forward in an effective and unencumbered manner. The timing of the next general elections may be important here.

Table 3 Political risk in Russia

Political Risk	25%			42.2
		Institutional permanence (30%)	46	
		Government stability (20%)	33	
		Political cohesion (30%)	49	
		External political threats (20%)	32	

Russia receives a rating of 33. Following the recent landslide victories for both the president and the pro-presidential party in their respective elections, the government currently benefits from a high level of stability. President Putin's emboldened administration also has attempted to rein in its critics, most notably by attempting to consolidate power over the regional governors, the oligarchs and, more worryingly, the media.

The government is currently popular with the electorate and receives widespread support for the ambitious reform programme that the administration has launched. In addition, the administration enjoys the backing of over two-thirds of the legislature who are willing to pass any given governmental legislation.

However, the biggest threat to long-term stability surrounds the need to find a successor to Putin when he steps down in 2008. Under the terms of the constitution, a president can serve for only two terms.

Political cohesion (weighting 30%)

Under this sub-risk category, we assess the degree to which the main political parties (as well as the population at large) share a broad political consensus, meaning that a change of government does not usually lead to a radical reversal in policy. Extremist groups may exist, but they will be in the minority and hold very little sway over public opinion.

Russia receives a rating of 49. Given that two-thirds of the legislature are prepared to support any given governmental legislation, the level of political cohesion and consensus with Russia's political system is high.

However, the continuing large level of electoral support for the far-left and increasingly xenophobic Communist Party and the ultra-nationalist Liberal Democratic Party shows that more extremist views still hold sway over large portions of the population.

External political threats (weighting 20%)

Under this sub-risk category, we assess the degree to which the country has poor relations and unresolved disputes of one type or another with other states. A worst-case scenario would see the country at war or in the state of high military alert.

Russia receives a rating of 32. While Russia has a number of disputes with various neighbouring states, these generally do not constitute a substantial risk to the domestic political system. However, tensions over issues such as Russia's continuing control of energy routes in the region and the EU and NATO's eastern expansion can escalate sporadically.

ECONOMIC RISK (OVERALL WEIGHTING 25%)

Under economic risk, we analyse the degree to which the economic system is flexible and does not buckle under stress. A stable system should be able to weather major internal or external shocks without experiencing a deep recession or severe financial crisis and should be able to quickly bounce back from less serious setbacks, such as a cyclical downturn or an oil price shock.

Our economic risk score is calculated by rating the following four weighted criteria:

Market orientation (weighting 20%)

Under this sub-risk category, we assess the degree to which a country's markets are free and flexible, and capable of adjusting smoothly in response to external shocks or major shifts in the economy's supply/demand curves.

Russia receives a rating of 47. Russia's economy is relatively open after having gone through an external sector liberalisation programme during its transition towards a market economy in the 1990s.

However, the energy sector remains largely in state hands, and this continues to undermine the efficiency of the economy's resource allocation. A crucial step towards liberalisation in that sector would be the break-up of the gas monopoly Gazprom. However, this seems more distant than ever following the announcement of the merger between Gazprom and Rosneft, whereby the state acquired a major stake in the energy giant.

Table 4 Economic risk in Russia

Economic risk	25%	46.7
	Market orientation (20%)	47
	Policy consistency and forward planning (30%)	41
	Diversity and resilience of economy (20%)	68
	Macroeconomic fundamentals (30%)	32

In addition, the domestic banking market needs more reform as it remains dominated by the state savings bank Sberbank, which holds more than 70% of household savings.

Policy consistency and forward planning (weighting 30%)

Under this sub-risk category, we assess the extent to which the country's economic policies are prudent, far-sighted, consistent and based on a sensible strategic framework with broad political support, thereby reducing the likelihood of major policy shifts in case of a change in government.

Russia receives a rating of 41. Russia's economic policies are generally prudent and there is little risk of significant policy shifts.

However, there is some concern that the current monetary and exchange-rate policies are mutually contradictory. Attempting to control inflation while simultaneously trying to prevent the rouble from strengthening (as petrodollars flood the currency markets) is not a sustainable policy. By targeting the rouble rate by increasing domestic money supply, the Russian Central Bank is actually contributing to inflationary pressures.

Diversity and resilience of economy (weighting 20%)

Under this sub-risk category, we assess the degree to which the economy's domestic income, employment and external flows are broadly based, rather than being overly dependent on a few sources. Diversity reduces the economy's volatility and makes it relatively immune to financial crisis, external shocks, natural disasters, wars, sanctions and trade conflicts. In general, the more developed and service-oriented economies are, the more diverse they are as well.

Russia receives a rating of 68. The Russian economy remains overly dependent on the energy sector, which accounts for over 40% of the country's export earnings, and for at least 13% of GDP by supply. Furthermore, the fiscal balance remains critically dependent on energy tariff receipts: the government relies on the energy sector for around 20% of its budget income, and a US$1 per barrel change in oil prices is estimated to have a US$1 billion impact on state revenues.

Russian GDP, exports (and thus foreign-exchange inflow) and fiscal position all remain heavily vulnerable to oil market volatility, and any extended period of lower world oil prices would have a significant negative impact on the economy.

In addition, the economy's market openness brings with it a high vulnerability to international capital flows, especially as the domestic banking sector remains underdeveloped.

Macroeconomic fundamentals (weighting 30%)

Under this sub-risk category, we assess the degree to which the overall economy is free of major macroeconomic imbalances and capable of weathering shocks and sustaining a GDP growth in line with its long-term potential, without the need for a severe correction.

Russia receives a rating of 32. Russia's GDP, current account, fiscal balance and debt solvency ratios are all in good condition, largely due to high oil prices boosting export revenues.

However, the financial sector remains weak and banking-sector reform remains a priority in order to increase the public's trust in banks and avoid further bank runs. There is also some concern regarding the narrowness of the tax base and its overreliance on export taxes.

LEGAL RISK (OVERALL WEIGHTING 15%)

Under legal risk, we analyse the degree to which the legal system successfully protects the rights of individuals, businesses and other bodies through effective legislation, precedents and a capable judiciary. This includes the extent to which the country's legal system is compatible with global best legal and business practice.

Our legal risk score is calculated by rating the following four weighted criteria:

Quality of legislation (weighting 25%)

Under this sub-risk category, we assess the extent to which legislation to protect the rights of individuals and other entities exists, and the adequacy and efficacy of this legislation, particularly with regard to business operations.

Table 5 Legal risk in Russia

Legal risk	15%		53.7
	Quality of legislation (25%)	36	
	Transparency of legal system (20%)	44	
	Independence/quality of judiciary (25%)	56	
	Enforcement of laws (30%)	68	

Russia receives a rating of 36. Russia has been honing its legislation to meet the needs of increasingly sophisticated and internationalised markets. There was a noticeable spate of new legislative initiatives in the first three years of Putin's first term, including a very much-improved company law, a new bankruptcy law, new intellectual property law, the much-publicised law on land sales and new codes.

There are signs that this drive is easing off now that the balance of forces behind the earlier, business-driven corporate governance improvements has changed. However, the trend is nevertheless likely to continue to be one of improvement, especially in the financial sector.

Transparency of legal system (weighting 20%)

Under this sub-risk category, we assess the clarity, openness and accessibility of the country's judicial processes, particularly in areas relating to commercial and criminal laws and precedents.

Russia receives a rating of 44. The boom in Russian use of the Internet has led to a major improvement in the dissemination of legal information, allowing both layers of bureaucracy and geographical distances to be leapfrogged and thus greatly improving transparency. A multiplicity of legal information sites, both government and commercial, have sprung up, abetted by new rules on the publication of regulations and judgments. Many of them are easily understandable to the public.

Changes to the general procedural codes have also made it more difficult for judgments that have an impact on company operations at headquarters to be gained in far-flung corners of the country where courts are more easily manipulated.

However, old habits die hard – and are in many cases reviving – as bureaucrats on all levels feel increasingly empowered in the "post-Yukos climate". It is far from certain that all judgments will be published in an open manner.

Independence/quality of judiciary (weighting 25%)

Under this sub-risk category, we assess the degree to which the country's judiciary is competent, respected and immune to outside influences, and the extent to which it arrives at its decisions objectively and without bribery or political favouritism.

Russia receives a rating of 56. The quality of the Russian judiciary has been improving, in the major cities at least. Indeed, many investors are likely to have no problem in gaining good-quality judgments at a reasonable speed. They will certainly have access to good-quality legal advice in what is a highly-competitive market. Efficiency and competence have been promoted by changes to the law on the judiciary and increased funding.

Independence is another matter, however. The ability of high-level or local power centres to influence the courts has always been relatively high, even if far from omnipresent. Now, however, in the post-Yukos climate and as the presidential administration strengthens its influence, there is a feeling that the gloves are increasingly off again at all levels when it comes to influencing the judiciary. Rulings in the Yukos case have seemingly been obtained to order from some of the country's highest courts, and the company does not appear to have received a fair hearing, especially as regards case preparation.

Enforcement of laws (weighting 30%)

Under this sub-risk category, we assess the degree to which existing legislation is practically enforceable, and whether the country has the organisational capacity and the political will to give effect to its laws.

Russia receives a rating of 68. Russia's dispute-resolution mechanism has undergone recent improvements, creating both a more efficient court system and improving arbitration mechanisms, although the country still does not apply fully with provisions for the enforcement of international arbitration awards. Particularly in cases involving government contracts, the experience of some investors indicates that domestic courts cannot be relied upon to implement international arbitration rulings.

The enforcement of arbitration or court judgments involving private contracts is also far from guaranteed, given the extent of influence that powerful local actors may have over the courts.

The workings of both the courts and the bailiffs' service have been improved by recent funding injections and legislative improvements, but bailiffs, too, can be notoriously open to influence.

TAX RISKS (OVERALL WEIGHTING 15%)

Under tax risk, we assess the degree to which the country's major political groups, opinion leaders and the wider population accept its tax system as an efficient, fair and legitimate means of financing the state. At the same time, the tax rates are not perceived to be too burdensome and do not act as a disincentive for work, entrepreneurship and foreign business activity.

Our tax risk score is calculated by rating the following four weighted criteria:

Quality of tax laws (weighting 25%)

Under this sub-risk category, we assess the extent to which the country's current body of tax laws are based on a clear and coherent framework, thereby allowing businesses to calculate their obligations and incorporate them into their plans. An incoherent tax system is likely to have an abundance of tax-collecting bodies with overlapping jurisdictions and no overarching organisational framework to coordinate their activities.

Russia receives a rating of 56. Tax legislation has improved significantly since the 1990s as it has been overhauled, but there is a significant degree of opacity. Together with capricious enforcement, this renders it hard to gauge whether tax strategies will be deemed to be compliant or not.

Despite the recently introduced simplifications of corporate and income tax, there continue to be too many regional taxes, increasing both the tax and administrative burdens on companies.

Corporate tax burden (weighting 40%)

Under this sub-risk category, we assess the extent to which a country's taxation rates weigh heavily on its economy by undermining corporate investment and entrepreneurship.

Russia receives a rating of 37. Corporate tax was reduced from 35% to 24% in early 2002, while small businesses now benefit from even lower rates and a much-simplified system. Payroll taxes have also been cut, and are being cut further in an effort to stimulate investment.

Table 6 Tax risk in Russia

Tax risk	15%			48.7
		Quality of tax laws (25%)	56	
		Corporate tax burden (40%)	37	
		Individual tax burden (15%)	31	
		Enforcement of taxes (20%)	67	

There have been moves to eliminate the tax-minimisation possibilities formerly used by companies, but, as the campaign waged on Yukos has shown, the use of such schemes can, especially in a climate of increasing state power, present the central or local administration with a stick with which to beat companies arbitrarily.

Individual tax burden (weighting 15%)

Under this sub-risk category, we assess the extent to which a country's taxation rates weigh heavily on its economy by undermining work incentives and/or discouraging saving and individual investment.

Russia receives a rating of 31. The introduction of a flat rate of income tax at only 13% was one of the most noted of the reforms made during Putin's first term. The favourable rate resulted in a large amount of capital being brought back to Russia for tax purposes, and together with the lower rate of corporate tax, resulted in a significant increase in revenues.

However, doubts have been voiced as to how long this low flat rate can be sustained, and there has been talk of increasing it. In addition, given the political popularity of a progressive scale there have been some attempts to reintroduce one.

Enforcement of taxes (weighting 20%)

Under this sub-risk category, we assess the extent of compliance with tax laws among the country's businesses and households. Compliance usually results from a combination of voluntary behaviour and effective enforcement of tax laws by the authorities.

Russia receives a rating of 67. It is in the sphere of enforcement that the attractiveness of the Russian tax system is let down. While arbitrary enforcement of tax law has always been an issue, in the past it has tended to be a matter for low-level corruption or ignorance.

However, the handling of Yukos has opened up the spectre of arbitrary (and retroactive) enforcement coming from the very highest echelons, and this has caused a general atmosphere of concern.

OPERATIONAL RISK (OVERALL WEIGHTING 10%)

Under operational risk, we analyse the degree to which business operations are impeded by obstacles such as an underdeveloped infrastructure, bureaucratic red tape, government and business corruption, labour constraints and turmoil, economic nationalism/

xenophobia, and targeting of business by political activists with various agendas.

Our operational risk score is calculated by rating the following five weighted criteria:

Attitudes to foreign business (weighting 15%)

Under this sub-risk category, we assess the degree of economic nationalism, xenophobia and antipathy directed against foreign business by the country's government, major political groups, opinion leaders and the broader public. This also includes any restrictions imposed on foreign businesses, ranging from minor regulatory hurdles all the way to outright prohibitions and asset confiscation.

Russia receives a rating of 57. While the Russian government's and public's attitudes towards foreign direct investment (FDI) has generally been positive, this is only just beginning to be reflected in legislation.

Restrictions have been lifted from the amount of FDI permitted within the banking and insurance sector as Russia makes progress towards membership of the WTO, but the contradictory nature of the Russian system – that of seeking privatisation revenues at the same time as enhancing state ownership – continues to create confusion among foreign investors who have been shaken by the Yukos investigation.

Business infrastructure (weighting 25%)

Under this sub-risk category, we assess the adequacy of the country's infrastructure for business operations, specifically in areas such as utilities, transportation and telecommunications. Adequacy is assessed in terms of sustainable capacity, quality of service, reliability and resiliency, rather than in terms of nominal capacity or density.

Table 7 Operational risk in Russia

Operational risk	10%			55.4
		Attitudes to foreign business (15%)	48	
		Business infrastructure (25%)	61	
		Labour quality/relations (30%)	53	
		Activism (10%)	28	
		Bureaucracy/corruption (20%)	66	

Russia receives a rating of 61. Russia's vast infrastructure has suffered greatly over the past 20 years, which continues to have a detrimental impact on the quality of its transportation, utilities and telecommunications systems.

The vast majority of Russia's roads, railways and ports have not undergone any extensive renovation programmes. While business infrastructure in Russia's major cities is adequate and has been targeted for investment, the situation in more remote areas is often dire.

Meanwhile, the long-predicted Internet boom is only now beginning to materialise as Internet costs fall and IT infrastructure finally catches up.

Labour quality/relations (weighting 30%)

Under this sub-risk category, we assess the extent to which labour unrest discourages business development, and the extent to which shortages of labour, scarcity of skills or high wages retard the country's business development.

Russia receives a rating of 63. Russia possesses a large pool of educated and skilled workers. However, the labour market continues to be highly fragmented, with Moscow still taking the lion's share of foreign investment.

A number of region-specific initiatives have been implemented, but unemployment is still believed to total 25% when all forms of official, partial and hidden unemployment figures are taken into account.

There has also been a noticeable increase in industrial action recently as the government has attempted to implement controversial welfare reforms. If the government cannot address labour concerns, such as social benefits and wage arrears, relations between the two parties will continue to deteriorate.

Activism (weighting 10%)

Under this sub-risk category, we assess the degree to which single-issue groups and political activists with various agendas target businesses operating in the country, and the extent to which foreign parent companies may face protests at home.

Russia receives a rating of 37. The degree of industrial pollution and the continuing use of nuclear energy have prompted some protests from local and transnational environmentalist groups, but their actions have tended to be non-violent, low-level and infrequent. Other single-issue action groups – such as animal rights protesters – are not a major concern in Russia.

Bureaucracy/corruption (weighting 20%)
Under this sub-risk category, we assess the extent to which the country's government bodies constrain business activities through inefficiency, red tape, intrusiveness or corruption, and the extent to which corrupt business practices are the norm.

Russia receives a rating of 66. The influence of government bureaucracy can still be felt at most levels of business operations in Russia despite measures that the Russian administration have implemented to curtail regional bureaucratic influence and poor enforcement of the rule of law.

Perceptions of corruption usually exaggerate the problems actually faced by foreign investors in Russia. Nevertheless, corruption is still widespread and is compounded by the influence of the bureaucracy on the registration and functioning of business. In a number of recent surveys conducted by respected Russian think tanks more than 60% of business owners and 50% of the general public have reported that paying bribes was a necessary part of their business or personal lives.

The government has earmarked corruption as a major obstacle to Russia's development, but to date there has been little tangible success in tackling it.

SECURITY RISK (OVERALL WEIGHTING 10%)
Under security risk, we analyse the degree to which the country is affected by physical security threats, such as crime, terrorism and internal/external political violence.

Our security risk score is calculated by rating the following four weighted criteria:

Table 8 Security risk in Russia

Security risk	10%			63.8
		Civil unrest (20%)	46	
		Crime (30%)	69	
		Terrorism (30%)	83	
		External security threats (20%)	28	

Civil unrest (weighting 20%)

Under this sub-risk category, we assess the country's susceptibility to various types of violent or disruptive civil unrest or escalation of such events (including coups, insurgencies, wars).

Russia receives a rating of 46. Following the violence that marked the power battle between President Yeltsin and the parliament in the early 1990s, political unrest and violence have been almost unheard of in the capital Moscow or in other major cities. Demonstrations and marches do take place, but they are almost always peaceful and often poorly attended.

However, ethnic unrest and violence is rife, particularly in the North Caucasus. This is particularly true in Chechnya, where separatist rebels continue to wage an armed campaign against Russian forces within the republic, as well as against other softer targets elsewhere in the region.

There is little prospect of an end to the unrest in Chechnya, and there is a significant risk that the violence will increasingly spill over into the neighbouring republics of Ingushetia, Dagestan, Karachai-Cherkessia, Kabardino-Balkaria and North Ossetia.

Crime (weighting 30%)

Under this sub-risk category, we assess the seriousness of the country's crime rates and the expected severity of their adverse consequences for businesses in terms of physical risks, higher operational costs and asset losses.

Russia receives a rating of 69. Crime levels may have dipped from the high levels recorded in the mid-1990s, but they remain a significant security (and business) threat. The Interior Ministry estimates that as much as 45% of the country's goods and services fall within the shadow economy.

There are a number of highly criminalised sectors, including the distribution, construction, retail and entertainment industries. Weak legislation in these fast-growing and profitable fields has led to the creation of powerful semi-criminal, semi-state-controlled networks that have little respect for legal mechanisms and market rules. Widespread corruption within the security services and regional administrations confounds the problem.

Terrorism (weighting 30%)

Under this sub-risk category, we assess the vulnerability of the country's political, social and economic system to terrorism and the potential adverse consequences for businesses, in terms of casualties, higher operating costs, revenue disruptions and asset losses. The likely scale and size of any terrorist attack also will be assessed.

Russia receives a rating of 83. Terrorism, originating from elements within the Chechen rebel movement, poses the most significant security risk to Russia. While the focal point of this instability is the North Caucasus region, Chechen terror groups have increasingly targeted Moscow in order to generate greater publicity.

They have not to date targeted foreign business directly, but the indiscriminate nature of their attacks (many of which are carried out by suicide bombers) has caused countless casualties. They have targeted public places (subways stations, hospitals, schools and theatres), but could decide to target foreign business if they perceived that such companies were in collusion with the Russian government in the rebuilding of Chechnya, or if such an attack would have far-reaching economic implications (such as an attack on a foreign-run airline or an oil refinery).

External security threats (weighting 20%)

Under this sub-risk category, we assess the likelihood of various types of violent interstate conflicts.

Russia receives a rating of 28. Putin's administration continues to emphasise the vulnerability of its external borders and the threat that other nations pose, but in reality Russia is relatively stable. There are tensions with Georgia – over Russian support for separatists in the Georgian republics of South Ossetia and Abkhazia – as well as territorial disputes with Ukraine and Japan. However, there is little likelihood that these will escalate into anything more than a diplomatic quarrel.

This final table shows how Russia compares to the rest of the top ten emerging markets.

Table 9 Operational risk in the top ten emerging markets

	Risk weighting (%)	Sub-risk weighting (%)	Argentina	Brazil	China	India	Indonesia	Mexico	Poland	Russia	South Africa	Turkey
1. *Political risk*	25		**47.8**	**40.4**	**49.1**	**43.2**	**58.4**	**42.7**	**27.8**	**42.2**	**32.3**	**39.4**
Institutional permanence		30	50	35	57	34	57	33	29	46	36	35
Government stability		20	47	48	38	48	67	43	27	33	24	35
Political cohesion		30	58	49	53	44	66	60	31	49	34	45
External political threats		20	20	20	39	49	34	15	21	32	31	41
2. *Economic risk*	25		**61.2**	**41.5**	**46.0**	**51.1**	**60.0**	**27.4**	**29.5**	**46.7**	**35.4**	**41.2**
Market orientation		20	55	39	53	58	57	18	26	47	36	33
Policy consistency and forward planning		30	62	40	47	52	62	29	28	41	30	34
Diversity and resilience of the economy		20	60	35	34	45	55	35	42	68	41	36
Macroeconomic fundamentals		30	65	48	47	49	63	25	22	32	36	54
3. *Legal risk*	15		**54.8**	**46.1**	**60.8**	**46.5**	**64.1**	**42.5**	**32.4**	**53.7**	**26.3**	**37.9**
Quality of legislation		25	50	41	62	40	66	38	25	36	25	29
Transparency of legal system		20	56	45	67	41	61	44	31	44	25	39

	Weight										
Independence/Quality of judiciary	25	49	48	63	39	67	41	34	56	31	42
Enforcement of laws	30	62	49	53	59	62	46	37	68	24	40
4. *Tax risk*	**15**	**48.3**	**47.8**	**53.8**	**42.4**	**53.4**	**43.3**	**29.8**	**48.7**	**28.7**	**42.6**
Quality of tax laws	25	45	38	57	38	59	36	26	56	30	39
Corporate tax burden	40	52	53	58	39	48	47	23	37	26	39
Individual tax burden	15	42	50	47	32	49	48	32	31	27	40
Enforcement of taxes	20	49	46	45	58	59	40	42	67	33	54
5. *Operational risk*	**10**	**52.3**	**46.0**	**52.9**	**52.4**	**64.3**	**39.2**	**30.3**	**55.4**	**34.2**	**37.7**
Attitudes to foreign business	15	52	39	48	58	69	21	26	48	27	32
Business infrastructure	25	57	50	53	61	68	41	30	61	29	41
Labour quality/Relations	30	37	40	55	38	51	30	29	53	41	37
Activism	10	62	42	32	37	49	42	18	28	27	32
Bureaucracy/Corruption	20	60	55	61	61	79	55	39	66	37	41
6. *Security risk*	**10**	**47.1**	**46.8**	**41.7**	**54.7**	**63.1**	**46.5**	**29.4**	**63.8**	**50.9**	**48.0**
Civil unrest	20	45	40	47	61	72	42	22	46	41	32
Crime	30	63	70	38	30	55	68	36	69	71	41
Terrorism	30	42	32	39	66	75	35	32	83	39	66
External security threats	20	22	22	45	58	42	17	19	28	38	38
Overall risk rating out of 100		**52.9**	**43.9**	**50.7**	**47.8**	**60.1**	**39.6**	**29.6**	**49.9**	**34.3**	**40.9**

Section 3

Managing a Country
Risk Portfolio

12

Best Practices in Country Risk Management

Michael Bates

Oxford Analytica

INTRODUCTION

One of the greatest challenges faced by country risk managers in major corporations is the lack of understanding of best practices. This is a reflection of the proprietary nature of the risk assessment function as a contributor to competitive advantage, but it is clear that there is a paucity of reliable information available to risk professionals that places them at a significant disadvantage when compared with other corporate functions. Lessons tend to be learned in isolation through trial and error, and, as we have witnessed in countries such as Argentina and Russia, the scale of the errors can threaten the viability of even the most venerable institution. Moreover, new entrants to the corporation are more likely to adopt an existing model than to refine or challenge it. Like an insurance policy that has been tucked away in a drawer for years, we fully understand what it covers and does not cover only when we are faced with a claim, by which time it is probably too late. The objective of this chapter is therefore to share some of the experiences and insights that Oxford Analytica has gleaned over many years of assessing, informing and challenging in-house country risk models in the hope that the science may be advanced and readers may use the information on best practices, as we see them, to stress-test their own systems and models.

In the first section of the chapter we explore the underlying causes and responses to the changing nature of risk, including globalisation, the regulatory environment, and the use of technology, and define the terminology of the world of financial risk. In the second section we examine some basic principles of best practice in country risk management and then seek to apply them to the process of selecting an appropriate risk assessment approach. Next we explore the tension between qualitative and quantitative inputs to risk models and the relative merits and demerits of each approach. We then move into some cases studies, which seek to identify best practices in the setting and reviewing of internal ratings and discuss the value of external ratings to the process. Finally, the chapter looks at organisational issues relating to effective risk management and again draws upon case studies to elucidate the answers. Of course, country risk will mean different things to different organisations, and especially different sectors, but in this chapter we shall focus particularly on the experiences of the financial sector, and in doing so hope that the basic principles of best practices explored will resonate with all country risk professionals.

THE RISK ENVIRONMENT
Globalisation of risk

During the last decade, an increasing number of countries have opened their capital account and financial systems to foreign participation. There has been a general shift from fixed to floating exchange rate regimes. Correspondingly, there has been a growth in the number of currency unions appearing (eg, EMU, CFA) to bring macroeconomic stability. This has brought changes to the nature of country risk, away from the transfer risk problems of the 1980s into currency-related crises. The nature of contemporary crises often involves the risk that problems within one sector of the economy, such as the government, the banking system or industry, triggers a run on the currency that, in turn, has a negative impact on other categories of counterparties: the sovereign, subnational governments, the banking system and the corporate sector. In response to the changing nature of risk and the growing sophistication of technology solutions, internal rating systems are becoming widely used to complement external ratings as part of overall risk-assessment methodologies. Alongside the more traditional macroeconomic developments, political, social and governance factors increasingly impact on a country's ability to service its foreign and domestic debt, in addition to affecting the more "operational" component of country risk – eg, the risk related to foreign direct investment (FDI), intra-company cross-border transactions, trade finance, and off-balance-sheet derivatives with both financial and non-financial enterprises.

The rapid expansion of the globalisation of trade, services and investment over the past fifteen years has transformed the nature of risk for country analysts. Information technology (IT) innovation and acceptance reduces time and shortens distance as traditional financial risk mitigation forces. Just as, when people come together physically, some risks decrease (for example, armed conflict reduces), while others (such as infectious disease transmission) increase, so it is with financial systems: there is greater transparency of operations, but less evidence of strong relationships between the lender and borrower. This can mean that previously isolated country financial crises can quickly turn into global systemic contagion. Business growth as a result of reduced communication and transport costs leads to new customers, markets and locations, and thus creates intense competition among all financial services as the process expands. Revised rules and regulations (local and international) are issued for accommodation of social and political consequences of this competition and volatility in finance. Dramatic changes ensue as a result for each firm's core business activity, for its client relationships, and for its leadership.

Changing regulatory environment
The regulatory framework of risk assessment in financial institutions is currently undergoing one of the most significant changes in decades and any consideration of best practices in country risk must therefore be seen in the context of Basel II. The original Basel Accord had two basic goals: (a) to establish a more level playing field for international competition among banks; and (b) to reduce the probability that such competition would lead to a bidding down of capital ratios to excessively low levels. The 1988 Accord made important progress towards these objectives, but it also had significant shortcomings. The most important problem has been the Accord's very limited sensitivity to risk. Categorising debtors into a few risk "buckets" gave rise to a significant gap between the regulatory measurement of the risk of a given transaction and its actual economic risk. The most troubling side effect of this gap has

been the distortion of financial decision making, including large amounts of regulatory arbitrage, or investments made on the basis of regulatory constraints rather than genuine economic opportunities. At best, this suggests a significant deadweight cost of regulation relative to an efficient market. At worst, it suggests that the purpose of the standards is itself being undermined, since the risk weighting that is formally assigned may bear little relation to that of the underlying transfer.

The new Accord has been designed with a view to encouraging more effective and comprehensive global risk-management practices, and to providing supervisors and the marketplace with more accurate measures of capital adequacy and risk. In practice this has led to an emphasis on increasing risk-sensitivity, especially for sovereign and corporate credit risk, and on using banks' own internal credit risk ratings, where possible, in the assessment of relative risk. There has also been greater recognition of the need for more extensive and explicit requirements for regulatory supervision and public disclosure.

Basel II's regulatory approach is based on three pillars. While the Basel Committee has emphasised that the three pillars are a package, it is the design of the first pillar that has generated the greatest attention. The most distinctive elements of the minimum capital requirements laid down in Basel II are the approach to credit risk and the inclusion of new capital requirements for operational risk. With respect to credit risk, it envisages three alternative approaches: the "standardised" approach and two (IRB) approaches based on internal ratings – "foundation" and "advanced". The Basel Committee has set the end of 2006 as the deadline for implementation of the basic methodology of Basel II, and the end of 2007 for the more advanced approach. One of the more immediate points of tension that will emerge during implementation is the difference in schedule and level of adoption between Europe and the United States. Protagonists of both blocs have claimed that their peers on the opposite side of the Atlantic will be advantaged by the transition to Basel II: the European Commission maintains that a new directive called the Capital Adequacy Directive (CAD 3) – via which Basel II will be adopted – will be implemented according to the deadlines set forth by the Basel Committee. However, this would seem to be more of an aspiration than a certainty. It is likely that the EU's implementation deadline will ultimately become January 2008. US regulators will conduct their own quantitative impact study later in 2004, tailored to the particular characteristics of the US banking industry. They have made it clear that the results of this study may prompt recalibration of Basel II as implemented in the US. Eight banks will be required to adopt the new regulation, with a further ten institutions expected to comply voluntarily. January 2008 is the tentative deadline for implementation. During 2007, banks will run their existing risk-based capital approach in parallel with a Basel II approach.

Categories of country risk

It is perhaps wise to address a complex area of operation by defining some basic terms in the context of the financial sector. For the sake of simplicity, the term "country" as used here may be interpreted as currency area, while the "sovereign" is the government behind the currency. While academic literature on country risk will point to "all factors" that could have a negative impact on the business, for all practical purposes these can be narrowed down to political, social, financial or economic factors or events. This includes structural fragility in a country, through which a counterparty in that country is unable to honour its debt obligations, predominantly through non-payment where that counterparty is the government, then it is referred to as sovereign because its distinct abilities to honour its obligations as well as its leadership and supervisory role among all counterparties in that jurisdiction. Sovereign risk involves foreign exchange transfer risk and credit risk, reflecting the sovereign's broader role in the integrity of the financial system, and also a political dimension where a government may have the ability to pay but for political reasons lacks the willingness to pay. In the case of cross-border lending there is introduced into the risk equation an additional country risk and that is due to the fact that the borrower is located in a different country from that of the lender; this additional resulting risk is termed *transfer risk* and it arises from the possibility that the borrower may not be able to secure the foreign exchange required to service its external debt, due either to currency restrictions or to exchange-rate movements.

An emerging category of risk is termed *structural fragility risk*, which came to the fore in the East Asian financial crises of the

1990s. In the East Asian crises it was often the case that borrowers could purchase foreign exchange to service the debt, and in this respect it does not fit with the classical definitions of transfer risk. The risk that was introduced in those turbulent times was that of the collapse in exchange rates and the surge in interest rates, as governments sought to respond to the crisis by imposing severe conditions on firms owing external debt. The severity of these conditions was exacerbated by collapsing banking systems and poor domestic bankruptcy laws, weak courts and ineffective enforcement, which meant that creditors were restricted in their ability to access collateral in the event of default.

To respond to these particular risks most financial institutions apply a ceiling to their lending or investment in a particular country. Differences tend to emerge between institutions where the ceiling, or cap, is set by the rating of the sovereign, or through the rating of the country for all counterparties of that country, including the sovereign. Default, as a term used by institutions predominantly active in the lending business, focuses on the inability of a counterparty to meet its debt-servicing obligations. The definition of default used by insurance institutions or investment and trading activities is connected to loss of value and can be triggered either by restrictions on the free flow of assets, or by asset performance risk.

Documenting basic principles

It will be critical for any institution that seeks to monitor and assess country risk to have a clearly written document containing an agreement on basic principles for country risk management, approved by the management, the board of directors, the audit team and country risk personnel. This document should clearly outline the scope of the task and where responsibility and authority rests. The document would serve as a benchmark for accountability between the risk support function and the business units. The document should also set out an agreed definition of country risk. In relation to sovereign risk, the document should differentiate between (a) liquidity or exchange rate risk and solvency or transfer risk (reintroduction of capital account regulation or introduction of transfer restrictions), and (b) the impact of such risk on a counterparty's ability to honour its obligations. The guidelines should note that *default* is a term legally defined by contract or by local custom, which may differ from the global market definitions referred to earlier. A careful distinction should be made between defaults linked to commercial risk, where the individual obligor fails to put in place appropriate mechanisms to address such issues as exchange-rate movements, and defaults linked to "political" or "country" risk, ie, systemic crises causing massive defaults among banks and corporates. Written policies should clarify whether local currency risk is included in the institution's definition of "country risk" as well as how the capital invested in local subsidiaries should be treated. There should be a codified definition that allows for the "dynamic" as opposed to "static" dimension of managing country risk. Definitions of country risk will be informed by experience and as the institution, its risk appetite, and the changing strategic objectives of the institution.

For these reasons, perhaps the greatest weakness in the present structure of country risk assessment methodologies is the limited extent by which they change. Hence, above all, the process of working through the applications of general principles in a particular institution will be a wholly beneficial one for the organisation in increasing their understanding of the risk profile of their business. The nature of risk continually changes and so do the methods of its assessment and the modalities by which this is done.

Selecting a risk assessment approach

In order to manage country risk effectively, institutions need to be able to measure and classify the level of risk associated with each country in which they operate. This section examines selected key elements of the risk-assessment methodologies employed by financial institutions, including their reliance on internal and external credit rating systems. This means:

❑ the level of formalisation characterising institutions' different approaches, ranging from pure statistical (key ratio-based or econometric) to less formalised methodologies. An important issue will be whether the rating methodology focuses on solvency issues or also seeks to integrate liquidity aspects such as the risk for a currency crisis.

❑ the extent to which risk assessment methodologies include only strictly macroeconomic data – such as economic growth, capital formation, foreign trade, current account balance, external debt and foreign reserves – or cover also factors such as the fiscal sustainability of public debt, the health of the banking system and the country's corporate indebtedness.

❑ the way in which countries' compliance with financial standards and codes is considered important for financial stability and therefore included in the risk-assessment methodology.

❑ the kind of qualitative factors taken into account (eg, political/social situation, legal system, economic/financial system, and development model) and the method whereby they are included in the risk assessment methodology.

❑ the sources of analytical judgement that feed into the risk-assessment models and support the credit risk decision-making process.

❑ the use and relevance of internal rating systems, with specific reference to the type of process applied to establish the rating, and the application of "sovereign ceiling" methodologies.

❑ the reliance on and observation of the external ratings of rating agencies – including their role within the internal rating system and the adequateness of external ratings in relation to different types of business – and on market based risk premiums.

In all these matters, country risk managers should not lose sight of the objective of all risk methodologies for a financial institution, which could be succinctly expressed as "to get our money back" and with as acceptable rates of return as possible. In order to achieve this goal, it is imperative to "know the country" in the way that financial regulations place an obligation on an institution to "know your client" before offering financial advice or accepting funds. Being familiar with local trading customs, etiquette and government protocol, and cultivating and maintaining business relationships, may be indispensable, especially for banks with a predominantly regional network of operations. Input from a country manager and country visits will also assume critical importance in understanding local issues while assessing risk. Tension will always exist between reliance on *quantitative*, data-driven assessments from head office and the *qualitative*, judgement-based assessments from managers in the field. Most financial institutions resolve this conflict by using both, and, managed correctly, this can be a creative tension that generates sound judgements.

Quantitative factors

There are essentially two quantitative approaches involved in the analysis of country risk. The first examines a series of indicators typically involving a series of economic ratios and runs them through an internal statistical model to determine creditworthiness. The most common indicators used are identified in Table 2. The problem with overrelying on a series of indicators is that they reflect a historical picture whereas investment and lending decisions require a more forward-looking approach. The alternative to the indicators approach is the widely used "principal scenario consistency analysis". This approach sets out a comprehensive forecast for macroeconomic and external account variables for the country being assessed over a medium-term time horizon (two to three years) and seeks to calculate the external financing needs against the projected availability of financing from foreign creditors and equity investors, and in so doing identifies a potential financing gap. This approach may be summarised as in Table 1.

In addition, the "principal scenario consistency analysis" includes stress testing by examining the implications of other scenarios for external financing requirements. Inputs include the Bank's assessment of country fundamentals in order to judge a country's ability to meet its debt servicing obligations over the medium term forecast period and its vulnerability to shocks eg, external events, policy shifts or political instability.

Of course it is one thing to list a range of indicators and it is another to obtain reliable sources of data to populate the fields in the quantitative model. This said, the absence of reliable datasets for a particular country is in itself an important indicator and should be regarded as a material fact when considering the risk profile of the jurisdiction. Moreover most, if not all, of the inputs

Table 1 Principal scenario risk analysis

Uses of FX	Sources of FX
Current account deficit	Current account surplus
Resident investment abroad	Return of resident capital
Outflows of foreign equity capital	Foreign equity investment in country
Amortisation payments due	New medium-term loans
Reduction in short-term debt	Increase in short-term borrowings

Table 2 Quantitative analysis factors

Fiscal			Balance of payments	
	Fiscal balance			Balance of payments
	General government revenue (% of GDP)			Trade balance
	Fiscal balance/GDP			FDI
	Public debt/GDP			Proportion of commodity exports/total exports
	Total public debt/central government revenues			Current account/GDP
Income				Current account
	GDP growth			Current account/ savings
	GDP per capita			Exports/GDP
Monetary				Savings/GDP
	Inflation (CPI) annual average			Investment/GDP
	Interest rates			
External financing	External debt		Exchange rate	Exchange rate valuation
	Short-term debt/ International reserves			Terms of trade
	Short-term debt/ total external debt		Other	
	External debt service ratio			External credit rating
	External debt to GDP			Banking sector risk
	Net external debt/ exports			Unemployment
	Reserves/imports			
	Debt service/exports			
	Growth in reserves			
	Foreign portfolio inflows			
	International reserves			
	GDP/reserves			

Source: OCC, IIF and OA

for macro-data will be produced by the countries themselves and must be treated with a certain degree of caution in some cases. By broadening the range of indicators and introducing certain key ratios as part of the analysis, lenders have tried to expose any inconsistencies in the data. The art of skilful use of quantitative data in country risk is in seeing the objective as not giving categorical answers, but in raising insightful questions for further exploration in the qualitative component of the exercise.

Qualitative factors

Most financial institutions take into consideration several "qualitative factors" when assessing country risk. This is often supported by use of a scoring model, sometimes combined with verbal analysis. The critical issue is how structured the qualitative judgement is – a comprehensive checklist under selected headings that deliver a score may be the most efficient way to integrate qualitative judgement with the quantitative analysis. Best practice suggests promoting discipline and order in the introduction and use of qualitative factors in order to avoid bias and to provide transparent, objective and independent considerations. Third-party objectivity on non-quantitative topics (corruption, corporate governance, human resources, management quality, ethics, auditing/accounting practices) plays a central role. Moreover, use of third-party assessments, such as ratings or indexes of political stability, corruption, political and economic freedom, allows the monitoring of developments that could affect those factors. These types of "meta-indicator" could signal an improvement or deterioration in a country's outlook. Country risk best practice should always seek out and use relevant qualitative factors, approaching new concepts and ideas for evaluations of country risks but constructed around some formal process of assessment. The most frequently used qualitative factors in preparing country risk are set out in Table 3.

Despite the discipline and organisational benefits of key ratio-based and econometric methodologies, a key aspect for effective country risk assessment remains the human intelligence input. This input into the statistical approach should be coupled with a direct link to the needs expressed by the business units and the wider strategic goals of the organisation. Best practices can be identified with the use of metrics that sharpen the business attention to

Table 3 Qualitative analytical factors

Political factors	Policy	
	Political stability	Quality of policymaking
	Political environment	Sanctity of contracts
	Risk of foreign war	Exchange rate regime
	Risk of civil war	Economic system
	Risk of revolution	Business climate
	Quality policy making	Labour practices
	External support	Taxation levels
	Membership of WTO	International cooperation
	Relations between central and local/regional government	Human rights
	IMF relations	Other
	Levels of corruption	Regulatory environment
	Independence of judiciary	

country environment issues *and* provide a reading of country exposure. Country risk systems work best when they are facilitated by an ongoing debate between business teams and country analysts, not least to broaden understanding by the former of the characteristics of country risk and by the latter to the risk characteristics of the financial instruments involved. This would facilitate a fruitful cooperation between the two with the aim of fostering business development. The inclusion of third-party analytical sources into the debate between business teams and country analysts can be useful for benchmarking purposes and critical for populating the qualitative components of country risk models.

Many financial institutions choose to employ a combination of research analysis and a statistical model output. Statistical datasets are computed to form ratios that can be compared and subjected to further interrogation before being transposed to produce a score. A selection of scores based on various ratios is put together to yield a combined or aggregate score, which is calibrated into a specific rating. The risk-assessment process is initiated by the bank's country risk research team, which also produces country reports at least once a year. These reports outline a brief macroeconomic and political analysis, and highlight the key risks (transfer risk, currency risk or collective debtor risk). Frequently, models can use as many as 50 to 60 different kinds of data input, which are combined and streamlined into 20 to 30 indicators. Forecasts for these indicators up to five years ahead are also formulated. The findings are usually augmented by research from the country risk department or the country/regional economists.

Factors based on international standards

There is also an increasing body of opinion that is wary of the risks inherent in relying solely on country-produced data. Following a series of financial difficulties in the 1990s, the international financial community came together to consider options that would reduce risk and increase transparency in the global financial system. The result was a report from the Financial Stability Forum in which it was recommended that the best practice standards in 12 key policy areas should be adopted by all countries. The standards-based approach provided considerable promise for achieving systemic reform. The monitoring of developments takes place through public-sector initiatives such as the IMF/World Bank Reports on Observance of Financial Standards and Codes (ROSCs), which now cover some 113 countries. Public-sector initiatives have been augmented by private-sector initiatives such as eStandards Forum, which monitors compliance with the core standards and codes in 85 countries (Table 4).[1]

There is some scepticism about the influence of standards and codes on country risk among financial institutions. However, closer examination of the causes of the Asian financial crises would require analysis of how the markets were caught in a panic when Thailand revealed undisclosed foreign-exchange liabilities leading to a complete erosion of foreign-exchange reserves. The reaction of investors and lenders was multiplied by the opacity of monetary policy and central banking practices in Thailand at the time. Again in Korea, the overvaluation of assets at the Daewoo Group by nearly US$40 billion resulted in large credit losses and investment write-offs. The central argument of those who promote the use of international standards and codes is that the integrity and transparency of macroeconomic policy, market infrastructure and

Table 4 International financial standards and codes

Standard	Purpose	Issuing body
1. Standards for publishing country statistics about GNP, balance of payments (called special data dissemination standard (SDDS))	To present clearly and transparently the current accurate position of country economies so that policymakers, lenders and investors act on the basis of truthful information about macroeconomic trends.	International Monetary Fund (IMF)
2. Monetary and fiscal policy transparency	To present accurately the patterns of monetary policy being carried out by the central bank and to avoid concealing risks such as off-balance-sheet financing of fiscal deficits; essential information to evaluate the quality of country macro-management	IMF
3. Fiscal policy transparency	To present a true picture of fiscal operations of the government, including the effect of off-balance-sheet activities; essential to evaluate the quality of country macro-management	IMF
4. International accounting standards	Common accounting standards that allow cross-border country/ institution comparisons on the same accounting basis; facilitate global financial activity and present risks accurately and transparently to lenders and investors.	International Accounting Standards Committee (IASC)
5. Auditing standards	To allow external audit of institutions globally according to common standards of evaluation; allow valid cross-country comparisons, facilitate global financial activity, and accurate representation of institutional risks.	International Federation of Accountants (IFAC)

Table 4 (continued)

Standard	Purpose	Issuing body
6. Corporate governance	Best practice standards for governance of private corporate/financial enterprises, covering responsibilities of the board of directors, management control groups, the regulators; assures proper ethical controlled management of enterprises and balance of stakeholder interests.	International Bank for Reconstruction and Development (World Bank), Organisation for Economic Cooperation and Development (OECD)
7. Insolvency	Best practice standards for the orderly bankruptcy/ reorganisation processes that allow enterprises to be efficiently restructured with fairness to all appropriate stakeholders.	World Bank
8. Systemically important payment systems	Standards to effectively regulate and control vital payment systems to assure orderly functioning of the payments markets; central bank responsibilities are clearly delineated.	Committee of Payment/Settlement Systems under the Bank of International Settlements (BIS)
9. Money laundering (described as market integrity)	Standards to control and eliminate illegal criminally sourced payments from and to a national financial system; to assure ethical financial climate	Financial Action Task Force (FATF)
10. Banking supervision	Core principles to effectively regulate commercial banks to assure safety and soundness, compliance with law and regulation, service to the community.	The Basel Committee on Banking Supervision under the Bank for International Settlements (BIS)

Table 4 (continued)

Standard	Purpose	Issuing body
11. Securities regulation	Standards for effective regulation of securities companies to assure safety and soundness, compliance with the law and regulation, service to the community.	International organisation of Securities Commissioners (IOSCO)
12. Insurance supervision	Principles for effective regulation of insurance companies, to assure safety and soundness, compliance with the law and regulation; service to the community.	International Association of Insurance Supervisors

Source: eStandards Forum

financial regulation are a fundamental component of best practices in assessing country risk. So far few investors factor these criteria into their assessments, an exception being the Californian Public Employees Retirement System (CalPERS), who assess compliance with international financial standards and codes, along with shareholder and creditor rights and a range of other qualitative and quantitative inputs as part of their annual review of markets in which they invest. This practice by CalPERS of due diligence of countries in which they are investing funds on behalf of their members is deemed controversial because it ranks countries and allocates investments accordingly. However, what is perhaps more extraordinary is that all funds do not do the same. This policy of reviewing financial governance as part of country risk assessments has had an impact on regulation, as a recent McKinsey report (2003) commented:

> Our recent discussions with regulators in Southeast Asia revealed that the investment actions of CalPERS – whether you agree with its investment criteria or not – have resonated throughout the region and had a major impact on standards and investor communications in those countries where they highlighted their concerns.

SETTING AND REVIEWING INTERNAL RATINGS

In order to manage country risk effectively, institutions need to have a process for making actionable decisions on country risk levels. This includes having timely risk reviews and the use of internal risk-rating systems, with specific reference to the type of process applied to establish the rating, and the application of country limit methodologies, as well as the potential use of external ratings for the purposes of benchmarking. This section reviews two case studies of leading global financial institutions and their processes for setting internal ratings.

Case Study 1

The first institution we shall examine is one that holds that the timeliness of indicators and analytical judgements is central to the sound operation of country risk processes. Country reports are often produced according to a set-frequency calendar based on annual, biannual and "irregular" reviews. Shorter "country overviews" are compiled when necessary. However, a country report or overview may also be prepared when there is a request from the business units, or following a crisis or default by a sovereign or a bank. The purpose of all assessments is to inform judgements. It is therefore essential that the data and reports prepared fit with the internal risk-management function. For instance, a common structure is that responsibility for assessing and approving country risks and country limits rests with the Country Risk Committees (CRCs). Input to the process comes from: (a) local representation and staff members with business experience, and, for countries where exposure is significant, regular in-country due diligence by risk management, and (b) research material from internal and external sources. As each country is reviewed, new forecasts are made to the main indicators that drive the econometric ratings model. Forecasts in this model would be presented to the CRC every month, along with the overall analysis.

The country forecasts that are fed into the ratings model produce a rating score for each country. The Country Risk Ratings model is based on the following three broad categories of indicator: economic structure, external structure and "soft" factors. The financial institution does not include cash-collateralised local currency exposure in the calculation of country risk. However, local currency exposure is treated like any other exposure from a credit point of view. Local currency exposure is monitored on a daily basis. Countries are graded at different levels of risk (very high, high, medium or low risk, frequently with levels in between). The country grade reflects the perception of a country's ability and/or willingness to service its external obligations, but rarely the risk of a currency crisis. Countries are also allocated a score in order of risk. The multi-category risk grade is applied based on the point score. All amendments to the risk category are to be ratified by the respective CRC at the next meeting. Country scores and grades are to be continually amended to reflect changes in underlying political and economic risk factors, regional and global influences. In some cases the Central Credit Committee (CCC) fixes the reference Maximum Country Risks (MCRs) that define the maximum limit for exposure/instruments/facilities.

Following this, the Country Limits Committee (CLC) breaks down this MCR into risk categories and ceilings, and also makes a final decision on the upgrading/downgrading of a country. Working under the CLC is the Credit Committee on Banks and Countries (CCBC), which manages ceilings and considers minor exceptions and bank ratings. The CLC recommends to the CCC the modifications of the country ceilings, and fixes the modalities of utilisation of the ceilings. The CCBC delegates powers within the assigned limits to the business areas that have representation on the CCBC. The executive committee has to approve transactions that exceed limits recommended by the CCC. Thus, this system allows for the rating to define maximum limits for lending/investment/trading in a country. This institution tends to apply the "sovereign ceiling" principle, although the sovereign may be rated lower than the country, and, in exceptional cases, above the country. The ceiling is applied strictly. A bank is at best given the same rating as its country of operation or the country of its parent group, normally depending on the currency regime of the country of operation. For local currency business, separate domestic/local ratings are applied.

In all cases, the role of research and analysis is a support role to the decision making. It is important, therefore, to ensure that data and analysis are collated as close to the point of decision as possible. In addition, the structure for risk evaluation should not be so

rigid as to exclude the likely possibility that significant developments impacting upon country risk may not fall neatly into the
rhythm of CRC meetings and as such any effective country risk
management system must have the capacity to monitor events on
a real-time basis and be flexible enough to generate alerts to the
CRC. In this respect the use of third-party sources is a vital part of
effective country risk practices, but, along with the information
that they generate, there must be a corresponding capacity to
absorb the information and to review decisions on a case-by-case
basis.

Case Study 2
The second institution we will consider is one which concerns the
trade-off between the size of the underlying business and the
resources that can be allocated to risk analysis (the portion of
analytical expenditure should not exceed the country risk premium). Global financial institutions appear to have a deeper
understanding of the local and cross-border risks attached to the
countries where they are active, while regional banks, operating
"from outside", can focus on cross-border-related factors that are
more easily quantified and translated into key ratios, to be combined with qualitative judgements (and some verbal analysis).
Even so, most systems allow for a "common sense factor".
Experience is a vital part of the internal rating system. One of the
most effective country risk management structures we have come
across is one in which the rating is established autonomously by
the Risk Management Department, within which economic
research conducts country analysis. (The efficiency of this structure, however, depends on the interplay between risk acceptance
and business culture within the organisation. Other approaches
may establish country risk analysis independent of both business
management and risk management.) The system is not scientific
but based substantially on experience.

The review process is gradually moving in the direction of capital allocation and will require more formalisation. There is no
automatic transmission from the rating to definition of maximum
policies (eg, instruments, limits, maturities) for lending/invest-
ment/trading on a country having that rating. The rating has an
impact on RAROC (risk-adjusted return on capital) that demands a

higher rate of return based on a higher level of risk. In this case the financial institution does not apply a "sovereign ceiling" but rather a "country ceiling", given that most business is not purely sovereign. The country rating is the main guide, but the sovereign rating is very close. Most of the time, the sovereign more or less determines the country ceiling. There are some exceptions, for instance, when the sovereign is already in default, but transfer risk has not materialised. The country ceiling is applied to banks, but not to corporates. Regarding the integration of country and counterparty rating, the connection among country/counterparty/transaction ratings is currently under review. Presently, there is a ceiling for banks, and corporates are stress-tested for their vulnerability to crisis. The entire process is augmented by the use of local knowledge through: (a) inputs from local offices (if any); and (b) extensive travelling by country risk officers to the countries concerned, with the aim of gathering first-hand information from politicians, officials and representatives of the local banking sector. In countries where this presents a particular challenge, embassy and consulate staff can often prove a valuable source of analysis. In those cases where extensive travelling is constrained by limited resources, reporting from the field can be crucial, and produces better results when there is a good relationship between the centralised country risk team and the local offices. In such cases, the person in the country feels that he/she is being provided with material that can be used to sell the company's services in that country. At the same time, the country risk officer can use productive information about the situation on the ground from the people who best understand the firm's involvement with that country.

Benchmarking against external ratings

Often financial institutions will express concern that external ratings are inadequate, too slow and reactive for their businesses or somewhat removed from local business realities. It is important to be reminded at the outset that rating systems have their origins in a world of currency controls, and measure the strengths and weaknesses of countries. This they do by looking at historical key ratios that constitute static information about the present solvency of the country, sovereign or counterparty. Most rating systems are not designed to predict currency crises, as shown by the way many of the currency crises of highly rated industrialised countries in the early 1990s crept up on financial markets under the radar of the rating agencies. Currency deregulation and financial globalisation make it necessary to complement or adjust them with systems measuring specifically the risk for currency crises. Rating agencies look primarily at sovereigns, while financial institutions need to tailor their views to specific business transactions, for example credit insurance. External ratings are also seen as lagging indicators. Despite this criticism, external ratings do have a significant impact on financial markets and for that reason most financial institutions must take external ratings into consideration within the risk-assessment methodology, although this may mainly be as an instrument for benchmarking/comparing internal results. Any significant divergence with internal risk assessment will need to be examined and justified to the satisfaction of the internal country risk management team.

The requirement to explain and to justify findings reminds us that effective risk managers must respond to an important function, which is to articulate the country risk premium in some forward-looking way. In such instances the manager must measure three additional components.

First is the risk from the market as measured by means of the sovereign spread. The sovereign spread represents additional interest paid by a foreign country to borrow US dollars in the Eurobonds market above that paid by the US Treasury. This spread reflects higher perceived risk associated to the country. Sources for this information are Eurobonds and Brady bond markets – when available. The strength of this measure is that it reflects the opinion of the marketplace about the probabilities of default in a straightforward and timely way. The first drawback is that the data for emerging markets do not always exist. Second is the risk appetite of the market, which will be reflected in the yield. Third, is the measure of risk from institutions: ranking on the basis of composite indices of macroeconomic fundamentals and political risk. The benefit is that there are exhaustive rankings available. The drawback is that they are ordinal and historical in view with limited forward-looking orientation. No clear indication of any preferred process for reaching these country risk premiums is indicated. Another interesting and increasing usage of external ratings is for internal audits. As the internal audit and risk review team, charged with the mandate of providing rigorous and independent assessment of the institution's risk and control environment, evaluate the performance of internal models, it will also frequently consider external ratings as a yardstick for evaluation.

BENCHMARKING FOR PORTFOLIO MANAGERS

External benchmarks can be used by private equity managers to identify arbitrage opportunities where for instance the internal system assesses a lower risk premium to the investment. In such cases sovereign spreads are used to set market rates for a country risk premium. It is more often necessary to estimate sovereign risk premiums in emerging markets. The methodology for this is to use market segmentation analysis and then select close proxy indicators. In industrialised countries, a zero sovereign risk premium is assumed. For emerging markets, sovereign spreads on Brady and Eurobonds issuances are referenced among countries with similar external ratings and/or similar sovereign risk characteristics. This analysis can also be used by private equity managers as a general framework to measure the risk premium required in order to accept investments in emerging markets. International portfolio managers require a higher rate of return on foreign investment, necessitating the establishment and use of a country risk premium. Forecasting this country risk premium is a major task for the portfolio manager. In such cases the risk-assessment methodology is geared to adjusting for sovereign risk in foreign investments. Using the private equity approach as an example, the *required rate of return* (RRR) is seen as the cost of equity. RRR is equal to the treasury bond yield for five-year bonds + a market risk premium + a sector risk premium + a country risk premium + a "lack of marketability" or liquidity premium.

ORGANISATIONAL ISSUES
Designing performance measures for risk assessment

The key objective for the risk manager is "loss containment" and to achieve this they must have in place a robust system for identifying risks via policy and country limits, and establish the framework to do business within some tolerable appetite for risk in each country. For this reason those institutions that evaluate performance of their risk assessment and risk management team by simple measures of "how much the institution loses" can often ensure that managers retain focus. In many cases this is the only internal method used to reward performance. There is often no direct linkage between sovereign risk or country risk assessment, and the institutions' overall productivity or profits, and this makes evaluation by normal business measures, ie, contribution to profitability, difficult. To attain some basis of performance some institutions benchmark against competitors. Performance of financial institutions is routinely compared to a relevant peer group; this is because, without a real risk-adjusted total return metric, there is no adequate way to make a fair and accurate evaluation.

It is axiomatic to say that, if risk is priced correctly, performance evaluation becomes transparent. Rewards are then linked to "units", but there is often no fully functioning management information system (MIS) or system to see a return by country. There is a highly "blended responsibility" for performance evaluation and reward. Business units and support staff work independently, and thus the performance is done by strict "silo" management evaluation – that is to say where various types of business within an institution pursue their own agenda without regard to how their efforts might influence the results of another product area. The disadvantages of this approach are that:

❑ there is no cross-evaluation among functions, business units or executive management agenda; and
❑ there is no specific and direct linkage between sovereign risk assessment and the institutions' profits and productivity, or between sovereign risk assessment and incentive based compensation.

There is a clear indirect linkage, however, in the fact that the front office must remain competitive in assessing and pricing country risk in order to meet the risk mitigation needs of its various clients – especially in the areas of exports, lending and providing other credit based services to its clients.

Regarding the linkage between country risk assessment and the bank's productivity and profitability, there is a distinct link via the capital adequacy ratio – if more capital has to be allocated to specific transactions, it will have a negative impact. An alternate approach, widely used, is to have performance of country or sovereign risk assessment evaluated directly by the management and the senior risk team. Critical input for performance evaluation will continue to be in the "results". Mechanisms need to be put in place so as to manage and evaluate country risk efforts more actively. In addition to "downside" risk evaluation, managers should seek to identify "upside" opportunities and be assessed on the net impact of both. There should be strong performance accountability for the country risk officer on the business results, on business efficiency/productivity, and especially on business profitability.

Country risk management is still seen by most financial institutions as a "loss-avoidance tool" to be employed *ex post* rather than an "opportunity/threat-identification tool" to be employed *ex ante*. In a business environment where risks are ever increasing because of globalisation, the risk officer should be held accountable and play a role in the business decisions of the firm – and be judged and held to performance standards accordingly. Moreover, systems should monitor the risk-adjusted total return on country exposures. This should be established and be a part of performance evaluations of the country risk officer.

Designing an organisational structure

Corporate structures for managing and assessing risk will vary significantly from organisation to organisation. However, an example of best practices in risk management structure by a global bank would be a case where risk assessments are the responsibility of the country risk research (CRR) team. The team consists of the head plus a group of economists, and a small team of documentation officers in charge of macroeconomic analysis. The CRR team is in charge of generating the country reviews and setting individual country limits, the head of risk management has the final say. The team's activity is independent: country risk analysis is not influenced by the business opportunities. The CRR team provides input to the country limits team that formulates policies and strategies. The team in charge of country limits management consists of the head and a small team. This team, covering 120 countries, defines the risk policy (ie, products/tenors/sectors) for each country on the basis of the risk analysis provided by the CRR team and on the basis of strategic considerations of the group. In this example countries attracting a low rating usually have no limits (these tend to be EU countries, the US, Canada and other developed economies); countries attracting a moderately high-risk rating are judged to present a low transfer risk, and are therefore monitored *ex post*, with limits set every three months. For countries attracting a high-risk rating, limits have to be in place *ex ante* and are advised by the country limits team to the highest credit risk committee of the bank, and set by this committee. Inputs to the process do not only consist of ratings, but also information on products, tenors and portfolio composition. The head of risk research oversees another small team that is in charge of quantitative credit and country risk research. The approach is strictly quantitative, aimed at building country and credit risk models to calculate default probabilities, and loss-given default models, as well as country risk correlations. The output of this team is used in RAROC based loan pricing and capital allocation models as well as the country VAR model. This team does not opine on the individual level of risk that a country is subject to. The head of risk management has the ultimate and global responsibility for all country risks and all counterparty risks (approval processes) as well as all credit and country risk quantification issues for activities such as loan pricing, customer profitability measurement, capital allocation, rating models and derivatives risk measurement.

The head of country risk research, the head of country limits management and the head of risk research all report to the head of risk management. In other words, the three functions are all "at the same level" and report to the head of risk management.

The current organisation structure is expressed in Figure 1. However, this organisation chart is to be restructured by dividing the institution's global risk management along the following five areas: (1) *approval process* (acceptance of credit risk transactions); (2) *credit systems* (specification and user support); (3) *research* (credit, country, portfolio modelling, loan pricing, limits, financial markets research); (4) *issuer risk* (acceptance of liquid/securitised credit risk); and (5) *portfolio management* (management of concentration risk). The institution's culture is based on responsibility for approval/monitoring, given to committees rather than individuals.

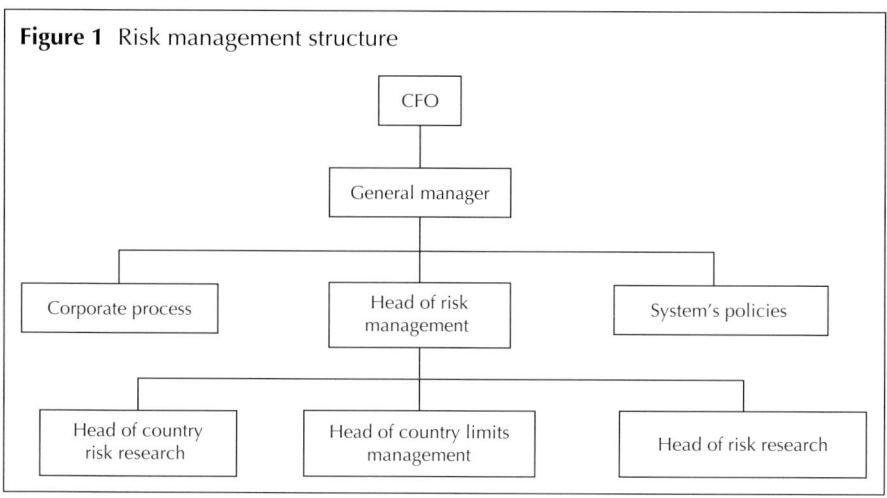

Figure 1 Risk management structure

This is based on the belief in collective responsibility and the fact that discussions within committees often lead to solutions that are better than individual solutions. This framework consists of local, regional and central credit committees. The country risk function refers only to the highest central credit risk committee, which meets once a week. Figure 2 describes the decision-making procedure for country and bank limits.

The risk assessment decision chain is structured as follows. Analysts provide the country ratings in agreement with relationship managers (who deal with banking relationships with the bank's bank counterparts); The Credit Committee International (CCI) and the Executive Credit Committee Corporate (ECCC) establish country limits for selected countries. A decision regarding individual credits or limits in these countries requires an allocation from the International Division under the country limit, The Credit Committee of the board decides on limits above a certain threshold. The Credit Committee responsible for emerging market risk is the TPFCC (Trade and Project Finance Credit Committee). Country ratings and limits are valid for all four banks that comprise the bank group. The international credit team, including country risk analysis, is part of the corporate banking credit organisation.

While working for a centralised risk-assessment function, the country risk analysis team is dispersed between various regional

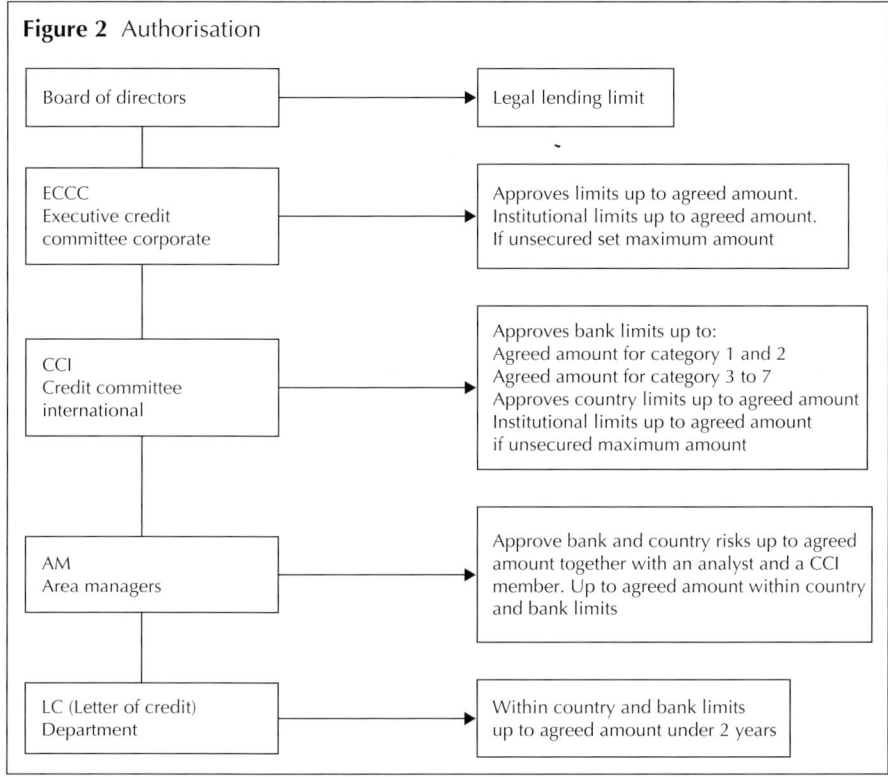

Figure 2 Authorisation

Board of directors	Legal lending limit
ECCC Executive credit committee corporate	Approves limits up to agreed amount. Institutional limits up to agreed amount. If unsecured set maximum amount
CCI Credit committee international	Approves bank limits up to: Agreed amount for category 1 and 2 Agreed amount for category 3 to 7 Approves country limits up to agreed amount Institutional limits up to agreed amount if unsecured maximum amount
AM Area managers	Approve bank and country risks up to agreed amount together with an analyst and a CCI member. Up to agreed amount within country and bank limits
LC (Letter of credit) Department	Within country and bank limits up to agreed amount under 2 years

cities that are the major business centres for country risk exposure. Foreign marketing strategies and risk tolerances are established/ managed by Country and Bank Risk Management and Relationship Managers (CBRM). CBRM is responsible for risk management (ie, definition of limits and risk management policies). The bank does have guidelines for translation of ratings into limits, but limits are normally, in practice, set independently below these guidelines based on business needs. Guidelines also apply for risk policies, but they are also set independently, based on business needs and within guidelines. TPFCC or ECCC authorise transactions that exceed limits. International units (branches, subsidiaries, rep offices) are responsible for keeping area managers, CBRM and other relevant units informed on relevant issues concerning countries, banks and corporates in their regions. International units also take decisions within the country and bank limits allocated to them.

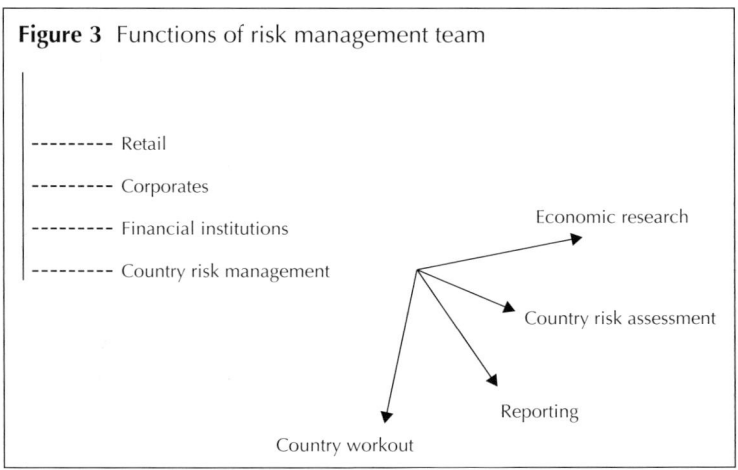

Figure 3 Functions of risk management team

The structure of the risk assessment/management team is as expressed in Figure 3. Economic research, country risk assessment, reporting and country workout are all components of the country risk management function. Limits are proposed by the country risk assessment team, recommended by the head of country risk management and then validated by senior management. The country risk limits are approved once a year, and reviewed at mid-year. For a group of around 20 countries that represent the bulk of the exposure of the bank, each individual set of limits is viewed and validated by senior management.

CONCLUSION
The globalisation of trade and capital flows has brought new challenges for risk managers and regulators alike. These changes require the refinement and restructuring of systems of assessment, control and surveillance – but to what? The proprietary function of country risk assessment models in the financial sector is being dragged, kicking and screaming, into the open, in full view of regulators and the corporate management functions of institutions. This creeping transparency will gather pace as the implementation date for Basel II approaches in January 2008 and will benefit all who seek to monitor and assess country risk. At the same time as new demands are being placed upon risk professionals by outside regulators, the sophistication of IT-based solutions is surpassing

them. The abilities of technology to further strengthen the support risk function within organisations is, and will continue to be, immense. However, the role of human intelligence, both in feeding the models with judgements and interpreting the outputs – discerning the signal from the noise – will continue to be decisive in the success of risk operations. There will always be a tension between quantitative inputs and qualitative inputs, but both are essential for best practice and, managed correctly, this can be a creative tension. Organisations striving for best practice should commence with the essential principles of the science of country risk assessment, but they must then be developed to reflect the strategic goals, corporate culture and the operational realities of the firm in order to be effective.

The process of developing the country risk guide for an organisation, conducted correctly, can be an enlightening one, which will enable the organisation to "know itself" and to "know its market". In knowing "oneself" one should know and understand the limitations of even the most sophisticated model or network of country managers, in this respect the risk manager should fully leverage the external resources to provide benchmarks for its judgments. This is not to blindly follow the assessments of others, but to invoke a discipline of constantly questioning and explaining variations.

This leads to a further point, which is the importance of ensuring that systems of risk assessment are dynamic and agile, rather than static. The pace of change of the past 15 years shows little sign of abating. Effective global trading and financial systems are essential for generating growth and relieving poverty in the developing world. To this end the international community governments and regulators have a fiduciary responsibility to ensure that international financial standards are applied across all markets and are effectively monitored. The international financial architecture is akin to the plumbing in an apartment block: it is seldom marveled at, but if it goes wrong on the top floor everyone is sure to know about it. This analogy is especially applicable to the world of country risk assessments, for when the plumbing bursts we all get flooded. It is for this reason that country risk analysis is too important to be practiced in isolation. Institutions and corporations must bring their learning and experience on best practices out into the open, and this publication is a worthy step in the right direction.

A final view would be this. We tend to think in terms of risk as being "loss prevention" and technically this will always be the case. We see an array of clouds looming on the horizon and seek to navigate organisations around the storms. The Chinese term for crisis – *wei ji* – has two meanings "danger" and "opportunity". The risk professional of the future may do well to see their role in serving their organisations by identifying both.

---

1   For further discussion of this table see also Chapter 6 of this book.

REFERENCE

McKinsey & Co, "A New Financial Architecture, Leadership in Turbulent Times", p. 29.

13

Why Firms Fail to Manage Political Risk: Explaining and Correcting Organisational Failures

J. Marc Michel Léonard

Aon Trade Credit

How do financial firms and corporations come to manage political risk in a specific manner? How are firm-wide policies developed, set and applied? This chapter looks at organisational failures in managing political risk – which over the years have resulted in billions of US dollars in lost earnings and assets – and asks how otherwise rational and successful firms fail to meet basic standards of organisational rationality and operate unprepared in the face of imminent and often expected crises.

Different models and approaches offer a variety of lenses through which to view the decision process, each offering assumptions about the appropriate unit of analysis, the meaning of interest and the logic of action. These approaches ask different questions about the decision process, improving the analyst's ability to understand how varied forces shape policies. In order to exemplify these models, this chapter uses the example of a hypothetical investment bank; let's call it "ACME". The example is based on a study of political risk management practices at more than 50 corporations and financial firms in the US, Japan and Europe (see Léonard, 2001).

The story of ACME could be that of many firms in a variety of different sectors. It is a vignette of political risk management, and provides the reader with an array of typical responses to political risk. While we use a financial firm, the case study and resulting recommendations are ultimately relevant to both financial and non-financial firms.

THE CASE OF ACME

A few years ago, ACME's CEO decided that the firm should do a better job at managing political risk. This was a direct result of the severe losses experienced by the firm's trading desks during the Asian financial crisis. Until then, the firm had no executive responsible for political risk. In order to achieve his goal, the CEO hired a risk management expert from another leading bank with a reputation for efficient risk management. The new risk manager rapidly followed up with the appointment of a special political risk adviser who was to produce a report on political risk management at peer firms. After six months, the report was presented to the firm's risk management committee, formed of the CEO, the head of risk management and senior managing directors from across the firm. The risk management committee agreed that risk management should be responsible for implementing a political risk framework that would draw on the experience of other firms, as outlined in the report, but that would address the firm's unique priorities, needs and structure. Once the report was submitted, the executive responsible for its publication left the company.

Following the example of other companies, the head of risk management created a small country risk department within the risk management department. The term "country risk" was chosen because of the firm's framing of political risk. For both market and credit risk experts, political risk has always been understood as part of country risk. As such, the country risk department's emphasis on political and country risk together worked well within the firm's managers' and traders' analytical framework. However, since resources were limited, and not wishing to overrule functions already maintained within the firm, the country risk department was to operate in conjunction with other established departments such as economics, government relations and the various sell-side research analysts. Outside sources were also used to provide a steady flow of political risk information as well as punctual reports on specific policy issues.

Within a year, the country risk department, under the guidance of the firm's head of risk management, had developed a country risk monitoring system that included both political and economic risk. A two-step country assessment process was put in place whereby countries were classified on the basis of the firm's own past experience as well as a compilation of major country risk indices from leading political risk information providers. Based on the former, some countries were deemed altogether inappropriate. The latter provided a more progressive measure of different countries' risk levels and was integrated in a value-at-risk (VAR) analysis. The new guidelines were presented by the head of risk management to the risk management committee and approved by the firm's executive board in order to provide legitimacy. This sent a clear signal to managers and traders that country risk was important to top management. In an effort to implement the new country risk management framework, the country risk department initiated a series of short seminars with the heads of the firm's different business units and trading desks explaining the new system and its practical implications for trading, VAR calculation and country ceilings. In addition, a written summary was sent to all traders.

Reactions were very positive, especially from those who experienced severe losses during the Asian and Russian crises. The country risk department's task was greatly facilitated by the fact that the firm already had a firm-wide global risk management system using VAR and monitoring risk exposure by trading desks and business units. However, both risk management and the country risk department had concerns over how this addition to the risk framework would work in practice. The head of risk management was concerned that traders' incentives were such that it would make it difficult to implement an additional component to the risk framework. This was nothing new: realigning conflicting incentives had been at the core of risk management's efforts to improve risk practices for five years. However, the new country risk guidelines, by imposing additional restrictions, would obviously highlight tensions and push the risk management's ability to influence behaviours.

On the other hand, the country risk department was concerned that traders would fail to monitor country risk. While traders and business managers recognised the importance of political risk, it remained an esoteric concept, even when made part of country risk. Most doubted the ability of any analysis to offer insights into political changes. Additionally, while economists recognised the need for integrating political variables into macroeconomic analysis, their professional training lead them to continue putting unrelenting faith into econometric modelling.

As part of its yearly risk management report, the risk management committee requested from the country risk department a review of the new country risk framework's performance. While the overall policy was declared a success, the country risk department identified key variables that acted as impediments to a fully efficient country risk management function. While the country risk department was assigned the specific responsibility to manage this type of risk, managers and traders were still getting cues from other internal sources. For example, because executives receive information from both the economics department and the country risk department, they were often confused about the actual situation in a given country. This undermined the ability of the country risk department to send clear signals and institute systematic firm-wide policies for a specific country. Additionally, managers and traders continued to rely extensively on nonspecialised information sources such as newspapers, and to conduct unsystematic and personal political and country risk assessments. Indeed, traders and managers did not see political and country risk as a professionalised function. Generally, while a politically informed workforce is a plus for the country risk department, it does create a false sense of security on the part of stakeholders, and decreases the self-perceived need for expert political and country risk information. Such self-reliance on personal analysis and the use of nonspecialised sources, coupled with the media's focus on headline events rather than underlying risks, often leads to large and unexpected risk exposure.

The country risk department of ACME also identified trends whereby different countries would suddenly become "the talk of the firm" and be identified as "safe" or "dangerous" zones. Employees would consume a limited but set group of information sources (the *Wall Street Journal*, the *New York Times* and *Bloomberg News*), so standard interpretations emerged. The country risk department's report also revealed specific departments that would frequently ignore country risk advisories. Traders and managers perceived themselves as risk-taking, impulsive and highly apt at operating under stress. However, such attitudes varied from one geographical location to another: within a global firm, the country risk department had to reconcile different national attitudes between its New York headquarters and the London, Tokyo and Frankfurt offices.

While the firm's risk management committee had taken strong actions to transform financial incentives, the ability of the country risk department to control risk behaviours was limited by the greater willingness of top management to overrule the head of risk management on country risk ceilings. This was especially the case when event-driven country risk analysis differed from econometric forecasts, or ran counter to perceptions of the risk levels in a certain country. Additionally, *de facto* versus official hierarchy – for instance, the willingness to relax risk constraints for high performing individuals – sent conflicting messages about the importance of sound risk practices.

What does the rational-actor approach tell us?

The "rational-actor" approach is widely used to explain the behaviour of companies. Everyday assumptions about individual human purpose are transferred to collective entities that are construed as unitary actors. When making a choice, a rational actor fully understands the benefits or costs associated with outcomes. For example, a growth-maximising corporation fully understands the values attached with the costs and benefits of a merger. As a result, a rational actor is capable of organising alternatives into a hierarchical set of preferences and to choose from a selection of outcomes that best serve its preferences.

Explaining ACME's behaviours: a first cut

One must assign to corporations a certain level of rationality. The crudest argument in favour of their ability to deal with political risk rationally is their basic survival. Firms have rarely suffered losses so great as a result of political and country risk that they had to cease all operations and fold. If one looks at major political crises to have hit different industries, such as the Iranian revolution, the 1980s debt crisis, and 1998's Asian financial crisis, there are very few cases where losses were so large that firms were driven into bankruptcy.

Firms are capable of surviving political crises because they have implemented political and country risk guidelines. ACME's risk management committee requested that the country risk department develop a system monitoring and limiting risk exposure using country risk ceilings and geographic diversification. This is the case in most firms in our survey; especially post the Asian, Russian and Indonesian crises, risk frameworks now incorporate political and country risk exposure.

In ACME's case, was the level of information used in making decisions sufficient to allow for rational behaviours? The answer is both yes and no, depending on the threshold one sets for rationality. ACME's country risk department uses both internal and external reports, and disseminates such information throughout the firm. The economics department, different business units and trading desks, research departments and the country risk department itself exchange information on political and country risk. All act as both consumer and producer of relevant information. For example, economics offers a specific type of information, econometric modelling, which in turn improves the analysis of the country risk department, research divisions and business units and trading desks. Similarly, the country risk department issues information that adds to the economics department, research divisions and business units and trading desks' own forecasts. Our survey reveals that multinationals, banks, asset managers and insurance companies all use a variety of information sources, from country risk reports to government sources, fellow executives and newspapers. However, as we shall see below, this information is often deficient, contradictory, or falls victim to short horizons (see Léonard, 2001).

Are firms well-oiled machines? In many ways, they generally are. At ACME, under the leadership of the risk management committee, the country risk department has been able to increase collaboration between the different stakeholders involved in managing political and country risk. The situation at ACME is indicative of data collected in our survey. However, as we shall also see below, collaboration is never perfect and many discrepancies remain.

The question with regard to rationality is not whether a firm actually takes actions to minimise political and country risk, but whether such actions are sufficient. The analyst may set a higher threshold for rationality than the mere presence of country risk guidelines, the consumption of some information and limited collaboration between a firm's different departments. Survival is not enough: risk management should be proactive and efficient. That so many firms fail to predict crisis or suffer considerable losses as a result of political and country risk reveals many failures.

In short, ACME experienced some significant deviations from a rational response to country and political risk. In order to explain these deviations, and correct them, we must look to other models of corporate behaviour.

What do organisational behaviour approaches tell us?

Individuals, who are limited in the complexity of the tasks they can complete, come together in organisations to overcome such limitations through collective efforts. The more complex the task, the more structured the organisation. Early economists asserted that organisations pursue suboptimal objectives and often develop preferences other than those they were created to serve. The mere presence of an organisation limits the realm of solutions and limits alternatives. (More formally, organisational behaviour models suggest a "logic of appropriateness", rather than the rational actor's "logic of consequences".)

During our survey, managers expressed in interviews that the main obstacles to developing coordination between their firms' different divisions were established practices, each division's own definition of its mission, and bridging professional identities. These three problems are all explained by organisational behaviour models.

Explaining ACME's behaviours: a second cut

Standard operational procedures

In bureaucratic settings, standard operational procedures (standard procedures) define the realm of available options. Organisations operate by dividing complex tasks into specialised operations conducted according to specific rules. In practice, this often results in less than rational outcomes. We have all experienced similar situations. For example, US social security regulations state that the only acceptable form of proper identification to replace a lost social security card is a valid passport. However, to receive a passport, one must have a valid social security card. An important consequence of standard procedures is cognitive blinders. "Cognitive blinders" refers to a situation where existing rules and procedures duplicate suboptimal behaviours and make innovations difficult or impossible. While a behaviour may be recognised as inefficient, it is nonetheless duplicated because it is correct within a specific set of rules.

Until ACME's risk management committee created the country risk department and developed a system to monitor political and country risk exposure, the review of the firm's risk exposures did not account for country risk. It was only after the firm experienced substantial losses during the Asian financial crisis that the CEO initiated a review of standard risk management procedures. However, the country risk department's task was greatly hindered by established risk management practices, which, acting as cognitive blinders, made it very difficult to reconcile qualitative information into a quantitative framework. For example, VAR and other quantitative tools used by risk managers, business unit managers and traders did not easily allow for the incorporation of qualitative analysis such as political and country risk analysis.

Additionally, standard procedures contributed to continuing the use of deficient information sources. Our survey revealed that even though executives perceive country risk reports to be the best source of country risk information, in practice, newspapers and magazines, such as the *New York Times* and the *Wall Street Journal*, are the primary sources of political and country risk information. Such practices are duplicated from one generation of executives to another and have evolved into unofficial but standard operational procedures. The short horizon of such information sources increases the inability of managers to monitor events beyond a two-week period and contributes to headline management.

Standard procedures also vary to reflect environmental, geographic and industry variables. For example, standard procedures in French companies favour the use of blanket government-sponsored insurance schemes rather than an actual review of political risk exposure.

Principal-agent limitations

Principal-agent issues further constrain the rational behaviours of organisations. "Principal-agent" refers to the difficulties of a principal to communicate its objectives to its agents and thereafter monitor the agent's behaviours (for instance, the inability of Enron shareholders to monitor and police the behaviour of Enron managers). Even when principals clearly define objectives, organisations may often come to perceive their mission differently or to espouse preferences other than their principals'.[1] This may be the result of involuntary misunderstandings between the principal and its agent. However, as they develop a sense of identity and mission, agents may come to interpret their mission differently even against the wishes of their principal. Political and country risk management suffers from many principal-agent limitations. Bureaucratic duplication is widespread and many departments issue political and country risk information. There is often a lack of coordination between different divisions, leading to conflicting reports about the extent of risk in any given country.

In the case of ACME and most firms in our survey, the principals are the company's top management and risk management committee. The agents are the firm's different departments: risk management, the country risk department, economics department, research analysts, business unit managers and traders. Each one understands its responsibility towards political and country risk differently. The country risk department looks at it from an analytical perspective integrating macroeconomics, political economy and foreign policy, while economics uses mostly econometric analysis. As such, they endeavour to meet their organisational missions in different ways.

Professionalisation

The professionalisation of the bureaucracy further reduces the realm of acceptable alternatives and increases tensions between principals and agents. Professional norms act in a manner similar to standard procedures, defining a variety of acceptable behaviours, from deductive patterns to speech and dress code. For example, lawyers are socialised through education and professional training to conceptualise problems in a specific manner and select solutions from a realm of predefined options. When professional routines clash with efficiency, the latter often loses. Rosabeth Moth Kanter refers to this process as the "homosexual reproduction of management" (see Kanter, 1991), pointing out that the same begets the same. We'll call this "isomorphism".

The professionalisation of key functions within ACME instituted different analytical frameworks that did not include political and country risk. Self-selection and firm-wide isomorphism duplicated an environment where political and country risk falls relatively low on corporate priorities or was understood differently across departments. This is especially clear when looking at the educational backgrounds of finance-industry MBAs or economists that place a strong emphasis on quantitative training but little on qualitative analysis. Executives seek professionals with similar education and backgrounds.

Because education and professional training define the realm of available options, this makes it more difficult to introduce new priorities. For example, our data indicated that when dealing with plant managers, who by profession are mostly engineers, risk managers found it especially difficult to raise concern for political and country risk (see Léonard, 2001). Engineers did not see how political and country risk should be of concern to them; nor did they comprehend how it related to their function, or what they could do to minimise exposure. The same was true for other divisions. While political and country risk should have been an important component of economic analysis, the evolution of economics in the last 30 years and the dominance of econometric modelling makes it very unlikely that political events and policy considerations would be incorporated by economists in their analysis. This phenomenon has been made more acute in recent years as a result of the professionalisation of the human resources (HR) function. In general, as an agent, HR's mission is to support the status quo, not to introduce change.

What can the bargaining-games approach tell us?

In the bargaining-games model, the logic is neither consequences nor appropriateness but rather bargaining. There is no single interest or consistent set of strategic objectives across the firm, but various conceptions of personal and organisational goals.[2] Executives or political leaders frame issues in terms of personal implications and resources. The outcome is the result of who is involved, their negotiating skills and the influence and power of different offices.[3]

Explaining ACME's behaviours: a third cut

The bargaining-games approach offers additional explanations of why corporate practices do not always meet the standards of rationality.

Agenda setting

According to the bargaining-games model, the power to influence an outcome rests not on understanding consequences, standard procedures or hierarchy, but in the ability of executives to influence the bargaining game (see Neustadt, 1990). Darman identifies four variables informing the bargaining process: quality, agenda setting, issue framing and rules (see Darman, 1996). Better solutions are stronger. Players will find it easier to advocate solutions that are thoroughly researched and original. However, the key to winning the bargaining game is setting the agenda and framing the issue correctly: the question often carries the answer.

Policy entrepreneurs will set the agenda by pushing forth those issues that will improve their relative positions.[4] Skilful players will be those more successful at occupying centre-stage by working within the rules to link those issues enhancing their relative importance to already established priorities. As a result of their success to bring attention to an issue specifically relevant to their area of expertise, they come to the centre of the stage and increase their ability to pursue their own priorities, whether that be prestige, influence or financial rewards.

In the case of ACME, the main actors are the members of the risk management committee, the head of risk management, the members of the country risk department, economists, analysts, business unit managers and traders. Goals may vary depending on the individual and are influenced by one's office. For example, some may value financial success over anything else, while others may seek recognition, prestige, influence or even power. In most cases, priorities will be set as the result of a combination of different goals.

Implementing political risk guidelines is not simply about curbing certain interests or behaviours. It is about altering the basic structure of the institutional framework and affecting the distribution of interests across departments and players. At ACME, this was achieved by shared ownership. However, for many actors, revenues from assets are secondary to salary, thus limiting the ability of shared ownership to realign interests beyond a certain level.

On the other end, curbing individual interests or realigning those of individuals and the firm is easier during crises. ACME's CEO used the aftershock of the Asian financial crisis to initiate a new political and country risk management framework. There is considerable literature on the role of crisis in facilitating reform.[5] Indeed, the most basic interests of all players also coincide with the firm's survival. Without the firm itself, the game would not continue. Individual and bureaucratic interests will be easier to restrain when survival is at stake, making reform more likely. On the other hand, discrepancies between individual and collective interests should be greater when there are no perceived threats.

The logic of bargaining games dictates that individuals would rather bring attention to issues for which they can take credit in the case of successes, but for which they can also deflect blame in case of failures. This limits risk managers' willingness to bring attention to political and country risk. Risk managers will only "surf" those issues for which they have effective solutions. Indeed, by raising the profile of certain risks for which they may yet be unprepared, risk managers may reveal their inability to manage all forms of risk and decrease their influence within the firm. This may explain why our data indicate that risk managers are often content with existing risk frameworks and take actions to include political and country risk only as a result of pressures from other corporate divisions or as a result of an outside crisis (see Léonard, 2001). Indeed, our data indicate that traditional risk managers do not consider political and country risk a priority, often downplaying its importance, focusing instead on financial risks that can be handled through the traditional tools of risk management, and incorporating economic information produced by the firm's macroeconomic department. The same logic applies to the other players involved in the corporate bargaining game, from vice presidents for government relations and international relations, to fund and plant managers. Unaware of the resources available to them to reduce exposure to political risk, each would rather deflect responsibility for political and country risk and focus on issues where they can be "part of the solution", not only of the problem.

This explains why in most cases the initial interest in developing political and country risk guidelines comes from a firm's CEO. At ACME, it was the CEO who created the risk management committee and called on risk management to develop political and country risk guidelines. This was the case for most firms in our survey, regardless of sector or country. CEOs can increase their own profile with shareholders only by showing their willingness to decrease political risk exposure, especially in the context of a major crisis. For a CEO, political risk offers a win–win situation: if other executives succeed in reducing risk exposure, or if the crisis simply goes away, they come across as visionaries who showed strong leadership in a time of crisis. On the other hand, if the firm actually experiences substantial losses, then responsibility can be deflected to other executives such as risk managers, legal counsel or different managers, further increasing the CEO's grasp on the firm. The CEO also has the necessary authority to implement the firm-wide guidelines necessary for political and country management to be effective.

Collective action problems

Bargaining games further decrease rationality through the complexity of joint action. The greater the number of actors involved in carrying out decisions, the less likely the resulting policy will follow the original intent. In a competitive bargaining game, the multiplicity of interests will ultimately make it impossible to agree on a straightforward policy or to produce coherent and coordinated actions. As Kenneth Arrow discussed, increasing the number of participants does not yield marginal increases in rationality but rather replaces value-maximising decisions by concessionary bargaining as some members' preferences come to dominate others (see Arrow, 1963). Furthermore, information asymmetries reduce the possibility of achieving consensus on a common goal.[6] The empirical evidence suggests that collective action limits the ability of groups to agree on policy outcomes that pursue rational behaviours.

Instead of rational action, decisions are made based on concessions between individual interests. For example, ACME's risk framework allows traders to appeal the country risk department's country risk limits. In the end, as a result of concessionary bargaining, the ultimate outcome does not entirely minimise political and country risk. Collective action problems are further increased by information asymmetries between the different actors involved in the process. For example, business unit managers and traders may use their greater understanding of VAR techniques as well as more instant information of risk exposures to take on risk positions that go unnoticed by the country risk department.

Groupthink

In the bargaining model, groups behave differently from individuals by creating collective patterns of defensive avoidance (see Janis and Mann, 1977). This creates a process often referred to as "groupthink" (see Janis, 1982), by producing personal tendencies to reject conflicting positions and to bolster consensus. Such tendencies are caused by differences in power among participants and personal conflict within each participant, increasing discomfort with confrontation, hesitations, uncertainty and emotional stress. The logic of decision making is no longer rationality or appropriateness but rather individual and group psychology. By arguing in favour of the consensus, actors engage in collective avoidance, shying away from personal responsibility. While herd behaviour may lead to collective failures, it is regarded as safer than being wrong alone.

Collective avoidance is greatly facilitated by information inbreeding. When any groups rely on the same information, consensus is much easier to reach and there is little responsibility in failing to identify variables that were overlooked by everyone.

Data from our survey suggest that political risk is a good example of groupthink, where negative expectations are downplayed and positive forecasts overvalued. In executive meetings, political risk is seen as a confrontational issue falling outside normative issues and provoking strong reactions from other managers. This logic is temporarily altered when specific instances of political risk come to dominate the agenda as the result of outside threats and repetitive headlines in the news media. Under such conditions, a new consensus may emerge, allowing for the discussion of specific instances of political risk.

Headline management and information inbreeding are essential components of groupthink. This phenomenon was observed in many of our data and was exemplified by ACME. As noted previously, our survey also reveals that managers use a very limited number of information sources, often the *New York Times* and the *Wall Street Journal*. While headline management allows for the deflation of threats, it also overvalues how dangerous certain countries are. Overnight, specific cases of political risk become the "talk of the town". This was the case with corruption in Russia at the beginning of 1999. However, while such a consensus decreased the confrontational nature of discussing this specific form of political risk, it did not affect the status of political risk in general terms, which continued to be perceived as a confrontational issue.

What can the critical-theory approach tell us?

Critical theory offers an alternative to understanding behaviours that may not be explained under the different logics of the previous approaches. It suggests that an individual's identity determines his or her interests. The logic driving decisions is identity: how people see themselves or others determines the alternatives they consider, their preferences and ultimately their choices. While critical theorists make it their agenda to challenge existing paradigms by revealing the underlying and hidden power structures leading us to embrace or reject certain identities, our goal here is to see how this logic of identity helps us understand the decision process.

Critical theory tells us that identities are the products of one's environment. Individuals select from a variety of socially sanctioned constructions. For example, the main construction in society is gender. In patriarchal polities, gender is largely informed by sex: what is associated with the masculine is emphasised while what is associated with the feminine is downplayed. Power and authority, as well as socially desirable means and ends, are the socially-constructed attributes of males. Individuals define their gender by espousing certain roles and behaviours. Their identity becomes a collection of decisions about those roles and behaviours most associated – or not – with a specific gender. By so doing, they reinforce or challenge their perception of themselves and, as others see them espousing specific attributes, they create a personal gender construction.

While paradigmatic gender constructions are constantly redefined and challenged, our society continues to associate certain roles, behaviours and expectations with specific activities. Activities *per se* continue to carry their own identity as both men and women engage in a process whereby they attempt to shape their own identity to the perceived characteristics of roles and activities in which they desire to engage. Critical theory's logic of identity suggests that executives will reject behaviours that are more rational but that clash with normative expectations about their roles.

Explaining ACME's behaviours: a fourth cut
Professions, risk and research

When asked to define a "successful executive", respondents in our survey identified four features: a willingness to take risks and to follow one's own instinct; a capacity to operate under minimal information; a competitive personality; and a drive towards success, ie, financial remuneration. The ability to espouse such behaviours is perceived as a key to success. On the other hand, when asked to define a typical risk manager, respondents identified different features: they are risk averse; maximise information through research; consider all options before making a decision; and favour collegial and consensus-oriented decisions.

The behaviours associated with risk-conscious decisions are in direct contradiction to the qualities respondents identified as key to an executive's success or defining the personality of the "typical" executive. For some respondents, the qualities required of risk managers were even likely to be a liability in other areas. Such constructions make it unlikely that executives outside of risk management would be willing to alter their approach to making decisions and embrace risk conscious behaviours. Indeed, the risk-conscious decision process is perceived as operating under premises that are in direct contradiction to what is needed to succeed in a corporate setting. Engaging in rational behaviours is not the key to success; espousing the right identity is.

From this perspective, basic or complex research is often understood as resulting from the inability to make decisions under stress. One executive clearly exemplified this analysis. In his eyes, corporate activities were similar to an American football game. The successful quarterback does not spend his time second-guessing his decision or in the library researching all options, but stays on the field with his teammates, ready to make decisions. When asked whether he had himself played football in high school or college, the executive answered that he was actually the library type and that he had never played football. Nevertheless, he believed that he would be a better executive had he played this game and it was very clear to him upon entering the corporate world that successful executives "are team players who don't pay too much attention to intellectual issues", such as political risk. Engaging in extensive research, and publicising such behaviour, puts one at odds with dominant identity constructions in corporate settings that value risk or impulsive behaviours (see Léonard, 2001).[7]

What can the prospect-theory approach tell us?

Prospect theory offers an alternative logic by focusing on individual behaviours towards risk (see Kahneman and Tversky, 1979; see also Allais, M., 1953; Arrow, 1982). In practice, prospect theory suggests that behaviours towards risk limit rationality and that individuals respond to probability in a nonlinear manner. Because it springs from empirical evidence looking at behaviours in investment firms, insurance companies and consumer practices, prospect theory's challenge to expected utility theory is especially relevant to this study (see Battalio, Kagel and Jiranyakul, 1985).

Prospect theory postulates that individuals evaluate alternatives with reference, not to current asset levels, but to changes in such levels. They consider gains and losses from this point of reference rather than by looking at absolute levels of wealth and welfare. This is called "reference dependence". As a result of reference dependence, when experiencing negative changes in asset levels, they become risk-acceptant. When experiencing positive changes, they become risk-averse. For example, confronted with severe losses, an individual may take additional risks that he or she would not otherwise consider rational to make up for the losses. However, when experiencing gains, his or her tolerance to risk decreases.

In equilibrium, prospect theory suggests that individuals tend to favour the status quo, espousing risk-averse behaviours.[8] Prospect theory's assumptions imply that individuals attach a higher value to what they have than to alternatives of equivalent value they do not have. Thaler (1980, pp. 43–7) refers to this phenomenon as the "endowment effect". It suggests that the disutility of giving up goods is greater than the utility of acquiring them.[9] Practically, this implies that individuals may often refuse to give up goods even at a price they would have never paid for it, in direct contradiction to rationality. Consequently, individuals will take more risks to maintain their position, authority and reputation than they would to enhance those positions.

Explaining ACME's behaviours: a fifth cut

Prospect theory casts a particularly powerful light on market behaviours, explaining risk behaviours throughout a boom–bust cycle. In the first phase, as a result of reference dependence, individuals are risk-averse. Initial gains are the result of the market's expansionary cycle. However, as the gains reach unsustainable levels, individuals develop risk-tolerant behaviours to sustain and protect gains. Because they attach such a high value to their gains, traders and business unit managers are willing to take on disproportional and additional risk to protect their previous gains. However, in the third phase, as a result once again of reference dependence, they become risk-prone and fail to react even after the burst has started.

This is exactly what happened in Asia. Prospect theory almost succeeds in explaining on its own why financial and non-financial firms, despite all the resources available, suffered such great losses in Russia, Asia and more recently in Indonesia. International diversification always takes place in periods of boom, when risk standards are already relaxing. Marginal asset allocation becomes riskier, and risk exposure increases. However, this is also facilitated by groupthink, which further deflates threats, and herd behaviour, which inflates opportunities while providing coverage. Additionally, information inbreeding, and the use of limited newspapers makes it very likely that early-warning signs will go unnoticed. Then, as the crisis evolves, there is a tendency to ignore risk management guidelines, and increase exposures even further, to protect gains that had been made.

ROAD MAP TO BETTER POLITICAL RISK MANAGEMENT

The first part of this chapter used the example of a hypothetical investment bank to demonstrate how otherwise rational organisations sometimes fail to manage political risk effectively. Building on the insights provided by the five different models, we now turn to providing practical solutions to overcome such obstacles. The core proposal is an information strategy aimed at changing the way stakeholders think and go about managing political and country risk.

Framing country risk issues

Framing the issues correctly is crucial to sound country risk management. Without properly relating country risk to existing conceptual frameworks, thereby increasing its importance by working within established individual and organisational priorities, a firm will be unable to implement effective country risk practices.

Recommendation 1: Relate country risk to
existing references

In order to overcome the tendency to isomorphism, and the bias in some professions against qualitative analysis and research, firms should integrate country risk within existing conceptual frameworks and references. By relating country risk to existing paradigms, senior management can reinvent analytical practices and increase the level of attention paid to this form of risk. For example, increasing awareness of country risk within an engineering firm, or among economists, will be achieved differently than within a bank or among brokers. Each organisation and profession has different analytical outlooks resulting in specific analytical priorities. What falls outside of such priorities is perceived as irrelevant. Therefore, country risk must first create a willing and receptive audience by identifying where and how country risk affects them, and only then use such "referential hooks" to successfully propose change-management strategies and implement new risk systems.

Recommendation 2: Leverage crisis

Individuals and organisations are averse to change. However, exogenous pressures such as financial, economic and political crises create organisational stress and opportunistic openness to change. As a result, crises provide windows of opportunity to alter established organisational and individual practices and implement new strategies. The importance of crisis is highly perceptual and varies across actors. Because the same crisis may produce largely different responses, senior management must publicise and enhance threats, identify specific causes and relate factors to policy priorities. For example, to leverage the Mexican peso crisis to implement new country risk practices, a firm must identify this event as an instance of country risk and show how proposed country risk policies could have minimised its impact.

Change management

Another important factor influencing a firm's ability to manage country risk is the presence of a coherent change-management strategy. A well-developed change-management strategy will monitor progress and ensure that initial policy recommendations be followed with adequate actions enabling successful implementation. Individuals and organisations often devote substantial resources to developing new systems, but fail to acknowledge the importance of follow-up actions focusing on implementation.

Recommendation 3: Increase accountability

To increase objectivity, policy implementation and assessment should be performed by different organisational units. A firm's risk management committee should issue organisational goals for country risk and instruct risk management to implement such policies. However, the committee should review how the solutions put forth by risk management bring the firm closer to its country risk management goals. If the risk management committee lacks the organisational capability to review the country risk unit's actions, it should rely on external review rather than on the country risk unit's analysis of its own performance.

Recommendation 4: Make strategic use of the human-resources function

Prospect theory gives insight into the conditions under which it will be easier to alter practices that limit rationality. Because it is easier to deter future behaviours than change existing practices, risk management should focus on the training of new executives in order to alter the "isomorphic" reproduction of the firm's harmful standard procedures.

Strategic HR should increase country risk expertise within the risk management function by hiring macro and political econo-mists. Additionally, it should develop similar, albeit more limited, expertise within business units and create pockets of "alien" expert-ise acting as translators between country risk management and information consumers. This process, which requires the reclassifi-cation of the criteria determining relevant experience, should be initiated by upper management. As a result of isomorphism, it is unlikely that the departments themselves will initiate such changes, while principal-agent limitations make HR ill-equipped to do so.

Actors

Three actors influence country risk management: managers, the firm and market forces. For this chapter, we are leaving out regula-tors. Successful country risk management must work within each actor's identity, logic and operational capabilities. Successful coun-try risk management will leverage the potential of all four actors, coordinating strategic actions across groups to better minimise risk.

Managers

Recommendation 5: Leverage individual interests
Prospect theory tells us that focusing on specific losses may lead to irrational responses. Risk management guidelines should be presented as a path to securing greater success for all, rather than controlling individual behaviours or making up for specific losses. At Lehman Brothers, for example, risk management firmly believes that "policing" individual executives and focusing on pre-empting losses is rarely successful. The path to success is, they argue, to con-vince all those involved that sound risk management is about cre-ating additional revenues, not just pre-empting or reducing losses.

When it comes to developing corporate guidelines regarding political risk, prospect theory suggests that it would be easier to deter executives from initiating new behaviours than to persuade them to stop or alter existing practices. It would also be easier to deter executives from making new gains than to persuade them not to try to recover past losses. Finally, it would be easier to implement guidelines focusing on protecting existing gains than reducing certain areas of activities. Because adaptation to losses tends to be slow, sunk costs frequently influence executives' calculations.

Senior management should enhance accountability and induce self-interested actors to engage in risk-conscious behaviours by integrating country risk management within performance reviews and remuneration structures. By doing so, it will harness the interests of the different actors, alter the distribution of interests across departments and players and change the structure of the institutional framework. Such policies should be driven by upper management: as a result of their own interests and organisational location, the firm's board and CEO are the only actors with both a personal stake in the firm's overall performance and the authority to implement the firm-wide guidelines necessary to increase coordination between risk management, research, public and government relations, and business managers.

Recommendation 6: Standardise risk tolerance through credit cycles
Prospect theory tells us that country risk is subject to the same cyclicality as other forms of risk. Risk tolerance should be standardised through business cycles, with special attention given to preserving country risk standards during expansionary credit and investment phases. In order to do so, a firm must reshape incentives and shield risk management techniques from arbitrary exclusions.

Firms
Recommendation 7: Create a country risk unit
Firms should create a country risk unit responsible for managing country risk. The country risk unit should be an autonomous department within risk management, distinct from credit and market risk. It should be responsible for disseminating information, preparing assessments and recommending management strategies aimed at integrating country risk within standard operations. It should provide requirements to include country risk within standard decisional processes and offer the means to do so effectively. To reduce exposure to concessionary bargaining and increase coordination between risk exposure and the firm's risk appetite, the country risk unit should answer directly to the head of global risk and be represented on a firm's risk management committee. It

should be organised as a research unit with experts bridging macroeconomics, political science and risk management. Analysts should focus on macro-environments across regions, applying insights from one country to another, rather than focusing solely on one country or region.

Recommendation 8: Put country risk within a standard
risk framework
Firms should isolate country risk from unnecessary vulnerability to concessionary bargaining by normalising country risk within the standard risk framework. Limits discounts should be standardised across types of risk and be similar for country, market and credit risk. Risk guidelines focusing on country risk should be standardised and systematically implemented within a firm's risk framework. Depending on the firm's operations and needs, aggregate exposures should be monitored across business units and presented to the risk management committee as part of ongoing exposure reviews.

Market forces
Recommendation 9: Increase expectations of industry
best practices and accountability
Markets should increase expectations of what constitutes acceptable country risk management practices. Actors such as shareholders, industry analysts and industry groups should include the quality of country risk management practices within their review of industry best practices and assessment of corporate performance. Firms that fail to live up to minimal industry standards of country risk management should be held accountable for their actions and punished through standard market mechanisms. Shareholders should seek to change managerial practices or replace leadership. Analysts should issue negative reviews and impose a discount on the value of the firm based on higher-than-necessary exposures to country risk and anticipated losses resulting from future financial, economic and political crisis. On the other hand, industry groups and think tanks should provide forums for debate and disseminate concrete solutions enabling senior management to enhance country risk management practices and meet such new expectations of industry best practices.

Four tools influence a firm's ability to manage country risk: (1) *information*, (2) *assessment models*, (3) *management techniques* and (4) *technology*. A firm's ability to withstand financial, economic, and political crises will be as strong as its weakest tool.

Tool 1: Information

Recommendation 10: Increase the transparency of country risk decisions

Firms should use information to minimise groupthink, information inbreeding and headlines management. Meetings should have clear objectives, use multiple information sources, empower the expression of alternative viewpoints and encourage new ideas. The chair should act more as a facilitator rather than an active participant with a vested interest in the outcome, and make sure that all stakeholders are part of the process. The use of a formal agenda or checklist should ensure that no specific variable or issue is overlooked or pushed under the rug because it is too confrontational. Outcomes can be discussed in relation to the organisation's greater goal-specific policies bring the organisation closer to its goals.

Recommendation 11: Use multiple sources

To further reduce the risk of groupthink, information inbreeding and headlines management, the country risk unit should use a variety information sources. Sources should provide legitimate, focused, reliable, available, expandable and normative data. Because risk managers yet unfamiliar with country risk information may find it difficult to assess the respective quality of different sources, senior management should initially secure the advice of an expert consultant prior to entering into costly relationships with information providers. Over time, the need for such expert opinion will decrease as the firm will develop its own internal expertise.

Recommendation 12: Employ triple relevance

Because of the opportunity cost of consuming information, the country risk unit should *sell* its utility to users. As managers are overwhelmed by information, only those tools that consistently succeed in making a clear contribution to the manager's function over time will become widely used. To do so, the country risk unit should engage in relational marketing and develop a branding strategy centred on "triple relevance". First, the country risk unit should identify and provide new information. Second, this information should focus on issues affecting the firm and be expressed as business contingencies. Third and finally, the information should alter decisions.

Recommendation 13: Use multiple distribution channels
The country risk unit should use four outreach tools: written reports, online information, country committees and seminars. Written reports, the most efficient channel to distribute information, should come in three formats: monitors, warnings and in-depth analysis. All reports should follow a similar format using different levels of summary outlining the nature of the information, stressing business contingencies and recommending alternative actions. Monitors should be published at regular intervals, for example each week or each month. Warnings should be issued sporadically to communicate changes in the macropolitical and macroeconomic environment of a country that requires attention. In-depth analyses should utilise downtimes, when few events require immediate attention, to discuss specific issues of major concern to the firm. All reports should be distributed electronically; in addition to facilitating distribution, e-reports decrease the opportunity cost of expanding information and provide scalability by offering links to additional data.

The country risk unit should utilise the Web to allow stakeholders access to additional data on specific countries, past research, information on a firm's country risk framework and updates on the country risk unit's activities. Their Web site should allow users to log onto a personalised interface offering customised country risk information and collect information about users' information consumption patterns. Country committees should bring together information providing and consuming stakeholders and provide opportunities for country risk managers to explain country-specific risk analyses and, by including feedback from end users, increase their stake in the risk-assessment process.

Finally, seminars should focus on increasing sensitivity to country risk by exemplifying its relevance to the firm's past, present and future operations and explaining the goals and structures of the firm's country risk framework.

Tool 2: Assessment models

*Recommendation 14: Improve model selection
and performance*

The key to increasing analytical and forecasting relevance is to choose those models that address the micro-priorities of a specific industry or company. A model's performance, beyond a certain threshold, is more a question of its being the *right* model given a firm's specific needs, rather than its being the *best* model. While they may use different assessment techniques, research reveals no significant differences in the accuracy of the leading assessment models (see Erb, Harvey and Viskanta, 1998).

Recommendation 15: Pay attention to both macro- and micro-components

Models must translate a country's macro-environment in terms of a firm's micro-exposures. Due to various factors such as the nature of a firm's activities and its identity, the same environment yields different levels of risk for different senior management. Macro- and micro-assessment techniques should be structured and systematic, allowing for standardisation and duplication across analysts.

While macro-assessments are available externally, senior management should supplement such information with internal assessments. Macro-assessments should utilise an analytical matrix integrating macroeconomic, financial and political variables within both the country and the region. Failure to integrate either economic or political variables, or to account for regional factors, will substantially decrease the model's explanatory power.

A review of different macro-models indicates that economic variables should include current accounts, trade balance, balance of payments, price and wage inflation, structural unemployment, export concentration, real GDP growth, GDP per capita, deficit over GDP, and debt service ration. Financial variables should include currency volatility, stock market volatility (when applicable), bank transparency and ownership concentration.

Political variables should include demographics (literacy rate, health practitioners per capita, poverty level, ethnic and religious factionalisation, income distribution), political (war and insurgencies, history of instability, regime legitimacy, free press, organised and open opposition in the country, free elections), judiciary (contract law, independence, rule of law, corruption), and government (policy coherence and flexibility, capability to mobilise resources, professional bureaucracy, commitment and integration to regional and international agreements and organisations).

Micro-assessments should regularly perform sensitivity and scenario stress tests and express results in terms of value, earnings, or assets-at-risk estimates. The probability of each scenario should be based on a firm's past experiences in a country, expert opinion, internal and external macro-assessments. Such estimates express the maximum expected loss of a firm or a unit for a given period and confidence interval. Because stress tests are more advanced in financial senior management, VAR estimates are the most common; however, non-financial senior management may find earnings and assets-at-risk measures highly insightful.

Tool 3: Management techniques
Recommendation 16: Use all available resources
Country risk can be managed through standard treasury and risk management operations such as hedging, short selling, straddling, and futures. Additional country risk techniques include country limits, diversification, government and public relations, partnerships, insurance, labour practices, technology, contractual provisions, and distribution.

All senior management should set country limits accounting for aggregate exposure across business units and develop a geographic diversification strategy. While country ceilings provide a passive measure, the latter offers an active means of minimising country risk. Because of regional contagion, simple country diversification is not a good indicator of aggregate country exposure.

Firms should use government relations, lobbying, and strategic relationships to minimise country risk. Even when explicit government guarantees are not an option, cultivating ties with government officials can provide useful communication channels and insights into the government's propensities, policies and attitudes.

Whenever possible, senior management should secure insurance from public or private providers. In addition to providing a variety of country, sovereign and political export and investment insurance, partnerships with multilateral and government agencies provide additional leverage vis-à-vis host governments.

Firms should use technology transfer and the withholding of such transfers to enhance their relative position vis-à-vis emerging markets and host countries. Whenever possible, labour practices should develop local constituencies and ensure that the economic benefits of their presence trickle down to local communities. This is especially important in countries where wealth redistribution mechanisms may not be fully efficient.

Firms should also use contractual provisions to define the post-investment environment by seeking adjustments to tariffs, waivers of sovereign immunity, pre-agreements on dispute resolution and arbitration, definition of acceptable political *force majeure*, and buy-out remedies. Similarly, payment structures can be used to protect revenues from restrictions on capital transfer. Finally, some senior management can attempt to control international distribution outlets for specific goods by developing monopsonies or oligopsonies.

Tool 4: Information technology

Recommendation 17: Use IT to disseminate information

As discussed earlier, IT systems should be an integral component of a firm's strategy to disseminate country risk information. Country risk should leverage online interactive channels such as the Web to interact with stakeholders. Risk management committee technology can be especially useful to identify information consumption patterns, allowing the country risk unit to deliver highly targeted information and ensuring that it actually reaches stakeholders.

Recommendation 18: Use IT for macro- and micro-risk assessments

Information systems should be used to perform complex macro-assessments and integrate national and regional variables. Similarly, senior management should use IT systems to perform stress tests. IT systems allow country risk to perform such tests with a high level of refinement that is both quantitatively and qualitatively superior to non-computerised tests.

Recommendation 19: Use IT to monitor risk exposures

Firms should use information systems to monitor risk exposures within and across units and product lines, offering estimates of aggregate exposures to changes in the financial, economic and political environments of specific countries and regions. Those with a greater need for ongoing risk monitoring should consider developing more refined systems capable of providing weekly, daily or hourly exposures.

Recommendation 20: Use IT to assess marginal
cost of risk minimisation
IT systems should identify the marginal and incremental risk minimisation benefits resulting from different management techniques. For example, IT systems should allow risk managers to compare modified risk exposures, with and without a specific management technique, thereby providing an assessment of the cost of risk management versus its benefits to the firm.

1   For more on principal-agent theory, see Pratt and Zeckhauser (1986).
2   See Allison *et al*, 1999.
3   See Allison *et al*, 1999.
4   For more on policy entrepreneurs, see Kingdom (1995).
5   For more on crisis and reform see Williamson (1994).
6   For an example of this process in practice, see Rakoe (1989).
7   See Léonard, 2001.
8   Levy, 1997, pp. 88.
9   Levy, 1997, pp. 89.

REFERENCES

Allais, M., 1953, "Le Comportement de l'homme rationel devant le risque: Critique des postulats de l'Ecole Americaine", *Econometrica*, **21**, pp. 503–16.

Allison, G., and P. Zelikow, 1999, *The Essence of Decision: Explaining the Cuban Missile Crisis*, 2nd edn (New York: Longman).

Arrow, K., 1963, *Social Choices and Individual Values* (New Haven, CT: Yale University Press).

Arrow, K. J., 1982, "Risk Perception in Psychology and Economics", *Economic Inquiry*, 20.

Battalio, R. C., J. H. Kagel, and K. Jiranyakul, 1985, "Testing Between Alternative Models of Choices under Uncertainty; Some Initial Results", *Journal of Risk and Uncertainty*, **3**, pp. 24–50.

Darman, R., 1996, *Who's in Control? Polar Politics and the Sensible Center* (New York: Simon & Schuster).

Erb, C., C. R. Harvey, and T. E. Viskanta, 1998, *Country Risk in Global Financial Management* (Charlottesville, VA: Research Foundation of the Institute of Chartered Financial Analysts).

Janis, I. L., 1982, *Groupthink* (Boston, MA: Houghton Mifflin).

Janis, I. L., and L. Mann, 1977, *Decision Making: A Psychological Analysis of Conflict, Choice and Polarization* (New York: Free Press).

Kahneman, D., and Tversky, A., 1979, "Prospect Theory: an Analysis of Decision under Risk", *Econometrica*, **47**, pp. 263–91

Kanter, R. M., 1991, "The Future of Bureaucracy and Hierarchy in Organisational Theory: A Report from the Field", in P. Bourdeiu and J. S. Coleman (eds.), *Social Theory for a Changing Society* (San Francisco, CA: Westview Press).

Kingdom, J. W., 1995, *Agendas, Alternatives, and Public Policies*, 2nd edn (New York: Longman).

Leonard, J. M. M., 2001, *Managing Global Political and Country Risk*, Doctoral Thesis, University of Virginia.

Levy, J. S., 1997, "Prospect Theory and Rational Choice", *International Studies Quarterly*, **41**.

Neustadt, R. E., 1990, *Presidential Power and the Modern Presidents: The Politics of Leadership from Roosevelt to Reagan*, 5th edn (New York: Free Press).

Pratt, J., and R. Zeckhauser, 1986, *Principals and Agents* (Boston, MA: Harvard University Press).

Rakoe, J., 1989, *Original Meanings: Politics and Ideas in the Making of the Constitution* (New York: Basic Books).

Thaler, R., 1980, "Towards a Positive Theory of Consumer Choice", *Journal of Economic Behavior and Organization*, **1**, pp. 39–60.

Williamson, J. (ed), 1994, *The Political Economy of Political Reform* (Washington, DC: Institute for International Economics).

14

*Pricing Political Risk within an Economic Capital Framework**

Jotaro Hamada, Henning Haugerudbraaten; Andrew Hickman, Ilya Khaykin

Multilateral Investment Guarantee Agency; ERisk

INTRODUCTION

Political risk insurance has been widely used over decades as an effective risk mitigation tool to protect foreign direct investments (FDIs) into developing countries. Historically, export credit agencies (ECAs) in the public sector were the major providers of political risk insurance for investment in developing countries. In the late 1990s, this niche insurance industry experienced a rapid growth, at an estimated rate of 20–30% a year, driven primarily by insurers in the private sector, such as AIG, Zurich, Lloyds of London and Sovereign Risk (a joint venture of ACE and XL).

Traditionally, pricing of political risk insurance has been considered an art rather than a science. It relies mainly on a qualitative approach, based on the expert judgement of experienced underwriters, rather than on a quantitative formula or a model. Underwriters in the industry have argued that pricing of political risk is not really actuarially based, unlike typical life or property and casualty (P&C) insurance products. This is not surprising considering the nature of the risks: each political risk event appears to have occurred by causes unique to a particular country – rendering risk assessment and

*The authors would like to thank Peter Nakada of ERisk and Amedee Prouvost at MIGA for their helpful comments and support. The findings, interpretations and conclusions expressed herein are the authors' own and do not necessarily reflect those of MIGA, The World Bank and its affiliated organisations, or those of the Executive Directors of MIGA/The World Bank or the governments they represent.

classification difficult. Most importantly, availability of industry data on historical claims is very limited.

Most providers of political risk insurance differentiate their premium rates according to risk, but in a qualitative manner. The majority of ECAs differentiate their premium rates by countries, using either their internal risk ratings or OECD's seven-category classification of countries, developed for the pricing of export credit insurance. Several ECAs further differentiate or adjust their premium rates based on industry sectors, such as manufacturing, financial and infrastructure. Some ECAs, however, apply a single low rate across the board, regardless of countries or sectors. Private insurers similarly differentiate their premium rates first by country (although they do not usually follow OECD's classification), and then adjust for investor types, project-specific risks and the demand and supply of political risk insurance capacity at the time of underwriting.

Today, political risk insurance coverage is increasingly available for large-scale investment projects such as those in the infrastructure sector, and even for very poor countries. Longer-term coverage is offered by both public and private insurers. Cooperation between public and private insurers has been increasingly common. At the same time, however, the industry has been affected over the past few years by the challenging global political environment and economic crises in some emerging markets. Many political risk insurers recently experienced an increased number of investment disputes, potential claims and actual claims. With inherently riskier offerings in, perhaps, a riskier environment, insurers should see greater potential benefits from improved risk assessment and management. In such an environment, a more systematic approach to political risk measurement, especially its pricing, could also play a valuable role in developing a robust political risk insurance industry that can promote needed FDI into developing countries.

While signs of demand for quantitative approaches to political risk insurance are encouraging, the field has long been neglected. A closer examination of existing industry data and available research literature suggests that there are many opportunities for quantitative approaches to be developed and applied to financial and insurance operations. Quantitative tools would strengthen, but by no means replace, traditional judgement-driven approaches in political risk underwriting.

This chapter proposes the use of a systematic pricing methodology, based on the concepts of *expected loss* and *economic capital*, supported by statistically derived risk parameters. It is organised in four sections: the proposed pricing methodology based on economic capital; a detailed discussion of a method for deriving key parameters, such as claims probability and correlations; a review of the business implications of the economic capital approach; and key concluding remarks.

Definitions

This chapter covers the three main political risks typically covered by investment insurance: *transfer restriction*, *expropriation*, and *war and civil disturbance*. As breach of contract coverage typically requires a case-by-case approach – and, to-date, sufficient historical data do not exist – it has not been included in the analysis.

❑ *Transfer restriction risk*: the inability to convert local currency (capital, interest, principal, profits, royalties and other remittances) into foreign exchange for transfer outside the host country.
❑ *Expropriation risk*: losses attributable to measures taken or approved by the host government that deprive the investor of its ownership or control over its investment, or, in the case of debt, results in the project enterprise being unable to meet its obligations to the lender.
❑ *War and civil disturbance risk*: loss from damage to, or the destruction or disappearance of, tangible assets and politically motivated acts of war or civil disturbance in the host country, including revolution, insurrection, *coups d'état*, sabotage and terrorism. It is also caused by an interruption of project operations essential to overall project financial viability and obligations to lenders.

CHOOSING A PRICING METHODOLOGY

The fields of financial engineering, corporate finance and actuarial science have contributed to the development of several methods for valuing and pricing risks. There are two broad families of pricing models: "arbitrage-free" and "economic". The following section briefly reviews the four most popular methods, the first being an arbitrage-free model, and the remaining three being different variations of economic models.

Figure 1 Methodology comparison				
Family	Methodology	Relevance	Practicality	Industry/ Academic acceptance
Arbitrage-free	Arbitrage-free	◆ ◆	◆	◆ ◆ ◆ ◆
Economic	CAPM	◆ ◆	◆ ◆	◆ ◆ ◆ ◆
	Standard-deviation	◆ ◆	◆ ◆ ◆ ◆	◆
	Economic capital	◆ ◆ ◆ ◆	◆ ◆ ◆	◆ ◆ ◆

To evaluate these methods, a set of criteria has been defined. Most importantly, a valuation model must be relevant to the needs of the organisation. For example, a model that focuses on the market value of an investment may be less relevant in an illiquid market or in cases where the investment's value to the organisation differs from its value to third parties. In addition, a model must be practical to implement, not only from the view point of the feasibility of model development, but also from the view point of day-to-day usability, and the appropriateness and measurability of model parameters. Lastly, to ensure acceptance of the model within the organisation and to third parties, the methodology must have a suitable level of acceptance within the narrow industry of interest and more broadly among other financial institutions and academics.

Figure 1 presents a summary of the methodology comparison, which the next sections will discuss in some detail. The proposed approach is one of the economic models, the *economic capital* method.

Arbitrage-free model

The "arbitrage-free" pricing model simply establishes the price of a policy as the market price of a basket of traded instruments that represents a "best hedge" for the policy. It is among the best known of the pricing methods. It is based on the simple foundation that a portfolio consisting of the risk to be priced and a perfectly offsetting hedge would be risk-less (such that the "basis risk" between the instrument to be priced and the hedge portfolio is insignificant or at least non-systematic, that is, not requiring a pricing premium) and should therefore earn the risk-free rate of return. The "arbitrage-free" price of the instrument is then equal to the cost of the hedge portfolio. In mathematical terms,

$$\text{Premium}_i = \text{Cost}_{\text{Hedge}}$$

where the hedge portfolio is designed such that

$$\text{Var}(\text{Claim}_i - \text{Return}_{\text{Hedge}}) \approx 0$$

or in weaker form,

$$\text{Covar}(\text{Claim}_i - \text{Return}_{\text{Hedge}}, m) \approx 0$$

where m is a broad "market basket" of all instruments requiring risk premia.

The arbitrage-free models are effective for assets for which there is an observable market – a requirement that is obviously a significant challenge for political risk. For potential application to political risk, the set of relevant market instruments is likely to include sovereign bonds (or perhaps certain corporate bonds), FX rate options and equity index options (one would need to use options to capture the downside-only nature of political risk insurance). However, the basis risk between these market instruments and political risk claims is likely to be extreme, with additional uncertainty due to the "model risk" of hedge ratios.

Another drawback is that arbitrage-free models are *not* sensitive to the risk contribution of a new transaction in relation to the existing portfolio of a political risk insurer. Thus arbitrage-free pricing models can lead to uneconomic concentrations where pricing appears attractive for the transaction itself, but risk concentrations within the portfolio make the deal unattractive for the insurer.

Economic models
"Economic" pricing models consist of two risk elements: expectations and compensation for risk, ie,

$$\text{Premium}_i = \text{Expected Loss}_i + \text{Expenses}_i + \text{Risk Load}_i$$

The expectations component is straightforward – it is the product of claims probability and mean claims severity, net of recovery. This "expected loss" represents the long-term average annual loss on insurance policies. The "expenses" component covers an insurer's operating expenses associated with issuing and maintaining insurance policies including overhead and staffing. The compensation for risk component, or "risk load", is the required return on risk stemming from the volatility in losses. It is more difficult to quantify this from a theoretical perspective. This section will review three popular economic approaches to determining the risk load: capital asset pricing model (CAPM), standard deviation, and economic capital.

CAPM

The corporate finance literature proposes that a risk should be compensated based on its covariance with the "market basket" risk and the excess return on that "market basket" as shown in the following equation.

$$\text{Risk Load}_i = \beta_{i,m}(E(R_m) - R_f)$$

where β is the covariance of the instrument to the market basket divided by the variance of the market basket, which is applied to the expected excess return for holding the market basket versus the risk-free rate. If the covariance is zero, this will result in a zero-risk premium.

While CAPM is also widely accepted in the finance industry and academia, its relevance to political risk is questionable. Like the arbitrage-free model, CAPM requires an observable market. In addition, the model requires the assumption that the risk-bearer chooses among an unconstrained menu of investment choices – a supposition that is clearly untenable for political risk insurers.

Standard deviation

The insurance literature proposes several analytical methods that assign risk loads based on contribution to variance or standard deviation of financial results. A typical formula is:

$$\text{Premium} = \text{Load Factor} \times \text{Standard Deviation}$$

While this method is operationally easy to implement and manage, it can be arbitrary in form, as well as in determining the appropriate load factor. In many cases, the load factor is determined by historical rules of thumb. This can be very problematic for non-standard lines such as political risk insurance, where each deal has many unique risk factors. As such, it is not very well accepted in the market or in academic literature.

Economic capital
The proposed approach is based on the concept of economic capital. This approach, unlike the arbitrage-free model and CAPM, provides a view of the cost of risk from the perspective of a specific insurer. Economic capital is the core measure of risk and is defined as the amount of capital that a business requires to support the economic risks it faces to a specified solvency standard or default probability (Figure 2).[1] Economic capital methods often require a greater amount of work to measure risk than more market-based methods, but allow for risk measurement in inefficient markets. They are calculated taking into account the specific risks in an insurer's portfolio and the ability of these risks to diversify among each other.

Risk-taking activities within the organisation contribute to the overall level of economic capital, which in turn may be allocated back to such activities. The risk contribution of a political risk insurance policy can be defined as its amount of allocated economic capital. Because shareholders demand a return on this capital, the cost of this risk (or negative value) can be defined as the allocated economic capital times some required return on capital.

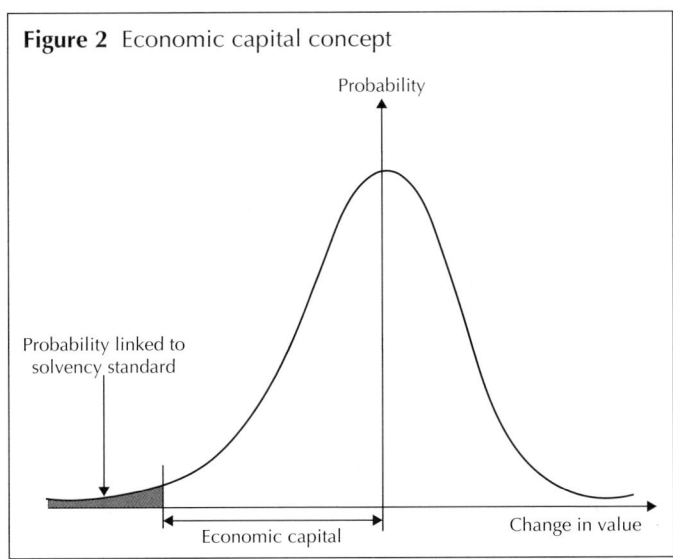

Figure 2 Economic capital concept

Then the "risk load" can be defined as the amount of this required return in excess of the risk-free rate earned by the capital:

$$\text{Risk Load} = \text{Allocated Capital} \times (H - R_f)$$

where H represents an insurer's "hurdle rate", and R_f is the risk-free rate.

Economic capital models are generally practical to implement. Structurally, political risk insurance shares a number of properties with credit risk; therefore, credit risk models may be adapted to accommodate political risk. Furthermore, the parameters used to populate such models can be calculated from historical data of political risk events. And the parameters provide valuable insights for the organisation beyond the context of economic capital modelling. While economic capital has not had the level of academic scrutiny of the arbitrage-free model or CAPM, it is widely used and accepted within financial institutions, particularly within banking institutions.

Adjusting for multi-year policies

As discussed, the minimum required premium for a particular policy for a particular political risk insurer is:

$$\text{Premium} = \text{Expected Loss} + \text{Expenses} + \text{Risk Load}$$

Most political risk insurance for investment is in the form of a multi-year policy, with a fixed annual premium rate over its term. To ensure profitability on such a multi-year policy, the multi-year cost must be determined.

As the timing of these premium components may differ significantly – eg, policies typically have large fixed underwriting costs at inception, and then a stream of ongoing annual premiums in later periods – a policy's profitability in any given year could be misleading relative to its overall lifetime profitability. The pricing model must therefore take into account all cashflows over the life of the policy. Thus the policy's profitability should be evaluated on the basis of present value of the expected value of all future cashflows. Over a multi-year period the costing equation is:

$$\text{PV(Premiums)} = \text{PV(Expected Loss} + \text{Expenses} + \text{Risk Load)}$$

$$\sum_{i=0}^{T} \text{Premium}_i/(1+r)^i = \sum_{i=0}^{T} (\text{Expected Loss}_i + \text{Expenses}_i + \text{Risk Load}_i)/(1+r)^i$$

where T = policy maturity and r = risk-free discount rate. Given the expenses, expected loss and risk load for every year, the required premium can be calculated.

Assuming that premium is a constant percentage of political risk exposure:

$$\text{Premium Rate} = \frac{\sum_{i=0}^{T}(\text{Expected Loss}_i + \text{Expenses}_i + \text{Risk Load}_i)/(1+r)^i}{\sum_{i=0}^{T}\text{Exposure}_i/(1+r)^i}$$

Furthermore, a political risk insurer can also incorporate the probability of policy cancellation by the policyholder during the term. Generally, a policyholder is given an option to cancel insurance coverage after a certain period, eg, three years following inception (insurers cannot cancel it). This option can impact the lifetime cost of the insurance. By converting year-by-year cancellation probabilities to "survival" rates, this can be incorporated into the premium formula. Survival rates are stated as the probability that a policy will survive (ie, not cancelled) in year i given that it has survived until year $i - 1$.

$$\text{Surv}_i = \text{Surv}_{i-1} \times (1 - \text{Cancel}_{i-1})$$

Then,

$$\text{Premium Rate} = \frac{\sum_{i=0}^{T}(\text{Expected Loss}_i + \text{Expenses}_i + \text{Risk Load}_i) \times \text{Surv}_i/(1+r)^i}{\sum_{i=0}^{T}\text{Exposure}_i \times \text{Surv}_i/(1+r)^i}$$

Note that the one-sided option to cancel may generate additional cost to the extent that policyholders exercise this option efficiently (ie, they tend to cancel when the risk improves, and not when it deteriorates).

ESTIMATING PARAMETERS

For the measurement of expected loss and risk load, the economic capital approach outlined above requires a number of parameters, including those for claims probability, severity, recovery likelihood and correlations.[2] These parameters may be derived in a variety of ways, including historical estimation, expert judgement and structural modelling. In low-data environments, such as the one for political risk insurance, the final parameters often require a combination of these methods.

To the extent possible, the use of empirical historical data is always the preferred approach as it generally produces more accurate and objective results. However, in many cases the use of these data should still be informed by the judgement of experts in the field. For example, if sufficient historical data are available, one may measure parameters over various time frames. The potentially higher relevance of more recent data should be traded off with the improved statistical confidence of using a longer series with more data points. The determination of the optimal time window is likely to involve the judgement of risk managers.

For political risk, it is usually important to take a long-term view, based on the observation that political risk events are rare: it may therefore be imprudent to infer absence of risk from absence of recent events. Given the long term of the policies, short-term trends from recent data may not be reflective of risk over the life of the policy.

The historical record demonstrates how the nature of political risk changes over time. For example, expropriation was the major risk in the early 1970s, while transfer restriction risk dominated the 1980s. The incidence of claims for all cover types declined in the 1990s (Figure 3). Given these shifts and the potential long-term nature of political risk policies (up to 15–20 years), using a period covering a variety of historical circumstances is more appropriate. Furthermore, the longer period covers a variety of conditions in the world economy, while the economic boom of the 1990s may be biased

Figure 3 OPIC political risk claims history (average number of claims per year)

	71–75	76–80	81–85	86–90	91–95	96–00
Transfer	4.2	8.8	16.8	4.2	0.4	0.0
Expropriation	3.4	2.2	2.6	0.8	0.6	1.4
War	0.8	1.0	0.4	0.8	0.9	1.0
Total	8.4	12.0	19.8	5.8	3.6	2.4

towards much more favourable conditions. Recent experiences of increases in disputes and possible claims relative to the 1990s further support this view.

Also note that the data exhibit some "clustering" of claims in certain time periods. This suggests that risk models should include some structural relationship to background factors or correlation among claims.

Parameter: claims probability

Generally, parameters should be measured for sub-portfolios within which they are relatively consistent from policy to policy. For example, claims probabilities vary by cover type and country risk rating. As a result, it is desirable to calibrate probabilities for all cover type/rating combinations. In many cases, the available data are too scarce to permit such direct measurement. Instead, historical data in the industry are used to estimate an average claims probability for each cover type. Claims probabilities can then be differentiated by country risk using econometric scoring models calibrated to the average probabilities.

Average claims probability

There are two primary sources of historical claims data: the Overseas Private Investment Corporation (OPIC) – a US government agency offering political risk insurance to American companies – and the Berne Union, an association of export credit and investment insurance agencies. Information on paid OPIC claims is publicly available, while the Berne Union data are available only to its members on a confidential basis.

OPIC claims data are useful as a starting point to estimate average claims probabilities for cover type. OPIC claims data from 1973 to 2000 were combined with estimates of the number of policies outstanding in each year to calculate the claims probabilities. The results are reported in Figure 4. Each insurer may consider making appropriate adjustments to these numbers. For example, the strength of the so-called "claim deterrence" effect varies from insurer to insurer (and also by cover type), and, depending on its relative effectiveness to that of OPIC, an insurer may consider increasing or decreasing the average claims probabilities.

Figure 4 Average claims probability by cover type	
Cover type	Average claims probability (%) (unadjusted estimates)
Transfer restrictions	0.60–0.80
Expropriation	0.30–0.50
War and civil disturbance	0.20–0.35

After defining average claims probabilities by cover type, the next step is to differentiate them between high-risk and low-risk countries.

Analogue scoring models
With respect to political risks, well-developed and contemporary statistical models for transfer restriction, expropriation and war and civil disturbance are not yet available either in academia or industry. Instead, analysis can be performed on "analogue events", ie, events that are believed to have a high correlation with the insured cover type, which would allow the development of a measure of its ability to differentiate country risk. There are more quantitative analyses and models available for these analogue events than the risks that political risk insurers specifically define and cover. Insurers can leverage the findings and insights from this research in developing their own scoring models, at least as a starting point.

The differentiation of claims probabilities is based on scoring models of political risk based on relevant analogue events. Such "analogue scoring models" assign a numerical score indicative of risk level for all "country-year" observations; eg, Argentina in 1991, Tanzania in 1995 and so on. The number of data points for analysis is significantly larger than actual claims: one scoring model covers as many as 70 countries over a 35-year period, providing us with more than 2,000 scores for the cover type. Those scores enable political risk insurers to quantitatively analyse the relative differences between high-risk, medium-risk and low-risk countries. Applying such relativity to the average claims probabilities produces differentiated claims probabilities by country risk rating.

Explanatory variables in the analogue scoring models are political, macroeconomic, demographic and other externally observable variables. Crucially, analogue scoring models are not used directly to determine claims probabilities, but only to make inferences about their differentiation. Further, as described later, the analogue models may provide insight about the behaviour of policy claims probabilities relative to each other (correlation) and over time (term structure).

Separate analogue scoring models have been developed for each type of insured risk. Each model uses a probit or logit link (the cumulative normal and the cumulative log odds ratio, respectively) between the score of a particular country in a specific year and the probability of a claim in that country-year. The estimation is carried out by maximising the log-likelihood function $\Sigma_i [Y_i \ln(p_i) + (1 - Y_i) \ln(1 - p_i)]$, where Y_i is zero in the country-years when no event occurred and one when an event occurred.

For transfer restriction and war and civil disturbance, suitable models of analogue events exist. For transfer restriction, currency crises appear appropriate as an analogue event under the hypothesis that they are closely linked to transfer events. Looking at OPIC's claims history, a significant overlap was observed between transfer claims and occurrences of currency crises. Furthermore, in evaluating transfer risk, political risk insurers generally look at a set of macroeconomic variables that have been shown to predict currency crises, eg, foreign debt, short-term debt, foreign currency reserves, etc. Lastly, political risk insurers tend to be more concerned with potential transfer claims during currency crises. For war and civil disturbance risk, the analogue model focuses on the risk of internal civil war. While coverage applies to all forms of political violence, including terrorist attacks and external wars, statistics show that a significant majority of major armed conflicts are internal.

For expropriation, while relevant academic papers exist, their data and analytic results are largely too old and country-specific for direct application today. Accordingly, a new model using recent historical data from OPIC and the Berne Union has been developed based on the study of theoretical frameworks and the explanatory variables used in existing literature. As an example, Figure 5 shows the summary of explanatory power (expressed in "power coefficient" as described in the power curve analysis section) of 16 variables

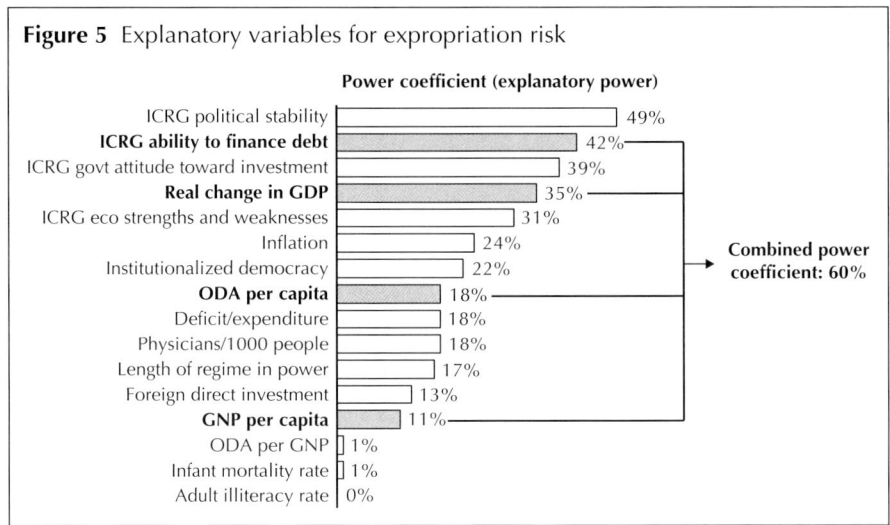

Figure 5 Explanatory variables for expropriation risk

for expropriation. As a result of testing various combinations and weightings of those variables, a certain weighted sum of the following four variables are found to be most robust: ICRG's index for ability to finance debt, real change in GDP, ODA (overseas development assistance) per capita and GNP per capita. The combined power coefficient is 60%, which is higher than the power coefficient of any individual variable.

A number of forms of testing analogue scores against historical experiences are available to validate the robustness of the models. The model parameters may be recalculated using a random subset of country-years. This re-derived model can then be applied to the subset of country-years not used in its creation. Its predictive ability in this case can be indicative of its ability to be applied to in the future and to countries not used in its original derivation. In addition, model scores can be compared with country ratings derived either by risk managers internal to an insurer or external rating services. Lastly, a comparison can be made between the analogue scores and actual claim and "near-claim" events experienced by the insurer. For example, in the case of one insurer, of six relevant near-claim events for expropriation, the scores for these countries are either on the high-risk side of the scale or in a declining trend starting 3–5 years prior to the events. In the case of one recent instance of a paid claim, the scores for that country were both on the high-risk side *and* declining.

Power curve analysis

To calculate risk-differentiated claims probabilities based on analogue scores, the model results are first converted into a specific representation of the model's predictive ability called a "power curve". A power curve is a graphic expression of how well a risk-rating system differentiates between high-risk and low-risk countries. Each point on the power curve represents a risk rating or score, with the x axis representing the cumulative proportion of country-year observations below that score, and the y axis representing the corresponding cumulative proportion of claims or analogue events from country-year observations below that score. Figure 6 shows a power curve for transfer restriction risk, using currency crises as the analogue event.

In this framework, the best rating system will have nearly all analogue events on the y axis occurring for only the worst-rated of the population on the x axis, resulting in a very steep power curve. Alternatively, if a rating system has no predictive power, ie, random assignment of ratings, its power curve is a straight diagonal line (neutral line), meaning that 20% of the population accounts for 20% of the analogue events, 50% for 50%, etc. In Figure 6, the riskiest 20% of the global sample, as measured by the risk-rating

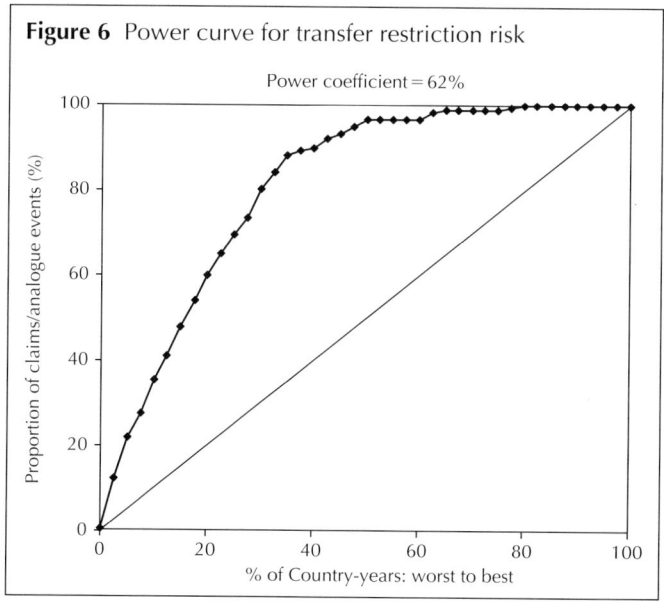

Figure 6 Power curve for transfer restriction risk

system, accounts for 60% of the claims. In the same way, the next 20% of countries are expected to generate an additional 36% of the claims. The explanatory power of the rating system is summed up by the power coefficient, measured as the ratio of the area between the actual power curve and the diagonal to the area of the triangle above the diagonal – 62% in this case.

The claims probabilities for each country rating can be determined by combining a power curve for each cover type with the average claims probability. The population on the x axis is divided into groups using the distribution of country-years according to the internal risk rating system; eg, the first x% of the population is A-rated countries. The power curve then determines the share of total analogue events that are expected to be generated by a certain ratings group. Dividing this number by the proportion of these countries to the population produces a ratio expressing the relative risk of the ratings groups. Graphically, this is the slope of the power curve in the area of the x axis corresponding to a rating. If the worst 20% of the population accounts for 60% of analogue events, and the next 40% account for a further 30%, the ratios will be 3.0 (60/20) and 0.75 (30/40), respectively. These ratios are multiplied with the average claims probability to generate a set of risk-differentiated claims probabilities across the risk-rating scale.

Term structure analysis
Another challenge for political risk pricing is the tenor, or the time horizon, of coverage. Typically, political risk insurance for investment provides risk coverage for 5–10 years or longer. It can be extremely difficult to accurately forecast or predict the political situation of any country over such a horizon. From an insurer's perspective, for a current low-risk country, basing the premium rate for the entire term of the insurance policy solely on the current level of risk (ie, claims probability) could result in undercharging to cover the actual lifetime risk. There is always some probability that the country's political situation would worsen over time. Likewise, from an insurance buyer's perspective, a premium rate would be too high for a high-risk country if the rate assumes the current risk level for the full tenor of the policy. Broadly, because the ability to predict country risks will be less robust as the time horizon increases, the ability to distinguish countries will be less effective over longer periods.

A common method for measuring risk development over time is through a ratings migration analysis. This type of analysis measures the probability of a country having a particular rating in one year as a function of its rating in the prior year. As the distribution of likely ratings spreads out in each future year, the mean – or expected rating – in future years approaches the portfolio average rating. As a result, the annual claims probability also converges over time to the portfolio average. This is referred to as mean reversion.

When a sufficient history of country risk ratings is available, an accurate migration matrix can be directly derived. Alternatively, the expected transition of analogue model scores can be used as a proxy for expected rating migration. This allows one to measure migration for more countries over a longer time horizon than would otherwise be possible. This is accomplished by converting analogue model scores to risk ratings according to a mapping system.[3] Historical movements of analogue scores then indicate the likelihood of various year-to-year transition paths of ratings; eg, the probability of a C+-rated country today moving up to B+ in Year 3, or the probability of moving down to C in Year 5. This analysis applied to all country-years provides the ratings migration matrix for each risk type. From this the "expected" (probability-weighted) rating in each year – given an initial rating – is obtained. This expected rating is then converted into a numerical claims probability. Finally, an expected marginal claims probability is calculated for every year of an insurance policy given an initial rating. This can be denoted the "term structure" of political risk claims probabilities.

Interestingly, the results show different degrees of mean reversion by risk, as Figure 7 shows. For transfer risk, the future expected claims probabilities converge faster to the mean probability than for expropriation or war risks. The movements of analogue scores, and thus ratings, are generally more stable from one year to another for expropriation and war risks than for transfer risk because the underlying risk drivers for transfer risk are more volatile. As a result, if a country has a high risk for expropriation and war today, the country is more likely to remain high-risk in future; if a country is low-risk, it is more likely to remain low-risk. In contrast, a country with a high level of transfer risk today is less likely to maintain its high level of risk.

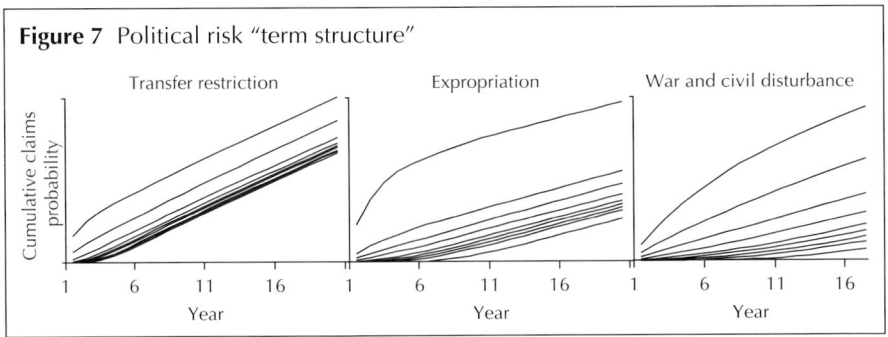

Figure 7 Political risk "term structure"

Parameter: claims severity and recovery likelihood

Severity and recovery likelihood can also be estimated using OPIC data. However, these can be measured only on the subset of actual claims. As a result, average severity by risk type is estimated across countries without further differentiation. Recovery likelihood is estimated based on OPIC's historical aggregate recovery rates by risk cover and on internal experience. Recovery is assumed to follow a Bernoulli distribution, ie, the insurer either recovers 100% with a certain probability, or does not recover at all. Partial restitution by countries is typically not in their economic interest. This approach is consistent with the historical experiences of many political risk insurers.

Parameter: claims correlations

In addition to the parameters required for the calculation of expected loss – claims probabilities, severities and recoveries – the calculation of risk load requires the measurement of correlation. Correlations describe the extent to which multiple claims are likely to occur simultaneously – within the same country, within the same region or across countries and regions. This drives the level of systematic claims variability, to which "idiosyncratic" claims risk due to simple random chance is added. Clustering of multiple claims over time increases the volatility of performance. This increased risk for a political risk insurer needs to be captured in the pricing of insurance policies through a higher risk load, as the insurer requires a higher amount of risk capital to support the policy.

Claims correlations, however, are not directly observable. The history of political risk events is not sufficient to measure correlations with an acceptable level of confidence. Actual political risk claims are generally very infrequent throughout most recent history. Especially in poor countries where FDI and/or political risk coverage were not available until recently, no historical claim data are available for meaningful correlation estimates.

Instead, the analogue scoring models provide a much larger quantity of data that enable us to quantify claim correlations. The analogue scores are available for a number of countries for an extended period of time, eg, 30 years, as long as the underlying macroeconomic and other indicators are available, regardless of their history of FDI or political risk insurance availability. Correlations between the underlying risk drivers for analogue scores are observable. The resulting correlation can be measured between composite analogue scores, and further translated into a correlation between claims.

The systematic risk for insurers exists at several levels: within a cover type in a given country (eg, an expropriatory governmental action affecting multiple investment projects), across multiple types of cover in a single country (eg, an economic crisis causing transfer restriction and also leading to property damage by civil unrest), and the so-called contagion effect across countries or even regions (eg, a regional economic crisis, or the Asia–Russia–Brazil contagion in the late 1990s). One efficient mechanism to accommodate these multiple levels of correlation is through a correlation tree (Figure 8). This hierarchical structure allows for the computation of correlation between any disparate policies.

In this framework, correlations are estimated at each of the four levels: a policy level with multiple risks; a country level with multiple policies; a region level with multiple countries; and a general "global" level with multiple regions. Correlation between two insurance policies can be computed by multiplying a series of correlations moving up, then down, the levels of the correlation tree using a chain rule.

Figure 8 also presents the country–region correlations as an example of results of this analysis. These figures can be loosely interpreted as the relative likelihood of the potential "contagion" within

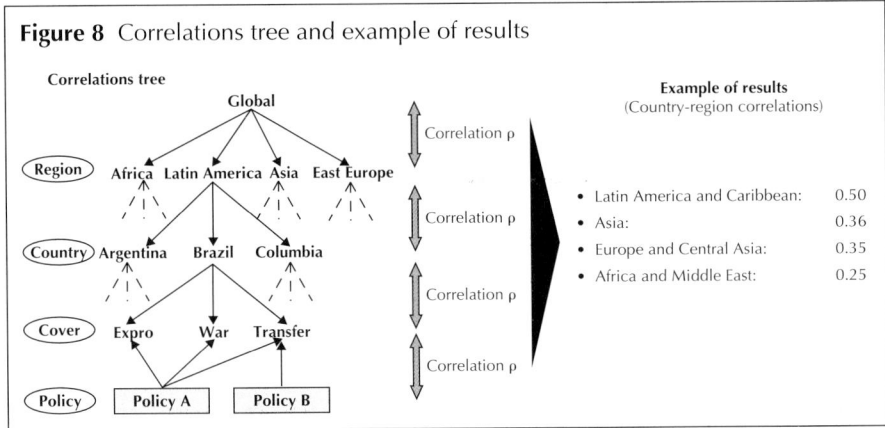

Figure 8 Correlations tree and example of results

each region. The analysis shows that the country–region correlation in Latin America is the highest among the four regions analysed.

In actual modelling, a framework similar to the Merton model has been applied. The model is usually applied to explain correlations between credit defaults of commercial borrowers. This method can be used for political risk insurance claims since both defaults and claims are Bernoulli variables (claim/default or not).

In this framework, each insurance policy is assumed to have a "latent factor" that acts as a driver to political risk claims. This latent factor can be mathematically expressed in terms of a "common factor", an idiosyncratic factor and a correlation to the common factor:

$$x_i = \rho_i m + \sqrt{1 - \rho_i^2}\, \varepsilon_i$$

where x_i is the latent factor, m is a common factor, ε_i is an idiosyncratic factor, and ρ_i is the latent factor's correlation to the common factor. In commercial credit risk, the common factor can be considered as a general economic condition that affects all borrowers. In the case of political risk, the common factor depends on the drivers of the type of cover, and the relation of those drivers between countries. For example, two insurance policies in Indonesia are correlated due to the dependence of claims probability on country-level factors shared by both. A risk in Uganda and a risk in Tanzania are correlated to the extent that their claims probabilities are driven by country-level factors that are in turn highly correlated to each other due to both countries being in Africa.

The correlation between claims is driven by the correlation between their latent factors. The correlation between two latent factors is the product of one latent factor's correlation to the common factor and the other latent factor's correlation to the same common factor, or $\rho_{i,j} = \rho_i \rho_j$. (This follows when the common and idiosyncratic factors are uncorrelated and assumed to be normally distributed with zero mean and unit variance, and the idiosyncratic factors are also uncorrelated to each other.) The same "chaining" relationship can be extended for higher-level factors in the correlation tree. Essentially, the correlation of an insurance policy to any common factor is the product of the correlations in the hierarchy path. For example, the correlation between Indonesia's expropriation risk and Egypt's transfer risk is the product of $\rho_{Expro,Indonesia}$, $\rho_{Indonesia,Asia}$, $\rho_{Asia,Global}$, $\rho_{Global,Africa}$, $\rho_{Africa,Egypt}$ and $\rho_{Egypt,Transfer}$ in the hierarchy path.

IMPLEMENTATION ISSUES FOR INSURERS

This section discusses some of the business implications of applying the economic capital approach to political risk insurance pricing: risk sensitivity of premium rates, in particular to exposure concentrations; and the difference between "costing" and "pricing" of insurance policies and the implications of the implementation of a "costing" model.

Risk sensitivity

Each component in this pricing methodology – expected loss, risk load and expenses – has its own drivers. The relative magnitude of these components depends not only on the attributes of individual policies, but also on the nature of the insurer. Although the details of calculations will differ between insurers, some general results follow more or less directly from the economic capital framework.

Claims probability effects

This pricing methodology produces results that are risk-sensitive. Differentiation in risk between policies is captured in the claims probabilities. This variable affects both expected loss and risk load, but in different ways.

Claims probability increases exponentially across the ratings scale from low- to high-risk, as is the case for default probabilities in commercial credit risk. As a result, all else equal, the expected loss component is significantly (dozens, perhaps hundreds, of times) higher in high-risk countries than in low-risk countries. However, the sensitivity of total cost to claims probability depends on the size of expected loss relative to other components. For example, if a policy covers a small project while the insurer's expenses have a high fixed cost that is independent of project size, the expense component may dominate, dwarfing the impact of the expected loss differences.

Sensitivity to risk is also reflected in the risk load component. Like expected loss, the risk load depends on claims probability: ie, high-risk countries obviously require higher risk loads than low-risk countries, all else equal. Claims probability determines a policy's "standalone" risk (ie, the risk without consideration of the rest of the portfolio). How standalone risk translates into portfolio risk – and therefore risk load – depends on the degree of concentration in the portfolio.

Concentration effects
Risk load also depends on a policy's interaction with the rest of the insurer's portfolio. Concentration risk arises from large exposures to a single policy, accumulation of exposures within a country, or accumulation within a region of correlated countries – all factors that prevent the portfolio from diversifying away "idiosyncratic" risks. There are a variety of ways to measure concentration risk in practice, but these are beyond the focus of this chapter. Conceptually, risk load can be calculated based on the total risk of a policy relative to the total risk of the insurer's portfolio. Specifically, this is done by allocating available capital to the policy according to its relative risk, a function of standalone risk and concentration risk:

$$\text{Risk Load} = \left(H - R_f \right) \times \text{Allocated Capital}$$

$$= \left(H - R_f \right) \times \text{Capital} \times \frac{\text{Standalone Risk} + \text{Concentration Risk}}{\text{Total Portfolio Risk}}$$

Risk load depends on the following factors, apart from the claims probability: (i) the size of the policy; (ii) the correlation of the policy with the rest of the portfolio; and (iii) the pre-existing exposure in the country and region where the covered project is located. The risk load can become particularly high if some of these factors simultaneously apply to a particular policy. The final impact of risk load on the total price depends on the relative size of the three components, as is the case with expected loss.

Thus, under this methodology, a large policy in a risky country that already has significant exposure may receive a high risk load. However, it is important to note that, on the same policy, the risk load (and thus the final price) for another insurer could be lower if the insurer has – relatively – less pre-existing exposure in the same country on its portfolio. This provides a useful incentive mechanism to political risk insurers to develop a well-diversified insurance portfolio. This could be achieved through its own business development and/or through the optimal use of reinsurance. From an insurance buyer's perspective, there may be opportunities to find an insurer that can price a transaction in more competitive terms because of its diversified portfolio.

Costing versus pricing

In putting the pricing methodology based on the economic capital into practice, political risk insurers should pay attention to the difference between "costing" and "pricing". In general, there are two sides in the task of pricing risk for insurance products: (1) determining the expected *cost* of the insurance product; and (2) determining the optimal *price* for the insurance product. These two tasks are distinct, but they are also closely interrelated.

The methodology that has been discussed in this chapter corresponds to the first task. It takes a supply-side perspective. The premium rate is primarily calculated by an insurer's view on risk, its existing insurance portfolio and its internal cost structure. The nature of this task is financial and/or actuarial, rather than market-driven. Strictly speaking, this is "costing", as opposed to "pricing", because a premium rate becomes a "price" only when business is transacted at that rate. Therefore, "pricing", the second of the tasks above, is an insurer's decision in a dynamic marketplace. It is affected by factors such as the demand-supply balance (for instance, capacity constraints), intensity of competition, and the customer's view of the economic value of the product.

As with any product – whether insurance, widgets or air travel – it is important to recognise the difference between average cost and marginal cost. Marginal cost is lower than average cost to the extent of allocated fixed expenses that would be incurred regardless of the marginal transaction. Similarly, because the shared capital base supports the diversified risk of all of the policies in the portfolio, the marginal capital – and corresponding marginal economic cost of risk – required for a new policy will be lower than the average allocated capital and risk load. While a particular transaction may be economically viable at marginal cost, the business will not be strategically viable unless transactions on average meet the average cost.

For an insurer, both the market and cost points of view are important. The cost view is important in setting a minimum price while the market price will (somewhat naturally) set the maximum possible price. Regardless of this market price, the insurer will not normally want to price below its costs – even if the cost-based price is above the market price. This results in a situation where the insurer will naturally do more business in markets where it has a comparative advantage. In this way the insurer is rewarding efficiency in operations, including a well-diversified portfolio of policies.

If, alternatively, the insurer did price to market only, it would be destroying value for shareholders when the cost is greater than the price. Note that the policy "cost" is not just expenses, which are relatively easy for underwriters to consider, but also risk and capital costs for the insurer, including the impact of concentrations and correlations. These concerns may be captured in the expert judgement of seasoned underwriters. However, without a tool to understand those effects reliably and accurately, an insurer may run the risk of destroying value by failing to charge enough for concentration risk, or by missing opportunities to do profitable business at lower prices if justified by diversification benefits.

Finally, there may be a non-economic factor that should also be considered in the pricing of political risk insurance, and that is policy-related considerations by public-sector providers of political risk insurance. Many national and multilateral insurers have an objective to pursue developmental contribution in developing countries. In addition, national insurers usually exist for the purpose of serving their national interests and, at times, foreign-policy goals. They may choose to use pricing as a tool to achieve these non-economic goals. For example, a public-sector insurer may price a policy in a way that promotes a particular type of developmentally positive foreign investment into target countries that struggle with poverty.

This policy-driven pricing should be a conscious management decision, with such pricing treated as exceptions from the cost-based view of pricing, such as the method based on economic capital. However, as long as those insurers want to maintain their long-term financial soundness and be accountable to their shareholders/taxpayers, the economic implications should clearly be understood and monitored against the cost of doing business. This will be possible only with a systematic and objective methodology of pricing political risks.

CONCLUSIONS

The quantitative pricing approach based on the economic capital concept would benefit insurers, investors and host countries. Insurers are able to take greater confidence in the long-term sustainability of their business by ensuring that they collect sufficient premium to fully cover all the costs of providing insurance, including both risk-related and expense-related costs. The quantitative approach also creates an opportunity to measure the economic impact of product features such as cover limits, deductibles, coinsurance, multi-country coverage and so forth, and thereby enable evaluation of trade-offs between these features and pricing as policies are structured and negotiated.

More risk-sensitive pricing has important implications for the availability and economics of political risk insurance in different risk segments. Insensitive pricing overcharges less risky policies and subsidises more risky policies. Without systematic risk-sensitive pricing, an insurers' only tool to manage the disequilibrium of this cross-subsidy is by rationing or avoiding coverage in the riskiest countries, failing to meet potential demand for economically fair-priced insurance in these segments. At the same time, overcharging may discourage economically attractive business for less risky policies, so that there is dead weight loss at both ends of the spectrum.

When investors consider using political risk insurance, they would feel more confident that the pricing is fair and consistent if they understand that a significant part of the pricing is based on objective data analysis. Host countries would benefit if this confidence resulted in broader availability and greater demand overall for political risk insurance, which in turn would facilitate much needed investment.

1 The tolerance for default can be calibrated as the default probability associated with a particular target debt rating.

2 Claims severity is the expected amount of a valid claim as a proportion of total coverage, which may be less than 100%. The recovery is the proportion of the amount paid out that is ultimately reimbursed either from the host government or from the sale of shares or other subrogated assets, adjusted for time value.

3 One way of producing such a mapping is by equating a distribution of country analogue scores to the distribution of ratings. For example, if the riskiest 10% of countries have a D rating, the lowest 10% of analogue scores then correspond to a D.

15

Managing Currency Inconvertibility and Exchange Transfer Risk: Identification, Assessment and Risk Transfer Issues

Martin Stone

Aon Political Risk

INTRODUCTION

Currency inconvertibility (CI) features only rarely in the academic literature for political risk. Along with its sister, exchange transfer (ET), it merits but a few passing mentions. Contrast this with the wealth of analysis and comment on currency crises more generally, most recently illustrated by the experience of Argentina in 2001–2. However, CI and ET risks differ substantially from general currency crisis risks. Not only are the definitions different but the causes can also differ substantially.

There is also a strong contrast with the volume of analysis on the other main components of political risk: expropriation and political violence. There are a number of papers, and even books, on expropriation risk, and a great deal of research on the causes of political violence events such as wars and revolutions.

Yet CI is rarely studied. This is despite the fact that CI and ET are risk events that occur relatively frequently. Although the data and statistics on political risk are notoriously incomplete and imprecise, insurers' claims records suggest that CI/ET ranks second after expropriation in terms of severity. According to OPIC, 21% of all OPIC claims between 1966 and 1999 were related to CI, while more than 74% related to expropriation and 5% to political violence.

Moreover, unlike other political risks, CI/ET remains as much a significant risk to international investors, traders and lenders in the

Figure 1 Companies' actual experience with various types of risks

Type of risk	Total sample % yes	122% not aware
Tax/regulatory risks	20	39
Expropriation risks	18	14
Operational environment risks	27	27
Political violence risks	19	15
Transfer risks	**34**	**25**
Trade risks	24	22
Government contract risks	15	29
Exchange rate risks	55	29
Unfair calling of contract-related bonds	8	32

Source: Aon Political Risk Management Survey, 2001

early 21st century as it did in the 1950s. Where the instances of confiscation and nationalisation are nowadays rare, the experience of Argentina in 2002 shows that the issue continues to present significant challenges to financiers and their client investors, exporters and contractors around the world.

Not surprisingly, investors and exporters often cite CI and ET as among their main concerns about international investment and cross-border trade. As long ago as 1984, 84% of respondents in an OPIC survey on political risk cited the issue as their number-one concern.[1] In 2001, 55% of respondents to a survey conducted by Deloitte & Touche cited "CI and exchange transfer problems" as of "first rank concern". A survey by Aon found similar results (see Figure 1).

This chapter attempts to remedy the lack of research in this area by providing an overview of CI and ET risks. The first section defines the two risks. The second and third sections address the causes of CI and ET risks, respectively. The fourth section describes risk assessment, the fifth exposure assessment, and the sixth concludes with technical considerations for risk transfer.

WHAT ARE CI AND EXCHANGE (NON-)TRANSFER?

By way of a definition, CI and ET risk constitutes changes in the foreign-exchange laws and practices prevailing at the time of the inception of an investment/contract.[2] In most cases, a government will enact legislation (or order a central bank, finance ministry or other regulatory monetary authority) that makes it impossible for a borrower or beneficiary to:

❑ convert local currency into foreign currency to meet debt service obligations;
❑ replenish debt service accounts through customary legal channels; or
❑ transfer offshore funds that have been converted within a specific period.

In other words, investors cannot transfer dividends, fees, profits, etc; pay local employees in hard currency; or service foreign currency debt obligations. Exporters cannot get paid. Bond issuers cannot transfer fixed-income payments. All these can lead to significant economic loss and/or asset devaluation. Investors and traders will also encounter an increased volume of paperwork to comply with the new controls.

The typical mechanism is for a central bank to fix the exchange rate at which it will buy foreign exchange and ration the amount of exchange available. This differs from a normal fixed exchange rate regime that regulates the supply and demand of foreign exchange. Alternatively, an authority might impose regulations that require it to approve all foreign exchange transactions. This approval might be declined, delayed or conditional.

Naturally, there are variations in the composition, timeframe, extent, severity and phasing of such legislation or regulations. A government's prime objective is to control the volume of foreign exchange in circulation. Whether one instance of legislation is sufficient, or whether it commences a series of similar, cumulative measures, depends very much on the perceived success of the measures in achieving the objective.

The precise composition of CI restrictions can range from nil to 100%, via many possible configurations of limits. For example, legislation or regulations might involve restricting dividends that could be returned in any one year to a percentage of a firm's registered capital plus reinvested earnings. However, when currency convertibility restrictions are imposed, they normally apply to both domestic and foreign entities.

WHERE DO CI/ET EVENTS OCCUR?

CI and ET problems are most often associated with emerging markets and developing economies. However, this is a relatively new phenomenon; such events occurred fairly often in Western Europe between 1945 and 1990, for example. The advent of the European Union, neo-liberal economics and globalisation have largely limited the problem to the former Soviet Union, Asia, Africa and Latin America. Figure 3 shows the wide range of countries that have undergone a CI and/or ET event.

WHAT CAUSES CURRENCY INCONVERTIBILITY?

CI can be categorised as an "active" blockage; as opposed to exchange non-transfer, a "passive" blockage. In the former circumstance, a government, usually through the agency of a central bank, deliberately enacts legislation that delays, prevents, limits or blocks indefinitely the conversion of dividends, fees, profits, share capital or debt service from the currency of the host country into a foreign currency.[3] This legislation might also affect the actual transfer from one currency to another.

Various causes for an active blockage have been observed over the past 40 years. A government is likely to impose some form of restrictive legislation, set specific limits and/or timeframes for

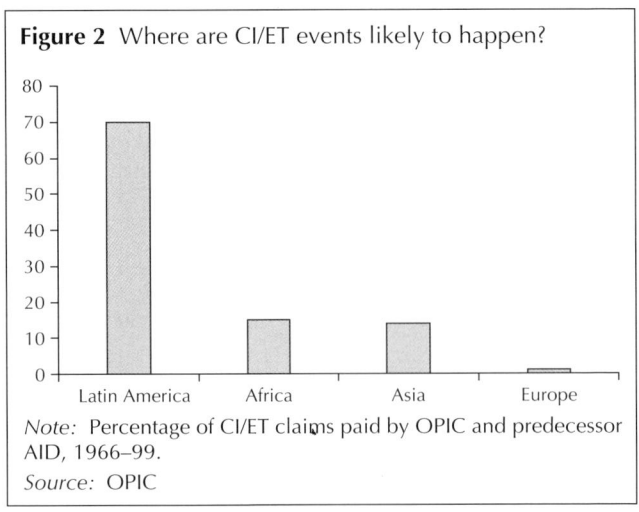

Figure 2 Where are CI/ET events likely to happen?

Note: Percentage of CI/ET claims paid by OPIC and predecessor AID, 1966–99.

Source: OPIC

Figure 3 Number of quarters of currency crises in selected countries, 1978–97

Source: Journal of International Money and Finance, 1998

currency conversion, or require specific permission for conversion, in the following circumstances:

❏ Currency crisis: for example, where a currency begins to depreciate due to over- or undervaluation, foreign reserve depletion, or its ability to borrow externally is doubted.
❏ Economic crisis: low levels of trade and investment, and high unemployment.
❏ Debt crisis: where governments are unable to service loans, resulting in slower internal development. This can be due to rising energy or other critical commodity prices, higher real interest rates, reduced lending, and declining exports. Argentina's experience of the late 1990s is an example.
❏ Politics: for example, where a government (often headed by an idiosyncratic and strong leader) feels it expedient to impose controls to gain political leverage by underlining his nationalist credentials. The Zimbabwe of President Robert Mugabe in the early 2000s provides an illustration.
❏ Punitive action against specific nationalities – a rare occurrence in modern times.

❑ Catastrophe: where a natural disaster, such as earthquake or major flood, or war, has a sudden and significant effect on foreign exchange reserves.

However, generally, governments tend to impose some form of CI regime in response to adverse trade conditions in the world, or where a currency has become significantly overvalued. In these circumstances, governments first resort to external borrowing and use (and therefore depletion) of reserves. Exchange controls are the next step if these fail to address the problem.

Analysis of the effect of CI/ET on the capital markets by the ratings agency Standard & Poor's shows that the probability that a government will interfere with a private organisation's foreign currency debt repayments is normally equivalent to the chance of the sovereign defaulting on its own foreign currency obligations. It calculates that 90% of sovereign interference events will last longer than one year; 80% will exceed two years; 70% more than three years; and so on.

ET problems, however, can in theory occur at any time. A currency crisis is the most commonly observed cause, yet there are many other potential reasons that involve a shortage of foreign currency. Currency crises are also the most common cause of convertibility restrictions. It is interesting to note that most political risk insurance claims result from "passive" situations – discussed in the next section.

WHAT CAUSES EXCHANGE (NON-)TRANSFER?

An exchange (non-)transfer event – a "passive" blockage – is where the conversion from local to foreign currency takes place, but there are insufficient amounts of foreign currency available to complete the transaction. The transfer is thus prevented completely, or delayed. It is "passive" because the authorities are not deliberately blocking transfer.

In most cases, this type of blockage results from a straightforward shortage of foreign currency. However, other reasons observed include:

❑ incompetence within the monetary agency;
❑ mismanagement;
❑ fraud and corruption;

❑ error;
❑ personnel change (decision-making and bureaucratic efficiency can halt in the run-up to, or, for some time after, executive change in highly centralised countries).
❑ catastrophe; and
❑ political factors: as with active blockage, a government or executive can deliberately restrict the amount of foreign exchange available.

ASSESSING CI/ET RISKS

Where the literature is reticent on CI/ET, it is much richer on the subject of suggesting forecasting and assessment models. Most models will attempt to identify the risk factors to be monitored for CI/ET. A classic analysis by Bunn and Mustafaoglu (1978) suggests two factors:

❑ balance of payments: "continuing deficits in the current account and lack of capital inflows result in the host country's participation in an embargo due to political reasons"; and
❑ economic development: "in order to encourage economic development, the host country forces the foreign firms to reinvest their profits domestically by restricting or prohibiting the transfer of those funds out of the country".

The ability to foresee a convertibility or transfer crisis is inextricably linked to the wider science of economic forecasting. As discussed above, currency, economic, debt and related crises tend to presage a convertibility or transfer problem. But as political risk is in large part a human risk (in that humans can, and do, act in unpredictable and sometimes mercurial ways), the analyst must consider a substantial element of uncertainty.

Why do some governments resort to convertibility and capital controls when others do everything to avoid them? Why do some administrations maintain such regimes for much longer than their neighbours? Politics is the main explanation: in addition to economic pressures, the decision is influenced by nationalism, economic ideology and orientation, internal political pressures, the political prospects of the ruling institution and so on. Malaysia's decision to impose convertibility and capital controls amid the Asian financial crisis of 1997–8, and to maintain them for many months, was at the time in part ascribed to then Prime Minister Mahathir's somewhat nationalistic and anti-Western orientation. Analysis of these signs is the province of the political risk analyst.

Reading the economic, financial and fiscal indicators is more straightforward. Economists cite the following as helpful:

Macro-environment
❑ exchange-rate patterns;
❑ GDP growth rates;
❑ industrial production;
❑ lending rate/deposit rate growth;
❑ bank deposit growth rate;
❑ stock price index;
❑ interest rates;
❑ liabilities to foreign banks;
❑ current account;
❑ foreign reserve levels;
❑ monetary policy; and
❑ currency speculation.

Micro-environment
❑ debtors' payment experience.

Regional experience is also often a strong signal. An inconvertibility and/or non-transfer event in one territory can often signal similar problems in neighbouring countries. Despite globalisation, regional ties (real or perceived) can play a strong role. Crises often have regional dynamics:

❑ the Tequila 'hangover' of 1994 (Mexico and neighbours);
❑ the Asian contagion of 1997 (Thailand, Malaysia, Hong Kong, etc); and
❑ Argentina, 2001, which had negative effects on larger neighbour Brazil and, disproportionately, on Uruguay, sandwiched between the two.

IDENTIFYING EXPOSURE TO CI/ET RISKS
CI and exchange non-transfer can affect the profitability of:

❑ investments and investment loans (project finance);

❑ cross-border trade; and
❑ capital markets transactions.

In the case of a foreign investment in an asset, a CI or ET event occurs when dividends, fees, profits, share capital or debt service are subject to active or passive blockage. On the capital markets, CI/ET would prevent or delay the conversion of the income generated by a local bond issue into the foreign investor's currency, for example. An exporter or contractor would suffer CI or ET when a foreign buyer is unable to convert his payment into the supplier's chosen currency.

Note that CI/ET events can also cause other problems for local operations. Usually, both foreign trading partners and local agents devise methods to circumvent the controls. This in turn tends to encourage increased official corruption, smuggling and other forms of crime. Residents, denied legal access to foreign exchange, will find alternative sources of funds in the form of a black market. In many cases, officials of the central bank or finance ministry are bribed to circumvent the restrictions.

Some countries, for example China, actually stockpile US dollars as a matter of economic policy. This is intended to keep exports cheap and influence trade relations with the US. The importance of US dollars to many emerging economies can make it difficult for an American company to repatriate US dollars from a foreign market,

Figure 4 Key events 1975–2001

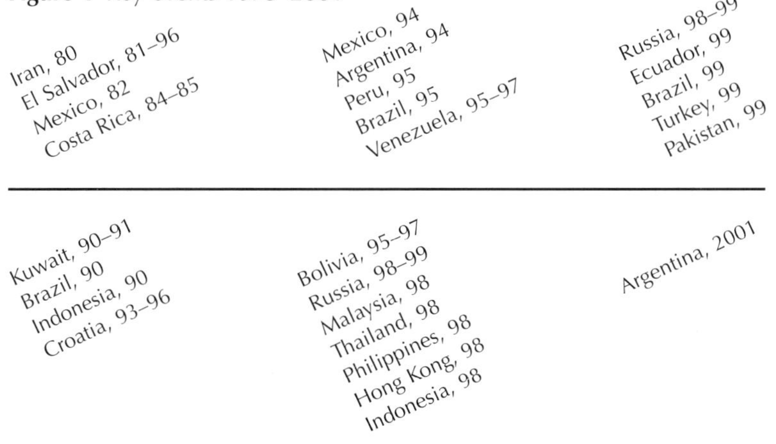

Iran, 80
El Salvador, 81–96
Mexico, 82
Costa Rica, 84–85

Mexico, 94
Argentina, 94
Peru, 95
Brazil, 95
Venezuela, 95–97

Russia, 98–99
Ecuador, 99
Brazil, 99
Turkey, 99
Pakistan, 99

Kuwait, 90–91
Brazil, 90
Indonesia, 90
Croatia, 93–96

Bolivia, 95–97
Russia, 98–99
Malaysia, 98
Thailand, 98
Philippines, 98
Hong Kong, 98
Indonesia,

Argentina, 2001

though some nations have long-term policies for controlling the flow of foreign currencies. In addition, US banking companies have learned how to work within these strictures, gradually taking out earnings, for example.

TRANSFERRING CI/ET RISKS

CI and ET are, of course, risks that can be transferred. A broker such as Aon Political Risk can source insurance policies that respond to CI/ET events. However, CI and ET are often erroneously equated with a range of other similar economic and financial risks, leading some investors and financiers to expect political risk insurers to cover a much wider range of perils than are normally available. It must be differentiated from exchange-rate risk – the risk of loss from movements in local currency values, or even devaluation. Similarly, it should be contrasted with accounting risk, which is the risk of loss due to the application of internationally accepted accounting standards for converting foreign currency liabilities.

There are several technical insurance issues that apply to CI and ET, and that might determine whether or not a situation is in fact an instance of inconvertibility and/or transfer.

Most commonly, an investor may lodge funds with a government institution and apply for its conversion, but the government may refuse both to convert and refund the amount. This would not constitute a claim for most underwriters, though clearly it would present significant problems for a project sponsor. A government seizure of funds in this manner would in this case constitute an expropriation (see Panel 1).

It is also relatively common for creditors to encounter transfer problems due to the incompetence or mismanagement of a bank. Exporters report officials losing or misdirecting documents, leading to delays. In many cases, pressure leads to eventual transfer.

Nevertheless, authorities tend to agree that the PRI market has a stronger record in paying CI/ET claims than for some other aspects. Standard & Poor's believes that "inconvertibility coverage provides the most significant potential for risk mitigation relative to other types of political risk coverage because of the severity of inconvertibility risk relative to the other risks covered by OPIC, as well as the better claims paying record and process for inconvertibility

PANEL 1 THE UNUSUAL CASE OF ARGENTINA IN 2002

The debt and currency crises in Argentina, which began in 2000 and lasted into 2002, provide the most recent example of a political situation that generated substantial losses for lenders and investors in the context of CI and ET. It is estimated that investors and banks (mainly North American) lost a total of US$20 billion.

After months of worsening economic instability, the Buenos Aires government introduced a series of regulatory measures between 2000 and 2002. In January 2002 it eliminated the parity between the Argentine peso and the US dollar.

Two years later it was estimated that political-risk-insurance policyholders had filed claims up to a total of US$1 billion. Some of these were standard claims. For instance, a Bermuda-based insurer paid a CI claim for a loss sustained in 2002 on a syndicated loan made by a commercial bank to a large Argentine corporate. "When a scheduled payment came due on the loan, the borrower had sufficient local currency to make the payment, but, due to exchange controls, was unable to convert the pesos to US dollars and remit the payment outside Argentina. The specific exchange controls were the Central Bank decrees requiring Central Bank approval for cross-border transfers to pay debt. For a lengthy period in 2002 and early 2003, such approvals were difficult, if not virtually impossible, to obtain."[4]

However, many other claims were unusual, because of the atypical nature of Argentina's crisis. For example, Argentine regulations restricted one US company's access to US$-denominated Certificates of Deposit that had been "pesified" (converted to pesos). However, here, as in many other cases, the claim upheld was for expropriation – not CI/ET – on the ground that the political event had caused "indirect expropriation of investors' assets".

claims compared to the other types of political risk insurance, such as expropriation" (S&P, 1999).

The information on CI/ET claims paid by the PRI insurance sector is incomplete. While ECAs such as OPIC and MLAs such as MIGA publish full details of settlements, the private market (primarily Lloyd's) normally makes confidentiality of the existence of cover, and of any claims arising, a condition of the policy.

---

1 Overseas Private Investment Corporation. Cited in Mandel, 1984.
2 Sometimes referred to as "exchange non-transfer".
3 The host country is that in which the investment is located, or where the buyer is domiciled.
4 Source: http://www.sovereignbermuda.com/claim2.html, consulted October 2004.

REFERENCES

Bunn, D. W., and M. M. Mustafaoglu, 1978, "Forecasting Political Risk", *Management Science*, **24**, pp. 1563–6, November.

Khamfula, Y., 2003, "The Impact of Currency Inconvertibility on Trade Flows", *International Trade Journal*, **17(4)**, p. 275.

Mandel, R., 1984, "The Overseas Private Investment Corporation and International Investment", *Columbia Journal of World Business*, **19(1)**, p. 89.

Standard and Poor, 1999, *Monthly Bulletin*, October.

Stern, R., 1982, "Insurance for Third World Currency Inconvertibility Protection", *Harvard Business Review*, **60(3)**, p. 62, May/June.

16

The Expanding Market for Sovereign Credit Default Swaps*

Frank Packer; Chamaree Suthiphongchai

BIS; Bank of Thailand

The market for credit derivatives, or financial contracts whose pay-offs are linked to changes in the credit quality of a reference asset, has expanded dramatically in recent years. According to the 2002 Credit Derivatives Report of the British Bankers' Association, the credit derivatives market grew from US$40 billion outstanding notional value in 1996 to an estimated US$1.2 trillion at the end of 2001, and is expected to reach US$4.8 trillion by the end of 2004.[1] The same report indicates that single-name credit default swaps (CDSs) accounted for roughly 45% of the overall credit derivatives market.

This chapter examines developments in the CDS market with a particular focus on the segments where the reference assets are sovereign obligations. Sovereign CDSs, which benefited from the standardisation of contract form and definitions in 1998 and 1999 as well as successful execution in the case of recent defaults, are considered the most liquid credit derivative instruments in emerging markets. Particularly as their liquidity increases, sovereign CDSs have the potential to supplement and increase efficiency in underlying sovereign bond markets.[2]

*This chapter was originally published in the BIS Quarterly Review, December 2003, under the title of "Sovereign Credit Default Swaps". Chamaree Suthiphongchai was seconded to the BIS by the Bank of Thailand while this chapter was being researched. The views expressed here are those of the authors and do not necessarily reflect those of the BIS or the Bank of Thailand. The authors wish to acknowledge the invaluable assistance of Anna Cobau.

This chapter begins by briefly outlining the function and structure of CDSs. We then review the data provided by CreditTrade, one of the major trading platforms for credit derivatives, and use this as a basis for comparing sovereign with corporate and bank CDSs across a number of dimensions, including concentration of quotes by name of the reference asset, rating composition, maturity and pricing.

BACKGROUND AND DATA SOURCE

CDSs are credit-protection contracts whereby one party agrees, in exchange for a periodic premium, to make a contingent payment in the case of a defined credit event. For buyers of credit protection, the CDS market offers the opportunity to reduce credit concentration and regulatory capital while maintaining customer relationships. For sellers of protection, it offers the opportunity to take credit exposure over a customised term and earn income without having to fund the position.

The quoting convention for CDSs is the annual premium payment as a percentage of the notional value of the reference obligation. Under certain conditions, this CDS premium should be approximately equal to the credit spread (yield minus risk-free rates) of the reference bond of the same maturity. In addition to confirming this stylised fact, empirical work suggests that the CDS premium maps the spread over US dollar swap rates more closely than the spread over US Treasury rates.[3]

The main data source for this chapter is CreditTrade, a major broker in the trading of credit and credit derivatives. The company's Market Prices database lists bids and offers of brokers and traders for CDSs, as well as other characteristics of the quote and reference asset. In addition to the price (premium) in basis points (bps), the database includes with each quote:

❑ the reference entity name;
❑ the notional amount and seniority of the reference asset;
❑ whether the quote is a bid or an offer;
❑ the date of the quote;
❑ the rating by both Moody's and Standard & Poor's;
❑ maturity; and
❑ type of restructuring clause.

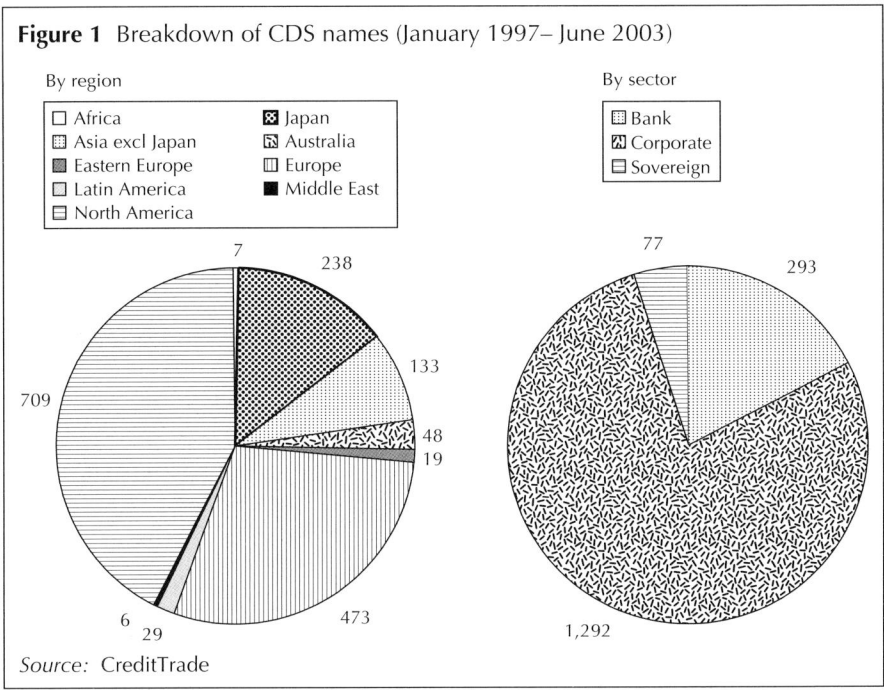

Figure 1 Breakdown of CDS names (January 1997– June 2003)

By region

- ☐ Africa
- ☒ Japan
- ☷ Asia excl Japan
- ▧ Australia
- ■ Eastern Europe
- ⊞ Europe
- ☐ Latin America
- ■ Middle East
- ⊟ North America

By sector

- ⊞ Bank
- ▨ Corporate
- ⊟ Sovereign

Source: CreditTrade

The database also identifies quotes that result in actual transactions through the system, and the number is not particularly large. For instance, in 2002 only 6% of quotes corresponded to actual transactions. Even so, quotes are more than indicative, since once submitted they are binding on participants. In what follows, we will use all quotes entered into the system as a metric for market activity.

In terms of chronological and geographical coverage, the database spans the period from January 1997 to June 2003, and contains slightly more than 400,000 quotes on 1,662 different reference entities from around the world. Of these entities, 1,292 are corporate names, 293 are banks, and 77 are sovereigns (see Figure 1).

GROWTH AND DEVELOPMENT

Table 1 lists the overall number of quotes on CDSs reported in the database each year, classified by category of the reference asset, ie, corporate, bank or sovereign. Clearly, the growth of quotes overall continues to be very strong, reaching 124% and 63.8% in 2001 and 2002, respectively. The overall number of quotes on CDSs for the

Table 1 Number of quotes by type of CDS

Type	Number of quotes						
	1997	1998	1999	2000	2001	2002	2003*
Corporate	196	1,892	11,726	22,538	55,679	102,039	88,817
Bank	394	2,715	8,021	6,854	16,844	25,490	8,615
Sovereign	771	2,283	8,169	8,133	11,535	10,124	7,844
Total	1,361	6,890	27,916	37,525	84,058	137,653	105,276
Type	% change of number of quotes and trades from the previous year						
Corporate	–	865.3	519.8	92.2	147.0	83.3	96.9
Bank	–	589.1	195.4	−14.5	145.8	51.3	−50.5
Sovereign	–	196.1	257.8	−0.4	41.8	−12.2	48.2
Total	–	406.2	305.2	34.4	124.0	−63.8	52.9

*First half; change over first half of 2002.
Source: CreditTrade

first six months of 2003 was nearly 53% greater than that registered over the same period in 2002.

Within the CDS market, quotes on sovereign CDSs occupy a relatively small share, in part reflecting the far smaller number of names being traded. Sovereign CDSs accounted for around 7.4% of all quotes in 2002 and 2003 to date. Corporates account for the lion's share of quotes over the same time frame at 78.6%, while banks account for roughly 14%. Even so, the resulting mean number of quotes per name is higher for sovereign CDSs than for the other categories, suggesting a higher degree of concentration in activity in sovereign names, as discussed further below.

Though the growth of sovereign CDSs has consistently been less than that of corporate CDSs, the first six months of 2003 recorded a robust 48.2% year-on-year rate of growth. This was a significant rebound from the decline in activity seen in 2002. More than one-third of this decline was due to the elimination of Argentina from the list of reference entities after its default in late 2001. Most of the rest of the drop was accounted for by a fall in transactions for Asian names such as China, Korea and Thailand. However, the decline in Asian names has levelled off in 2003, while growth in other Latin American names such as Brazil and Mexico has continued.

Similar patterns can be noted in the overall *volume* of quoted CDS contracts, where the volume is defined as available quotes

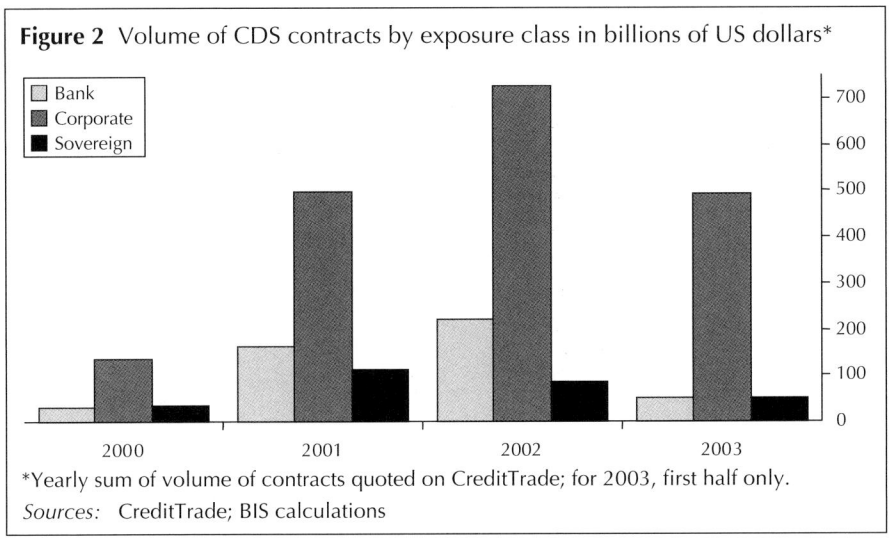

Figure 2 Volume of CDS contracts by exposure class in billions of US dollars*

*Yearly sum of volume of contracts quoted on CreditTrade; for 2003, first half only.

Sources: CreditTrade; BIS calculations

weighted by the size of the notional reference debt obligation (see Figure 2). Thus defined, the volume of sovereign CDSs for the first six months of 2003 was higher than that for the first six months of 2002, although the rate of expansion was lower than that for the volume of CDSs on corporate obligations. At the same time, the growth rate was well above that observed for CDS volume on bank obligations, which fell into negative territory.

Relative to the corporate sector, the concentration of quotes on sovereign CDSs by name is very marked. The five leading names are Brazil, Mexico, Japan, the Philippines and South Africa, which together account for more than 40% of listed quotes on sovereign names. The addition of Colombia and China brings the total to more than 50% (see Table 2). By contrast, the top five names in corporate CDSs yield only 7.7% of all quotes on CreditTrade.

The concentration of sovereign CDSs among emerging market sovereign names is for the most part consistent with the composition of TRAC-X Emerging Markets, the new credit default swap index from JPMorgan Chase and Morgan Stanley. For instance, the weighting of the top three names in the TRAC-X index, Mexico, Russia and Brazil, is slightly higher than 37%, while the most actively quoted sovereign names for 2003 in CreditTrade, Mexico, Brazil and South Africa, comprise more than 35% of the

Table 2 Concentration of quotes on sovereign CDSs

Name	Number of quotes					Percentage		Average rating*			
	2000	2001	2002	2003	Total	%	Cumulative (%)	2000	2001	2002	2003
Brazil	1,080	1,352	1,293	868	4,593	12.2	12.2	B+	B+	B	B
Mexico	748	1,010	1,644	933	4,335	11.5	23.7	BBB−	BBB−	BBB	BBB
Japan	418	1,062	628	205	2,313	6.1	29.9	AA+	AA−	A+	A+
Philippines	821	740	436	209	2,206	5.9	35.7	BB+	BB+	BB+	BB
South Africa	94	518	717	683	2,012	5.3	41.1	BBB−	BBB−	BBB−	BBB
Colombia	93	345	801	556	1,795	4.8	45.8	BB	BB	BB	BB
China	743	672	140	62	1,617	4.3	50.1	BBB+	BBB+	BBB+	BBB+
Korea	533	636	138	287	1,594	4.2	54.4	BBB	BBB	A−	A−
Poland	329	388	406	420	1,543	4.1	58.5	BBB+	BBB+	A−	A−
Venezuela	155	521	497	319	1,492	4.0	62.4	B	B+	B	B
Turkey	146	471	475	380	1,472	3.9	66.4	B+	B	B−	B−
Malaysia	302	685	256	85	1,328	3.5	69.9	BBB	BBB	BBB+	BBB+
Argentina	851	461	0	6	1,318	3.5	73.4	B+			
Thailand	494	562	121	37	1,214	3.2	76.6	BB−	BBB−	BBB−	BBB−
Russia	16	395	365	377	1,153	3.1	79.7	B−	B−	BB	BB
Other countries	1,310	1,717	2,207	2,417	7,651	20.3	100.0				
All emerging markets	7,523	10,283	9,218	7,053	34,077	90.5					
Total	8,133	11,535	10,124	7,844	37,636	100.0					

*End-year average of Moody's and Standard & Poor's ratings from CreditTrade transactions.

2003 sample. Though quotes on non-emerging-market entities constitute less than 10% of the total quotes on sovereigns, one country that has had a significant presence as a reference entity in the CreditTrade dataset is Japan. CDSs on Japanese bonds make up more than 6% of all observed quotes on CreditTrade during 2000–3.

Unlike CDSs written on bank and corporate obligations, the vast majority of outstanding sovereign CDSs remain under the old restructuring clause of the ISDA Credit Derivatives Definitions of 1999 (see Figure 3). Among CDS contracts drafted under this clause, there had been several cases where protection buyers had claimed compensation based on relatively harmless "credit events". These unjustified claims were behind the development of a modified restructuring clause in 2001 (with further refinement in 2003). Though many protection sellers included the new clause in corporate and bank CDS contracts, CDSs on sovereign obligations do not seem to have been similarly affected. This is reportedly because the likelihood of restructuring occurring in the absence of a real deterioration in financial status is believed to be very rare in the case of sovereign CDSs. Most emerging-market sovereign CDSs are bond-oriented in terms of the credit event indication and the deliverable obligation, and opportunistic restructuring is viewed as less feasible in the case of widely held bond obligations. Another reason is that sovereign restructuring-related credit events tend to be initiated by the government, which is the borrower rather than the lender.

The sovereign-linked CDSs tend to be on lower-credit-quality assets than the other categories of CDS. Figure 4 documents the composition of CDS volume by rating category for our three classes of reference asset.[4] Just below 40% of sovereign obligations that provide the underlying asset for CDSs are sub-investment-grade (BB and below), more than in the case of either corporate or bank reference assets. Similarly, 10–15% of the reference assets for sovereigns tend to be highly rated at AAA or AA, a smaller proportion than the 20% rates seen for bank CDSs, though larger than is the case for corporates.[5]

PREMIA ON SOVEREIGN CDSs

As discussed above, the premium should roughly correspond to the spread of the reference obligation of equal maturity over the

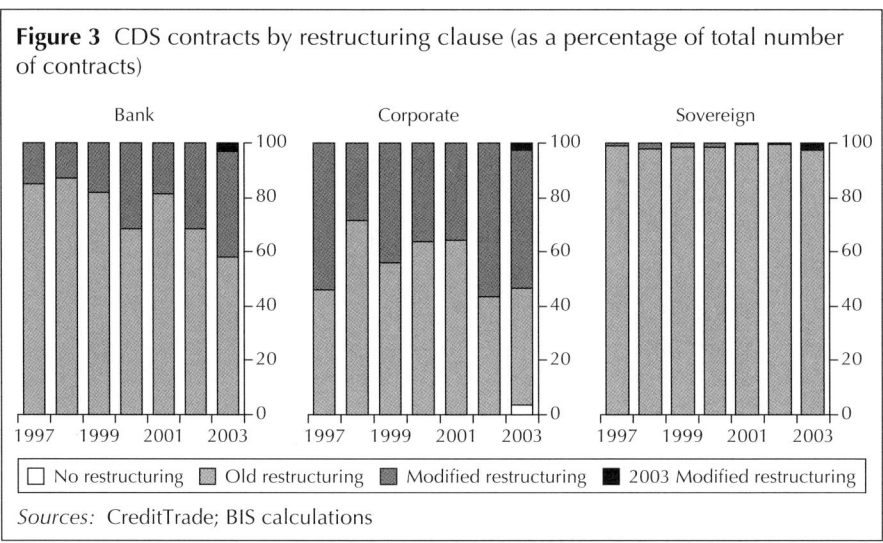

Figure 3 CDS contracts by restructuring clause (as a percentage of total number of contracts)

Bank | Corporate | Sovereign

1997 1999 2001 2003

☐ No restructuring ▨ Old restructuring ▨ Modified restructuring ■ 2003 Modified restructuring

Sources: CreditTrade; BIS calculations

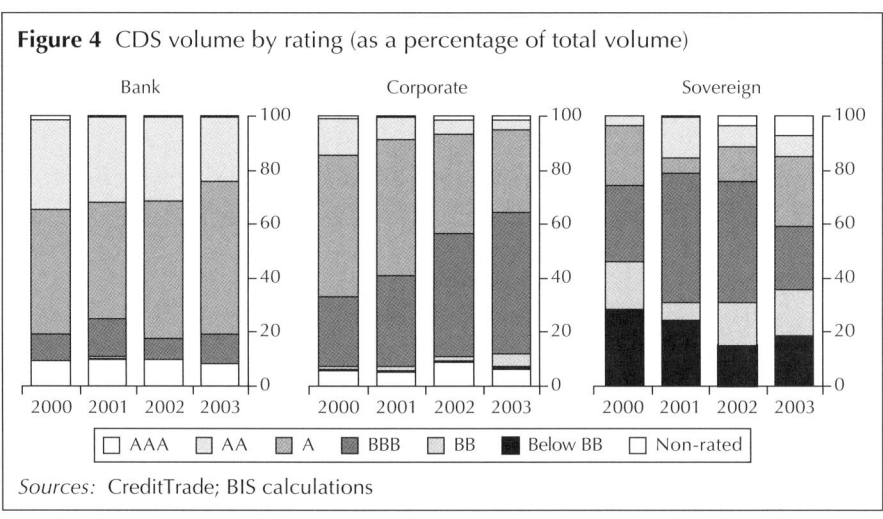

Figure 4 CDS volume by rating (as a percentage of total volume)

Bank | Corporate | Sovereign

2000 2001 2002 2003

☐ AAA ☐ AA ▨ A ■ BBB ☐ BB ■ Below BB ☐ Non-rated

Sources: CreditTrade; BIS calculations

risk-free rate. For this reason, we should expect the premium to show a fairly close cross-sectional relationship with the credit risk of the underlying reference asset as measured by credit rating agencies. Indeed, there appears to be a consistently negative relationship between ratings and premia on sovereign CDSs (see Figure 6).

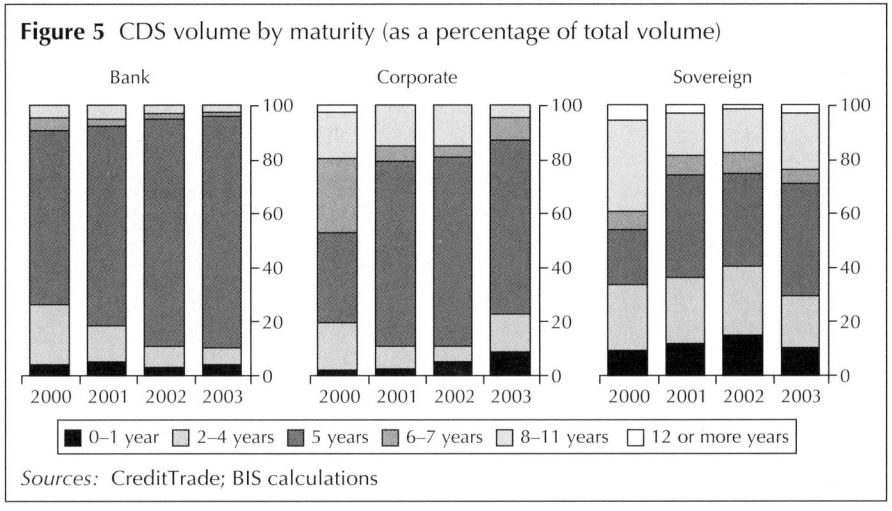

Figure 5 CDS volume by maturity (as a percentage of total volume)

Bank   Corporate   Sovereign

■ 0–1 year   ☐ 2–4 years   ▨ 5 years   ▨ 6–7 years   ☐ 8–11 years   ☐ 12 or more years

Sources: CreditTrade; BIS calculations

One question of interest is how the premia on sovereign CDSs might match up relative to other CDS segments, holding the credit rating constant. In the mid-1990s, Cantor and Packer (1995) documented a tendency for lower-grade sovereign bonds to be priced at higher spreads than corporate bonds. This stylised fact would still appear to hold many years later at the letter-grade rating levels of B and below; the Bloomberg fair market curve is significantly higher for the US dollar sovereign B sector than the US dollar industrial B2 sector. Do we see a similar result holding for CDS premia as well? In Figure 6, we chart the monthly average CDS premia for all categories between January 2000 and June 2003 for six different rating classes.

A number of results are evident. In the upper rating classes of single A or higher, quoted premia for corporate CDSs have tended to be consistently higher than those for the sovereign credits. For instance, in 2003 the spread of AAA-rated corporate-linked CDSs has been around 30 bps over that of comparably rated sovereigns; for AA- and A-rated obligations, the average difference has been around 40 and 50 bps, respectively.

The results may be explained by the small sample of highly rated sovereigns for which CDS quotes are available, combined with the relatively broad letter-grade rating categories for which the comparisons have been made. For instance, in the case of

Figure 6 Five-year CDS premia by rating (monthly average, in bps)

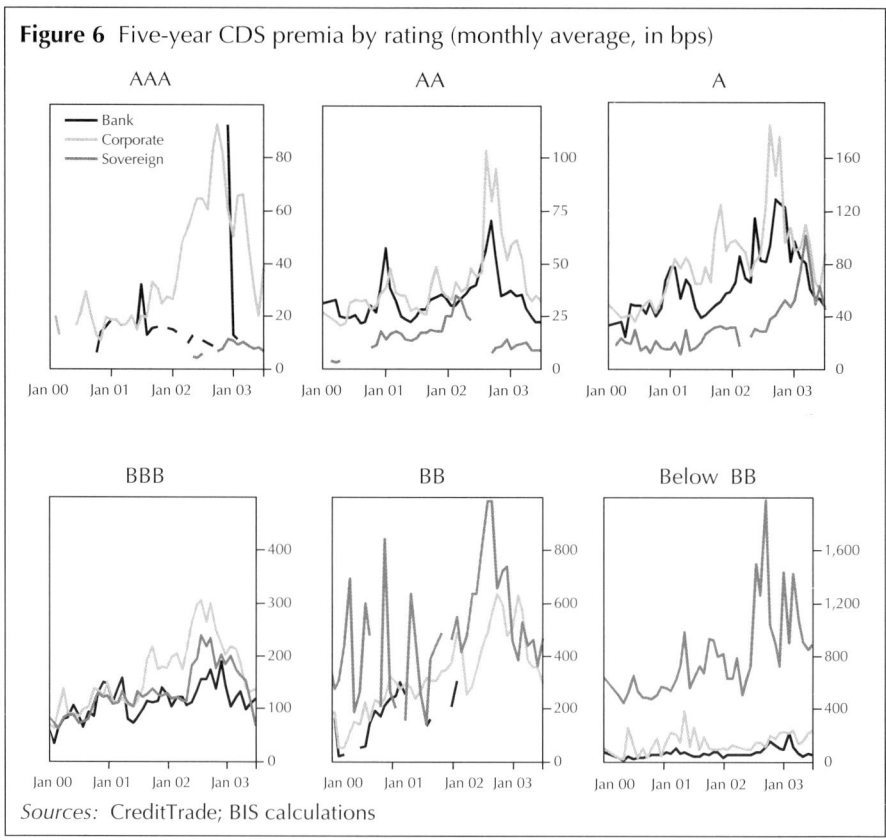

Sources: CreditTrade; BIS calculations

AAA-rated reference obligations, the two sovereigns, Germany and France, comprise virtually the entire sample of quotes. But these sovereigns arguably represent credits that would be rated over AAA were such a rating available, so that the sovereign CDSs would naturally be trading at lower premia than a sample of corporations. Similarly, in the case of AA- and A-rated credits, specific characteristics of the small sample of sovereign obligations that serve as the underlying asset might explain the difference between the average premia at different rating categories.[6]

The situation changes when we move to lower-grade reference assets, however. The difference between sovereigns and corporates in the premium appears to be virtually indistinguishable for the lower-grade categories of BBB and BB, suggesting greater similarity in the pricing of sovereign and industrial credits than was found in the 1990s. Even so, for reference assets rated below BB, sovereign credit still appears to be priced higher, with the average sovereign premium at times more than 1,000 bps above the corporate average. In the very lowest-grade categories, in which countries such as Argentina, Brazil and Turkey are prominent, the argument can be made that the market is less sure about the returns in the event of default to sovereign credits, and thus has demanded a higher premium than for similarly rated CDSs on corporate credits.[7]

CONCLUSION

Sovereign CDSs constitute a minor though growing part of the CDS market. After falling off in 2002, observed quotes on sovereign CDSs have risen markedly in 2003, with more than 90% of them linked to so-called emerging market sovereign credits. Our examination of the quotes available for sovereign CDSs suggests that trading is more concentrated in fewer names than for corporate or bank CDSs, and also tends to be concentrated in underlying assets of relatively short maturity, which is consistent with the relative frequency of low-rated sovereigns that can issue only at short maturities.

With regard to the pricing of sovereign CDSs relative to the pricing of those written on corporate or bank obligations, there is a striking asymmetry between cases depending on whether the underlying is high- or low-rated. On the one hand, the premia for sovereign CDSs are generally lower than for similarly rated corporates at high rating levels. Whether there is a liquidity-based reason for this, or whether it is simply due to the small sample of sovereigns and the crude grouping by letter-grade rating, remains to be seen. By contrast, the mean premia for CDSs written on very low-rated sovereigns appear much higher than those for CDSs written on low-rated corporates. This result is consistent with the market being less sure about returns in the event of sovereign default.

---

1 In a more recent survey of around 200 financial institutions, Fitch Ratings (2003) identified derivatives-related sold credit protection of around US$1.7 trillion.

2 Although some work has found bid–ask spreads of the CDSs in the more liquid sovereign names to be 10–20 bps, generally wider than those observed in the cash market, increasing volumes in the CDS market could narrow the differential going forward. For a detailed analysis, see Dresdner Kleinwort Wasserstein Research (2002). Earlier work on the topic is to be found in JPMorgan (2001).

3 See, for example, the discussions in Zhu (2003) and Hull, Predescu and White (2003).

4   When the reference obligation has two different ratings from Moody's and Standard & Poor's, the average rating is taken.

5   The distinction between sovereign and corporate CDSs in the investment-grade category appears to have become sharper over the past few years. Among corporates, there has been a modest shift to lower investment-grade reference assets (ie, rated A and BBB). By contrast, the past few years have seen the introduction of quotes on very highly rated countries such as France, Germany and Italy. This has compensated for the movement of Japan to the A category from AA in 2002.

6   In the case of AA-rated reference obligations, quotes from Japan dominated in 2001 and 2002, and were replaced by Italy, Belgium and Spain in 2003. These three countries are rated AA+ and are thus at the higher end of the AA range; Japan is one case where a number of observers have suggested that the market has a more sanguine view of the country's credit-worthiness than that of the major rating agencies. Similarly, the lower premia for CDSs in the A category might be explained by Japan, which had a prominent place in this category in 2002 and 2003 subsequent to its rating agency downgrades.

7   To check that outlying observations were not driving the outcome, we also charted the median premia for each rating and sector segment, with similar results.

REFERENCES

Bowler, T., and J. F. Tierney, 1999, "Credit Derivatives and Structured Credit: A Survey of Products, Applications and Market Issues", *Deutsche Bank Global Markets Research*, October.

British Bankers' Association, 2002, *Credit Derivatives Report 2002*, September.

Cantor, R., and F. Packer, 1995, "Sovereign Credit Ratings", *Current Issues in Economics and Finance*, Federal Reserve Bank of New York, June.

Dresdner Kleinwort Wasserstein Research, 2002, "Credit Default Swaps: A Product Overview", September.

Fitch Ratings, 2003, "Global Credit Derivatives: A Qualified success", 24 September.

Hull, J., M. Predescu, and A. White, 2003, "The Relationship between Credit Default Swap Spreads, Bond Yields and Credit Rating Announcement", forthcoming, *Journal of Banking and Finance*.

International Swaps and Derivatives Association, 2002, "2002 Year-end Market Survey".

JP Morgan, 2001, "Emerging Market Credit Derivatives", November.

Xu, D., and C. Wilder, 2003, "Emerging Market Credit Derivatives: Market Overview, Product Analyses, and Applications", *Deutsche Bank Global Markets Research*, May.

Zhu, H., 2004, "An Empirical Comparison of Credit Spreads Between the Bond Market and the CDS market", Bank for International Settlements, Working paper 160, August.

Index